RACE, LAW, AND PUBLIC POLICY

RACE, LAW, AND PUBLIC POLICY

THIRD EDITION

*Cases and Materials on Law
and the Public Policy of Race*

Robert Johnson, Jr.

INPRINT EDITIONS

BALTIMORE

Race, Law and Public Policy
Cases and Materials on Law and the Public Policy of Race

Copyright @2008 by Robert Johnson, Jr.

First Black Classic Press Edition 2000
Second Edition 2003
Third Edition 2009

Library of Congress Number: 2009925840

ISBN-13 978-1-58073-042-6

Printed by BCP Digital Printing, Inc.
An affiliate company of Black Classic Press

To review or purchase Black Classic Press and INPRINT EDITIONS
books, visit: www.blackclassicbooks.com

You may also obtain a list of titles by writing to:
Black Classic Press
c/o List
P.O. Box 13414
Baltimore, MD 21203

PREFACE

From the first day that Africans set foot on American soil, the relationship of law and racism has been a pressing social concern. This relationship, which continues to be viewed differently by blacks and whites, has never been fully explored within the context of the colonial period to the present. Professor Derrick Bell and Judge Leon Higginbotham, however, have written pioneering works that have opened up a tremendously rich field of study, particularly in the law school curriculum. Outside of the law school classroom there is very little material available for instruction at the graduate school and college levels. This book has been written to fill that void and has done so through three editions.

For nine years I have used this text in my class: Race and the American Legal System at the University of Massachusetts Boston. During this period a number of pressing legal issues pertaining to race have developed in the United States. First, the question of the death penalty and its unequal use among African-Americans and the poor has continued to escalate. Issues relating to the disenfranchisement of African-American voters in the Bush/Gore presidential election have gripped the nation and the world. Finally, the question of racial profiling has now been expanded to include Arab-Americans, which has placed at risk civil liberties of individuals of the Islamic faith. This third edition, therefore, becomes necessary in order to sharpen the debate over law and its relationship to public policy questions pertaining to race in a global context.

Essentially, this edition continues to analyze the evolution of racism in American law and its impact upon public policy strategies for achieving economic justice for African-Americans. It critically analyzes key court decisions, both state and federal, that legitimized the subordination of African-Americans and other people of color in American society. Moreover, it considers the effects of racism upon legal reasoning through an examination of decisions of the United States Supreme Court from 1841 to 2009.

ACKNOWLEDGMENTS

I owe my highest gratitude to my mother, Louise Guyton, who despite tremendous obstacles, provided me the love and support that continues to sustain my being. Unfortunately, she passed on to be with the ancestors on February 18, 2001.

While on sabbatical during academic year 2000-2001, I was a visiting scholar in Afro-American studies at Vanderbilt University. While there, I met Joe Ingle who has been a pastor to inmates on Tennessee's death row for twenty years and two death row inmates: Ndume Olatushani (Erkskine Johnson) and Phillip Workman (executed by the State of Tennessee, 2007). Through visits with Ndume and Phillip, I heightened my understanding about the death penalty and the unequal use of state resources to convict and kill individuals who would not ordinarily be on death row but for their economic status, color and ethnic backgrounds. More importantly, I witnessed the personal determination that each of these men exerted against seemingly insurmountable odds as they struggled through the courts to vindicate themselves and obtain their freedom. Unfortunately, Philip lost his struggle, while Ndume's sentence has been changed from death to life imprisonment although he continues to fight for his release and total vindication.

While on sabbatical during academic year 2008-2009, I researched the poisoning of Ambrose Madison, grandfather of President James Madison and the subsequent arrest of three slaves. Without the support of the Carter G. Woodson Institute for African-American and African Studies at University of Virginia, I would not have been able to complete my research into the trial of three slaves (Pompey, Turk and Dido) who, in 1732, struck out for their freedom. I also acknowledge the assistance and encouragement of Valerie Ann Todd while I continued my research in Charlotte, North Carolina. Without her generosity I would not have been able to complete this edition of the book.

CONTENTS

Chapter One

THE SLAVERY ERA

A.
Pro-Slavery Constitution

In order to understand racism in America, one must have a clear understanding of the development of slavery and its effects upon American values and legal institutions. In the early history of the country, at the Constitutional Convention in 1787, the nation faced the question of whether Blacks should be admitted into the union as free men or as slaves. After much debate in the Constitutional Convention, the founding fathers adopted a pro-slavery platform that went into effect in 1789. The vote was clear: Article I, Section 9 of the Constitution would prohibit Congress from interfering with the Atlantic slave trade until 1808. James Madison argued that the clause was necessary in order to create a strong union of states. He was afraid that Georgia and South Carolina would not join the union, except with the clause. Madison further argued that slavery would be protected by the fugitive slave clause and the prohibition against the imposition of taxes on slave sales. What accounted for their inability to adopt an anti-slavery platform? Would there have been a union if slavery had not been accepted? What political and economic forces drove the founding fathers to this reactionary conclusion?

The union of the states had to be at the cost of African freedom. As a matter of public policy, many states rejected slavery as early as the revolutionary war. In 1777, the Vermont Constitution abolished slavery, and subsequently enacted legislation implementing the constitutional provision. In Massachusetts, court decisions were rendered in favor of slaves, on the grounds that slavery conflicted with the state constitution's provision of universal rights of man. By 1793, slavery was illegal in Massachusetts. In New Hampshire, slaves sued for their freedom under the state's constitution, with the same result. In 1778, Rhode Island passed its first bill which freed slaves gradually. A similar bill took effect in Connecticut on March 1, 1784.

These statutes and court decisions led to a sharp increase in the number of free Blacks in the North, and many states passed laws that made the trade in slaves more expensive. Higher duties on the importation as well as the criminalization of the trade, forced a change. In 1787, Rhode Island made the trade a crime. These advancements, during the period of the revolutionary war, created an impression that independence would mean the elimination of slavery.

Such was not the case. The compromise of counting three-fifths of the slaves, for purposes of representation, strengthened the political power of the Southern states. The Southern delegates clearly stated their case on the economic value of slavery. Charles Pinckney of South Carolina argued that, without slavery, his state would "...become a desert waste..." The compromise at the convention, however, satisfied him:

> "We have secured an unlimited importation of negroes for twenty years. Nor is it declared that the importation shall be then stopped; it may be continued. We have a security that the general government can never emancipate them, for no such authority is granted ... We have obtained a right to recover our slaves in whatever part of America they may take refuge, which is a right we had not before."[1]

---

1 Herbert J. Storing, Ed. *Complete Anti-Federalist, V.5*, (Chicago: 1981), pp. 158-159n

In order to obtain the support of racist Southerners, such as Thomas Jefferson, Northerners listened, then compromised Black freedom. In February, 1787, Thomas Jefferson published his *Notes on the State of Virginia,* in which he stated his belief that Blacks were inferior. He raised, therefore, no objections to the pro-slavery Constitution. The failure of these so-called moderate patriots to object to racism in the Constitution, helped instill white supremacy into the political and legal institutions of America.

While the Southern states differed on whether slaves were property, they were unanimous in their dispensation of punishment. Punishment was swift and cruel, as required in the following Mississippi statute:

> Sec. 54. When any negro or mulatto slave shall be convicted of any felony, not punishable with death, such negro or mulatto slave, shall be burnt in the hand by the sheriff, in open court, and suffer such other corporal punishment as the court shall think fit to inflict, except where he or she shall be convicted of a second offence of the same nature, in which case such negro or mulatto slave shall suffer death.

> Sec. 59. If any negro or mulatto shall be found, upon due proof made to any county or corporation court of this state, to have given false testimony, every such offender shall, without further trial, be ordered by the said court, to have one ear nailed to the pillory, and there to stand for the space of one hour, and then the said ear to be cut off, and thereafter the other ear nailed in like manner and cut off at the expiration of one other hour, and moreover to receive thirty-nine lashes on his or her bare back, well laid on, at the public whipping post, or such other punishment as the court shall think proper, not extending to life or limb.[2]

If a slave was not *subject* to adverse punishment under the criminal code, he was subject to arbitrary and discriminatory treatment under

---

2 *Laws of Mississippi* (1840), Chapter 92, Sections 54, 59, passed June 18, 1822.

the civil law. One of the most inhumane experiences faced by many slaves was the auction. The auction was a day of festivities for the white slaver and the white community in general. Men, women and children would gather at the steps of the courthouse to witness the disposition of human beings. Professor James Oakes describes in graphic terms the inhumanity of the process: "...Ceremonies of degradation, symbolic reenactment of the violence of original enslavement, potent reminders of the slave's powerlessness and dishonor...."[3] Furthermore, the vast majority of these auction sales of slaves in South Carolina were court supervised.[4] Most of these sales were the result of credit transactions, and the second largest a result of probate proceedings.

Public policy toward Black people had its genesis, for the most part, in the slavery era. It was borne of institutional racism, which had its foundation deeply rooted in early capitalist development. In *The World and Africa,* the late historian W.E.B. Du Bois argued that capital accumulation was achieved at the expense of human labor. According to Du Bois, the African slave trade served as catalyst for the growth and expansion of capitalism.[5] The bulk of this trade was controlled by the British Crown, through the Royal African Company, until pressure by British merchants led to the establishment of free trade in 1750. This led to an immediate boom in slave trafficking until 1771, when almost one-third of all shipping in England was related to the slave trade.[6]

---

3 James Oakes, *Slavery and Freedom An Interpretation of the Old South* (New York: Knopf, 1990), page 24.

4 Thomas D. Russell, "South Carolina's Largest Slave Auctioneering Firm,"68 *Chicago-Kent Law Review* (1993), pp. 1241-82.

5 W.E.B. Du Bois, *The World and Africa*, (New York, International Publishers, 1972), page 44.

6 Du Bois, page 54. Du Bois stated that within the first nine years of this free trade, 160,950 Blacks were shipped to the sugar plantations. He wrote that the British colonies imported over two million slaves between 1680 and 1786.

This international slave trade had a tremendous impact upon the development of England as the late historian, Walter Rodney argued in his *How Europe Underdeveloped Africa.*[7] One direct result of the trade was the growth of the shipping and ship building industries. Between 1690 and 1714, the tonnage of goods shipped between England and the Caribbean Islands increased from 13,600 tons to 122,000 tons.[8] This shipping trade indirectly enhanced the fishing, rum and woolen trades in England. For instance, in 1788, Manchester exported to Africa 200,000 pounds of cheap goods which gave employment to thousands of British citizens.[9] The birth and expansion of racism was the result of this trade. As Eric Williams pointed out, Blacks were not enslaved because of the color of their skin, but because they constituted an essential lynch-pin in the economic master plan of Europe. As the number of slaves imported into the United States continued to increase, racism developed as an intellectual justification for the institution of slavery. Law, therefore, with its inherent ideals of justice and fair play, became compromised by these economic imperatives. Racism facilitated the economic exploitation of Black people by rationalizing that "A Negro is not a man" and thus is inferior to white people.[10]

---

7 Eric Williams' *Capitalism and Slavery* is a leading work on the impact of slavery on the development of the West. The more recent *How Europe Underdeveloped Africa,* by the late Walter Rodney is also a pioneering work in this area.

8 Eric Williams, *Capitalism and Slavery* (New York, Capricorn Books, 1944, 1966), page 58.

9 Williams, page 70.

10 Cochin, Augustin, *Results of Slavery*, (Freeport, Books for Libraries Press, 1863, 1970), page 100.

This thinking, according to Du Bois, created a paradox in the intellectual and institutional fabric of early America; a paradox best typified by contradictory thinking on questions of liberty and slavery. Even the founding fathers were not immune to this paradox. Many believed that Blacks were sub-human.[11] George Washington, the founding President of the United States, attended many discussions on slavery but did not speak out in opposition to proposals to classify Africans as property. This would be understandable, given that he came from a family of three generations of slave owners. Here was an opportunity to attack slavery as a violation of basic human rights, yet he acquiesced to the exploitation of Black labor. George Washington was not alone. Racism was also manifest in the actions of other key political figures of the eighteenth century. Ironically, many drafters of the *Declaration of Independence* held deep rooted feelings that Black people were inferior; and of the five men responsible for the document, three were lawyers.[12] What should have been the role of law during the slavery era? Were the ideals of justice and liberty incorporated into American law? Slavery was a key to the early development of capitalist institutions in America. Slave labor on the Southern cotton plantations led to the development of manufacturing, marketing, financing and transportation industries in the North.[13]

---

11 Matthew T. Mellon, *Early American View of Negro Slavery,* (Boston, Meador Publishing Co., 1970), page 73.

12 Barnett Hollander, *Slavery in America: Its Legal History,* (New York, Barnes and Noble, 1963), page 22. The three lawyers were Thomas Jefferson, John Adams and Roger Sherman. The remaining two were Benjamin Franklin and Robert Livingston.

13 Barrington Moore, Jr. *The Social Origins of Dictatorship and Democracy*, (Boston: Beacon Press, 1967), page 33.

Law was therefore used by capitalists to establish and maintain the subordinate position of Blacks in American society. Should slaves or their descendants have been compensated for over three hundred years of free labor? Should families be compensated for years of rape and murder? Should the descendants of slaves be compensated for the unjust enrichment that a segment of the American population experienced as a direct result of slavery? Did the law have any other choice, but to rationalize slavery?

B.
The Legitimization of Segregation in the North

One of the first challenges to segregation in Northern schools was brought by white abolitionist and attorney Charles Sumner and Robert Morris, Jr., the second Black Attorney admitted to practice law in the United States. The first was Macon Bolling Allen, who was admitted to the Massachusetts Bar on May 5, 1845.[14] *They argued before the Supreme Judicial Court that segregated schools were inferior and inconvenient to Black children. Many Black students had to bypass white schools to get to the Black schools. Although the Court rejected the claim of Sarah Roberts, a young Black girl who sought entrance on a non-segregated basis, the Massachusetts Legislature passed a law in 1855 barring the use of race in school admissions. (Mass. Laws 1855, Ch. 256, s 1). Could the Supreme Judicial Court of the Commonwealth of Massachusetts have decided the case of Roberts v. City of Boston any differently, given the fact that Boston was the first slave trading port in the "new world?"*

---

14 Charles Walker, "Fighting for Freedom and Equality: Blacks and the Law in Early Massachusetts," *The Journal of the Supreme Judicial Court Historical Society*, Vol. 4 (1998), pages 82-92.

SARAH C. ROBERTS v. THE CITY OF BOSTON
Supreme Judicial Court
59 Mass. (5 Cush.) 198 (1850)

This was an action on the case, brought by Sarah C. Roberts, an infant, who sued by Benjamin F. Roberts, her father and next friend, against the city of Boston, under the statute of 1845, c. 214, which provides that any child, unlawfully excluded from public school instruction in this commonwealth, shall recover damages therefor against the city or town by which such public instruction is supported...

"...The regulations of the primary school committee contain the following provisions:

"Admissions. No pupil shall be admitted into a primary school without a ticket of admission from a member of the district committee.

"Admissions of Applicants. Every member of the committee shall admit to his school, all applicants, of suitable age and qualifications, residing nearest to the school under his charge, (excepting those for whom special provision has been made,) provided the number in his school will warrant the admission.

"Scholars to go to the Schools Nearest Their Residences. Applicants for admission to the Schools, (with the exception and provision referred to in the preceding rule,) are especially entitled to enter the schools nearest to their places of residence.

"At the time of the plaintiff's application, as hereinafter mentioned, for admission to the primary school, the city of Boston had established, for the exclusive use of colored children, two primary schools, one in Belknap Street, in the eighth school district and one in Sun Court Street in the second school district.

"The colored population of Boston constitutes less than one sixty-second part of the entire population of the city. For half a century, separate schools have been kept in Boston for colored children, and the primary school for colored children in Belknap street was established in 1820, and has been kept there ever since. The teachers of this school have the same compensation and qualifications as in other like schools in the city. Schools for colored children were originally established at the request of colored citizens, whose children could not attend the public schools, on account of the prejudice then existing against them.

"The plaintiff is a colored child, of five years of age, a resident of Boston, and living with her father, since the month of March, 1847, in Andover Street, in the sixth primary school district. In the month of April, 1847, she being of suitable age and qualifications, (unless her color was a disqualification,) applied to a member of the district primary school committee, having under his charge the primary school nearest to her place of residence, for a ticket of admission to that school, the number of scholars therein warranting her admission, and no special provision having been made for her, unless the establishment of the two schools for colored children exclusively, is to be so considered.

"The member of the school committee, to whom the plaintiff applied, refused her application, on the ground of her being a colored person, and of the special provision made as aforesaid. The plaintiff thereupon applied to the primary school committee of the district, for admission to one of their schools, and was in like manner refused admission, on the ground of her color and the provision aforesaid. She thereupon petitioned the general primary school committee, for leave to enter one of the schools nearest her residence. That committee referred the subject to the committee of the district, with full powers, and the committee of the district thereupon again refused the plaintiff's application, on the sole ground of color and the special provision aforesaid, and the plaintiff has not since attended any school in Boston. Afterwards, on the 15th of February, 1848, the plaintiff went into the primary school nearest her residence, but without any ticket of admission or other leave granted, and was on that day ejected from the school by the teacher.

"The school established in Belknap Street is twenty-one hundred feet distant from the residence of the plaintiff, measuring through the streets; and in passing from the plaintiff's residence to the Belknap Street School, the direct route passes the ends of two streets in which there are five primary schools. The distance to the school in Sun Court is much greater. The distance from the plaintiff's residence to the nearest primary school is nine hundred feet. The plaintiff might have attended the school in Belknap Street, at any time, and her father was so informed, but he refused to have her attend there.

"In 1846, George Putnam and other colored citizens of Boston petitioned the primary school committee, that exclusive schools for colored children might be abolished, and the committee, on the 22d of June, 1846, adopted the report of a sub-committee, and a resolution appended thereto, which was in the following words:

"Resolved, that in the opinion of this board, the continuance of the separate schools for colored children, and the regular attendance of all such children upon the schools, is not only legal and just, but is best adapted to promote the education of that class of our population..."

C. SUMNER and R. MORRIS, JR., for the Plaintiff.

Mr. Sumner argued as follows:
    1. According to the spirit of American institutions, and especially of the Constitution of Massachusetts, (Part First, Articles I and VI,) all men, without distinction of color or race, are equal before the law.

2. The legislation of Massachusetts has made no discrimination of color or race in the establishment of the public schools. The laws establishing public schools speak of "schools for the instruction of children," generally, and "for the benefit of all the inhabitants of the town," not specifying any particular class, color, or race. Rev. Sts. c.23; Colony Law of 1647, (Anc. Ch. c.186.)....

3. The courts of Massachusetts have never admitted any discrimination, founded on color or race, in the administration of the common schools, but have recognized the equal rights of all the inhabitants. *Commonwealth v. Dedham,* 16 Mass. 141, 146; *Withington v. Eveleth,* 7 Pick. 106; *Perry v. Dover,* 12 Pick. 206, 213.

4. The exclusion of colored children from the public schools, which are open to white children, is a source of practical inconvenience to them and their parents, to which white persons are not exposed, and

5. The separation of children in the public schools of Boston, on account of color or race, is in the nature of caste, and is, therefore, a violation of equality.

6. The school committee has no power, under the constitution and laws of Massachusetts, to make any discrimination on account of color or race, among children in the public schools... The power to determine the "qualifications" of the scholars must be restrained to the qualifications of age, sex, and moral and intellectual fitness. The fact, that a child is black, or that he is white, cannot of itself be considered a qualification, or a disqualification.

The regulations and by-laws of municipal corporations must be reasonable, or they are inoperative and void. *Commonwealth v. Worcester,* 3 Pick. 462; *Vandine's Case,* 6 Pick. 187; Shaw v. Boston, 1 Met.130. So, the regulations and by-laws of the school committee must be reasonable; and their discretion must be exercised in a reasonable manner. The discrimination made by the School Committee of Boston, on account of color, is not legally reasonable... It is clear, that the committee may classify scholars, according to age and sex, for these distinctions are inoffensive, and recognized as legal (Rev. Sts. c. 23, '63); or according to their moral and intellectual qualifications, because such a power is necessary to the government of schools. But the committee cannot assume, without individual examination, that an entire race possess certain moral or intellectual qualities, which render it proper to place them all in a class by themselves.

But it is said, that the committee, in thus classifying the children, has not violated any principle of equality, inasmuch as they have provided a school with competent instructors for the colored children, where they enjoy equal advantages of instruction with those enjoyed by the white children. To this there are several answers: 1st, The separate school for colored children is not one of the schools established by the law relating to public schools, (Rev. Sts. c. 23,) and having no legal existence, cannot be a legal equivalent. 2d. It is not in fact an equivalent. It is the occasion of inconveniences to the colored children, to which they would not be exposed if they had access to the nearest public schools; it inflicts upon them the stigma of caste; and although the matters taught in the two schools may be precisely the same, a school exclusively devoted to one class must differ essentially, in its spirit and character, from that public school known to the law, where all classes meet together in equality. 3d. Admitting that it is an equivalent, still the colored children cannot be compelled to take it. They have an equal right with the white children to the general public schools.

7. The court will declare the by-law of the school committee, making a discrimination of color among children entitled to the benefit of the public schools, to be unconstitutional and illegal, although there are no express words of prohibition in the constitution and laws. Slavery was abolished in Massachusetts, by virtue of the declaration of rights in our constitution without any specific words of abolition in that constitution, without any specific words of abolition in that instrument, or in any subsequent legislation. *Commonwealth v. Aves*, 18 Pick. 193, 210. The same words, which are potent to destroy slavery, must be equally potent against any institution founded on caste.....

The fact, that the separation of the schools was originally made at the request of the colored parents, cannot affect the rights of the colored people, or the powers of the school committee. The separation of the schools, so far from being for the benefit of both races, is an injury to both. It tends to create a feeling of degradation in the blacks, and of prejudice and uncharitableness in the whites.

SHAW, C.J. ...The question therefore is, whether, upon the facts agreed, the plaintiff has been unlawfully excluded from such instruction...

By the agreed statement of facts, it appears, that the defendants support a class of schools called primary schools, to the number of about one hundred and sixty, designed for the instruction of children of both sexes, who are between the ages of four and seven years. Two of these schools are appropriated by the primary school committee, having charge of that class of schools, to the exclusive instruction of colored children, and the residue to the exclusive instruction of white children.

The plaintiff, by her father, took proper measures to obtain admission into one of these schools appropriated to white children, but pursuant to the regulations of the committee, and in conformity therewith, she was not admitted. Either of the schools appropriated to colored children was open to her; the nearest of which was about a fifth of a mile or seventy rods more distant from her father's house than the nearest primary school. It further appears, by the facts agreed, that the committee having charge of that class of schools had, a short time previously to the plaintiff's application, adopted a resolution, upon a report of a committee, that in the opinion of that board, the continuance of the separate schools for colored children, and the regular attendance of all such children upon the schools, is not only legal and just, but is best adapted to promote the instruction of that class of the population....

The plaintiff, had access to a school, set apart for colored children, as well conducted in all respects, and as well fitted, in point of capacity and qualification of the instructors, to advance the education of children under seven years old, as the other primary schools; the objection is, that the schools thus open to the plaintiff are exclusively appropriated to colored children, and are at a greater distance from her home. Under these circumstances, has the plaintiff been unlawfully excluded from public school instruction? Upon the best consideration we have been able to give the subject, the court are all of opinion that she has not....

The great principle, advanced by the learned and eloquent advocate of the plaintiff, is, that by the constitution and laws of Massachusetts, all persons without distinction of age or sex, birth or color, origin or condition, are equal before the law. This, as a broad general principle, such as ought to appear in a declaration of rights, is perfectly sound; it is not only expressed in terms, but pervades and animates the whole spirit of our constitution of free government. But, when this great principle comes to be applied to the actual and various conditions of persons in society, it will not warrant the assertion, that men and women are legally clothed with the same civil and political powers, and that children and adults are legally to have the same functions and be subject to the same treatment; but only that the rights of all, as they are settled and regulated by law, are equally entitled to the paternal consideration and protection of the law, for their maintenance and security. What those rights are, to which individuals, in the infinite variety of circumstances by which they are surrounded in society, are entitled, must depend on laws adapted to their respective relations and conditions.

Conceding, therefore, in the fullest manner, that colored persons, the descendants of Africans, are entitled by law, in this commonwealth, to equal rights, constitutional and political, civil and social, the question then arises, whether the regulation in question, which provides separate schools for colored children, is a violation of any of these rights.

The power of general superintendence vests a plenary authority in the committee to arrange, classify, and distribute pupils, in such a manner as they think best adapted to their general proficiency and welfare. If it is thought expedient to provide for very young children, it may be, that such schools may be kept exclusively by female teachers, quite adequate to their instruction, and yet whose services may be obtained at a cost much lower than that of more highly-qualified male instructors. So if they should judge it expedient to have a grade of schools for children from seven to ten, and another for those from ten to fourteen, it would seem to be within their authority to establish such schools. So to separate male and female pupils into different schools. It has been found necessary, that is to say, highly expedient, at times, to establish special schools for poor and neglected children, who have passed the age of seven, and have become too old to attend the primary school, and yet have not acquired the rudiments of learning, to enable them to enter the ordinary schools. If a class of youth, of one or both sexes, is found in that condition, and it is expedient to organize them into a separate school, to receive the special training, adapted to their condition, it seems to be within the power of the superintending committee, to provide for the organization of such special school.

In the absence of special legislation on this subject, the law has vested the power in the committee to regulate the system of distribution and classification; and when this power is reasonably exercised, without being abused or perverted by colorable presences, the decision of the committee must be deemed conclusive. The committee, apparently upon great deliberation, have come to the conclusion, that the good of both classes of schools will be best promoted, by maintaining the separate primary schools for colored and for white children, and we can perceive no ground to doubt, that this is the honest result of their experience and judgment.

It is urged, that this maintenance of separate schools tends to deepen and perpetuate the odious distinction of caste, founded in a deep-rooted prejudice in public opinion. This prejudice, if it exists, is not created by law, and probably cannot be changed by law. Whether this distinction and prejudice, existing in the opinion and feelings of the community, would not be as effectually fostered by compelling colored and white children to associate together in the same schools, may well be doubted; at all events, it is a fair and proper question for the committee to consider and decide upon, having in view the best interests of both classes of children placed under their superintendence, and we cannot say, that their decision upon it is not founded on just grounds of reason and experience, and in the results of a discriminating and honest judgment.

The increased distance, to which the plaintiff was obliged to go to school from her father's house, is not such, in our opinion, as to render the regulation in question unreasonable, still less illegal.

On the whole the court are of the opinion, that upon the facts stated, the action cannot be maintained.

Plaintiff nonsuit.

► Notes & Questions

1. Are the arguments advanced by the attorneys for Ms. Roberts compelling?

2. If all people are equal before the law, how did the Court arrive at its decision?

3. What about the argument that separation of children is a form of caste? Is that argument compelling? Why? If not? Why not?

4. Do you agree with the Court's decision?

5. Why is separation according to race different from that on the basis of wealth or gender?

6. Should the Court have deferred to the authority of the School Committee?

7. What public policy purpose is served by the Court allowing the committee to make decisions, such as these, as long as they are reasonable?

C.
The Legitimization of Racism in the Nation

1.) <u>Militant Demand for African Repatriation</u>

In the Amistad case, the United States Government compromised with slavery by capitulating to the widespread belief that, because of their inferiority, Black people should be removed to Africa. The Supreme Court, in general, refused to depart from this popular sentiment. When the African Cinque and his other enslaved brothers seized the slave ship Amistad, the Court supported their militant demands for a return to Africa. The United States Government, however, held firm to its support of white supremacy and refused to support the claims of the Africans for freedom and repatriation. Despite these gains for the African, both the United States Congress and this same Supreme Court refused to recognize the humanity of Africans in two separate legal pronouncements: The Fugitive Slave Act of 1850 and the Dred Scott case.

Shortly after the Roberts case the Federal Government established national policies for the dehumanization of African people. The Amistad case, decided in 1841, represented a widespread belief in America that Africans should be resettled in Africa. In 1816 the American Colonization Society was founded by Northern industrialists and Southern plantation owners to transport Blacks to the colony of Liberia.

UNITED STATES v. AMISTAD
Supreme Court of the United States
40 U.S. 518 (1841)

Mr. Justice STORY delivered the opinion of the Court.

This is the case of an appeal from the decree of the Circuit Court of the District of Connecticut, sitting in admiralty. The leading facts, as they appear upon the transcript of the proceedings, are as follows: On the 27th of June, 1839, the schooner L'Amistad, being the property of Spanish subjects, cleared out from the port of Havana, in the island of Cuba, for Puerto Principe, in the same island. On board of the schooner were the captain, Ransom Ferrer, and Jose Ruiz, and Pedro Montez, all Spanish subjects. The former had with him a negro boy, named Antonio, claimed to be his slave. Jose Ruiz had with him forty-nine negroes, claimed by him as his slaves, and stated to be his property, in a certain pass or document, signed by the Governor General of Cuba. Pedro Montez had with him four other negroes, also claimed by him as his slaves, and stated to be his property, in a similar pass or document, also signed by the Governor General of Cuba. On the voyage, and before the arrival of the vessel at her port of destination, the negroes rose, killed the captain, and took possession of her. On the 26th of August, the vessel was discovered by Lieutenant Gedney, of the United States brig Washington, at anchor on the high seas, at the distance of half a mile from the shore of Long Island. A part of the negroes were then on shore at Culloden Point, Long Island; who were seized by Lieutenant Gedney, and brought on board. The vessel, with the negroes and other persons on board, was brought by Lieutenant Gedney into the district of Connecticut, and there libelled for salvage in the District Court of the United States. A libel for salvage was also filed by Henry Green and Pelatiah Fordham, of Sag Harbour, Long Island. On the 15th of September, Ruiz and Montez filed claims and libels, in which they asserted their ownership of the negroes as their slaves, and of certain parts of the cargo, and prayed that the same might be "delivered to them, or to the representatives of her Catholic majesty, as might be most proper." On the 19th of September, the Attorney of the United States, for the district of Connecticut, filed an information or libel, setting forth, that the Spanish minister had officially presented to the proper department of the government of the United States, a claim for the restoration of the vessel, cargo, and slaves, as the property of Spanish subjects, which had arrived within the jurisdictional limits of the United States, and were taken possession of by the said public armed brig of the United States; under such circumstances as made it the duty of the United States to cause the same to be restored to the true proprietors, pursuant to the treaty between the

United States and Spain: and praying the Court, on its being made legally to appear that the claim of the Spanish minister was well founded, to make such order for the disposal of the vessel, cargo, and slaves, as would best enable the United States to comply with their treaty stipulations. But if it should appear, that the negroes were persons transported from Africa, in violation of the laws of the United States, and brought within the United States contrary to the same laws; he then prayed the Court to make such order for their removal to the coast of Africa, pursuant to the laws of the United States, as it should deem fit...

On the 7th of January, 1840, the negroes, Cinque and others, with the exception of Antonio, by their counsel, filed an answer, denying that they were slaves, or the property of Ruiz and Montez, or that the Court could, under the Constitution or laws of the United States, or under any treaty, exercise any jurisdiction over their persons, by reason of the premises; and praying that they might be dismissed. They specially set forth and insist in this answer, that they were native born Africans; born free, and still of right ought to be free and not slaves; that they were, on or about the 15th of April, 1839, unlawfully kidnapped, and forcibly and wrongfully carried on board a certain vessel on the coast of Africa, which was unlawfully engaged in the slave trade, and were unlawfully, transported in the same vessel to the island of Cuba, for the purpose of being there unlawfully sold as slaves; that Ruiz and Montez, well knowing the premises, made a pretended purchase of them: that afterwards, on or about the 28th, of June, 1839, Ruiz and Montez, confederating with Ferrer, (captain of the Amistad,) caused them, without law or right, to be placed on board of the Amistad to be transported to some place unknown to them, and there to be enslaved for life; that, on the voyage, they rose on the master, and took possession of the vessel, intending to return therewith to their native country, or to seek an asylum in some free state; and the vessel arrived, about the 26th of August, 1839, off Montauk Point, near Long Island; a part of them were sent on shore, and were seized by Lieutenant Gedney, and carried on board; and all of them were afterwards brought by him into the district of Connecticut...

The cause has been very elaborately argued, as well upon the merits, as upon a motion on behalf of the appellees to dismiss the appeal. On the part of the United States, it has been contended, 1. That due and sufficient proof concerning the property has been made to authorize the restitution of the vessel, cargo, and negroes to the Spanish subjects on whose behalf they are claimed pursuant to the treaty with Spain, of the 27th of October, 1795. 2. That the United States had a right to intervene in the manner in which they have done, to obtain a decree for the restitution of the property, upon the application of the Spanish minister. These propositions have been strenuously denied on the other side. Other collateral and incidental points have been stated, upon which it is not necessary at this moment to dwell.

Before entering upon the discussion of the main points involved in this interesting and important controversy, it may be necessary to say a few words as to the actual posture of the case as it now stands before us. In the first place, then, the only parties now before the Court on one side, are the United States, intervening for the sole purpose of procuring restitution of the property as Spanish property, pursuant to the treaty, upon the grounds stated by the other parties claiming the property in their respective libels. The United States do not assert any property in themselves, or any violation of their own rights, or sovereignty, or laws, by the acts complained of. They do not insist that these negroes have been imported into the United States, in contravention of our own slave trade acts. They do not seek to have these negroes delivered up for the purpose of being transported to Cuba as pirates or robbers, or as fugitive criminals found within our territories, who have been guilty of offences against the laws of Spain. They do not assert that the seizure, and bringing the vessel, and cargo, and negroes into port, by Lieutenant Gedney, for the purpose of adjudication, is a tortious act. They simply confine themselves to the right of the Spanish claimants to the restitution of their property, upon the facts asserted in their respective allegations.

In the next place, the parties before the Court on the other side as appellees, are Lieutenant Gedney, on his libel for salvage, and the negroes, (Cinque, and others,) asserting themselves, in their answer, not to be slaves, but free native Africans, kidnapped in their own country, and illegally transported by force from that country; and now entitled to maintain their freedom.

No question has been here made, as to the proprietary interests in the vessel and cargo. It is admitted that they belong to Spanish subjects, and that they ought to be restored. The only point on this head is, whether the restitution ought to be upon the payment of salvage or not? The main controversy is, whether these negroes are the property of Ruiz and Montez, and ought to be delivered up; and to this, accordingly, we shall first direct our attention.

It has been argued on behalf of the United States, that the Court are bound to deliver them up, according to the treaty of 1795, with Spain, which has in this particular been continued in full force, by the treaty of 1819, ratified in 1821... To bring the case within the article, it is essential to establish, First, That these negroes, under all the circumstances, fall within the description of merchandise, in the sense of the treaty. Secondly, That there has been a rescue of them on the high seas, out of the hands of the pirates and robbers; which, in the present case, can only be, by showing that they themselves are pirates and robbers; and, Thirdly, That Ruiz and Montez, the asserted proprietors, are the true proprietors, and have established their title by competent proof.

If these negroes were, at the time, lawfully held as slaves under the laws of Spain, and recognised by those laws as property capable of being lawfully bought and sold; we see no reason why they may not justly be deemed within the intent of the treaty, to be included under the denomination of merchandise, and, as such, ought to be restored to the claimants: for, upon that point, the laws of Spain would seem to furnish the proper rule of interpretation. But, admitting this, it is clear, in our opinion, that neither of the other essential facts and requisites has been established in proof; and the onus probandi of both lies upon the claimants to give rise to the casus foederis. It is plain beyond controversy, if we examine the evidence, that these negroes never were the lawful slaves of Ruiz or Montez or of any other Spanish subjects. They are natives of

Africa, and were kidnapped there, and were unlawfully transported to Cuba, in violation of the laws and treaties of Spain, and the most solemn edicts and declarations of that government. By those laws, and treaties, and edicts, the African slave trade is utterly abolished; the dealing in that trade is deemed a heinous crime; and the negroes thereby introduced into the dominions of Spain, are declared to be free. Ruiz and Montez are proved to have made the pretended purchase of these negroes, with a full knowledge of all the circumstances. And so cogent and irresistible is the evidence in this respect, that the District Attorney has admitted in open Court, upon the record, that these negroes were native Africans, and recently imported into Cuba, as alleged in their answers to the libels in the case. The supposed proprietary interest of Ruiz and Montez, is completely displaced, if we are at liberty to look at the evidence or the admissions of the District Attorney.

If, then, these negroes are not slaves, but are kidnapped Africans, who, by the laws of Spain itself, are entitled to their freedom, and were kidnapped and illegally carried to Cuba, and illegally detained and restrained on board of the Amistad; there is no pretence to say, that they are pirates or robbers. We may lament the dreadful acts, by which they asserted their liberty, and took possession of the Amistad, and endeavoured to regain their native country; but they cannot be deemed pirates or robbers in the sense of the law of nations, or the treaty with Spain, or the laws of Spain itself; at least so far as those laws have been brought to our knowledge. Nor do the libels of Ruiz or Montez assert them to be such.

This posture of the facts would seem, of itself, to put an end to the whole inquiry upon the merits. But it is argued, on behalf of the United States, that the ship, and cargo, and negroes were duly documented as belonging to Spanish subjects, and this Court have no right to look behind these documents; that full faith and credit is to be given to them; and that they are to be held conclusive evidence in this cause, even although it should be established by the most satisfactory proofs, that they have been obtained by the grossest frauds and impositions upon the constituted authorities of Spain. To this argument we can, in no wise, assent. There is nothing in the treaty which justifies or sustains the argument. We do not here meddle with the point, whether there has been any connivance in this illegal traffic, on the part of any of the colonial authorities or subordinate officers of Cuba; because, in our view, such an examination is unnecessary, and ought not to be pursued, unless it were indispensable to public justice, although it has been strongly pressed at the bar. What we proceed upon is this, that although public documents of the government, accompanying property found on board of the private ships of a foreign nation, certainly are to be deemed prima facie evidence of the facts which they purport to state, yet they are always open to be impugned for fraud; and whether that fraud be in the original obtaining of these documents, or in the subsequent fraudulent and illegal use of them, when once it is satisfactorily established, it overthrows all their sanctity, and destroys them as proof. Fraud will vitiate any, even the most solemn transactions; and an asserted title to property, founded upon it, is utterly void. The very language of the ninth article of the treaty of 1795 requires the proprietor to make due and sufficient proof of his property. And how can that proof be deemed either due or sufficient, which is but a connected and stained tissue of fraud? This is not a mere rule of municipal jurisprudence. Nothing is more clear in the law of nations, as an established rule to regulate their rights, and duties, and intercourse, than the doctrine, that the ship's papers are but prima facie evidence, and that, if they are shown to be fraudulent, they are not to be held proof of any valid title... Upon the merits of the case, then, there does not seem to us to be any ground for doubt, that these negroes ought to be deemed free; and that the Spanish treaty interposes no obstacle to the just assertion of their rights...

...Upon the whole, our opinion is, that the decree of the Circuit Court, affirming that of the District Court, ought to be affirmed, except so far as it directs the negroes to be delivered to the President, to be transported to Africa, in pursuance of the act of the 3d of March, 1819; and, as to this, it ought to be reversed: and that the said negroes be declared to be free, and be dismissed from the custody of the Court, and go without day.

► Notes & Questions

1. Why did the United States take up the position of the Spanish crown? Why didn't the United States support the claims of the Africans that they were free and should be returned to Africa?

2. What public policy issues were at stake in the case?

3. John Quincy Adams represented the Africans before the Court. Why did some white Americans take up the cause of Black freedom? What public policy issues were they raising by actively getting involved in the struggle for Black freedom?

4. What was the rationale for the Court's decision? How do you distinguish this decision from others that upheld the inferiority of Blacks within the United States?

5. Why couldn't Blacks, who were brought into the United States prior to 1808, argue that they had been unlawfully kidnapped and therefore deserved to be free?

2.) **Fugitive Slave Act (1850)**

This law was designed to control the movement of slaves throughout the country, and to provide slave masters with legal assistance in their efforts to reclaim slaves who had escaped from racial oppression. The first federal extradition statute, upon which the Act of 1850 was based, was enacted in 1793. The earlier law did not provide for court costs, attorney's fees and travel costs associated with the attempts to capture an escaped slave. After a United States Supreme Court case in 1842, Prigg v. Pennsylvania, many states passed legislation entitled "personal liberty laws," which made it extremely difficult for extradition proceedings to prevail. In 1843, Massachusetts enacted a statute which prohibited judges from hearing fugitive slave cases and state officials from arresting fugitive slaves.

This federal law of 1850 strengthened law enforcement by authorizing the appointment of federal commissioners in each county of the United States. The law authorized the imposition of fines up to $2,000.00 and imprisonment for up to six months for interfering with rendition proceedings. A slave could not adjudicate that he was entitled to freedom. The master needed only to produce an affidavit signed by an officer of a court confirming that the slave was owned by the master. The slave could not allege mistaken identity and neither was the trial public. Obviously, there was no requirement that the slave be offered legal assistance.

The following excerpts from the Fugitive Slave Act of 1850 provide examples of the sweeping nature of the statute:

"Chap. LX- An Act to Amend, and Supplementary to the Act Entitled "An Act Respecting Fugitives from Justice, and Persons Escaping from the Services of their Masters," approved February twelfth, one thousand seven hundred and ninety-three.

"Be it enacted by the Senate and House of Representatives of the United States of America in congress assembled....

Marshalls are Liable for Loss of Slaves

"Sec. 5. And be it further enacted, That it shall be the duty of all marshalls and deputy marshalls to obey and execute all warrants and precepts issued under the provisions of this act, when to them directed; and should any marshall or deputy marshall refuse to receive such warrant, or other process, when tendered, or to use all proper means diligently to execute the same, he shall, on conviction thereof, be fined in the sum of one thousand dollars, to the use of such claimant, on the motion of such claimant, by the Circuit or District Court for the district of such marshall; and after arrest of such fugitive, by such marshall or deputy, or whilst at any time in his custody under the provisions of this act, should such fugitive escape, whether with or without the assent of such marshall or his deputy, such marshall shall be liable, on his official bond, to be prosecuted for the benefit of such claimant, for the full value of the service or labor of said fugitive in the State, Territory, or District whence he escaped;

Punishment for Those who Hinder Recapture or Aid Escape

"Sec. 7. And be it further enacted, That any person who shall knowingly and willingly obstruct, hinder, or prevent such claimant, his agent or attorney, or any person or persons lawfully assisting him, her, or them, from arresting such fugitive from service or labor either with or without process as aforesaid, or shall rescue, or attempt to rescue, such fugitive from service or labor, from the custody of such claimant, his or her agent or attorney, or other person or persons lawfully assisting as aforesaid, when so arrested, pursuant to the authority herein given and declared; or shall aid, abet, or assist such person so owing service or labor as aforesaid, directly or indirectly, to escape from such claimant, his agent or attorney, or other person or persons legally authorized as aforesaid; or shall harbor or conceal such fugitive, so as to prevent the discovery and arrest of such person, after notice or knowledge of the fact that such person was a fugitive from service or labor as aforesaid, shall, for either of said offence, be subject to a fine not exceeding one thousand dollars, and imprisonment not exceeding six months, by indictment and conviction before the District Court of the United States for the district in which such offence may have been committed, or before the proper court of criminal jurisdiction, if committed within any one of the organized Territories of the United States; and shall moreover forfeit and pay, by way of civil damages to the party injured by such illegal conduct, the sum of one thousand dollars, for each fugitive so lost as aforesaid, to be recovered by action of debt, in any of the District or Territorial Courts aforesaid, within whose jurisdiction the said offence may have been committed...

Right of Marshall to Conscript a Posse to Prevent Rescue

"Sec.9. And be it further enacted, That, upon affidavit made by the claimant of such fugitive, his agent or attorney, after such certificate has been issued, that he has reason to apprehend that such fugitive will be rescued by force from his or their possession before he can be taken beyond the limits of the State in which the arrest is made, it shall be the duty of the officer making the arrest to retain such fugitive in his custody, and to remove him to the State when he fled, and there to deliver him to said claimant, his agent, or attorney. And to this end, the officer aforesaid is hereby authorized and required to employ so many persons as he may deem necessary to overcome such force, and to retain them in his service so long as circumstances may require. The said officer, and his assistants, while so employed, to receive the same compensation, and to be allowed the same expenses, as are now allowed by law for compensation, and to be allowed the same expenses, as are now allowed by law for transportation of criminals, to be certified by the judge of the district within which the arrest is made, and paid out of the treasury of the United States..."

▶ Notes & Questions

1. Why was it necessary for the Federal Government to pass the Fugitive Slave Act?

2. Under the statute Federal marshalls are made personally liable for loss of fugitives in their custody. What effect does this have upon the business practices of bonding companies?

3. Marshalls are given the right to conscript posses for an unlimited period. What effects did this law have upon that section of the population that normally opposed slavery?

4. What rights did the new law infringe upon?

3.) **The Case of Anthony Burns**

The impact of the Fugitive Slave Act was quickly felt throughout the nation, particularly in the northern states. In the Commonwealth of Massachusetts the implementation of the statute was challenged in the case of Anthony Burns, a runaway slave. On May 24, 1854, Charles Suttles of Alexandria County, Virginia appeared before Commissioner Loring and presented an affidavit from a Virginia court, indicating that Anthony Burns had escaped from servitude on March 24, 1854. Witnesses appeared for Burns and testified that he was in Boston before the date of the alleged escape. Despite this testimony, Loring issued a warrant for the arrest of Burns. On May 24, 1854, Burns was arrested and taken to the Federal courthouse where Suttles asked him: "Why did you run away from me?" Burns responded: "I fell sleep on board the vessel where I worked, and before I woke up she set sail and carried me off."[15]

On May 25, 1854, Anthony Burns went on trial before Commissioner Edward Loring. The commission had to determine whether Burns was the run away described in the affidavit. Loring had hoped that the trial would be quick and Burns would be on his way out of Boston. However, Attorney Richard Henry Dana, Jr. was passing the courthouse and noticed that a slave was being presented under the statute. The court officers tried to bar Dana from Burns, but Dana made it to Burns and offered his services. Burns refused his services, but Dana convinced Commissioner Loring to delay the proceedings until Burns could reconsider whether he wanted counsel. The Commissioner agreed and adjourned proceedings for two days.

During this period, the word about the trial spread throughout the abolitionist community. Two Black leaders, Reverend Leonard A. Grimes and Coffin Pitts went to the court to visit Burns. They took with them, Wendell Phillips, a leading abolitionist attorney in an effort to convince Burns to have his case tried.

---

15 Charles Emory Stevens, *Anthony Burns: A History* (Boston: John P. Jewett and Co.), p. 18-19.

Other abolitionists decided to resort to direct action. A mass meeting was held at Faneuil Hall, and a group of Blacks, under the leadership of Reverend Thomas Wentworth Higginson stormed the jail in an attempt to rescue Burns. After the unsuccessful attempt to rescue the prisoner, heavy chains were draped around the courthouse as soldiers and militiamen stood guard.

Ironically, Suttles had agreed to sell Burns to a group of Boston businessmen for $1,200.00, but the sale was averted by United States District Attorney Benjamin F. Hallett. Hallett kept President Franklin Pierce informed of the proceedings. Pierce, though from New England, was a pro-slavery president who wanted to demonstrate to the Southerners that he could be tough on runaway slaves.

The trial, therefore, proceeded for four days, ending in a verdict against Burns on June 2. On that same day, Burns was placed on a ship to Virginia. Despite his extradition, hundreds of Bostonians raised funds to purchase his freedom. It was not until February, 1855, that Burns returned to Boston a free man.[16] While in Virginia, Burns was kept in jail for four months under inhumane conditions which caused him to become ill and permanently lame.

One result of the new Fugitive Slave Law was that liberal states, such as Massachusetts, had to enforce it despite widespread opposition. The law, as represented in this case, became an instrument for the destruction of Black people's liberties.

---

16 Stevens, page 181-97

▶ Notes & Questions

The Anthony Burns case was a major test case for the new statute. President Franklin Pierce was determined to put liberal Massachusetts in its right place. Massachusetts was one of a growing number of states that had passed laws which prohibited its court officers and personnel from cooperating with slave catchers.

4.) **Blacks as Property under the Constitution.**

For more than a century, the controversy raged in America over whether Africans were property or human beings, endowed with the same rights as all others. While most states by 1857 had adopted laws that governed the condition and status of slaves, the highest court in the land had not decided the definitive question of whether Africans were, in fact, human beings under the Constitution.

Before bringing his action in the Federal Court, Dred Scott first sought his freedom in the state courts of Missouri. Dr. John Emerson died, after he brought the Scott family back from Illinois to Missouri in 1838. Legal title to the Scotts then passed to Dr. Emerson's wife, Irene. In 1846, Dred Scott asked Ms. Emerson if he could pay for his family's freedom, but she refused. He then filed suit in the Circuit Court of St. Louis, seeking his family's freedom on the grounds that he and his family had resided in a free state. On January 23, 1850, the court ruled in favor of the family. The Supreme Court of Missouri, on the other hand, determined that he and his family were not entitled to their freedom. *Scott v. Emerson*, 15 Mo. 576, *Sylvia v. Kirby*, 17 Mo. 434.

This decision of the state court appeared to be contrary to other decisions in which Blacks had successfully sued for their freedom on similar grounds. *Winny v. Whitesides*, 1 Mo. R. 472; *Rachel, a Woman of Color v. Walker,* 4 Mo. 350, 354; *Nat (A Man of Color) v. Ruddle*, 3 Mo. 400, 402. Just as Rosa Parks made her courageous stand against segregation in the South in 1954, Dred Scott sought relief for himself and his family from violence and slavery in 1853. Irene Emerson subsequently transferred ownership of the Scotts to her brother John F.A. Sanford, who periodically whipped them. Dred and Harriet Scott declared their freedom as individuals and refused to serve their new master, John F.A. Sandford. The Scotts contended in their new complaints, filed in the Circuit Court of the United States, essentially the same claims that they had asserted in the state courts. The legal papers were filed on November 2, 1853. According to the Scotts, John Sandford, a citizen of the State of New York assaulted and held them as slaves, and in prison for more than six hours on January 1, 1853.[17] After their release from prison, the Scotts alleged that John Sandford threatened to beat them and by such threats put them in fear. Dred Scott alleged that he was deprived of "... society, companion and assistance of his wife..." as a result of the beatings and detention. Finally, Dred Scott alleged that John Sandford, on the same day, assaulted, imprisoned and held as slaves the Scotts' two infant children, Eliza Scott and Lizzie Scott.

In their legal papers, the attorneys for Sandford, attacked the jurisdiction of the Court. They alleged that the Court could not hear the complaints of the Scotts because "... he is a negro of African descent, his ancestors were of pure African blood, and were brought into this country and sold as negro slaves."[18]

On April 25, 1854, the Court sustained Scott's objection to Sandford's plea of lack of jurisdiction. On May 4, 1854, the attorneys filed with the Court an agreed upon statement of the facts in the case. Sandford, represented by H.A. Garland, stated that his client was not guilty of any of the charges brought against him. In answer to Scott's allegations that Sandford had assaulted and imprisoned him, Sandford, through his attorney, stated that because Scott was a Negro slave and lawfully his property, that he could lawfully restrain him. With respect to Harriet, Eliza and Lizzi, Sandford stated that he had a right to restrain them because they were also his slaves.

The Decision of the United States Supreme Court

The decision of the high court rendered on March 6, 1857 demonstrated the thinking of nine of the most prominent and influential white men in the country. The majority (five) of the justices were from slave holding states and the two dissenting justices (Benjamin R. Curtis: Massachusetts, John McLean: Ohio) were from the North. Chief Justice Roger Brooke Taney hailed from the State of Maryland. The justices who voted with Taney

---

17 *Scott v. Sandford*, 60 U.S. 691, 692 (1857).

18 *Scott v. Sandford*, 60 U.S. 691, 693.

were Justice Samuel Nelson of New York, Justice James W. Wayne of Georgia, Justice Robert G. Grier of Pennsylvania, Justice Peter V. Daniel of Virginia, Justice James A. Campbell of Alabama and Justice John Catron of Tennessee. They were split on what legal issues the Court had to consider in order to decide the case. Justices Wayne and Daniel agreed with Justice Taney that the key question was the one of citizenship. Justice Nelson of New York reasoned that the Court could consider whether Scott had become emancipated as a result of being taken into Northwest Territory.[19] What was the basis of their decision? Was the decision racist? If so, how did law perpetuate racism? Was the decision just? Did the decision compromise the philosophical concept of justice? Was justice blind? Were there two systems of justice? Should there be two systems of justice?

DRED SCOTT v. JOHN F.A. SANDFORD
60 U.S. (19 How.)393 (1857)

Mr. Chief Justice Taney delivered the opinion of the court:

This case has been twice argued. After the argument at the last term, differences of opinion were found to exist among the members of the court; and as the questions in controversy are of the highest importance, and the court was at that time much pressed by the ordinary business of the term, it was deemed advisable to continue the case, and direct a re-argument on some of the points, in order that we might have an opportunity of giving to the whole subject a more deliberate consideration. It has accordingly been again argued by counsel, and considered by the court; and I now proceed to deliver its opinion.

There are two leading questions presented by the record:

1. Had the Circuit Court of the United States jurisdiction to hear and determine the case between these parties? And,

---

19 Mindy Frankel, *Dred Scott v. Sandford: How It Was Decided and Where It Stands Today*, unpublished, 1996, page 6.

2. If it had jurisdiction, is the judgment it has given erroneous or not? The plaintiff in error, who was also the plaintiff in the court below, was with his wife and children, held as slaves by the defendant, in the State of Missouri, and he brought this action in the Circuit Court of the United States for that district, to assert the title of himself and his family to freedom.

A. *Jurisdiction*

Did the federal courts have the power to hear Dred Scott's case? Judge Taney discusses the nature of federal jurisdiction.

...This difference arises, as we have said, from the peculiar character of the government of the United States. For although it is sovereign and supreme in its appropriate sphere of action, yet it does not possess all the powers which usually belong to the sovereignty of a nation. Certain specified powers, enumerated in the Constitution, have been conferred upon it: and neither the Legislative, Executive nor Judicial Departments of the Government can lawfully exercise any authority beyond the limits marked out by the Constitution. And in regulating the Judicial Department, the cases in which the courts of the United States shall have jurisdiction are particularly and specifically enumerated and defined; and they are not authorized to take cognizance of any case which does not come within the description therein specified. Hence, when a plaintiff sues in a court of the United States, it is necessary that he should show, in his pleading that the suit he brings is within the jurisdiction of the court, and that he is entitled to sue there. And if he omits to do this, and should, by any oversight of the Circuit Court, obtain a judgment in his favor, the judgment would be reversed in the appellate court for want of jurisdiction in the court below. The jurisdiction would not be presumed, as in the case of a common law, English, or state court, unless the contrary appeared. But the record, when it comes before the appellate court, must show, affirmatively, that the inferior court had authority, under the Constitution, to hear and determine the case. And if the plaintiff claims a right to sue in a circuit court of the United States, under that provision of the Constitution which gives jurisdiction in controversies between citizens of different states, he must distinctly aver in his pleading that they are citizens of different states; and he cannot maintain his suit without showing that fact in the pleadings... And this being the case in the present instance, the plea in abatement is necessarily under consideration; and it becomes, therefore, our duty to decide whether the facts stated in the plea are or are not sufficient to show that the plaintiff is not entitled to sue as a citizen in a court of the United States.

This is certainly a very serious question, and one that now for the first time has been brought for decision before this court. But it is brought here by those who have a right to bring it, and it is our duty to meet it and decide it.

The question is simply this: can a negro, whose ancestors were imported into this country and sold as slaves, become a member of the political community formed and brought into existence by the Constitution of the United States, and as such become entitled to all the rights, and privileges, and immunities, guarantied by that instrument to the citizen. One of these rights is the privilege of suing in a court of the United States in the cases specified in the Constitution.

It will be observed, that the plea applies to that class of persons only whose ancestors were negroes of the African race, and imported into this country, and sold and held as slaves. The only matter in issue before the court, therefore, is, whether the descendants of such slaves, when they shall be emancipated, or who are born of parents who had become free before their birth, are citizens of a state, in the sense in which the word "citizen"is used in the Constitution of the United States. And this being the only matter in dispute on the pleadings, the court must be understood as speaking in this opinion of that class only; that is, of those persons who are the descendants of Africans who were imported into this country and sold as slaves...

B. *Citizenship*
   Ultimately the Court had to decide whether Dred Scott was

a citizen who was empowered by the Constitution to bring suit in federal courts?

1.) *Who Were Citizens?*

The Court discussed the concept of citizens within the context of the Constitution.

...The words "people of the United States" and "citizens" are synonymous terms, and mean the same thing. They both describe the political body who, according to our republican institutions, form the sovereignty, and who hold the power and conduct the government through their representatives. They are what we familiarly call the "sovereign people," and every citizen is one of the people, and a constituent member of this sovereignty. The question before us is, whether the class of persons described in the plea in abatement compose a portion of this people, and are constituent members of this sovereignty. We think they are not, and that they are not included, and were not intended to be included, under the word "citizen" in the Constitution, and can, therefore, claim none of the rights and privileges which that instrument provides for and secures to citizens of the United States. On the contrary, they were at that time considered as a subordinate and inferior class of beings, who had been subjugated by the dominant race, and whether emancipated or not, yet remained subject to their authority, and had no rights or privileges but such as those who held the power and the government might choose to grant them....

2.) *The Court Should Not Make Judgments On Policy*

The Court states that it should not make moral judgments, but rather interpret the Constitution. Is the Court, however, making a moral judgment by rendering this decision?

...It is not the province of the court to decide upon the justice or injustice, the policy or impolicy of these laws. The decision of that question belonged to the political or law-making power; to those who formed the sovereignty and framed the Constitution. The duty of the court is to interpret the instrument they have framed, with the best lights we can obtain on the subject, and to administer it as we find it, according to its true intent and meaning when it was adopted....

3.) *State Citizenship*

Why does the Court go to such a length to acknowledge the rights of states to confer citizenship?

...In discussing this question, we must not confound the rights of citizenship which a state may confer within its own limits, and the rights of citizenship as a member of the Union. It does not by any means follow, because he has all the rights and privileges of a citizen of a State, that he must be a citizen of the United States. He may have all of the rights and privileges of the citizen of a State, and yet not be entitled to the rights and privileges of a citizen in any other State. For previous to the adoption of the Constitution of the United States, every State had the undoubted right to confer on whomever it pleased the character of a citizen, and to endow him with all its rights. But this character, of course, was confined to the boundaries of the State, and gave him no rights or privileges in other States beyond those secured to him by the laws of nations and the comity of States. Nor have the several States surrendered the power of conferring these rights and privileges by adopting the Constitution of the United States. Each State may still confer them upon an alien, or any one it thinks proper, or upon any class or description of persons; yet he would not be a citizen in the sense in which that word is used in the Constitution of the United States, nor entitled to sue as such in one of its courts, nor to the privileges and immunities of a citizen in the other States....

It is very clear, therefore, that no State can, by any Act or law of its own, passed since the adoption of the Constitution, introduce a new member into the political community created by the Constitution of the United States. It cannot make him a member of this community by making him a member of its own. And for the same reason it cannot introduce any person, or description of persons, who were not intended to be embraced in this new political family, which the Constitution brought into existence, but were intended to be excluded from it.

The question then arises, whether the provisions of the Constitution, in relation to the personal rights and privileges to which the citizen of a state should be entitled, embraced the negro African race, at that time in this country, or who might afterwards be imported, who had then or should afterwards be made free in any State; and to put it in the power of a single State to make him a citizen of the United States, and endue him with the full rights of citizenship in every other State without their consent. Does the Constitution of the United States act upon him whenever he shall be made free under the laws of a State and raised there to the rank of citizen, and immediately clothe him with all the privileges of a citizen in every other State, and in its own courts?

This court thinks the affirmative of these propositions cannot be maintained. And if it cannot, the plaintiff in error could not be a citizen of the State of Missouri, within the meaning of the Constitution of the United States, and, consequently, was not entitled to sue in its courts.

It is true, every person, and every class and description of persons, who were at the time of the adoption of the Constitution recognized as citizens in the several States, became also citizens of this new political body: but none other; it was formed by them, and for them and their posterity, but for no one else. And the personal rights and privileges guarantied to the citizens of this new sovereignty were intended to embrace those only who were then members of the several state communities, or who should afterwards, by birthright or otherwise, become members, according to the provisions of the Constitution and the principles on which it was founded. It was the union of those who were at that time members of distinct and separate political communities into one political family, whose power for special purposes, was to extend over the whole territory of the United States. And it gave to each citizen rights and privileges outside of his State which he did not before possess, and placed him in every other State upon a perfect equality with its own citizens as to rights of person and rights of property; it made him a citizen of the United States.

It becomes necessary, therefore, to determine who were citizens of the several States when the Constitution was adopted. And in order to do this, we must refer to the governments and institutions of the thirteen Colonies, when they separated from Great Britain and formed new sovereignties, and took their places in the family of independent nations. We must inquire who, at that time, were recognized as the people or citizens of a State, whose rights and liberties had been outraged by the English Government; and who declared their independence, and assumed the powers of government to defend their rights by force of arms.

In the opinion of the court, the legislation and histories of the times, and the language used in the Declaration of Independence show, that neither the class of persons who had been imported as slaves, nor their descendants, whether they had become free or not, were then acknowledged as part of the people, nor intended to be included in the general words used in that memorable instrument.

It is difficult at this day to realize the state of public opinion in relation to that unfortunate race, which prevailed in the civilized and enlightened portions of the world at the time of the Declaration of Independence, and when the Constitution of the United States was framed and adopted. But the public history of every European nation displays it, in a manner too plain to be mistaken.

They had for more than a century before been regarded as beings of an inferior order; and altogether unfit to associate with the white race, either in social or political relations; and so far inferior, that they had no rights which the white man was bound to respect; and that the negro might justly and lawfully be reduced to slavery for his benefit. He was bought and sold, and treated as an ordinary article of merchandise and traffic, whenever a profit could be made by it. This opinion was at that time fixed and universal in the civilized portion of the white race. It was regarded as an axiom in morals as well as in politics, which no one thought of disputing, or supposed to be open to dispute; and men in every grade and position in society daily and habitually acted upon it in their private pursuits, as well as in matters of public concern, without doubting for a moment the correctness of this opinion.

And in no nation was this opinion more firmly fixed or more uniformly acted upon than by the English government and English people. They not only seized them on the coast of Africa, and sold them or held them in slavery for their own use; but they took them as ordinary articles of merchandise to every country where they could make a profit on them, and were far more extensively engaged in this commerce than any other nation in the world.

The opinion thus entertained and acted upon in England was naturally impressed upon the colonies they founded on this side of the Atlantic. And, accordingly, a negro of the African race was regarded by them as an article of property, and held, and bought and sold as such in every one of the thirteen Colonies which united in the Declaration of Independence and afterwards formed the Constitution of the United States. The slaves were more or less numerous in the different Colonies, as slave labor was found more or less profitable. But no one seems to have doubted the correctness of the prevailing opinion of the time....

4.) *Reliance Upon Colonial Law to Uphold the Inferiority of Africans*

Why does the Court go back to the colonial laws to establish that Africans were considered inferior by whites? Why doesn't the Court overrule these precedents? Shouldn't justice and morality play a key role in law?

...We give both of these laws in the words used by the respective legislative bodies, because the language in which they are framed, as well as the provisions contained in them, show, too plainly to be misunderstood, the degraded condition of this unhappy race. They were still in force when the Revolution began, and are a faithful index to the state of feeling towards the class of persons of whom they speak, and of the position they occupied throughout the thirteen colonies, in the eyes and thoughts of the men who framed the Declaration of Independence and established the State constitutions and governments. They show that a perpetual and impassable barrier was intended to be erected between the white race and the one which they had reduced to slavery, and governed as subjects with absolute and despotic power, and which they then looked upon as so far below them in the scale of created beings, that intermarriages between the white persons and negroes or mulattoes were regarded as unnatural and immoral, and punished as crimes, not only in the parties, but in the persons who joined them in marriage. And no distinction in this respect was made between the free negro or mulatto and the slave, but this stigma, of the deepest degradation, was fixed upon the whole race.

We refer to these historical facts for the purpose of showing the fixed opinions concerning that race, upon which the statesmen of that day spoke and acted. It is necessary to do this, in order to determine whether the general terms used in the Constitution of the United States, as to the rights of man and the rights of the people, was intended to include them, or to give to them or their posterity the benefit of any of its provisions....

5. *Reliance Upon the Declaration of Independence to Uphold the Inferiority of Africans*

Even though this document outlined broad philosophical concepts of freedom and equality, the Court made clear that the document did not apply to Africans.

...The language of the Declaration of Independence is equally conclusive.

It begins by declaring that, "when in the course of human events it becomes necessary for one people to dissolve the political bonds which have connected them with another, and to assume among the powers of the earth the separate and equal station to which the laws of nature and nature's God entitle them, a decent respect for the opinions of mankind requires that they should declare the causes which impel them to the separation."

It then proceeds to say: "We hold these truths to be self-evident: that all men are created equal; that they are endowed by their Creator with certain inalienable rights; that among them is life, liberty, and pursuit of happiness; that to secure these rights, governments are instituted, deriving their just powers from the consent of the governed."

The general words above quoted would seem to embrace the whole human family, and if they were used in a similar instrument at this day, would be so understood. But it is too clear for dispute, that the enslaved African race were not intended to be included, and formed no part of the people who framed and adopted this Declaration; for if the language, as understood in that day, would embrace them, the conduct of the distinguished men who framed the Declaration of Independence would have been utterly and flagrantly inconsistent with the principles they asserted; and instead of the sympathy of mankind, to which they so confidently appealed, they would have deserved and received universal rebuke and reprobation...

But there are two clauses in the Constitution which point directly and specifically to the negro race as a separate class of persons, and show clearly that they were not regarded as a portion of the people or citizens of the government then formed.

One of these clauses reserves to each of the thirteen States the right to import slaves until the year 1808, if it thinks proper. And the importation which it thus sanctions was unquestionably of persons of the race of which we are speaking, as the traffic in slaves in the United States had always been confined to them. And by the other provision the States pledge themselves to each other to maintain the right of property of the master, by delivering up to him any slave who may have escaped from his service, and be found within their respective territories. By the first above-mentioned clause, therefore, the right to purchase and hold this property is directly sanctioned and authorized for twenty years by the people who framed the Constitution. And by the second, they pledge themselves to maintain and uphold the right of the master in the manner specified, as long as the government they then formed should endure. And these two provisions show, conclusively, that neither the description of persons therein referred to, nor their descendants, were embraced in any of the other provisions of the Constitution; for certainly these two clauses were not intended to confer on them or their posterity the blessings of liberty, or any of the personal rights so carefully provided for the citizen....

6.) *Congressional Intent*

Why does the Court draw upon Congressional enactments to support its rationale?

...To all this mass of proof we have still to add, that Congress has repeatedly legislated upon the same construction of the Constitution that we have given. Three laws, two of which were passed almost immediately after the government went into operation, will be abundantly sufficient to show this. The first two are particularly worthy of notice, because many of the men who assisted in framing the Constitution, and took an active part in procuring its adoption, were then in the halls of legislation, and certainly understood what they meant when they used the word "people of the United States" and "citizen" in that well considered instrument.

The first of these Acts is the Naturalization Law, which was passed at the second session of the first Congress, March 26, 1790, and confines the right of becoming citizens "to aliens being free white persons."

Now the Constitution does not limit the power of Congress in this respect to white persons. And they may, if they think proper, authorize the naturalization of anyone, of any color, who was born under allegiance to another government. But the language of the law above quoted shows that citizenship at that time was perfectly understood to be confined to the white race; and that they alone constituted the sovereignty in the government....

Another of the early laws of which we have spoken, is the first Militia Law, which was passed in 1792, at the first session of the second Congress. The language of this law is equally plain and significant with the one just mentioned. It directs that every "free able-bodied white male citizen" shall be enrolled in the militia. The word "white" is evidently used to exclude the African race, and the word "citizen" to exclude unnaturalized foreigners, the latter forming no part of the sovereignty; owing it no allegiance, and therefore under no obligation to defend it. The African race, however, born in the country, did owe allegiance to the government, whether they were slave or free; but it is repudiated, and rejected from the duties and obligations of citizenship in marked language.

The third Act to which we have alluded is even still more decisive; it was passed as late as 1813 (2 Stat., 809) and it provides: "That from and after the termination of the war in which the United States are now engaged with Great Britain, it shall not be lawful to employ, on board of any public or private vessels of the United States, any person or persons except citizens of the United States, or persons of color, natives of the United States."

Here the line of distinction is drawn in express terms. Persons of color, in the judgment of Congress, were not included in the word "citizen," and they are described as another and different class of persons, and authorized to be employed, if born in the United States.

And even as late as 1820 (chap. 104, sec.8) in the charter to the City of Washington, the Corporation is authorized "to restrain and prohibit the nightly and other disorderly meetings of slaves, free negroes, and mulattoes," thus associating them together in its legislation; and after prescribing the punishment that may be inflicted on the slaves, proceeds in the following words: "And to punish such free negroes and mulattoes by penalties not exceeding twenty dollars for any one offense; and in case of the inability of any such free negro or mulatto to pay any such penalty and cost thereon, to cause him or her to be confined to labor for any time not exceeding six calendar months." And in a subsequent part of the same section, the Act authorizes the Corporation "to prescribe the terms and conditions upon which free negroes and mulattoes may reside in the city."

This law, like the laws of the States, shows that this class of persons were governed by special legislation directed expressly to them, and always connected with provisions for the government of slaves, and not with those for the government of free white citizens.

And after such an uniform course of legislation as we have stated, by the Colonies, by the States, and by the Congress, running through a period of more than a century, it would seem to call persons thus marked and stigmatized, "citizens" of the United States, "fellow-citizens," a constituent part of the sovereignty, would be an abuse of terms, and not calculated to exalt the character of an American citizen in the eyes of other nations....

7.) *Executive Branch of Government*

Judge Taney adds to his argument evidence of racism within the Executive Branch of government.

...The conduct of the Executive Department of the government has been in perfect harmony upon this subject with this course of legislation. The question was brought officially before the late William Wirt, when he was the Attorney-General of the United States, in 1821, and he decided that the words "citizens of the United States" were used in the Acts of Congress in the same sense as in the Constitution; and that free persons of color were not citizens, within the meaning of the Constitution and laws; and this opinion has been confirmed by that of the late Attorney-General, Caleb Cushing, in a recent case, and acted upon by the Secretary of State, who refused to grant passports to them as "citizens of the United States....

8.) *Strict Construction*

Did the Constitution and the nation's founding legal documents support racism?

...No one, we presume, supposes that any change in public opinion or feeling in relation to this unfortunate race, in the civilized nations of Europe or in this country, should induce the court to give to the words of the Constitution a more liberal construction in their favor than they were intended to bear when the instrument was framed and adopted. Such an argument would be altogether inadmissible in any tribunal called on to interpret it. If any of its provisions are deemed unjust, there is a mode prescribed in the instrument itself by which it may be amended; but while it remains unaltered, it must be construed now as it was understood at the time of its adoption. It is not only the same in words, but the same in meaning, and delegates the same powers to the government, and reserves and secures the same rights and privileges to the citizen; and as long as it continues to exist in its present form, it speaks not only in the same words, but with the same meaning and intent with which it spoke when it came from the hands of its framers, and was voted on and adopted by the people of the United States. Any other rule of construction would abrogate the judicial character of this court and make it the mere reflex of the popular opinion or passion of the day. This court was not created by the Constitution for such purposes. Higher and graver trusts have been confided to it, and it must not falter in the path of duty.

What the construction was at that time, we think can hardly admit of doubt. We have the language of the Declaration of Independence and of the Articles of Confederation, in addition to the plain words of the Constitution itself; we have the legislation of the different States, before, about the time, and since the Constitution was adopted; we have the legislation of Congress, from the time of its adoption to a recent period; and we have the constant and uniform action of the Executive Department, all concurring together, and leading to the same result. And if anything in relation to the construction of the Constitution can be regarded as settled, it is that which we now give to the word "citizen" and the word "people....

C. *Decision*

The Court's decision is more than a legal decision, it is a political judgment that squarely places the United States Government in support of racism. More importantly, it stood for the proposition that law sanctioned the dehumanization of a people.

...And upon a full and careful consideration of the subject, the court is of the opinion that, upon the facts stated in the plea in abatement, Dred Scott was not a citizen of Missouri within the meaning of the Constitution of the United States, and not entitled as such to sue in its courts; and, consequently, that the Circuit Court had no jurisdiction of the case, and that the judgment on the plea in abatement is erroneous....

D. *Entitlement to Freedom*

After ruling in favor of Sandford, why does the Court take this additional step to determine whether Dred Scott and his family are entitled to freedom?

...We proceed, therefore, to inquire whether the facts relied on by the plaintiff entitled him to his freedom. In considering this part of the controversy, two questions arise: 1st. Was he, together with his family, free in Missouri by reason of the stay in the territory of the United States hereinbefore mentioned? And 2nd. If they were not, is Scott himself free by reason of his removal to Rock Island, in the State of Illinois, as stated in the above admissions?

We proceed to examine the first question....

Now, as we have already said in an earlier part of this opinion, upon a different point, the right of property in a slave is distinctly and expressly affirmed in the Constitution. The right to traffic in it, like an ordinary article of merchandise and property, was guarantied to the citizens of the United States, in every State that might desire it, for twenty years. And the government in express terms is pledged to protect it in all future time, if the slave escapes from his owner. This is done in plain words, too plain to be misunderstood. And no word can be found in the Constitution which gives Congress a greater power over slave property, or which entitles property of that kind to less protection than property of any other description. The only power conferred is the power coupled with the duty of guarding and protecting the owner in his rights.

Upon these considerations, it is the opinion of the court that the Act of Congress which prohibited a citizen from holding and owning property of this kind in the territory of the United States north of the line therein mentioned, is not warranted by the Constitution, and is therefore void; and that neither Dred Scott himself, nor any of his family, were made free by being carried into this territory: even if they had been carried there by the owner, with the intention of becoming a permanent resident.

We have so far examined the case, as it stands under the Constitution of the United States, and the powers thereby delegated to the Federal Government.

But there is another point in the case which depends on state power and state law. And it is contended, on the part of the plaintiff, that he is made free by being taken to Rock Island, in the State of Illinois, independently of his residence in the territory of the United States; and being so made free, he was not again reduced to a state of slavery by being brought back to Missouri....

So in this case: as Scott was a slave when taken into the State of Illinois by his owner, and was there held as such, and brought back in that character, his status, as free or slave, depended on the laws of Missouri, and not of Illinois....

Upon the whole, therefore, it is the judgment of this court, that it appears by the record before us that the plaintiff in error is not a citizen of Missouri, in the sense in which that word is used in the Constitution; and that the Circuit Court of the United States, for that reason, had no jurisdiction in the case, and could give no judgment in it....

► **Notes & Questions**

1. Do you agree with the Court's decision that Dred Scott was property? If we accept the Court's reasoning as indicative of both the moral and legal viewpoints of the white majority in the nineteenth century, what conclusions can we draw from such realizations?

2. The Court writes that black people are so inferior, that they have no rights which the white race should respect. If the most sophisticated levels of society have adopted these types of views towards blacks, what views would you expect the white working class to hold?

3. Are the affects of this decision still present today? Explain.

4. What impact did Dred Scott have upon other state court decisions relating to black freedom?

5. On February 24, 2007 Virginia became the first state to pass a resolution expressing 'profound regret' for slavery. The resolution stated in part that state-sanctioned slavery "ranks as the most horrendous of all depredations of human rights and violations of our founding ideals in our nation's history, and the abolition of slavery was followed by systematic discrimination, enforced segregation, and other insidious institutions and practices toward Americans of African descent that were rooted in racism, racial bias, and racial misunderstanding." (Larry O'Dell, "Va-lawmakers air 'profound regret' for slavery," *The Boston Globe*, February 25, 2007)

D.
The Legitimization of Racial Genocide

Not only was the United States Government and its legal establishment confronted with the paradox of slavery (the theft of human beings), but also with Native American genocide (murder of human beings). How would the courts rationalize the taking of the land that had been "discovered" by Europeans? Should the native people be treated as sovereign nations? Would treaties and other agreements be enforced and given the same effect as those entered into by European nations? What should the role of law be, both on the state and national levels, when Native American claims of national autonomy conflict with European material expansion? Was the forced removal of the Cherokee Nation from their lands a form of national genocide? What role did law and public policy play in precipitating the genocide of the Cherokee and other Indians?

On December 30, 1828, the State of Georgia passed a law entitled: "An act to add the territory lying within this state and occupied by the Cherokee Indian, to the counties of Carroll, Dekalb, Gwinett, Hall and Habersham, and to extend the laws of this state over the same, and for other purposes."

On December 19, 1829 an additional act was passed which purported to annul all laws and ordinances made by the Cherokee Nation.

By these laws the Cherokees were placed on notice that the State of Georgia, with the support of President Andrew Jackson, planned to uproot them from their ancestral lands. The legal challenge of the Cherokees reached the Supreme Court of the United States.

THE CHEROKEE NATION v. STATE OF GEORGIA
Supreme Court of the United States
30 U.S. 1 (1831)

This case came before the court on a motion on behalf of the Cherokee Nation of Indians for a subpoena, and for an injunction, to restrain the state of Georgia, the governor, attorney-general, judges, justices of the peace, sheriffs, deputy sheriffs, constables, and others the officers, agents, and servants of that state, from executing and enforcing the laws of Georgia or any of these laws, or serving process, or doing any thing; towards the execution or enforcement of those laws, within the Cherokee territory, as designated by treaty between the United States and the Cherokee nation....

The bill set forth the complainants to be "the Cherokee nation of Indian, a foreign state, not owing allegiance to the United States, nor to any state of this union, nor to any prince, potentate or state, other than their own."

"That from time immemorial the Cherokee nation have composed a sovereign and independent state, and in this character have been repeatedly recognized, and still stand recognized by the United States, in the various treaties subsisting between their nation and the United States."

That the Cherokees were the occupants and owners of the territory in which they now reside, before the first approach of the white men of Europe to the western continent; "deriving their title from the Great Spirit, who is the common father of the human family, and to whom the whole earth belongs." Composing the Cherokee nation, they and their ancestors have been and are the sole and exclusive masters of this territory, governed by their own laws, usages, and customs....

Mr Chief Justice MARSHALL delivered the opinion of the Court.

This bill is brought by the Cherokee nation, praying an injunction to restrain the state of Georgia from the execution of certain laws of that state, which, as is alleged, go directly to annihilate the Cherokees as a political society, and to seize, for the use of Georgia, the lands of the nation which have been assured to them by the United States in solemn treaties repeatedly made and still in force.

If courts were permitted to indulge their sympathies, a case better calculated to excite them can scarcely be imagined. A people once numerous, powerful, and truly independent, found by our ancestors in the quiet and uncontrolled possession of an ample domain, gradually sinking beneath our superior policy, our arts and our arms, have yielded their lands by successive treaties, each of which contains a solemn guarantee of the residue, until they retain no more of their formerly extensive territory than is deemed necessary to their comfortable subsistence. To preserve this remnant, the present application is made.

Before we can look into the merits of the case, a preliminary inquiry presents itself. Has this court jurisdiction of the cause?

The third article of the constitution describes the extent of the judicial power. The second section closes an enumeration of the cases to which it is extended, with "controversies" " between a state or the citizens thereof, and foreign states, citizens, or subjects." A subsequent clause of the same section gives the Supreme Court original jurisdiction in all cases in which a state shall be a party. The party defendant may then unquestionably be sued in this court. May the plaintiff sue in it? Is the Cherokee nation a foreign state in the sense in which that term is used in the constitution?

The counsel for the plaintiffs have maintained the affirmative of this proposition with great earnestness and ability. So much of the argument as was intended to prove the character of the Cherokees as a state, as a distinct political society, separated from others, capable of managing its own affairs and governing itself, has, in the opinion of the majority of the judges, been completely successful. They have been uniformly treated as a state from the settlement of our country. The numerous treaties made with them by the United States recognize them as a people capable of maintaining the relations of peace and war, of being responsible in their political character for any violation of their engagements, or for any aggression committed on the citizens of the United States by any individual of their community. Laws have been enacted in the spirit of these treaties. The acts of our government plainly recognize the Cherokee nation as a state, and the courts are bound by those acts.

A question of much more difficulty remains. Do the Cherokees constitute a foreign state in the sense of the constitution?

The counsel have shown conclusively that they are not a state of the union, and have insisted that individually they are aliens, not owing allegiance to the United States. An aggregate of aliens composing a state must, they say, be a foreign state. Each individual being foreign, the whole must be foreign.

This argument is imposing, but we must examine it more closely before we yield to it. The condition of the Indian in relation to the United States is perhaps unlike that of any other two people in existence. In the general, nations not owing a common allegiance are foreign to each other. The term foreign nation is, with strict propriety, applicable by either to the other. But the relation of the Indian to the United States is marked by peculiar and cardinal distinctions which exist no where else.

The Indian territory is admitted to compose a part of the United States. In all our maps, geographical treatises, histories, and laws, it is so considered. In all our intercourse with foreign nations, in our commercial regulations, in any attempt at intercourse between Indian and foreign nations, they are considered as within the jurisdictional limits of the United States, subject to many of those restraints which are imposed upon our own citizens. They acknowledge themselves in their treaties to be under the protection of the United States; they admit that the United States shall have the sole and exclusive right of regulating the trade with them, and managing all their affairs as they think proper; and the Cherokees in particular were allowed by the treaty of Hopewell, which preceded the constitution, "to send a deputy of their choice, whenever they think fit, to congress." Treaties were made with some tribes by the state of New York, under a then unsettled construction of the confederation, by which they ceded all their lands to that state, taking back a limited grant to themselves, in which they admit their dependence.

Though the Indian are acknowledged to have an unquestionable, and, heretofore, unquestioned right to the lands they occupy, until that right shall be extinguished by a voluntary cession to our government; yet it may well be doubted whether those tribes which reside within the acknowledged boundaries of the United States can, with strict accuracy, be denominated foreign nations. They may, more correctly, perhaps, be denominated domestic dependent nations. They occupy a territory to which we assert a title independent of their will, which must take effect in point of possession when their right of possession ceases. Meanwhile they are in a state of pupilage. Their relation to the United States resembles that of a ward to his guardian....

When forming this article, the convention considered them as entirely distinct. We cannot assume that the distinction was lost in framing a subsequent article, unless there be something in its language to authorize the assumption... The court has bestowed its best attention on this question, and, after mature deliberation, the majority is of opinion that an Indian tribe or nation within the United States is not a foreign state in the sense of the constitution, and cannot maintain an action in the courts of the United States....

If it be true that the Cherokee nation have rights, this is not the tribunal in which those rights are to be asserted. If it be true that wrongs have been inflicted, and that still greater are to be apprehended, this is not the tribunal which can redress the past or prevent the future.

The motion for an injunction is denied.

Dissenting Opinion of Justice Thompson

...Testing the character and condition of the Cherokee Indian by these rules, it is not perceived how it is possible to escape the conclusion, that they form a sovereign state. They have always been dealt with as such by the government of the United States both before and since the adoption of the present constitution. They have been admitted and treated as a people governed solely and exclusively by their own laws, usages, and customs within their own territory, claiming and exercising exclusive dominion over the same; yielding up by treaty, from time to time, portions of their land, but still claiming absolute sovereignty and self government over what remained unsold. And this has been the light in which they have, until recently been considered from the earliest settlement of the country by the white people. And indeed, I do not understand it is denied by a majority of the court, that the Cherokee Indian form a sovereign state according to the doctrine of the law of nations; but that, although a sovereign state, they are not considered a foreign state within the meaning of the constitution... But such was not the condition and character of the Cherokee nation, in any respect whatever, in the year 1802, or at any time since. It was a numerous and distinct nation, living under the government of their own laws, usages, and customs, and in no sense under the ordinary jurisdiction of the state of Georgia; but under the protection of the United States, with a solemn guarantee by treaty of the exclusive right to the possession of their lands. This guarantee is to the Cherokees in their national capacity. Their land is held in common, and every invasion of their possessory right is an injury done to the nation, and not to any individual. No private or individual suit could be sustained: the injury done being to the nation, the remedy sought must be in the name of the nation. All the rights secured to these Indian, under any treaties made with them, remain unimpaired. These treaties are acknowledged by the United States to be in full force, by the proviso to the seventh section of the act of the 28th May 1830; which declares, that nothing in this act contained shall be construed as authorizing or directing the violation of any existing treaty between the United States and any Indian tribes.

That the Cherokee nation of Indian have, by virtue of these treaties, an exclusive right of occupancy of the lands in question, and that the United States are bound under their guarantee, to protect the nation in the enjoyment of such occupancy; cannot, in my judgment, admit of a doubt: and that some of the laws of Georgia set out in the bill are in violation of, and in conflict with those treaties and the act of 1802, is to my mind equally clear....

Upon the whole, I am of opinion,

1. That the Cherokees compose a foreign state within the sense and meaning of the constitution, and constitute a competent party

to maintain a suit against the state of Georgia.

2. That the bill presents a case for judicial consideration, arising under the laws of the United States, and treaties made under their authority with the Cherokee nation, and which laws and treaties have been, and are threatened to be still further violated by the laws of the state of Georgia referred to in this opinion.

3. That an injunction is a fit and proper writ to be issued, to prevent the further execution of such laws, and ought therefore to be awarded.

And I am authorised by my brother Story to say, that he concurs with me in this opinion.

► **Notes & Questions**

1. Why did the State of Georgia attempt to extend their laws over the Cherokee Nation? What process did they engage in to ascertain whether the Cherokee assented to this action?

2. By what authority did the State of Georgia derive the power to annul the laws of the Cherokee Nation?

3. Do you agree with the opinion of Justice Marshall?

4. How do you distinguish the opinion of Justice Marshall from the dissenting opinion of Justice Thompson?

5. In the early part of the 1830's, the State of Georgia passed a series of acts that were designed to control the land that had been historically occupied by the Creek and Cherokee nations. The act barred Indians from litigating this blatant confiscation of their land by stating that no Indian or descendant of an Indian residing upon the subject land could be a witness against a white person. It also required all white people residing upon the land to obtain a license from the state. Samuel A. Worcester, a white man and a resident of the State of Vermont and others, refused to leave the land and to comply with the statute. In September, 1831 Samuel Worcester and six other white people were indicted by a grand jury of the county of Gwinnett. Samuel Worcester challenged the validity of the proceedings against himself by stating that on July 15, 1831, the date on which he was told to vacate the property, he was in New Echota, capital of the Cherokee Nation and that Georgian courts had no jurisdiction over him. On September 15, 1831, Samuel Worcester was found guilty by a jury and sentenced to hard labor for four (4) years by the superior court of the county of Gwinnett. The matter was appealed to the Supreme Court of the United States.

WORCESTER v. STATE OF GEORGIA
Supreme Court of the United States
31 U.S. 515 (1832)

This was a writ of error to the superior court for the county of Gwinnett, in the state of Georgia.

On the 22nd December 1830, the legislature of the state of Georgia passed the following act:

"An act to prevent the exercise of assumed and arbitrary power, by all persons, under pretext of authority from the Cherokee Indian and their laws, and to prevent white persons from residing within that part of the chartered limits of Georgia, occupied by the Cherokee Indian, and to provide a guard for the protection of the gold mines, and to enforce the laws of the state within the aforesaid territory.

"Be it enacted by the senate and house of representatives of the state of Georgia in general assembly met, and it is hereby enacted by the authority of the same, that, after the 1st day of February 1831, it shall not be lawful for any person or persons, under colour or pretence of authority from said Cherokee tribe, or as headmen, chief or warriors of said tribe, to cause or procure by any means the assembling of any council or other pretended legislative body of the said Indian or others living among them, for the purpose of legislating (or for any other purpose whatever). And persons offending against the provisions of this section shall be guilty of a high misdemeanour, and subject to indictment therefor, and, on conviction, shall be punished by confinement at hard labour in the penitentiary for the space of four years...."

It has been said at the bar, that the acts of the legislature of Georgia seize on the whole Cherokee country, parcel it out among the neighbouring counties of the state, extend her code over the whole country, abolish its institutions and its laws, and annihilate its political existence....

The first step, then, in the inquiry, which the constitution and laws impose on this court, is an examination of the rightfulness of this claim....

The great maritime powers of Europe discovered and visited different parts of this continent at nearly the same time. The object was too immense for any one of them to grasp the whole; and the claimants were too powerful to submit to the exclusive or unreasonable pretensions of any single potentate. To avoid bloody conflicts, which might terminate disastrously to all, it was necessary for the nations of Europe to establish some principle which all would acknowledge, and which should decide their respective rights as between themselves. This principle, suggested by the actual state of things, was, "that discovery gave title to the government by whose subjects or by whose authority it was made, against all other European governments, which title might be consummated by possession." 8 Wheat. 573.

This principle, acknowledged by all Europeans, because it was the interest of all to acknowledge it, gave to the nation making the discovery, as its inevitable consequence, the sole right of acquiring the soil and of making settlements on it. It was an exclusive principle which shut out the right of competition among those who had agreed to it; not one which could annul the previous rights of those who had not agreed to it. It regulated the right given by discovery among the European discoverers; but could not affect the rights of those already in possession, either as aboriginal occupants, or as occupants by virtue of a discovery made before the memory of man. It gave the exclusive right to purchase, but did not found that right on a denial of the right of the possessor to sell.

The relation between the Europeans and the natives was determined in each case by the particular government which asserted and could maintain this pre-emptive privilege in the particular place. The United States succeeded to all the claims of Great Britain, both territorial and political; but no attempt, so far as is known, has been made to enlarge them. So far as they existed merely in theory, or were in their nature only exclusive of the claims of other European nations, they still retain their original character, and remain dormant. So far as they have been practically exerted, they exist in fact, are understood by both parties, are asserted by the one, and admitted by the other....

The Cherokee nation, then, is a distinct community occupying its own territory, with boundaries accurately described, in which the laws of Georgia can have no force, and which the citizens of Georgia have no right to enter, but with the assent of the Cherokees themselves, or in conformity with treaties, and with the acts of congress. The whole intercourse between the United States and this nation, is, by our constitution and laws, vested in the government of the United States.

The act of the state of Georgia, under which the plaintiff in error was prosecuted, is consequently void, and the judgment a nullity....

The forcible seizure and abduction of the plaintiff in error, who was residing in the nation with its permission, and by authority of the president of the United States, is also a violation of the acts which authorise the chief magistrate to exercise this authority....

It is the opinion of this court that the judgment of the superior court for the county of Gwinnett, in the State of Georgia, condemning Samuel A. Worcester to hard labour, in the penitentiary of the state of Georgia, for four years, was pronounced by that court under colour of a law which is void, as being repugnant to the constitution, treaties, and laws of the United States, and ought, therefore, to be reversed and annulled.

▶ Notes & Questions

1. How do you reconcile *Cherokee Nation v. State of Georgia* with this case? Why is there a different opinion here? Does it make a difference if the plaintiff is a white man or an Indian?

2. What public policy did the act serve for the State of Georgia? Why was the Georgia law used to bring about this type of social change?

3. Assuming that the Georgia statute was valid, what arguments would you make that the Cherokee were entitled to compensation? Can one adequately compensate the Cherokee for the loss of their land?

4. What public policy arguments could you make that they are not entitled to any compensation? If you have difficulties with formulating an argument, what additional factual information would help you to make the argument?

5. Why did the law state that a Cherokee or his descendant could not be a witness against a white man?

6. The Cherokee Nation recently voted to expel black freedmen from the Cherokee Nation. Is this a form of racism or is it merely a depressed nation seeking to find a scapegoat for their continued oppression?

Chapter Two

JIM CROW ERA

A.
Crisis over Civil Rights

In 1850, the Supreme Judicial Court of Massachusetts issued a crucial decision, which paved the way in which people of color would be treated throughout the rest of the country. Chief Justice Shaw delivered the opinion for the Court, which laid the foundation for the "separate but equal" doctrine which would later become the law of the land. Forty seven years later, Shaw's opinion would become precedence for the United States Supreme Court case of *Plessy v. Ferguson,* decided in 1896. The case arose in the State of Louisiana over the issue of whether a State could require passengers to sit in segregated public transportation facilities. Plessy, a black man who sat in a white section of a railroad car, was ordered by the conductor to take another seat in the black section of the train. When Plessy refused, he was taken by the police and held in the county jail. Mr. Plessy used the Fourteenth Amendment as his defense, but Judge Ferguson failed to see the relevance in his argument. The judge found the defendant guilty as charged. Mr. Plessy filed a petition with the United States Supreme Court seeking a reversal. The Court concluded that the Fourteenth Amendment did not apply to this case and cited the decision of the Massachusetts Supreme Judicial Court in *Roberts v. the City of Boston* as its precedent.

"Separate but Equal" became the law of the land until another landmark case appeared in the mid-twentieth century. In 1953,

Brown v. the Board of Education appeared on the United States Supreme Court docket. *Brown* resembled the *Roberts* case of Massachusetts, but this time a group of states was being sued and the case was heard by the United States Supreme Court. Thurgood Marshall was the attorney for the plaintiffs as well as a representative for the National Association for the Advancement of Colored People. Marshall used both the Thirteenth and Fourteenth Amendments as the basis of his case. He argued that while schools may be separating Black and white children, they are not creating equal school systems. Black children, he argued, were receiving inadequate education, leaving them scarred with feelings of inferiority.

Chief Justice Warren delivered the opinion of the Court. In his opinion, Warren, not only changed a precedent in the Supreme Court, but also gave impetus to the civil rights movement. Warren went even further in *Brown II* in 1955. In *Brown II* the Chief Justice ordered that there be remedies for the injustices that stemmed from the policy of separate but equal. One such remedy was court ordered busing, which was to be used as a tool for achieving desegregation.

Although the Brown case proved to be a landmark decision for civil rights in the United States, there continued to be inequities in the delivery of educational services to children of color. For instance, in 1968, Demetrio Rodriguez, a resident of San Antonio, Texas, led a group of parents in a lawsuit against the government, *San Antonio School District v. Rodriguez,* 411 U.S. 1 (1973). Rodriguez's suit argued that there was unequal distribution of funds for schools and that this violated the Equal Protection Clause. A federal trial judge agreed initially, but the United States Supreme Court reversed, ruling that public education is not a guaranteed right. Instead, the Court ruled that public education is a benefit. Even today there continues to be disparities in the public education system. In the inner cities, lower property taxes mean that less money is available for education, therefore resulting in poor children receiving an inferior education, compared to rich children receiving superior education.

Should public funding for public schools be based upon property taxes? What are the problems with this approach? Should vouchers be used to allow students to go to the school where their dollar takes them? Has desegregation in education been successful? Should Blacks and other people of color have their own, publicly funded schools? Should students be allowed to attend school outside their districts, when there has been no finding of discrimination outside their school districts? Should the law prohibit discrimination on the basis of class in providing education? What argument would you advance to justify such a position? Is there anything singularly important about education that would constitute a compelling justification for such a policy?

B.
Emancipation and Racism

Even though slavery was legally abolished on December 18, 1865, by the 13th Amendment, its progeny, racism, continued to flourish within the society and the law. After President Lincoln's executive order (Emancipation Proclamation) and the defeat of the South in the Civil War, very little was left of slavery. The Emancipation Proclamation which was issued on September 22, 1862, and took effect on January 1, 1863, abolished slavery in Confederate states at war with the Union, and enlisted slaves in the war effort. The Amendment, therefore merely codified in constitutional terms what had already been achieved on the battlefield. However, what was to be done with the Africans, who found themselves free? Would the adoption of the post-war Amendments change the hearts and minds of America, given the pervasive racism that had been documented by Justice Taney in his decision in *Dred Scott*? If Africans were free, how would others define their freedom? How far would this freedom go? Could whites be required to associate with Africans in places of public accommodation, in education and employment? In short, how does government insure that racism does not perpetuate the effects of slavery? Should the government have acknowledged to

Africans that they had been unjustly treated and therefore provide restitution? Did emancipation fundamentally change the master-slave relationship?

1. Elimination of Slavery Status

On February 1, 1865, the Thirteenth Amendment to the Constitution of the United States was proposed by the Thirty-eighth Congress. On December 18, 1865, the Secretary of State declared that it had been ratified by twenty-seven of the thirty-six states.

CONSTITUTION OF THE UNITED STATES

AMENDMENT XIII
"§ 1. **Slavery Abolished**
Section 1. Neither slavery nor involuntary servitude, except as a punishment for crime whereof the party shall have been duly convicted, shall exist within the United States, or any place subject to their jurisdiction.

"§ 2. **Enforcement**
Section 2. Congress shall have Power to enforce this article by appropriate legislation."

2. Creation of Citizenship Rights

On June 16, 1866, the Thirty-ninth Congress proposed to the legislatures of several States the Fourteenth Amendment. On July 21, 1868, Congress adopted a concurrent resolution which declared that at least-three-fourths of the States had ratified the fourteenth article of amendment to the Constitution of the United States. On July 28, 1868, the Secretary of State issued a proclamation that the amendment had been ratified by thirty of the thirty-six states.

AMENDMENT XIV.
"§ 1. **Citizenship rights not to be abridged by states**
Section 1. All persons born or naturalized in the United States,

and subject to the jurisdiction thereof, are citizens of the United States and of the State wherein they reside. No State shall make or enforce any law which shall abridge the privileges or immunities of citizens of the United States; nor shall any State deprive any person of life, liberty, or property, without due process of law; nor deny to any person within its jurisdiction the equal protection of the laws."

3. Creation of Substantive Right to Vote for Black Men

The Fifteenth Amendment (1870) won the ballot for Black men in the North and the Civil Rights Act of 1875 provided remedies against discrimination in public accommodations. These new laws were only as good as the politicians who enforced them. By 1877 white Democrats came to power and started to chip away at the rights gained by Blacks. The United States Supreme Court struck down the Civil Rights Act of 1875 in 1883 (*The Civil Rights Cases*, 109 U.S. 1 (1883)), which further eroded substantive rights.

4. Establishment of Limitations on Social Equality

A. **Intrastate Commerce**

The law in the southern states began to reflect this new conservative control of political power. Many states passed laws segregating all aspects of public life, including transportation and education. In Louisiana, Black and white citizens formed the American Citizens' Equal Rights Association that denounced the new laws, in particular Acts 1890, No. 111, and brought suit challenging its constitutionality. These groups found unexpected success in their challenge of the Jim Crow statute. *In State of Louisiana ex rel. Abbott v. Hicks*, 44 La. Annual 770 (1892), the Supreme Court of Louisiana struck down the statute on interstate commerce grounds. However, the United States Supreme Court established dangerous national precedence when it decided that intrastate segregation did not violate the Fourteenth Amendment.

PLESSY v. FERGUSON
Supreme Court of the United States
163 U.S. 537 (1896)

MR. JUSTICE BROWN, after stating the case, delivered the Opinion of the court.

This case turns upon the constitutionality of an act of the General Assembly of the State of Louisiana, passed in 1890, providing for separate railway carriages for the white and colored races. Acts 1890, No. 111, p. 152.

The first section of the statute enacts "that all railway companies carrying passengers in their coaches in this State, shall provide equal but separate accommodations for the white, and colored races, by providing two or more passenger coaches for each passenger train, or by dividing the passenger coaches by a partition so as to secure separate accommodations: Provided, That this section shall not be construed to apply to street railroads. No person or persons shall be admitted to occupy seats in coaches, other than, the ones, assigned, to them on account of the race they belong to."

By the second section it was enacted "that the officers of such passenger trains shall have power and are hereby required to assign each passenger to the coach or compartment used for the race to which such passenger belongs; any passenger insisting upon going into a coach or compartment to which by race he does not belong, shall be liable to a fine of twenty-five dollars, or in lieu thereof to imprisonment for a period of not more than twenty days in the parish prison, and any officer of any railroad insisting on assigning a passenger to a coach or compartment other than the one set aside for the race to which said passenger belongs, shall be liable to a fine of twenty-five dollars, or in lieu thereof to imprisonment for a period of not more than twenty days in the parish prison; and should any passenger refuse to occupy the coach or compartment to which he or she is assigned by the officer of such railway, said officer shall have power to refuse to carry such passenger on his train, and for such refusal neither he nor the railway company which he represents shall be liable for damages in any of the courts of this State."

The third section provides penalties for the refusal or neglect of the officers, directors, conductors and employes of railway companies to comply with the act, with a proviso that "nothing in this act shall be construed as applying to nurses attending children of the other race." The fourth section is immaterial...

The petition for the writ of prohibition averred that petitioner was seven eighths Caucasian and one eighth African blood; that the mixture of colored blood was not discernible in him, and that he was entitled to every right, privilege and immunity secured to citizens of the United States of the white race; and that, upon such theory, he took possession of a vacant seat in a coach where passengers of the white race were accommodated, and was ordered by the conductor to vacate said coach and take a seat in another assigned to persons of the colored race, and having refused to comply with such demand he was forcibly ejected with the aid of a police officer, and imprisoned in the parish jail to answer a charge of having violated the above act.

The constitutionality of this act is attacked upon the ground that it conflicts both with the Thirteenth Amendment of the Constitution, abolishing slavery, and the Fourteenth Amendment, which prohibits certain restrictive legislation on the part of the States.

1. That it does not conflict with the Thirteenth Amendment, which abolished slavery and involuntary servitude, except as a punishment for crime, is too clear for argument. Slavery implies involuntary servitude- a state of bondage; the ownership of mankind as a chattel, or at least the control of the labor and services of one man for the benefit of another, and the absence of a legal right to the disposal of his own person, property and services. This amendment was said in the *Slaughter-house cases*, 16 Wall. 36, to have been intended primarily to abolish slavery, as it had been previously known in this country, and that it equally forbade Mexican peonage or the Chinese coolie trade, when they amounted to slavery or involuntary servitude, and that the use of

the word "servitude" was intended to prohibit the use of all forms of involuntary slavery, of whatever class or name. It was intimated, however, in that case that this amendment was regarded by the statesmen of that day as insufficient to protect the colored race from certain laws which had been enacted in the Southern States, imposing upon the colored race onerous disabilities and burdens, and curtailing their rights in the pursuit of life, liberty and property to such an extent that their freedom was of little value; and that the Fourteenth Amendment was devised to meet this exigency.

So, too, in the *Civil Rights Cases*, 109 U.S. 3, 24, it was said that the act of a mere individual, the owner of an inn, a public conveyance or place of amusement, refusing accommodations to colored people, cannot be justly regarded as imposing any badge of slavery or servitude upon the applicant, but only as involving an ordinary civil injury, properly cognizable by the laws of the State, and presumably subject to redress by those laws until the contrary appears. "It would be running the slavery argument into the ground," said Mr. Justice Bradley, "to make it apply to every act of discrimination which a person may see fit to make as to the guests he will entertain, or as to the people he will take into his coach or cab or car, or admit to his concert or theatre, or deal with in other matters of intercourse or business."

A statute which implies merely a legal distinction between the white and colored races-a distinction which is founded in the color of the two races, and which must always exist so long as white men are distinguished from the other race by color-has no tendency to destroy the legal equality of the two races, or reestablish a state of involuntary servitude. Indeed, we do not understand that the Thirteenth Amendment is strenuously relied upon by the plaintiff in error in this connection.

2. By the Fourteenth Amendment, all persons born or naturalized in the United States, and subject to the jurisdiction thereof, are made citizens of the United States and of the State wherein they reside; and the States are forbidden from making or enforcing any law which shall abridge the privileges or immunities of citizens of the United States, or shall deprive any person of life, liberty or

property without due process of law, or deny to any person within their jurisdiction the equal protection of the laws.

The proper construction of this amendment was first called to the attention of this court in the *Slaughter-house cases*, 16 Wall. 36, which involved, however, not a question of race, but one of exclusive privileges. The case did not call for any expression of opinion as to the exact rights it was intended to secure to the colored race, but it was said generally that its main purpose was to establish the citizenship of the negro; to give definitions of citizenship of the United States and of the States, and to protect from the hostile legislation of the States the privileges and immunities of citizens of the United States, as distinguished from those of citizens of the States.

The object of the amendment was undoubtedly to enforce the absolute equality of the two races before the law, but in the nature of things it could not have been intended to abolish distinctions based upon color, or to enforce social, as distinguished from political equality, or a commingling of the two races upon terms unsatisfactory to either. Laws permitting, and even requiring, their separation in places where they are liable to be brought into contact do not necessarily imply the inferiority of either race to the other, and have been generally, if not universally, recognized as within the competency of the state legislatures in the exercise of their police power. The most common instance of this is connected with the establishment of separate schools for white and colored children, which has been held to be a valid exercise of the legislative power, even by courts of States where the political rights of the colored race have been longest and most earnestly enforced....

Laws forbidding the intermarriage of the two races may be said in a technical sense to interfere with the freedom of contract, and yet have been universally recognized as within the police power of the State. *State v. Gibson*, 36 Indiana, 389.

The distinction between laws interfering with the political equality of the negro and those requiring the separation of the two races in schools, theatres and railway carriages has been frequently drawn by this court. Thus in *Strauder v. West Virginia*, 100 U.S.

303, it was held that a law of West Virginia limiting to white male persons, 21 years of age and citizens of the State, the right to sit upon juries, was a discrimination which implied a legal inferiority in civil society, which lessened the security of the right of the colored race, and was a step toward reducing them to a condition of servility. Indeed, the right of a colored man that, in the selection of jurors to pass upon his life, liberty and property, there shall be no exclusion of his race, and no discrimination against them because of color, has been asserted in a number of cases....

While we think the enforced separation of the races, as applied to the internal commerce of the State, neither abridges the privileges or immunities of the colored man, deprives him of his property without due process of law, nor denies him the equal protection of the laws, within the meaning of the Fourteenth Amendment, we are not prepared to say that the conductor, in assigning passengers to the coaches according to their race, does not act at his peril, or that the provision of the second section of the act, that denies to the passenger compensation in damages for a refusal to receive him into the coach in which he properly belongs, is a valid exercise of the legislative power. Indeed, we understand it to be conceded by the State's attorney, that such part of the act as exempts from liability the railway company and its officers is unconstitutional. The power to assign to a particular coach obviously implies the power to determine to which race the passenger belongs, as well as the power to determine who, under the laws of the particular State, is to be deemed a white, and who a colored person. This question, though indicated in the brief of the plaintiff in error, does not properly arise upon the record in this case, since the only issue made is as to the unconstitutionality of the act, so far as it requires the railway to provide separate accommodations, and the conductor to assign passengers according to their race.

It is claimed by the plaintiff in error that, in any mixed community, the reputation of belonging to the dominant race, in this instance the white race, is *property*, in the sense that a right of action, or of inheritance, is property. Conceding this to be so, for the purposes of this case, we are unable to see how this statute deprives him of, or in any way affects his right to, such property. If he be a white man and assigned to a colored coach, he may have his action for damages against the company for being deprived of his so called property. Upon the other hand, if he be a colored man and be so assigned, he has been deprived of no property, since he is not lawfully entitled to the reputation of being a white man....

So far then, as a conflict with the Fourteenth Amendment is concerned, the case reduces itself to the question whether the statute of Louisiana is a reasonable regulation, and with respect to this there must necessarily be a large discretion on the part of the legislature. In determining the question of reasonableness it is at liberty to act with reference to the established usages, customs and traditions of the people, and with a view to the promotion of their comfort, and the preservation of the public peace and good order. Gauged by this standard, we cannot say that a law which authorizes or even requires the separation of the two races in public conveyances is unreasonable or more obnoxious to the Fourteenth Amendment than the acts of Congress requiring separate schools for colored children in the District of Columbia, the constitutionality of which does not seem to have been questioned, or the corresponding acts of state legislatures.

We consider the underlying fallacy of the plaintiff's argument to consist in the assumption that the enforced separation of the two races stamps the colored race with a badge of inferiority. If this be so, it is not by reason of anything found in the act, but solely because the colored race chooses to put that construction upon it. The argument necessarily assumes that if, as has been more than once the case, and is not unlikely to be so again, the colored race should become the dominant power in the state legislature, and should enact a law in precisely similar terms, it would thereby relegate the white race to an inferior position. We imagine that the white race, at least, would not acquiesce in this assumption. The argument also assumes that social prejudices may be overcome by legislation, and that equal rights cannot be secured to the negro except by an enforced commingling of the two races. We cannot accept this proposition. If the two races are to meet upon terms of social equality, it must be the result of natural affinities, a mutual appreciation of each other's merits and a voluntary consent of individuals... Legislation is powerless to eradicate racial instincts or to abolish distinctions based upon physical differences, and the attempt to do so can only result in accentuating the difficulties of the present situation. If the civil and political rights of both races be equal one cannot be inferior to the other civilly or politically. If one race be inferior to the other socially, the Constitution of the United States cannot put them upon the same plane.

It is true that the question of the proportion of colored blood necessary to constitute a colored person, as distinguished from a white person, is one upon which there is a difference of opinion in the different States, some holding that any visible admixture of black blood stamps the person as belonging to the colored race, (*State v. Chavers,* 5 Jones, [N.C.] 1, p.11;) others that it depends upon the preponderance of blood, (*Gray v. State*, 4 Ohio, 354; *Monroe v. Collins,* 17 Ohio St. 665); and still others that the predominance of white blood must only be in the proportion of three fourths. *People v. Dean,* 14 Michigan, 406; *Jones v. Commonwealth,* 80 Virginia, 538.) But these are questions to be determined under the laws of each State and not properly put in issue in this case. Under the allegations of his petition it may undoubtedly become a question of importance whether, under the laws of Louisiana, the petitioner belongs to the white or colored race.

The judgment of the court below is, therefore,

Affirmed.

MR. JUSTICE HARLAN dissenting.

...In respect of civil rights, common to all citizens, the Constitution of the United States does not, I think, permit any public authority to know the race of those entitled to be protected in the enjoyment of such rights. Every true man has pride of race, and appropriate circumstances when the rights of others, his equals before the law, are not to be affected, it is his privilege to express such pride and to take such action based upon it as to him seems proper. But I deny that any legislative body or judicial tribunal may have regard to the race of citizens when the civil rights of those citizens are involved. Indeed, such legislation, as that here in question, is inconsistent not only with that equality of rights which pertains to citizenship, National and State, but with the personal liberty enjoyed by every one within the United States.

The Thirteenth Amendment does not permit the withholding or the deprivation of any right necessarily inhering in freedom. It not only struck down the institution of slavery as previously existing in the United States, but it prevents the imposition of any burdens or disabilities that constitute badges of slavery or servitude. It decreed universal civil freedom in this country. This court has so adjudged. But that amendment having been found inadequate to the protection of the rights of those who had been in slavery, it was followed by the Fourteenth Amendment, which added greatly to the dignity and glory of American citizenship, and to the security of personal liberty, by declaring that "all persons born or naturalized in the United States and of the State wherein they reside," and that "no State shall make or enforce any law which shall abridge the privileges or immunities of citizens of the United States; nor shall any State deprive any person of life, liberty or property without due process of law, nor deny to any person within its jurisdiction the equal protection of the laws." These two amendments, if enforced according to their true intent and meaning, will protect all the civil rights that pertain to freedom and citizenship. Finally, and to the end that no citizen should be denied, on account of his race, the privilege of participating in the political control of his country, it was declared by the Fifteenth Amendment that "the right of citizens of the United States to vote shall not be denied or abridged by the United States or by any State on account of race, color or previous condition of servitude."

These notable additions to the fundamental law were welcomed by the friends of liberty throughout the world. They removed the race line from our governmental systems. They had, as this court has said, a common purpose, namely, to secure "to a race recently emancipated, a race that through many generations have been held in slavery, all the civil rights that the superior race enjoy..." ...The white race deems itself to be the dominant race in this country. And so it is, in prestige, in achievements, in education, in wealth and in power. So I doubt not, it will continue to be for all time, if it remains true to its great heritage and holds fast to the principals of constitutional liberty. But in view of the Constitution, in the eye of the law, there is in this country no superior, dominant, ruling class of citizens. There is no caste here. Our Constitution is color-blind, and neither knows nor tolerates classes among citizens. In respect of civil rights, all citizens are equal before the law. The humblest is the peer of the most powerful. The law regards man as man, and takes no account of his surroundings or of his color when his civil rights as guaranteed by the supreme law of the land are involved. It is, therefore, to be regretted that this high tribunal, the final expositor of the fundamental law of the land, has reached the conclusion that it is competent for a State to regulate the enjoyment by citizens of their civil rights solely upon the basis of race.

In my opinion, the judgment this day rendered will, in time, prove to be quite as pernicious as the decision made by this tribunal in the *Dred Scott case*...The present decision, it may well be apprehended, will not only stimulate aggressions, more or less brutal and irritating, upon the admitted rights of colored citizens, but will encourage the belief that it is possible, by means of state enactments, to defeat the beneficent purposes which the people of the United States had in view when they adopted the recent amendments of the Constitution, by one of which the blacks of this country were made citizens of the United States and of the States in which they respectively reside, and whose privileges and immunities, as citizens, the States are forbidden to abridge. Sixty millions of whites are in no danger from the presence here of eight millions of blacks. The destinies of the two races, in this country, are indissolubly linked together, and the interests of both require that the common government of all shall not permit the seeds of race hate to be planted under the sanction of law. What can more certainly arouse race hate, what more certainly create and perpetuate a feeling of distrust between these races, than state enactments, which, in fact, proceed on the ground that colored citizens are so inferior and degraded that they cannot be allowed to sit in public coaches occupied by white citizens? That, as all will admit, is the real meaning of such legislation as was enacted in Louisiana....

The arbitrary separation of citizens, on the basis of race, while they are on a public highway, is a badge of servitude wholly inconsistent with the civil freedom and the equality before the law established by the Constitution. It cannot be justified upon any legal grounds....

▶ Notes & Questions

1. What was Plessy trying to accomplish by sitting in the white section of the train? If the facilities for Blacks and whites were equal, what was he trying to prove?

2. In 1896, Booker T. Washington, a recognized leader of Black America had recently made a speech in Atlanta in which he urged Blacks to accept racial separatism for the time being. Through gradualism, Washington believed that Blacks would advance. Why didn't Plessy follow Washington's advice? Was Plessy trying to bring about social change too soon? Was America willing, at such an early point after the end of slavery, to accept Blacks as social equals?

3. How could Justice Harlan take such a "color-blind" view of the Constitution, while the majority upheld segregation? What principals did Justice Harlan base his decision upon?

4. What is his view of the Thirteenth Amendment? Should it be interpreted to make social distinctions based upon race unconstitutional?

5. What was Justice Harlan's response to the argument that the Louisiana statute was colorblind?

6. Does he see a conflict between state's rights and national rights?

B. **Interstate Commerce**

Ms. Morgan, an African-American woman, refused to go to the back of a bus that was traveling from Virginia to Maryland. She was subsequently arrested, charged and convicted of violating a Virginia law that required segregation on the motor buses. Her conviction was affirmed by the Supreme Court of Appeals of Virginia. Her conviction was appealed to the United States Supreme Court by William H. Hastie and Thurgood Marshall of the National Association for the Advancement of Colored People (N.A.A.C.P.). Friends of the court briefs were filed by the American Civil liberties Union and the Workers Defense League.

MORGAN v. VIRGINIA
Supreme Court of the United States
328 U.S. 373 (1946)

MR. JUSTICE REED delivered the opinion of the Court.

This appeal brings to this Court the question of the constitutionality of an act of Virginia, (note omitted) which requires all passenger motor vehicle carriers, both interstate and intrastate, (note omitted) to separate without discrimination (note omitted) the white and colored passengers in their motor buses so that contiguous seats will not be occupied by persons of different races at the same time. A violation of the requirement of separation by the carrier is a misdemeanor. (Note omitted). The driver or other person in charge is directed and required to increase or decrease the space allotted to the respective races as may be necessary or proper and may require passengers to change their seats to comply with the allocation. The operator's failure to enforce the provisions is made a misdemeanor.

These regulations were applied to an interstate passenger, this appellant, on a motor vehicle then making an interstate run or trip. According to the statement of fact by the Supreme Court of Appeals of Virginia, appellant, who is a Negro, was traveling on a motor common carrier, operating under the above-mentioned statute, from

Gloucester County, Virginia, through the District of Columbia, to Baltimore, Maryland, the destination of the bus. There were other passengers, both white and colored. On her refusal to accede to a request of the driver to move to a back seat, which was partly occupied by other colored passengers, so as to permit the seat that she vacated to be used by white passengers, a warrant was obtained and appellant was arrested, tried and convicted of a violation of § 4097dd of the Virginia Code. (Note omitted). On a writ of error the conviction was affirmed by the Supreme Court of Appeals of Virginia. 184 Va. 24. The Court of Appeals interpreted the Virginia statute as applicable to appellant since the statute "embraces all motor vehicles and all passengers, both interstate and intrastate." The Court of Appeals refused to accept appellant's contention that the statute applied was invalid as a delegation of legislative power to the carrier by a concurrent holding "that no power is delegated to the carrier to legislate.... The statute itself condemns the defendant's conduct as a violation of law and not the rule of the carrier." Id., at 38. No complaint is made as to these interpretations of the Virginia statute by the Virginia court. (Note omitted).

The errors of the Court of Appeals that are assigned and relied upon by appellant are in form only two. The first is that the decision is repugnant to Clause 3, § 8, Article I of the Constitution of the United States, (note omitted) and the second the holding that powers reserved to the states by the Tenth Amendment include the power to require an interstate motor passenger to occupy a seat restricted for the use of his race. Actually, the first question alone needs consideration for, if the statute unlawfully burdens interstate commerce, the reserved powers of the state will not validate it. (Note omitted).

We think, as the Court of Appeals apparently did, that the appellant is a proper person to challenge the validity of this statute as a burden on commerce. (Note omitted). If it is an invalid burden, the conviction under it would fail. The statute affects appellant as well as the transportation company. Constitutional protection against burdens on commerce is for her benefit on a criminal trial for violation of the challenged statute. (Citation omitted).

The precise degree of a permissible restriction on state power cannot be fixed generally or indeed not even for one kind of state legislation, such as taxation or health or safety. (Note omitted). There is a recognized abstract principle, however, that may be taken as a postulate for testing whether particular state legislation in the absence of action by Congress is beyond state power. This is that the state legislation is invalid if it unduly burdens that commerce in matters where uniformity is necessary -- necessary in the constitutional sense of useful in accomplishing a permitted purpose. (Note omitted). Where uniformity is essential for the functioning of commerce, a state may not interpose its local regulation. (Note omitted). Too true it is that the principle lacks in precision. Although the quality of such a principle is abstract, its application to the facts of a situation created by the attempted enforcement of a statute brings about a specific determination as to whether or not the statute in question is a burden on commerce. Within the broad limits of the principle, the cases turn on their own facts.

In the field of transportation, there has been a series of decisions which hold that where Congress has not acted and although the state statute affects interstate commerce, a state may validly enact legislation which has predominantly only a local influence on the course of commerce. (Note omitted). It is equally well settled that, even where Congress has not acted, state legislation or a final court order is invalid which materially affects interstate commerce. (Note omitted). Because the Constitution puts the ultimate power to regulate commerce in Congress, rather than the states, the degree of state legislation's interference with that commerce may be weighed by federal courts to determine whether the burden makes the statute unconstitutional. (Note omitted). The courts could not invalidate federal legislation for the same reason because Congress, within the limits of the Fifth Amendment, has authority to burden commerce if that seems to it a desirable means of accomplishing a permitted end. (Note omitted)....

Interstate passengers traveling via motor buses between the north and south or the east and west may pass through Virginia on through lines in the day or in the night. The large buses approach the comfort of pullmans and have seats convenient for rest. On such interstate journeys the enforcement of the requirements for reseating would be disturbing.

Appellant's argument, properly we think, includes facts bearing on interstate motor transportation beyond those immediately involved in this journey under the Virginia statutory regulations. To appraise the weight of the burden of the Virginia statute on interstate commerce, related statutes of other states are important to show whether there are cumulative effects which may make local regulation impracticable. Eighteen states, it appears, prohibit racial separation on public carriers. (Note omitted). Ten require separation on motor carriers. (Note omitted). Of these, Alabama applies specifically to interstate passengers with an exception for interstate passengers with through tickets from states without laws on separation of passengers. (Note omitted). The language of the other acts, like this Virginia statute before the Court of Appeals' decision in this case, may be said to be susceptible to an interpretation that they do or do not apply to interstate passengers.

In states where separation of races is required in motor vehicles, a method of identification as white or colored must be employed. This may be done by definition. Any ascertainable Negro blood identifies a person as colored for purposes of separation in some states. (Note omitted). In the other states which require the separation of the races in motor carriers, apparently no definition generally applicable or made for the purposes of the statute is given. Court definition or further legislative enactments would be required to clarify the line between the races. Obviously there may be changes by legislation in the definition. (Note omitted).

The interferences to interstate commerce which arise from state regulation of racial association on interstate vehicles has long been recognized. Such regulation hampers freedom of choice in selecting accommodations. The recent changes in transportation brought about by the coming of automobiles does not seem of great significance in the problem. People of all races travel today more extensively than in 1878 when this Court first passed upon state regulation of racial segregation in commerce. The factual situation set out in preceding paragraphs emphasizes the soundness of this Court's early conclusion in *Hall v. DeCuir*, 95 U.S. 485…

In weighing the factors that enter into our conclusion as to whether this statute so burdens interstate commerce or so infringes the requirements of national uniformity as to be invalid, we are mindful of the fact that conditions vary between northern or western states such as Maine or Montana, with practically no colored population; industrial states such as Illinois, Ohio, New Jersey and Pennsylvania with a small, although appreciable, percentage of colored citizens; and the states of the deep south with percentages of from twenty-five to nearly fifty per cent colored, all with varying densities of the white and colored races in certain localities. Local efforts to promote amicable relations in difficult areas by legislative segregation in interstate transportation emerge from the latter racial distribution. As no state law can reach beyond its own border nor bar transportation of passengers across its boundaries, diverse seating requirements for the races in interstate journeys result. As there is no federal act dealing with the separation of races in interstate transportation, we must decide the validity of this Virginia statute on the challenge that it interferes with commerce, as a matter of balance between the exercise of the local police power and the need for national uniformity in the regulations for interstate travel. It seems clear to us that seating arrangements for the different races in interstate motor travel require a single, uniform rule to promote and protect national travel. Consequently, we hold the Virginia statute in controversy invalid.

Chapter Three

Desegregation Era

The Brown Case

The *Brown* case brought about several important changes in the political and social fabric of the United States. Almost a century after the Emancipation Proclamation, it ended legally sanctioned segregation in the South. It set in motion a national policy that required, not only desegregation, but also integration. But did the *Brown* decision go too far? Was the Court correct in its reasoning that separate facilities are inherently unequal? What are the implications of such a decision for predominantly state Black colleges and universities?

Many Blacks believed that *Brown v. Board of Education* and the Civil Rights Act of 1964 would usher in an era of opportunity. The law was therefore looked to as a crucible for destroying segregation and providing a federal right to equal education and employment opportunity. Even though, the young attorney for the N.A.A.C.P., Thurgood Marshall, had successfully argued and won a landmark United States Supreme Court case, the decision failed to fundamentally change the living condition of Blacks. Rather than providing Blacks with the means to achieve redress for centuries of brutal and uncompensated labor, *Brown* merely stood for the legal proposition that segregated (though equal) schools deprived Blacks of educational opportunity. The message from the court was clear: Black schools, though equal in physical facilities and other tangible factors, were, nevertheless, inferior. The decision therefore caused a generation of Blacks to believe that their liberation could be achieved through court ordered integration. The *Brown* decision raised false expectations that the law would provide the lever for achieving freedom and justice. This belief, however, was short lived as many Blacks engaged in massive demonstrations in an effort to secure more sweeping human rights, rather than just civil rights.

A.
Right to Integrated Education

BROWN ET AL. v. BOARD OF EDUCATION OF TOPEKA ET AL.
Supreme Court of the United States
347 U.S. 483 (1954)

MR. CHIEF JUSTICE WARREN delivered the opinion of the Court.

These cases come to us from the States of Kansas, South Carolina, Virginia, and Delaware. They are premised on different facts and different local conditions, but a common legal question justifies their consideration together in this consolidated opinion. (Footnote omitted).

In each of the cases, minors of the Negro race, through their legal representatives, seek the aid of the courts in obtaining admission to the public schools of their community on a nonsegregated basis. In each instance, they had been denied admission to schools attended by white children under laws requiring or permitting segregation according to race. This segregation was alleged to deprive the plaintiffs of the equal protection of the laws under the Fourteenth Amendment. In each of the cases other than the Delaware case, a three-judge federal district court denied relief to the plaintiffs on the so-called "separate but equal" doctrine announced by this Court in *Plessy v. Ferguson*, 163 U.S. 537...

The plaintiffs contend that segregated public schools are not "equal"and cannot be made "equal," and that hence they are deprived of the equal protection of the laws...

The most avid proponents of the post-War Amendments undoubtedly intended them to remove all legal distinctions among "all persons born or naturalized in the United States." Their opponents, just as certainly, were antagonistic to both the letter and the spirit of the Amendments and wished them to have the most limited effect. What others in Congress and the state legislatures had in mind cannot be determined with any degree of certainty.

An additional reason for the inconclusive nature of the Amendment's history, with respect to segregated schools, is the status of public education at that time. (Footnote omitted). In the South, the movement toward free common schools, supported by general taxation, had not yet taken hold. Education of white children was largely in the hands of private groups. Education of Negroes was almost nonexistent, and practically all of the race were illiterate. In fact, any education of Negroes was forbidden by law in some states. Today, in contrast, many Negroes have achieved outstanding success in the arts and sciences as well as in the business and professional world. It is true that public school education at the time of the Amendment had advanced further in the North, but the effect of the Amendment on Northern States was generally ignored in the congressional debates. Even in the North, the conditions of public education did not approximate those existing today. The curriculum was usually rudimentary; ungraded schools were common in rural areas; the school term was but three months a year in many states; and compulsory school attendance was virtually unknown. As a consequence, it is not surprising that there should be so little in the history of the Fourteenth Amendment relating to its intended effect on public education.

In the first cases in this Court construing the Fourteenth Amendment, decided shortly after its adoption, the Court interpreted it as proscribing all state-imposed discriminations against the Negro race". (Footnote omitted)...

In the instant cases that question is directly presented. Here unlike *Sweatt v. Painter*, there are findings below that the Negro and white schools involved have been equalized or are being equalized with respect to buildings, curricula, qualifications and salaries of teachers and other "tangible" factors. (Footnote omitted). Our decision therefore cannot turn on merely a comparison of these tangible factors in the Negro and white schools involved in each of the cases. We must look instead to the effect of segregation itself on public education.

In approaching this problem we cannot turn the clock back to 1868 when the Amendment was adopted or even to 1896 when *Plessy v. Ferguson* was written. We must consider public education in the light of its full development and its present place in American life throughout the Nation. Only in this way can it be determined if segregation in public schools deprives these plaintiffs of the equal protection of the laws. Today education is perhaps the most important function of state and local governments. Compulsory school attendance laws and the great expenditures for education both demonstrate our recognition of the importance of education to our democratic society. It is required in the performance of our most basic public responsibilities even service in the armed forces. It is the very foundation of good citizenship. Today it is a principal instrument in awakening the child to cultural values in preparing him for later professional training and in helping him to adjust normally to his environment. In these days, it is doubtful any child may reasonably be expected to succeed in life if he is denied the opportunity of an education. Such an opportunity, where the state has undertaken to provide it, is a right which must be made available to all on equal terms.

We come then to the question presented: Does segregation of children in public schools solely on the basis of race even though the physical facilities and other tangible factors may be equal, deprive the children of the minority group of equal educational opportunities? We believe that it does.

In *Sweatt v. Painter*, supra, in finding that a segregated law school for Negroes could not provide them equal educational opportunities, this Court relied in large part on "those qualities which are incapable of objective measurement but which make for greatness in a law school." In *McLaurin v. Oklahoma State Regents, supra*, the Court in requiring that a Negro admitted to a white graduate school be treated like all other students again resorted to intangible considerations: "...his ability to study, to engage in discussions and exchange views with other students and in general to learn his profession."

Such considerations apply with added force to children in grade and high schools. To separate them from others of similar age and qualifications solely because of their race generates a feeling of inferiority as to their status in the community that may affect their hearts and minds in a way unlikely ever to be undone. The effect of this separation on their educational opportunities was well stated by a finding in the Kansas case by a court which nevertheless felt compelled to rule against the Negro plaintiffs:

> "Segregation of white and colored children in public schools has a detrimental effect upon the colored children. The impact is greater when it has the sanction of the law; for the policy of separating the races is usually interpreted as denoting the inferiority of the negro group. A sense of inferiority affects the motivation of a child to learn. Segregation with the sanction of law therefore has a tendency to (retard) the educational and mental development of negro children and to deprive them of some of the benefits they would receive in a racial(ly) integrated school system." (Footnote omitted).

Whatever may have been the extent of psychological knowledge at the time of *Plessy v. Ferguson*, this finding is amply supported by modern authority. (Footnote omitted) Any language in *Plessy v. Ferguson contrary* to this finding is rejected.

We conclude that in the field of public education the doctrine of "separate but equal" has no place. Separate educational facilities are inherently unequal. Therefore, we hold that the plaintiffs and others similarly situated for whom the actions have been brought are by reason of the segregation complained of deprived of the equal protection of the laws guaranteed by the Fourteenth Amendment. This disposition makes unnecessary any discussion whether such segregation also violates the Due Process Clause of the Fourteenth Amendment". (Footnote omitted)... *It is so ordered.*

▶ **Notes & Questions**

1. Are segregated schools always unequal? Why does the Court move in the direction of holding that segregated schools are inherently unequal?

2. Can Black colleges and universities ever be the equal of white ones?

3. From what four states did the appeals come?

4. What did the appellants allege?

5. Did the Court look at "tangible factors" such as buildings, curricula, qualifications and salaries of teachers?

6. Why did the Court weigh the "effect of segregation upon public education"?

7. Why did the Court look at public education in light of its full development?

8. Do you agree with the Court that education is the most important function of state and local government?

9. *Desegregation of Public Higher Education*

   If a state operates a dual system of higher education, should it be required under the Fourteenth Amendment to create a unitary system? Should traditionally Black colleges be dismantled to achieve this result?

   In April, 2001, the State of Mississippi agreed to spend $500 million to upgrade its Black colleges and expedite integration of White students. The state had been sued by Blacks in 1975 alleging that their colleges and universities (Jackson State, Alcorn State and Mississippi Valley State) were unfairly under-

▶ Notes & Questions

funded as compared to the state's White institutions. In 1992 the United States Supreme Court ruled that Mississippi had to adopt new spending and educational policies, which would include an affirmative action program for White students.

Since the State of Mississippi had been found responsible for discriminating against Blacks by failing to appropriate equal funds to Black colleges and universities, should not the remedy solely be an order to appropriate equal funds? Is there a convincing rationale for requiring an affirmative action program for White students? Should the historic character of the Black schools be sacrificed to achieve the goal of integration?

10. *The Impetus of Social Movements*

African-American women led in the struggle to achieve human rights in America. In December, 1955, Rosa Parks stepped forward and initiated a social movement that galvanized a grass roots revolt against the socio-economic conditions that stifled and oppressed people of color. The speech of Rev. Martin Luther King, Jr., upon the arrest of Rosa Parks, reflected the frustration and impatience of a people determined to take their destiny into their own hands, rather than rely upon the law for redress:

> "There comes a time when people get tired. We are here this evening to say to those who have mistreated us so long that we are tired—tired of being segregated and humiliated, tired of being kicked about by the brutal feet of oppression..."[1]

1 Sitkoff, Harvard, *The Struggle for Black Equality, 1954–1980,* (New York, Hill and Wang, 1981), page 51.

▶ Notes & Questions

This movement to end oppression raised fundamental questions regarding racial discrimination and economic inequality. Dr. King moved the conscience of America by exposing the social/racial contradictions in this society to the international community. The world witnessed such atrocities as the lynching of Emmett Till, a fourteen year old Chicago youth who had visited Mississippi in 1955, the murder of Medgar Evers, the Jackson, Mississippi N.A.A.C.P. Field Secretary on June 11, 1963; and the March on Washington in the same year. The Congress quickly passed the Civil Rights Act of 1964 in direct response to this grass roots militancy and the non-violent leadership that had precipitated the march.

B.
Right to Freedom of Marriage

Part of the process of desegregation was the breaking down of racist ideas and values that had been imbedded in the South and the nation. Not only were Blacks to be kept separate in political activities, but also in matters that were social. At the heart of this social separation was the fear of interracial romance and marriage. The fears of the Southern whites were reflected in their laws on fornication and marriage. Therefore, the law was forced to take the lead in breaking down social prohibitions that were based upon race.

LOVING v. VIRGINIA
Supreme Court of the United States
388 U.S. 1 (1967)

MR. CHIEF JUSTICE WARREN delivered the opinion of the Court.

This case presents a constitutional question never addressed by this Court: whether a statutory scheme adopted by the State of Virginia to prevent marriages between persons solely on the basis of racial classifications violates the Equal Protection and Due Process Clauses of the Fourteenth Amendment. (Footnote omitted). For reasons which seem to us to reflect the central meaning of those constitutional commands, we conclude that these statutes cannot stand consistently with the Fourteenth Amendment.

In June 1958, two residents of Virginia, Mildred Jeter, a Negro woman, and Richard Loving, a white man, were married in the District of Columbia pursuant to its laws. Shortly after their marriage, the Lovings returned to Virginia and established their marital abode in Caroline County. At the October Term, 1958, of the Circuit Court of Caroline County, a grand jury issued an indictment charging the Lovings with violating Virginia's ban on interracial marriages. On January 6, 1959, the Lovings pleaded guilty to the charge and were sentenced to one year in jail; however, the trial judge suspended the sentence for a period of 25 years on the condition that the Lovings leave the State and not return to Virginia together for 25 years. He stated in an opinion that:

> "Almighty God created the races white, black, yellow, malay and red, and he placed them on separate continents. And but for the interference with his arrangement there would be no cause for such marriages. The fact that he separated the races shows that he did not intend for the races to mix."

After their convictions, the Lovings took up residence in the District of Columbia. On November 6, 1963, they filed a motion in the state trial court to vacate the judgment and set aside the sentence on the ground that the statutes which they had violated were repugnant to the Fourteenth Amendment. The motion not having been decided by October 28, 1964, the Lovings instituted a class action in the United States District Court for the Eastern District of Virginia requesting that a three-judge court be convened to declare the Virginia anti-miscegenation statutes unconstitutional and to enjoin state officials from enforcing their convictions. On January 22, 1965, the state trial judge denied the motion to vacate the sentences, and the Lovings perfected an appeal to the Supreme Court of Appeals of Virginia. On February 11, 1965, the three-judge District Court continued the case to allow the Lovings to present their constitutional claims to the highest state court.

The Supreme Court of Appeals upheld the constitutionality of the anti-miscegenation statutes and, after modifying the sentence, affirmed the convictions. (Footnote omitted). The Lovings appealed this decision, and we noted probable jurisdiction on December 12, 1966, 385 U.S. 986.

The two statutes under which appellants were convicted and sentenced are part of a comprehensive statutory scheme aimed at prohibiting and punishing interracial marriages. The Lovings were convicted of violating ' 20-58 of the Virginia Code:

> *"Leaving State to evade law.*—If any white person and colored person shall go out of this State, for the purpose of being married, and with the intention of returning, and be married out of it, and afterwards return to and reside in it, cohabiting as man and wife, they shall be punished as provided in '20-59, and the marriage shall be governed by the same law as if it had been solemnized in this State. The fact of their cohabitation here as man and wife shall be evidence of their marriage."

Section 20-59, which defines the penalty for miscegenation, provides:

> *"Punishment for marriage.*—If any white person intermarry with a colored person, or any colored person intermarry with a white person, he shall be guilty of a felony and shall be punished by confinement in the penitentiary for not less than one nor more than five years."

Other central provisions in the Virginia statutory scheme are ' 20-57, which automatically voids all marriages between "a white person and a colored person" without any judicial proceeding, (Footnote omitted) and ' 20-54 and 1-14 which, respectively, define "white persons" and "colored persons and Indians" for purposes of the statutory prohibitions. (Footnote omitted). The Lovings have never disputed in the course of this litigation that Mrs. Loving is a "colored person" or that Mr. Loving is a "white person" within the meanings given those terms by the Virginia statutes.

Virginia is now one of 16 States which prohibit and punish marriages on the basis of racial classifications. (Footnote omitted). Penalties for miscegenation arose as an incident to slavery and have been common in Virginia since the colonial period. (Footnote omitted). The present statutory scheme dates from the adoption of the Racial Integrity Act of 1924, passed during the period of extreme nativism which followed the end of the First World War.

The central features of this Act, and current Virginia law, are the absolute prohibition of a "white person" marrying other than another "white person," (Footnote omitted) a prohibition against issuing marriage licenses until the issuing official is satisfied that the applicants' statements as to their race are correct, (Footnote omitted) certificates of "racial composition" to be kept by both local and state registrars, (Footnote omitted) and the carrying forward of earlier prohibitions against racial intermarriage". (Footnote omitted).

In upholding the constitutionality of these provisions in the decision below, the Supreme Court of Appeals of Virginia referred to its 1955 decision in *Naim v. Naim*, 197 Va. 80, 87 S. E. 2d 749, as stating the reasons supporting the validity of these laws. In *Naim*, the state court concluded that the State's legitimate purposes were "to preserve the racial integrity of its citizens," and to prevent "the corruption of blood," "a mongrel breed of citizens," and "the obliteration of racial pride," obviously an endorsement of the doctrine of White Supremacy. *Id.*, at 90, 87 S. E. 2d, at 756. The court also reasoned that marriage has traditionally been subject to state regulation without federal intervention, and, consequently, the regulation of marriage should be left to exclusive state control by the Tenth Amendment.

While the state court is no doubt correct in asserting that marriage is a social relation subject to the State's police power, *Maynard v. Hill*, 125 U.S. 190 (1888), the State does not contend in its argument before this Court that its powers to regulate marriage are unlimited notwithstanding the commands of the Fourteenth Amendment. Nor could it do so in light of *Meyer v. Nebraska v. Hill*, 262 U.S. 390 (1923), and *Skinner v. Oklahoma*, 316 U.S. 535 (1942). Instead, the State argues that the meaning of the Equal Protection Clause, as illuminated by the statements of the Framers, is only that state penal laws containing an interracial element as part of the definition of the offense must apply equally to whites and Negroes in the sense that members of each race are punished to the same degree. Thus, the State contends that, because its miscegenation statutes punish equally both the white and the Negro participants in an interracial marriage, these statutes, despite their reliance on racial classifications, do not constitute an invidious discrimination based upon race. The second argument advanced by the State assumes the validity of its equal application theory. The argument is that, if the Equal Protection Clause does not outlaw miscegenation statutes because of their reliance on racial classifications, the question of constitutionality would thus become whether there was any rational basis for a State to treat interracial marriages differently from other marriages. On this question, the State argues, the scientific evidence is substantially in doubt and, consequently, this Court should defer to the wisdom of the state legislature in adopting its policy of discouraging interracial marriages.

Because we reject the notion that the mere "equal application" of a statute containing racial classifications is enough to remove the classifications from the Fourteenth Amendment's proscription of all invidious racial discriminations, we do not accept the State's contention that these statutes should be upheld if there is any possible basis for concluding that they serve a rational purpose...

There can be no question but that Virginia's miscegenation statutes rest solely upon distinctions drawn according to race. The statutes proscribe generally accepted conduct if engaged in by members of different races. Over the years, this Court has consistently repudiated "[distinctions between citizens solely because of their ancestry" as being "odious to a free people whose institutions are founded upon the doctrine of equality." *Hirabayashi v. United States*, 320 U.S. 81, 100 (1943). At the very least, the Equal Protection Clause demands that racial classifications, especially suspect in criminal statutes, be subjected to the "most rigid scrutiny," *Korematsu v. United States*, 323 U.S. 214, 216 (1944), and, if they are ever to be upheld, they must be shown to be necessary to the accomplishment of some permissible state objective, independent of the racial discrimination which it was the object of the Fourteenth Amendment to eliminate. Indeed, two members of this Court have already stated that they "cannot conceive of a valid legislative purpose... which makes the color of a person's skin the test of whether his conduct is a criminal offense." *McLaughlin v. Florida, supra*, at 198 (STEWART, J., joined by DOUGLAS, J., concurring).

There is patently no legitimate overriding purpose independent of invidious racial discrimination which justifies this classification. The fact that Virginia prohibits only interracial marriages involving white persons demonstrates that the racial classifications must stand on their own justification, as measures designed to maintain White Supremacy. (Footnote omitted). We have consistently denied the constitutionality of measures which restrict the rights of citizens on account of race. There can be no doubt that restricting the freedom to marry solely because of racial classifications violates the central meaning of the Equal Protection Clause.

II.

These statutes also deprive the Lovings of liberty without due process of law in violation of the Due Process Clause of the Fourteenth Amendment. The freedom to marry has long been recognized as one of the vital personal rights essential to the orderly pursuit of happiness by free men.

Marriage is one of the "basic civil rights of man," fundamental to our very existence and survival. *Skinner v. Oklahoma*, 316 U.S. 535, 541 (1942). See also *Maynard v. Hill*, 125 U.S. 190 (1888). To deny this fundamental freedom on so unsupportable a basis as the racial classifications embodied in these statutes, classifications so directly subversive of the principle of equality at the heart of the Fourteenth Amendment, is surely to deprive all the State's citizens of liberty without due process of law. The Fourteenth Amendment requires that the freedom of choice to marry not be restricted by invidious racial discriminations. Under our Constitution, the freedom to marry, or not marry, a person of another race resides with the individual and cannot be infringed by the State.

These convictions must be reversed.

It is so ordered.

MR. JUSTICE STEWART, concurring.

I have previously expressed the belief that "it is simply not possible for a state law to be valid under our Constitution which makes the criminality of an act depend upon the race of the actor." *McLaughlin v. Florida*, 379 U.S. 184, 198 (concurring opinion). Because I adhere to that belief, I concur in the judgment of the Court.

▶ Notes & Questions

1. Why did so many states have laws making it a crime to marry someone from the Black race? What were the state legislatures trying to protect? What led them to develop these laws? Why did it take until 1967 for the Supreme Court to hold that such laws were unconstitutional?

2. Are there any circumstances where the state would be justified in regulating who married whom?

3. Does the Constitution forbid discrimination on the basis of a marriage between consenting adult homosexuals? What should be the public policy concerning such marriages?

4. Can a private university be prohibited, under federal law, from outlawing mixed racial dating on its college campus? See *Bob Jones University v. United States*, 461 6-5-574 (1983).

5. Can a homosexual couple rely upon *Lovings* to support their position that the Fourteenth Amendment prohibits discrimination based upon sexual preference? See *Baehr v. Lewin*, 74 Haw. 530 (1993).

6. The Supreme Court of Massachusetts ruled in *Goodridge v. Department of Public Health* 440 Mass. 309 (2003) that the prohibition against same-sex marriages violated the Massachusetts Constitution. Should other states follow Massachusetts?

C.

Right to Vote

One of the most tenacious aspects of segregation and institutional racism was the denial to vote. The denial of the right to vote was premised upon the fear that equal access to the polls for African-Americans would impact political power in the South and the material benefits that flow to those in power. The efforts to use law, therefore, to desegregate had to confront the state public policy barriers to voting.

1. State Laws Denying the Right to Vote

Nixon v. Herndon **ET AL.**
Supreme Court of the United States
273 U.S. 536 (1927)

MR. JUSTICE HOLMES delivered the opinion of the Court.

This is an action against the Judges of Elections for refusing to permit the plaintiff to vote at a primary election in Texas. It lays the damages at five thousand dollars. The petition alleges that the plaintiff is a negro, a citizen of the United States and of Texas and a resident of El Paso, and in every way qualified to vote, as set forth in detail, except that the statute to be mentioned interferes with his right; that on July 26, 1924, a primary election was held at El Paso for the nomination of candidates for a senator and representatives in Congress and State and other offices, upon the Democratic ticket; that the plaintiff, being a member of the Democratic party, sought to vote but was denied the right by defendants; that the denial was based upon a Statute of Texas enacted in May, 1923, and designated Article 3093a, by the words of which "in no event shall a negro be eligible to participate in a Democratic party primary election held in the State of Texas,"& c., and that this statute is contrary to the Fourteenth and Fifteenth Amendments to the Constitution of the United States. The defendants moved to dismiss upon the ground that the subject matter of the suit was political and not within the jurisdiction of the Court and that no violation of the Amendments was shown. The suit was dismissed and a writ of error was taken directly to this Court. Here no argument was made on behalf of the defendants but a brief was allowed to be filed by the Attorney General of the State.

The objection that the subject matter of the suit is political is little more than a play upon words. Of course the petition concerns political action but it alleges and seeks to recover for private damage. That private damage may be caused by such political action and may be recovered for in a suit at law hardly has been doubted for over two hundred years, since *Ashby v. White*, (Citation omitted). If the defendants' conduct was a wrong to the plaintiff the same reasons that allow a recovery for denying the plaintiff a vote at a final election allow it for denying a vote at the primary election that may determine the final result.

The important question is whether the statute can be sustained. But although we state it as a question the answer does not seem to us open to a doubt. We find it unnecessary to consider the Fifteenth Amendment, because it seems to us hard to imagine a more direct and obvious infringement of the Fourteenth. That Amendment, while it applies to all, was passed, as we know, with a special intent to protect the blacks from discrimination against them. *Slaughter House Cases*, 16 Wall. 36. *Strauder v. West Virginia*, 100 U.S. 303. That Amendment "not only gave citizenship and the privileges of citizenship to persons of color, but it denied to any State the power to withhold from them the equal protection of the laws... What is this but declaring that the law in the States shall be the same for the black as for the white; that all persons, whether colored or white, shall stand equal before the laws of the States, and, in regard to the colored race, for whose protection the amendment was primarily designed, that no discrimination shall be made against them by law because of their color?" (Citation omitted). The statute of Texas in the teeth of the prohibitions referred to assumes to forbid negroes to take part in a primary election the importance of which we have indicated, discriminating against them by the distinction of color alone. States may do a good deal of classifying that it is difficult to believe rational, but there are limits, and it is too clear for extended argument that color cannot be made the basis of a statutory classification affecting the right set up in this case.

Judgment reversed.

2. Political Parties Denying the Right to Vote

NIXON v. CONDON
Supreme Court of the United States
286 U.S. 536 (1932)

MR. JUSTICE CARDOZO delivered the opinion of the Court.

The petitioner, a Negro, has brought this action against judges of election in Texas to recover damages for their refusal by reason of his race or color to permit him to cast his vote at a primary election.

This is not the first time that he has found it necessary to invoke the jurisdiction of the federal courts in vindication of privileges secured to him by the Federal Constitution.

In *Nixon v. Herndon*, 273 U.S. 536, decided at the October Term, 1926, this court had before it a statute of the State of Texas (Article 3093a, Revised Civil Statutes, afterwards numbered 3107) whereby the legislature had said that "in no event shall a negro be eligible to participate in a democratic party primary election [held in that State]," and that "should a negro vote in a democratic primary election, the ballot shall be void," and election officials were directed to throw it out. While the mandate was in force, the Negro was shut out from a share in primary elections, not in obedience to the will of the party speaking through the party organs, but by the command of the State itself, speaking by the voice of its chosen representatives. At the suit of this petitioner, the statute was adjudged void as an infringement of his rights and liberties under the Constitution of the United States.

Promptly after the announcement of that decision, the legislature of Texas enacted a new statute (L. 1927, c. 67) repealing the article condemned by this court; declaring that the effect of the decision was to create an emergency with a need for immediate action; and substituting for the article so repealed another bearing the same number. By the article thus substituted, "every political party in this State through its State Executive Committee shall have the power to prescribe the qualifications of its own members and shall in its own way determine who shall be qualified to vote or otherwise participate in such political party; provided that no person shall ever be denied the right to participate in a primary in this State because of former political views or affiliations or because of membership or non-membership in organizations other than the political party."

Acting under the new statute, the State Executive Committee of the Democratic party adopted a resolution "that all white democrats who are qualified under the constitution and laws of Texas and who subscribe to the statutory pledge provided in Article 3110, Revised Civil Statutes of Texas, and none other, be allowed to participate in the primary elections to be held July 28, 1928, and August 25, 1928," and the chairman and secretary were directed to forward copies of the resolution to the committees in the several counties.

On July 28, 1928, the petitioner, a citizen of the United States, and qualified to vote unless disqualified by the foregoing resolution, presented himself at the polls and requested that he be furnished with a ballot. The respondents, the judges of election, declined to furnish the ballot or to permit the vote on the ground that the petitioner was a Negro and that by force of the resolution of the Executive Committee only white Democrats were allowed to be voters at the Democratic primary. The refusal was followed by this action for damages. In the District Court there was a judgment of dismissal, (Citation omitted), which was affirmed by the Circuit Court of Appeals for the Fifth Circuit, (Citation omitted). A writ of certiorari brings the cause here.

Barred from voting at a primary the petitioner has been, and this for the sole reason that his color is not white. The result for him is no different from what it was when his cause was here before. The argument for the respondents is, however, that identity of result has been attained through essential diversity of method. We are reminded that the Fourteenth Amendment is a restraint upon the States and not upon private persons unconnected with a State. (Citation omitted). This line of demarcation drawn, we are told that a political party is merely a voluntary association; that it has inherent power like voluntary associations generally to determine its own membership; that the new article of the statute, adopted in place of the mandatory article of exclusion condemned by this court, has no other effect than to restore to the members of the party the power that would have been theirs if the lawmakers had been silent; and that qualifications thus established are as far aloof from the impact of constitutional restraint as those for membership in a golf club or for admission to a Masonic lodge...

We do not impugn the competence of the legislature to designate the agencies whereby the party faith shall be declared and the party discipline enforced. The pith of the matter is simply this, that when those agencies are invested with an authority independent of the will of the association in whose name they undertake to speak, they become to that extent the organs of the State itself, the repositories of official power. They are then the governmental instruments whereby parties are organized and regulated to the end that government itself may be established or continued. What they do in that relation, they must do in submission to the mandates of equality and liberty that bind officials everywhere. They are not acting in matters of merely private concern like the directors or agents of business corporations. They are acting in matters of high public interest, matters intimately connected with the capacity of government to exercise its functions unbrokenly and smoothly. Whether in given circumstances parties or their committees are agencies of government within the Fourteenth or the Fifteenth Amendment is a question which this court will determine for itself. It is not concluded upon such an inquiry by decisions rendered elsewhere. The test is not whether the members of the Executive Committee are the representatives of the State in the strict sense in which an agent is the representative of his principal. The test is whether they are to be classified as representatives of the State to such an extent and in such a sense that the great restraints of the Constitution set limits to their action.

With the problem thus laid bare and its essentials exposed to view, the case is seen to be ruled by *Nixon v. Herndon*, supra. Delegates of the State's power have discharged their official functions in such a way as to discriminate invidiously between white citizens and black. The Fourteenth Amendment, adopted as it was with special solicitude for the equal protection of members of the Negro race, lays a duty upon the court to level by its judgment these barriers of color.

The judgment below is reversed and the cause remanded for further proceedings in conformity with this opinion.

Reversed.

▶ Notes & Questions

In the above case the Court found violations of constitutional rights even though the actions appeared to be private. What rationale did the Court use to reach this result? Do you agree with its holding? How far should it be taken? Is the Court stretching the intentions of the 14th Amendment?

Chapter Four

EQUAL OPPORTUNITY ERA: MYTH or REALITY?

March on Washington

The 1963 March on Washington, led by Rev. Martin Luther King, Jr. and A. Philip Randolph confronted the nation about its discriminatory past. The more than two hundred thousand Americans said to government leadership and the captains of industry that the nation had to undergo fundamental changes in how it addressed issues of discrimination, especially in employment.

Civil Rights Act of 1964

As a result of this massive show of public discontent, Congress passed comprehensive legislation designed to eliminate the vestiges of discrimination in public affairs. As A. Philip Randolph stressed in his address at the March on Washington, jobs are critical to the advancement of Black people. After the end of slavery, Blacks had been denied access to economic security, by being relegated to inferior and low paying employment. Title VII of the Act was intended to break down these barriers and usher in an era of equal opportunity in employment, which would substantially change the economic condition of Blacks.

To what extent has the purpose of Title VII been achieved within the work place? Are Blacks and other people of color afforded the dignity that legitimate employment bestows upon individuals and communities? Title VII was designed to reconcile the paradox of the American dream that was crafted in the slavery era. Has the American dream become the American reality for those who had suffered both psychological and physical debasement? The specific problems that the new law was designed to address were the failure to hire and promote and the failure to develop and maintain work environments free of discriminatory conditions.

Civil Rights Act of 1991

This amendment to the 1964 legislation strengthened the sanctions against discrimination. Under this act plaintiffs are able to seek greater damages, amounting to $300,000.00 per person in compensatory and punitive damages. Under the 1964 statute, plaintiffs could only seek back pay awards, costs and attorneys fees.

A.
Rationalization for Non-Discrimination in Employment and Voting

Civil Rights Act of 1964

" ' 703. Unlawful employment practices

... (a) It shall be an unlawful employment practice for an employer

(1) to fail or refuse to hire or to discharge any individual, or otherwise to discriminate against any individual with respect to his compensation, terms, conditions, or privileges of employment, because of such individual's race, color, religion, sex, or national origin; or...

" ' 704. Other unlawful employment practices

(a) It shall be an unlawful employment practice for an employer to discriminate against any of his employees or applicants for employment, for an employment agency, or joint labor-management committee controlling apprenticeship or other training or retraining, including on -the-job training programs, to discriminate against any individual, or for a labor organization to discriminate against any member thereof or applicant for membership, because he has opposed any practice made an unlawful employment practice by this Title, or because he has made a charge, testified, assisted, or participated in any manner in an investigation, proceeding, or hearing under this Title."

1. Legal Theories of Discrimination in Employment

A. Disparate Impact

How is the disparate impact theory different from the disparate treatment theory? Does this theory provide greater remedies? If the employer is a governmental entity would this require the plaintiff to prove intent to discriminate?

GRIGGS ET AL. v. DUKE POWER CO.
Supreme Court of the United States
401 U.S. 424, 91 S.Ct. 849 (1971)

MR. CHIEF JUSTICE BURGER delivered the opinion of the Court.

We granted the writ in this case to resolve the question whether an employer is prohibited by the Civil Rights Act of 1964, Title VII, from requiring a high school education or passing of a standardized general intelligence test as a condition of employment in or transfer to jobs when (a) neither standard is shown to be significantly related to successful job performance, (b) both requirements operate to disqualify Negroes at a substantially higher rate than white applicants, and (c) the jobs in question formerly had been filled only by white employees as part of a longstanding practice of giving preference to whites. (Citation omitted).

Congress provided, in Title VII of the Civil Rights Act of 1964, for class actions for enforcement of provisions of the Act and this proceeding was brought by a group of incumbent Negro employees against Duke Power Company. All the petitioners are employed at the Company's Dan River Steam Station, a power generating facility located at Draper, North Carolina. At the time this action was instituted, the Company had 95 employees at the Dan River Station, 14 of whom were Negroes; 13 of these are petitioners here.

The District Court found that prior to July 2, 1965, the effective date of the Civil Rights Act of 1964, the Company openly discriminated on the basis of race in the hiring and assigning of employees at its Dan River plant. The plant was organized into five operating departments: (1) Labor, (2) Coal Handling, (3) Operations, (4) Maintenance, and (5) Laboratory and Test. Negroes were employed only in the Labor Department where the highest paying jobs paid less than the lowest paying jobs in the other four "operating" departments in which only whites were employed. (Citation omitted). Promotions were normally made within each department on the basis of job seniority. Transferees into a department usually began in the lowest position.

In 1955 the Company instituted a policy of requiring a high school education for initial assignment to any department except Labor, and for transfer from the Coal Handling to any "inside" department (Operations, Maintenance, or Laboratory). When the Company abandoned its policy of restricting Negroes to the Labor Department in 1965, completion of high school also was made a prerequisite to transfer from Labor to any other department. From the time the high school requirement was instituted to the time of trial, however, white employees hired before the time of the high school education requirement continued to perform satisfactorily and achieve promotions in the "operating" departments. Findings on this score are not challenged.

The Company added a further requirement for new employees on July 2, 1965, the date on which Title VII became effective. To qualify for placement in any but the Labor Department it became necessary to register satisfactory scores on two professionally prepared aptitude tests, as well as to have a high school education. Completion of high school alone continued to render employees eligible for transfer to the four desirable departments from which Negroes had been excluded if the incumbent had been employed prior to the time of the new requirement. In September 1965 the Company began to permit incumbent employees who lacked a high school education to qualify for transfer from Labor or Coal Handling to an "inside" job by passing two tests—the Wonderlie Personnel Test, which purports to measure general intelligence, and the Bennett Mechanical Comprehension Test. Neither was directed or intended to measure the ability to learn to perform a particular job or category of jobs. The requisite scores used for both initial hiring and transfer approximated the national median for high school graduates. (Citation omitted).

The District Court had found that while the Company previously followed a policy of overt racial discrimination in a period prior to the Act, such conduct had ceased. The District Court also concluded that Title VII was intended to be prospective only and, consequently, the impact of prior inequities was beyond the reach of corrective action authorized by the Act.

The Court of Appeals was confronted with a question of first impression, as are we, concerning the meaning of Title VII. After careful analysis a majority of that court concluded that a subjective test of the employer's intent should govern, particularly in a close ease, and that in this case there was no showing of a discriminatory purpose in the adoption of the diploma and test requirements. On this basis, the Court of Appeals concluded there was no violation of the Act.

The Court of Appeals reversed the District Court in part, rejecting the holding that residual discrimination arising from prior employment practices was insulated from remedial action. (Citation omitted). The Court of Appeals noted, however, that the District Court was correct in its conclusion that there was no showing of a racial purpose or invidious intent in the adoption of the high school diploma requirement or general intelligence test and that these standards had been applied fairly to whites and Negroes alike. It held that, in the absence of a discriminatory purpose, use of such requirements was permitted by the Act. In so doing, the Court of Appeals rejected the claim that because these two requirements operated to render ineligible a markedly disproportionate number of Negroes, they were unlawful under Title VII unless shown to be job related. (Citation omitted). We granted the writ on these claims. 399 U.S. 926.

The objective of Congress in the enactment of Title VII is plain from the language of the statute. It was to achieve equality of employment opportunities and remove barriers that have operated in the past to favor an identifiable group of white employees over other employees. Under the Act, practices, procedures, or tests neutral on their face, and even neutral in terms of intent, cannot be maintained if they operate to "freeze" he status quo of prior discriminatory employment practices...

The Act proscribes not only overt discrimination but also practices that are fair in form, but discriminatory in operation. The touchstone is business necessity. If an employment practice which operates to exclude Negroes cannot be shown to be related to job performance, the practice is prohibited.

On the record before us, neither the high school completion requirement nor the general intelligence test is shown to bear a demonstrable relationship to successful performance of the jobs for which it was used. Both were adopted, as the Court of Appeals noted, without meaningful study of their relationship to job-performance ability. Rather, a vice president of the Company testified, the requirements were instituted on the Company's judgment that they generally would improve the over-all quality of the work force.

The evidence, however, shows that employees who have not completed high school or taken the tests have continued to perform satisfactorily and make progress in departments for which the high school and test criteria are now used. (Citation omitted). The promotion record of present employees who would not be able to meet the new criteria thus suggests the possibility that the requirements may not be needed even for the limited purpose of preserving the avowed policy of advancement within the Company. In the context of this case, it is unnecessary to reach the question whether testing requirements that take into ac-count capability for the next succeeding position or related future promotion might be utilized upon a showing that such long-range requirements fulfill a genuine business need. In the present case the Company has made no such showing.

The Court of Appeals held that the Company had adopted the diploma and test requirements without any "intention to discriminate against Negro employees." 420 F. 2d, at 1232. We do not suggest that either the District Court or the Court of Appeals erred in examining the employer's intent; but good intent or absence of discriminatory intent does not redeem employment procedures or testing mechanisms that operate as "built-in headwinds" for minority groups and are unrelated to measuring job capability.

The Company's lack of discriminatory intent is suggested by special efforts to help the undereducated employees through Company financing of two-thirds the cost of tuition for high school training. But Congress directed the thrust of the Act to the consequences of employment practices, not simply the motivation. More than that, Congress has placed on the employer the burden of showing that any given requirement must have a manifest relationship to the employment in question.

The facts of this case demonstrate the inadequacy of broad and general testing devices as well as the infirmity of using diplomas or degrees as fixed measures of capability. History is filled with examples of men and women who rendered highly effective performance without the conventional badges of accomplishment in terms of certificates, diplomas, or degrees. Diplomas and tests are useful servants, but Congress has mandated the commonsense proposition that they are not to become masters of reality...

Nothing in the Act precludes the use of testing or measuring procedures; obviously they are useful. What Congress has forbidden is giving these devices and mechanisms controlling force unless they are demonstrably a reasonable measure of job performance. Congress has not commanded that the less qualified be preferred over the better qualified simply because of minority origins. Far from disparaging job qualifications as such, Congress has made such qualifications the controlling factor, so that race, religion, nationality, and sex become irrelevant. What Congress has commanded is that any tests used must measure the person for the job and not the person in the abstract.

The judgment of the Court of Appeals is, as to that portion of the judgment appealed from, reversed.

B: Disparate Treatment

What are the steps that one must take to prove discrimination in employment under Title VII of the Civil Rights Act of 1964? Is the remedy afforded under the statute sufficient? What are the problems with seeking relief under the statute?

McDONNELL DOUGLAS CORP. v. GREEN
Supreme Court of the United States
411 U.S. 792, 93 S.Ct. 1817 (1973)

MR. JUSTICE POWELL delivered the opinion of the Court.

The case before us raises significant questions as to the proper order and nature of proof in actions under Title VII of the Civil Rights Act of 1964, 78 Stat. 253, 42 U.S. C. ' 2000e et seq.

Petitioner, McDonnell Douglas Corp., is an aerospace and aircraft manufacturer headquartered in St. Louis, Missouri, where it employs over 30,000 people. Respondent, a black citizen of St. Louis, worked for petitioner as a mechanic and laboratory technician from 1956 until August 28, 1964 (Citation omitted) when he was laid off in the course of a general reduction in petitioner's work force.

Respondent, a long-time activist in the civil rights movement, protested vigorously that his discharge and the general hiring practices of petitioner were racially motivated. (Citation omitted). As part of this protest, respondent and other members of the Congress on Racial Equality illegally stalled their cars on the main roads leading to petitioner's plant for the purpose of blocking access to it at the time of the morning shift change. The District Judge described the plan for, and respondent's participation in, the "stall-in" as follows:

"Five teams, each consisting of four cars would 'tie up' five main access roads into McDonnell at the time of the morning rush hour. The drivers of the cars were instructed to line up next to each other completely blocking the intersections or   roads. The drivers were also instructed to stop their cars, turn off the engines, pull the emergency brake, raise all windows, lock the doors, and remain in their cars until the police arrived. The plan was to have the cars remain in position for one hour.

"Acting under the 'stall-in' plan, plaintiff respondent in the present action, drove his car on to Brown Road, a McDonnell access road, at approximately 7:00 a.m., at the start of the morning rush hour. Plaintiff was aware of the traffic problems that would result. He stopped his car with the intent to block traffic. The police arrived shortly and requested plaintiff to move his car. He refused to move his car voluntarily. Plaintiff's car was towed away by the police, and he was arrested for obstructing traffic. Plaintiff pleaded guilty to the charge of obstructing traffic and was fined." 318 F. Supp. 846, 849.

On July 2, 1965, a "lock-in" took place wherein a chain and padlock were placed on the front door of a building to prevent the occupants, certain of petitioner's employees, from leaving. Though respondent apparently knew beforehand of the "lock-in," the full extent of his involvement remains uncertain. (Citation omitted).

Some three weeks following the "lock-in," on July 25, 1965, petitioner publicly advertised for qualified mechanics, respondent's trade, and respondent promptly applied for re-employment. Petitioner turned down respondent, basing its rejection on respondent's participation in the "stall-in" and "lock-in." Shortly thereafter, respondent filed a formal complaint with the Equal Employment Opportunity Commission, claiming that petitioner had refused to rehire him because of his race and persistent involvement in the civil rights movement, in violation of ' 703 (a)(l) and 704 (a) of the Civil Rights Act of 1964, 42 U. S. C. ' 2000e-2 (a)(l) and 2000e-3(a). (Citation omitted). The former section generally prohibits racial discrimination in any employment decision while the latter forbids discrimination against applicants or employees for attempting to protest or correct allegedly discriminatory conditions of employment.

The Commission made no finding on respondent's allegation of racial bias under ' 703(a)(1), but it did find reasonable cause to believe petitioner had violated ' 704 (a) by refusing to rehire respondent because of his civil rights activity. After the Commission unsuccessfully attempted to conciliate the dispute, it advised respondent in March 1968, of his right to institute a civil action in federal court within 30 days.

On April 15, 1968, respondent brought the present action, claiming initially a violation of ' 704 (a) and, in an amended complaint, a violation of ' 703(a)(1) as well. (Citation omitted). The District Court dismissed the latter claim of racial discrimination in petitioner's hiring procedures on the ground that the Commission had failed to make a determination of reasonable cause to believe that a violation of that section had been committed. The District Court also found that petitioner's refusal to rehire respondent was based solely on his participation in the illegal demonstrations and not on his legitimate civil rights activities. The court concluded that nothing in Title VII or s704 protected "such activity as employed by the plaintiff in the `stall in' and `lock in' demonstrations." 318 F. Supp., at 850.

On appeal, the Eighth Circuit affirmed that unlawful protests were not protected activities under ' 704 (a), (Citation omitted) but reversed the dismissal of respondent's ' 703 (a)(l) claim relating to racially discriminatory hiring practices, holding that a prior Commission determination of reasonable cause was not a jurisdictional prerequisite to raising a claim under that section in federal court. The court ordered the case remanded for trial of respondent's claim under ' 703 (a)(1).

In remanding, the Court of Appeals attempted to set forth standards to govern the consideration of respondent's claim. The majority noted that respondent had established a prima facie case of racial discrimination; that petitioner's refusal to rehire respondent rested on "subjective" criteria which carried little weight in rebutting charges of discrimination; that, though respondent's participation in the unlawful demonstrations might indicate a lack of a responsible attitude toward performing work for that employer, respondent should be given the opportunity to demonstrate that petitioner's reasons for refusing to rehire him were mere pretext. (Note omitted). In order to clarify the standards governing the disposition of an action challenging employment discrimination, we granted certiorari, 409 U.S. 1036 (1972).

I.

We agree with the Court of Appeals that absence of a Commission finding of reasonable cause cannot bar suit under an appropriate section of Title VII and that the District Judge erred in dismissing respondent's claim of racial discrimination under ' 703 (a)(l). Respondent satisfied the jurisdictional prerequisites to a federal action (i) by filing timely charges of employment discrimination with the Commission and (ii) by receiving and acting upon the Commission's statutory notice of the right to sue, 42 U.S. C. ' 2000e-5(a) and 2000e-5(e). The Act does not restrict a complainant's right to sue to those charges as to which the Commission has made findings of reasonable cause, and we will not engraft on the statute a requirement which may inhibit the review of claims of employment discrimination in the federal courts...

II.

The critical issue before us concerns the order and allocation of proof in a private, non-class action challenging employment discrimination. The language of Title VII makes plain the purpose of Congress to assure equality of employment opportunities and to eliminate those discriminatory practices and devices which have fostered racially stratified job environments to the disadvantage of minority citizens... (Citation omitted).

The complainant in a Title VII trial must carry the initial burden under the statute of establishing a prima facie case of racial discrimination. This may be done by showing (i) that he belongs to a racial minority; (ii) that he applied and was qualified for a job for which the employer was seeking applicants; (iii) that, despite his qualifications, he was rejected; and (iv) that, after his rejection, the position remained open and the employer continued to seek applicants from persons of complainant's qualifications. (Note omitted). In the instant case, we agree with the Court of Appeals that respondent proved a prima facie case. 463 F.2d 337, 353. Petitioner sought mechanics, respondent's trade, and continued to do so after respondent's rejection. Petitioner, moreover, does not dispute respondent's qualifications (Note omitted) and acknowledges that his past work performance in petitioner's employ was "satisfactory." (Note omitted).

The burden then must shift to the employer to articulate some legitimate, nondiscriminatory reason for the employee's rejection. We need not attempt in the instant case to detail every matter which fairly could be recognized as a reasonable basis for a refusal to hire. Here petitioner has assigned respondent's participation in unlawful conduct against it as the cause for his rejection. We think that this suffices to discharge petitioner's burden of proof at this stage and to meet respondent's prima facie case of discrimination...

Respondent admittedly had taken part in a carefully planned "stall-in," designed to tie up access to and egress from petitioner's plant at a peak traffic hour. (Note omitted). Nothing in Title VII compels an employer to absolve and rehire one who has engaged in such deliberate, unlawful activity against it. (Note omitted)...

Petitioner's reason for rejection thus suffices to meet the prima facie case, but the inquiry must not end here. While Title VII does not, without more, compel rehiring of respondent, neither does it permit petitioner to use respondent's conduct as a pretext for the sort of discrimination prohibited by ' 703 (a)(1). On remand, respondent must, as the Court of Appeals recognized, be afforded a fair opportunity to show that petitioner's stated reason for respondent's rejection was in fact pretext. Especially relevant to such a showing would be evidence that white employees involved in acts against petitioner of comparable seriousness to the "stall-in" were nevertheless retained or rehired. Petitioner may justifiably refuse to rehire one who was engaged in unlawful, disruptive acts against it, but only if this criterion is applied alike to members of all races.

Other evidence that may be relevant to any showing of pretext includes facts as to the petitioner's treatment of respondent during his prior term of employment; petitioner's reaction, if any, to respondent's legitimate civil rights activities; and petitioner's general policy and practice with respect to minority employment. (Note omitted). On the latter point, statistics as to petitioner's employment policy and practice may be helpful to a determination of whether petitioner's refusal to rehire respondent in this case conformed to a general pattern of discrimination against blacks. (Citation omitted). (Note omitted). In short, on the retrial respondent must be given a full and fair opportunity to demonstrate by competent evidence that the presumptively valid reasons for his rejection were in fact a coverup for a racially discriminatory decision...

III.

In sum, respondent should have been allowed to pursue his claim under ' 703 (a)(1). If the evidence on retrial is substantially in accord with that before us in this case, we think that respondent carried his burden of establishing a prima facie case of racial discrimination and that petitioner successfully rebutted that case. But this does not end the matter. On retrial, respondent must be afforded a fair opportunity to demonstrate that petitioner's assigned reason for refusing to re-employ was a pretext or discriminatory in its application. If the District Judge so finds, he must order a prompt and appropriate remedy. In the absence of such a finding, petitioner's refusal to rehire must stand.

The judgment is vacated and the cause is hereby remanded to the District Court for further proceedings consistent with this opinion.

So ordered.

▶ Notes & Questions

1.) Texaco Discrimination Suit

In November, 1996, a racial incident at Texaco, Inc. made Americans realize that despite the proliferation of anti-discrimination laws, discrimination in employment continued to plague Black Americans. The incident ignited an otherwise silent lawsuit that had been brought by six named employees and 1500 unnamed class action employees several years earlier. The plaintiffs had alleged that a racially hostile work environment existed at the company. They alleged that they had been called monkeys, Aunt Jemima and other derogatory words. In August, 1994 four senior executives met to discuss the lawsuit. One executive, who had the responsibility of taking notes during the meeting, tape recorded the conversations. When he was fired in 1996 due to corporate reorganization, he turned over the tapes to the Black plaintiffs. The plaintiffs' attorneys immediately made the tapes available to the press. The Texaco executives could be heard using language that many thought consisted of racial epithets. Blacks were referred to as "Black jelly beans" at the bottom of the jar.

The revelation created a public affairs nightmare for the $40 billion dollar oil company. Immediately civil rights leaders called for a national boycott of its products. As a result, investors became nervous as the price of shares dropped by $3.00 per share. The Chairman of the Board, Peter I. Bijur moved to limit damage to the company's image by promising to settle the class action lawsuit soon. Despite these promises Reverend Jesse Jackson, Reverend Al Sharpton and others started picketing Texaco service stations. Emanuel Cleaver 2d, President of National Conference of Black Mayors urged consumers to cut up their Texaco credit cards. Not all Black leaders supported this strategy, however. Kwesi Mfume, President of the National Association for the Advancement of Colored People (NAACP) called for more moderate action.

► **Notes & Questions**

As a result of the mounting pressure, the company announced on November 15, 1996 that it would settle the discrimination lawsuit for approximately $40 million dollars. Chairman Bijur stated that the company would establish policies, including goals and timetables that would eliminate any discrimination at the company. Texaco also agreed to establish a committee to monitor its affirmative action program. Many key members of the committee would be appointed by individuals from outside the company. The key would be changing attitudes and making managers accountable for the actions of their subordinates.

2.) Discrimination Against Black Farmers

One month after the Texaco bias suit was settled Black farmers marched in Washington, D.C., where they complained about racial bias in the administration of loan programs of the Department of Agriculture. The Black farmers alleged that they were given smaller loans than white farmers, given loans late in the crop season, or denied technical assistance. In the case of Welchel Long, a 74 year old Black farmer, from Dewey Rose, Georgia, the Department had concluded that he had been charged 18 percent for a loan, while a nearby white farmer had been charged only 3 percent. Despite this internal finding, the Department proceeded with foreclosure proceedings against Long. Agriculture Secretary Don Glickman agreed to set up a "civil rights action team" to investigate the problems and make recommendations to him by February, 1997.

The problem appeared to be widespread. Robert Williams, Jr. from Roscoe, Texas received word from the Department three years earlier that it had discriminated against him, but he had yet to receive any compensation. Many of these farmers alleged that government inaction had caused the number of Black farms to dwindle from 18,800 in 1982 to 33,300 in 1992.

▶ Notes & Questions

In 2002, the Bush Administration was forced to settle the lawsuits against many of these farmers and paid millions of dollars in damages.

3.) Ann Smith, a Black woman, of fifty-six years of age began work at a state agency after coming to Boston at the age of forty-five. She immediately enrolled in a part-time program that would lead to a Master's Degree in Social Work. Five years later, she completed her degree and informed her employer of its award. She told her boss that since she had obtained the degree, she wanted to take on more challenging assignments that would, in the long run, lead to promotions to higher levels of responsibility.

Her supervisor promised Ms. Smith that she would be given additional work. Despite these promises, the supervisor ignored Ms. Smith and did not assign her additional work for over a year. In fact, Ms. Smith was not given any work to do. She was merely left alone. Ms. Smith decided to write the Director of the unit and complain that she was not being given any work. This letter did not result in any meaningful changes. Ms. Smith subsequently hired a lawyer and brought suit under Title VII in the United States District Court alleging discrimination in terms and conditions of employment and failure to promote. In the meantime, Ms. Smith continued to draw a check from the agency. What factual issues must Ms. Smith produce at court in order to support her claims? Should there be a legal right to a job? Should the courts compel the employer to put Ms. Smith to work? How is Ms. Smith damaged by not being given work? How should the court rule on this problem? Shouldn't Ms. Smith be happy that she is getting a pay check?

4.) Bill Smith had worked in a public hospital for twenty-five years. He began as a radiologist assistant and quickly advanced

▶ Notes & Questions

to the position of Budget Director. He is Black. When the hospital became eligible for several federal contracts totaling over 25 million dollars, Mr. Smith's competency was questioned for the first time by other managers. Although he had never been given a written evaluation, he was given a letter of termination, effective in two months. Mr. Smith has indicated in his complaint to the Equal Employment Opportunity Commission (EEOC) that he had applied for a position of Fiscal Director and that the person who was Acting Fiscal Director, had written the letter of termination. Mr. Smith also stated that he had been called "nigger" by the Acting Fiscal Director during a private meeting between the two.

How should Mr. Smith begin developing his case for presentation to the EEOC? What kind of testimonial and physical evidence would be useful to his case? If you were the hearing officer in the case, what would be the critical evidence that you would want to see produced? What should the remedy be for Mr. Smith if the hearing officer rules in his favor? Can money compensate sufficiently an individual who has been damaged by unfair treatment? If not, what other sanctions should be available to compensate victims?

5.) Lester Smith graduated from one of the most prestigious business schools in the nation. Upon returning to his home town, he obtained a job in a major financial institution as an account manager. He was the only Black account manager in a division of fifty individuals. The financial institution had a policy of forwarding "new calls" to specific account managers for follow up. In the year that Lester worked at the firm, he was never given a "new call," while five white employees in his immediate group were given four each. The "new calls" resulted in each of the white co-workers obtaining new clients with substantial portfolios.

▶ Notes & Questions

Sensing that he was not being treated well, Lester met with his boss to discuss the matter. His boss told him to increase his number of "cold calls" to friends, relatives and other associates in the Black community. Lester took his boss' advice, but the "cold calls" did not result in a significant increase in the number of new clients brought into the firm.

Several weeks later, Lester received a letter from his boss indicating that if he did not increase the volume of his work by fifty percent, within six months, that he would be terminated. Upon receiving the letter, Lester marched into the office and confronted his boss. A shouting match resulted. When the boss tried to leave, he brushed up against Lester, whereupon Lester pushed him into the wall. Security was called and Lester was arrested. He was immediately fired for insubordination. Should the company cooperate in the criminal prosecution of Lester? Should Lester bring an action against the company under Title VII? How could the company have avoided the problem? Should Lester be given his job back? What facts would be necessary to mount a claim of discrimination?

2. Voting Rights Act of 1965

Even though the 15th Amendment declared that the right to vote could not be abridged on the basis of race, color and previous condition of servitude, southern communities adopted numerous policies and practices to prevent Blacks from voting. In 1965, President Lyndon Johnson signed the Voting Rights Act which guaranteed greater political participation of Blacks, and made unlawful, devices that were designed to limit participation. The Voting Rights Act was amended in 1970 when Congress extended the ban on the use of literacy tests to include the entire country. In 1982, Congress amended it again to clarify whether proof of discriminatory intent was necessary to establish a violation.

As a result of the statute, many Blacks were able to seek election, particularly to Congress, for the first time since Reconstruction. In 1902, George White left the House as representative from North Carolina and it was not until 1972, that Barbara Jordan was elected from Texas, followed by Andrew Young from Georgia (who was elected from a majority-white House district). In 1992 alone, thirteen African-Americans were elected to the House from the South. Cynthia McKinney became the first Black woman elected to Congress from Georgia. In 1992, she was elected from the 11th District that was 60.4 percent Black, but after a federal court ruling, the District was re-shaped to contain a Black voting population of 11 percent. Representative McKinney decided to run in the 4th District where the Black voting population was 33 percent. She successfully retained her position in the new district.

3. Legal Enforcement of the Voting Rights Act

The following cases address issues of the constitutionality of the Voting Rights Act and re-districting. When can the racial make-up of a neighborhood constitute a legitimate factor in creating legislative districts? Should state governments take affirmative steps to insure that sufficient numbers of Blacks are included within districts in order to insure the election of more Blacks? Is cumulative voting or proportional representation the appropriate measure?

STATE OF SOUTH CAROLINA v. KATZENBACH
Supreme Court of the United States
383 U.S. 301 (1966)

Mr. Chief Justice WARREN delivered the opinion of the Court.

By leave of the Court, 382 U.S. 898, 86 S.Ct.229, South Carolina has filed a bill of complaint, seeking a declaration that selected provisions of the Voting Rights Act of 1965 (Note omitted) violate the Federal Constitution, and asking for an injunction against enforcement of these provisions by the Attorney General. Original jurisdiction is founded on the presence of a controversy between a State and a citizen of another State under Art. III, ' 2, of the Constitution. (Citation omitted). Because no issues of fact were raised in the complaint, and because of South Carolina's desire to obtain a ruling prior to its primary elections in June 1966, we dispensed with appointment of a special master and expedited our hearing of the case.

Recognizing that the questions presented were of urgent concern to the entire country, we invited all of the States to participate in this proceeding as friends of the Court. A majority responded by submitting or joining in briefs on the merits, some supporting South Carolina and others the Attorney General. (Note omitted). Seven of these States also requested and received permission to argue the case orally at our hearing. Without exception, despite the emotional overtones of the proceeding, the briefs and oral arguments were temperate, lawyer-like and constructive. All viewpoints on the issues have been fully developed, and this additional assistance has been most helpful to the Court.

The Voting Rights Act was designed by Congress to banish the blight of racial discrimination in voting, which has infected the electoral process in parts of our country for nearly a century. The Act creates stringent new remedies for voting discrimination where it persists on a pervasive scale, and in addition the statute strengthens existing remedies for pockets of voting discrimination elsewhere in the country. Congress assumed the power to prescribe these remedies from ' 2 of the Fifteenth Amendment, which authorizes the National Legislature to effectuate by "appropriate" measures the constitutional prohibition against racial discrimination in voting. We hold that the sections of the Act which are properly before us are an appropriate means for carrying out Congress' constitutional responsibilities and are consonant with all other provisions of the Constitution. We therefore deny South Carolina's request that enforcement of these sections of the Act be enjoined.

I.

The constitutional propriety of the Voting Rights Act of 1965 must be judged with reference to the historical experience which it reflects. Before enacting the measure, Congress explored with great care the problem of racial discrimination in voting. The House and Senate Committees on the Judiciary each held hearings for nine days and received testimony from a total of 67 witnesses. (Note omitted). More than three full days were consumed discussing the bill on the floor of the House, while the debate in the Senate covered 26 days in all. (Note omitted). At the close of these deliberations, the verdict of both chambers was overwhelming. The House approved the bill by a vote of 328-74, and the measure passed the Senate by a margin of 79-18.

Two points emerge vividly from the voluminous legislative history of the Act contained in the committee hearings and floor debates. First: Congress felt itself confronted by an insidious and pervasive evil which had been perpetuated in certain parts of our country through unremitting and ingenious defiance of the Constitution. Second: Congress concluded that the unsuccessful remedies which it had prescribed in the past would have to be replaced by sterner and more elaborate measures in order to satisfy the clear commands of the Fifteenth Amendment...

The Fifteenth Amendment to the Constitution was ratified in 1870. Promptly thereafter Congress passed the Enforcement Act of 1870, (Note omitted) which made it a crime for public officers and private persons to obstruct exercise of the right to vote. The statute was amended in the following year (Note omitted) to provide for detailed federal supervision of the electoral process, from registration to the certification of re-turns. As the years passed and fervor for racial equality waned, enforcement of the laws became spotty and ineffective, and most of their provisions were repealed in 1894...

Meanwhile, beginning in 1890, the States of Alabama, Georgia, Louisiana, Mississippi, North Carolina, South Carolina, and Virginia enacted tests still in use which were specifically designed to prevent Negroes from voting. (Note omitted). Typically, they made the ability to read and write a registration qualification and also required completion of a registration form. These laws were based on the fact that as of 1890 in each of the named States, more than two-thirds of the adult Negroes were illiterate while less than one-quarter of the adult whites were unable to read or write. (Note omitted). At the same time, alternate tests were prescribed in all of the named States to assure that white illiterates would not be deprived of the franchise. These included grandfather clauses, property qualifications, "good character" tests, and the requirement that registrants "understand" or "interpret" certain matter.

The course of subsequent Fifteenth Amendment litigation in this Court demonstrates the variety and persistence of these and similar institutions designed to deprive Negroes of the right to vote. Grandfather clauses were invalidated in Guinn v. United States, 238 U.S. 347, 35 S. Ct. 926, 59 L. Ed. 1340, and Myers v. Anderson, 238 U.S. 368, 35 S. Ct. 932, 59 L. Ed. 1349. Procedural hurdles were struck down in Lane v. Wilson, 307 U.S. 268, 59 S. Ct. 872, 83 L. Ed. 1281. The white primary was outlawed in Smith v. Allwright, 321 U.S. 649, 64 S. Ct. 757, 88 L. Ed. 987, and Terry v. Adams, 345 U.S. 461, 73 S. Ct. 809, 97 L. Ed. 1152. Improper challenges were nullified in United States v. Thomas, 362 U.S. 58, 80 S. Ct. 612, 4 L. Ed. 2d 535. Racial gerrymandering was forbidden by Gomillion v. Lightfoot, 364 U.S. 339, 81 S.Ct. 125, 5 L.Ed. 2d 110. Finally, discriminatory application of voting tests was condemned in Schnell v. Davis, 336 U.S. 933, 69 S.Ct. 749, 93

L.Ed. 1093; Alabama v. United States, 371 U.S. 37, 83 S.Ct. 145, 9 L.Ed.2d 112, and Louisiana v. United States, 380 U.S. 145, 85 S.Ct. 817.

According to the evidence in recent Justice Department voting suits, the latter stratagem is now the principal method used to bar Negroes from the polls. Discriminatory administration of voting qualifications has been found in all eight Alabama cases, in all nine Louisiana cases, and in all nine Mississippi cases which have gone to final judgment. (Note omitted). Moreover, in almost all of these cases, the courts have held that the discrimination was pursuant to a widespread "pattern or practice." White applicants for registration have often been excused altogether from the literacy and understanding tests or have been given easy versions, have received extensive help from voting officials, and have been registered despite serious errors in their answers. (Note omitted). Negroes, on the other hand, have typically been required to pass difficult versions of all the tests, without any outside assistance and without the slightest error. (Note omitted). The good-morals requirement is so vague and subjective that it has constituted an open invitation to abuse at the hands of voting officials. (Note omitted). Negroes obliged to obtain vouchers from registered voters have found it virtually impossible to comply in areas where almost no Negroes are on the rolls. (Note omitted)...

II.

The Voting Rights Act of 1965 reflects Congress' firm intention to rid the country of racial discrimination in voting. (Note omitted). The heart of the Act is a complex scheme of stringent remedies aimed at areas where voting discrimination has been most flagrant. Section 4 (a)-(d) lays down a formula defining the States and political subdivisions to which these new remedies apply. The first of the remedies, contained in ' 4 (a), is the suspension of literacy tests and similar voting qualifications for a period of five years from the last occurrence of substantial voting discrimination. Section 5 prescribes a second remedy, the suspension of all new voting regulations pending review by federal authorities to determine whether their use would perpetuate voting discrimination. The third remedy, covered in ' 6(b), 7, 9, and 13(a), is the assignment of federal examiners on certification by the Attorney General to list qualified applicants who are thereafter entitled to vote in all elections…

Federal examiners.

In any political subdivision covered by ' 4(b) of the Act, the Civil Service Commission shall appoint voting examiners whenever the Attorney General certifies either of the following facts: (1) that he has received meritorious written complaints from at least 20 residents alleging that they have been disenfranchised under color of law because of their race, or (2) that the appointment of examiners is otherwise necessary to effectuate the guarantees of the Fifteenth Amendment. In making the latter determination, the Attorney General must consider, among other factors, whether the registration ratio of non-whites to whites seems reasonably attributable to racial discrimination, or whether there is substantial evidence of good-faith efforts to comply with the Fifteenth Amendment. ' 6(b). These certifications are not reviewable in any court and are effective upon publication in the Federal Register. ' 4(b).

The examiners who have been appointed are to test the voting qualifications of applicants according to regulations of the Civil Service Commission prescribing times, places, procedures, and forms. ' 7(a) and 9(b). Any person who meets the voting requirements of state law, insofar as these have not been suspended by the Act, must promptly be placed on a list of eligible voters. Examiners are to transmit their lists at least once a month to the appropriate state or local officials, who in turn are required to place the listed names on the official voting rolls. Any person listed by an examiner is entitled to vote in all elections held more than 45 days after his name has been transmitted. ' 7(b)…

On October 30, 1965, the Attorney General certified the need for federal examiners in two South Carolina counties, (Note omitted) and examiners appointed by the Civil Service Commission have been serving there since November 8, 1965. Examiners have also been assigned to 11 counties in Alabama, five parishes in Louisiana, and 19 counties in Mississippi. (Note omitted). The examiners are listing people found eligible to vote, and the challenge procedure has been employed extensively. No political subdivision has yet sought to have federal examiners withdrawn through the Attorney General or the District Court for the District of Columbia.

III.

These provisions of the Voting Rights Act of 1965 are challenged on the fundamental ground that they exceed the powers of Congress and encroach on an area reserved to the States by the Constitution...

[11] The ground rules for resolving this question are clear. The language and purpose of the Fifteenth Amendment, the prior decisions construing its several provisions, and the general doctrines of constitutional interpretation, all point to one fundamental principle. As against the reserved powers of the States, Congress may use any rational means to effectuate the constitutional prohibition of racial discrimination in voting...

[12-15] Section 1 of the Fifteenth Amendment declares that "(t)he right of citizens of the United States to vote shall not be denied or abridged by the United States or by any State on account of race, color, or previous condition of servitude." This declaration has always been treated as self-executing and has repeatedly been construed, without further legislative specification, to invalidate state voting qualifications or procedures which are discriminatory on their face or in practice. (Citations omitted). These decisions have been rendered with full respect for the general rule, reiterated last Term in *Carrington v. Rash*, 380 U.S. 89, 91, 85 S. Ct. 775, 777, 13 L. Ed. 2d 675, that States "have broad powers to determine the conditions under which the right of suffrage may be exercised." The gist of the matter is that the Fifteenth Amendment supersedes contrary exertions of state power. "When a State exercises power wholly within the domain of state interest, it is insulated from federal judicial review. But such insulation is not carried over when

state power is used as an instrument for circumventing a federally protected right." *Gomillion v. Lightfoot*, 364 U.S., at 347, 81 S. Ct., at 130...

The basic test to be applied in a case involving ' 2 of the Fifteenth Amendment is the same as in all cases concerning the express powers of Congress with relation to the reserved powers of the States. Chief Justice Marshall laid down the classic formulation, 50 years before the Fifteenth Amendment was ratified:

"Let the end be legitimate, let it be within the scope of the constitution, and all means which are appropriate, which are plainly adapted to that end, which are not prohibited, but consist with the letter and spirit of the constitution, are constitutional." McCulloch v. Maryland, 4 Wheat. 316, 421, 4 L. Ed. 579...

We therefore reject South Carolina's argument that Congress may appropriately do no more than to forbid violations of the Fifteenth Amendment in general terms-that the task of fashioning specific remedies or of applying them to particular localities must necessarily be left entirely to the courts. Congress is not circumscribed by any such artificial rules under ' 2 of the Fifteenth Amendment...

IV.

Coverage formula.

We now consider the related question of whether the specific States and political subdivisions within ' 4(b) of the Act were an appropriate target for the new remedies...

To be specific, the new remedies of the Act are imposed on three States—Alabama, Louisiana, and Mississippi—in which federal courts have repeatedly found substantial voting discrimination. (Note omitted). Section 4(b) of the Act also embraces two other States—Georgia and South Carolina—plus large portions of a third State—North Carolina—for which there was more fragmentary evidence of recent voting discrimination mainly adduced by the Justice Department and the Civil Rights Commission. (Citations omitted). All of these areas were appropriately subjected to the new remedies. In identifying past evils, Congress obviously may avail itself of information from any probative source. (Citations omitted)...

After enduring nearly a century of widespread resistance to the Fifteenth Amendment, Congress has marshalled an array of potent weapons against the evil, with authority in the Attorney General to employ them effectively. Many of the areas directly affected by this development have indicated their willingness to abide by any restraints legitimately imposed upon them. (Note omitted). We here hold that the portions of the Voting Rights Act properly before us are a valid means for carrying out the commands of the Fifteenth Amendment. Hopefully, millions of non-white Americans will now be able to participate for the first time on an equal basis in the government under which they live. We may finally look forward to the day when truly "[t]he right of citizens of the United States to vote shall not be denied or abridged by the United States or by any State on account of race, color, or previous condition of servitude."

The bill of complaint is dismissed.

Bill dismissed.

4. **<u>Re-Districting</u>**

Given the history of pervasive discrimination against Blacks in the area of voting rights, wouldn't it be necessary for states to develop re-districting strategies that are designed to ameliorate the effects of this past discrimination? What are some compelling arguments for developing race-based plans? In order for Blacks to experience true democracy, isn't it necessary for states to draw districts to maximize Black political participation?

SHAW v. RENO
Supreme Court of the United States
113 S.Ct. 2816 (1993)

Justice O'CONNOR delivered the opinion of the Court.

This case involves two of the most complex and sensitive issues this Court has faced in recent years: the meaning of the constitutional "right" to vote, and the propriety of race-based state legislation designed to benefit members of historically disadvantaged racial minority groups. As a result of the 1990 census, North Carolina became entitled to a twelfth seat in the United States House of Representatives. The General Assembly enacted a reapportionment plan that included one majority black congressional district. After the Attorney General of the United States objected to the plan pursuant to ' 5 of the Voting Rights Act of 1965, 79 Stat. 439, as amended, 42 U.S.C. ' 1973c, the General Assembly passed new legislation creating a second majority-black district. Appellants allege that the revised plan, which contains district boundary lines of dramatically irregular shape, constitutes an unconstitutional racial gerrymander. The question before us is whether appellants have stated a cognizable claim.

I.

The voting age population of North Carolina is approximately 78% white, 20% black, and 1% Native American; the remaining 1% is predominantly Asian. (Citation omitted). The black population is relatively dispersed; blacks constitute a majority of the general population in only 5 of the State's 100 counties. (Citation omitted). Geographically, the State divides into three regions: the eastern Coastal Plain, the central Piedmont Plateau, and the western mountains. H. Lefler & A. Newsom, The History of a Southern State: North Carolina 18-22 (3d ed. 1973). The largest concentrations of black citizens live in the Coastal Plain, primarily in the northern part. O. Gade & H. Stillwell, North Carolina: People and

Environments 6568 (1986). The General Assembly's first redistricting plan contained one majority-black district centered in that area of the State.

Forty of North Carolina's one hundred counties are covered by ' 5 of the Voting Rights Act of 1965, 42 U.S.C. ' 1973c, which prohibits a jurisdiction subject to its provisions from implementing changes in a "standard, practice, or procedure with respect to voting" without federal authorization. The jurisdiction must obtain either a judgment from the United States District Court for the District of Columbia declaring that the proposed change "does not have the purpose and will not have the effect of denying or abridging the right to vote on account of race or color" or administrative preclearance from the Attorney General. Because the General Assembly's reapportionment plan affected the covered counties, the parties agree that ' 5 applied. (Citation omitted). The State chose to submit its plan to the Attorney General for preclearance.

The Attorney General, acting through the Assistant Attorney General for the Civil Rights Division, interposed a formal objection to the General Assembly's plan. The Attorney General specifically objected to the configuration of boundary lines drawn in the south-central to southeastern region of the State. In the Attorney General's view, the General Assembly could have created a second majority-minority district "to give effect to black and Native American voting strength in this area" by using boundary lines "no more irregular than [those] found elsewhere in the proposed plan," but failed to do so for "pretextual reasons." (Citation omitted).

Under ' 5, the State remained free to seek a declaratory judgment from the District Court for the District of Columbia notwithstanding the Attorney General's objection. It did not do so. Instead, the General Assembly enacted a revised redistricting plan, 1991 N.C. Extra Sess.Laws, ch. 7, that included a second majority-black district. The General Assembly located the second district not in the south-central to southeastern part of the State, but in the north-central region along Interstate 85. (Citation omitted).

The first of the two majority-black districts contained in the revised plan, District 1, is somewhat hook shaped. Centered in the northeast portion of the State, it moves southward until it tapers to a narrow band; then, with finger-like extensions, it reaches far into the southern-most part of the State near the South Carolina border...

The second majority-black district, District 12, is even more unusually shaped. It is approximately 160 miles long and, for much of its length, no wider than the I-85 corridor. It winds in snake-like fashion through tobacco country, financial centers, and manufacturing areas "until it gobbles in enough enclaves of black neighborhoods" (Citation omitted). Northbound and southbound drivers on I-85 sometimes find themselves in separate districts in one county, only to "trade" districts when they enter the next county. Of the 10 counties through which District 12 passes, five are cut into three different districts; even towns are divided. At one point the district remains contiguous only because it intersects at a single point with two other districts before crossing over them. (Citation omitted). One state legislator has remarked that " ' [i]f you drove down the interstate with both car doors open, you'd kill most of the people in the district.'" (Citation omitted). The district even has inspired poetry: "Ask not for whom the line is drawn; it is drawn to avoid thee." Grofman, Would Vince Lombardi Have Been Right If He Had Said: "When It Comes to Redistricting, Race Isn't Everything, It's the Only Thing"?, 14 Cardozo L. Rev. 1237, 1261, n. 96 (1993) (internal quotation marks omitted).

The Attorney General did not object to the General Assembly's revised plan. But numerous North Carolinians did. The North Carolina Republican Party and individual voters brought suit in Federal District Court alleging that the plan constituted an unconstitutional political gerrymander under Davis v. Bandemer, 478 U.S. 109, 106 S.Ct. 2797, 92 L.Ed.2d 85 (1986). That claim was dismissed. (Citation omitted). Shortly after the complaint in Pope v. Blue was filed, appellants instituted the present action in the United States District Court for the Eastern District of North Carolina. Appellants alleged not that the revised plan constituted a political gerrymander, nor that it violated the "one person, one vote" principle, (Citation omitted), but that the State had created an unconstitutional racial gerrymander. Appellants are five residents of Durham County, North Carolina, all registered to vote in that county. Under the General Assembly's plan, two will vote for congressional representatives in District 12 and three will vote in neighboring District 2. Appellants sued the Governor of North Carolina, the Lieutenant Governor, the Secretary of State, the Speaker of the North Carolina House of Representatives, and members of the North Carolina State Board of Elections (state appellees), together with two federal officials, the Attorney General and the Assistant Attorney General for the Civil Rights Division (federal appellees).

Appellants contended that the General Assembly's revised reapportionment plan violated several provisions of the United States Constitution, including the Fourteenth Amendment. They alleged that the General Assembly deliberately "create[d] two Congressional Districts in which a majority of black voters was concentrated arbitrarily—without regard to any other considerations, such as compactness, contiguousness, geographical boundaries, or political subdivisions" with the purpose "to create Congressional Districts along racial lines" and to assure the election of two black representatives to Congress. App. to Juris. Statement 102a. Appellants sought declaratory and injunctive relief against the state appellees. They sought similar relief against the federal appellees, arguing, alternatively, that the federal appellees had misconstrued the Voting Rights Act or that the Act itself was unconstitutional.

The three judge District Court granted the federal appellees' motion to dismiss. 808 F. Supp. 461 (EDNC 1992). The court agreed unanimously that it lacked subject matter jurisdiction by reason of ' 14(b) of the Voting Rights Act, 42 U.S. C. ' 19731 (b), which vests the District Court for the District of Columbia with exclusive jurisdiction to issue injunctions against the execution of the Act and to enjoin actions taken by federal officers pursuant thereto.

By a 2-to 1 vote, the District Court also dismissed the complaint against the state appellees. The majority found no support for appellants' contentions that race-based districting is prohibited by

Article I, ' 4, or Article I, ' 2, of the Constitution, or by the Privileges and Immunities Clause of the Fourteenth Amendment. It deemed appellants' claim under the Fifteenth Amendment essentially sub-sumed within their related claim under the Equal Protection Clause. (Citation omitted). That claim, the majority concluded, was barred by United Jewish Organizations of Williamsburgh, Inc. v. Carey, 430 U.S. 144, 97 S.Ct. 996, 51 L.Ed.2d 229 (1977) (UJO).

The majority first took judicial notice of a fact omitted from appellants' complaint: that appellants are white. It rejected the argu-ment that race-conscious redistricting to benefit minority voters is per se unconstitutional. The majority also rejected appellants' claim that North Carolina's reapportionment plan was impermissible...

We noted probable jurisdiction. (Citation omitted).

II.
A.

"The right to vote freely for the candidate of one's choice is of the essence of a democratic society..." Reynolds v. Sims, 377 U.S., at 555, 84 S.Ct., at 1378. For much of our Nation's history, that right sadly has been denied to many because of race. The Fifteenth Amendment, ratified in 1870 after a bloody Civil War, promised unequivocally that "[t]he right of citizens of the United States to vote" no longer would be "denied or abridged... by any State on account of race, color, or previous condition of servitude." U.S.Const., Amdt. 15, ' 1...

B.

It is against this background that we confront the questions presented here.

In our view, the District Court properly dismissed appellants' claims against the federal appellees. Our focus is on appellants' claim that the State engaged in unconstitutional racial gerryman-dering. That argument strikes a powerful historical chord: It is unsettling how closely the North Carolina plan resembles the most egregious racial gerrymanders of the past.

An understanding of the nature of appellants' claim is critical to our resolution of the case. In their complaint, appellants did not claim that the General Assembly's reapportionment plan unconstitutionally "diluted" white voting strength. They did not even claim to be white. Rather, appellants' complaint alleged that the deliberate segregation of voters into separate districts on the basis of race violated their constitutional right to participate in a "color- blind" electoral process. (Citation omitted).

Despite their invocation of the ideal of a "color-blind" Constitution, (Citation omitted), appellants appear to concede that race-conscious redistricting is not always unconstitutional. (Citation omitted). That concession is wise: This Court never has held that race-conscious state decisionmaking is impermissible in all circumstances. What appellants object to is redistricting legislation that is so extremely irregular on its face that it rationally can be viewed only as an effort to segregate the races for purposes of voting, without regard for traditional districting principles and without sufficiently compelling justification. For the reasons that follow, we conclude that appellants have stated a claim upon which, relief can be granted under the Equal Protection Clause. See Fed. Rule Civ.Proc. 12(b)(6).

III.
A.

The Equal Protection Clause provides that "[n]o State shall... deny to any person within its jurisdiction the equal protection of the laws." (Citation omitted). Its central purpose is to prevent the States from purposefully discriminating between individuals on the basis race. (Citation omitted). Laws that explicitly distinguish between individuals on racial grounds fall within the core of that prohibition...

Classifications of citizens solely on the basis of race "are by their very nature odious to a free people whose institutions are founded upon the doctrine of equality. (Citation omitted). They threaten to stigmatize individuals by reason of their membership in a racial group and to incite racial hostility. (Citation omitted)...

The difficulty of proof, of course, does not mean that a racial gerrymander, once established, should receive less scrutiny under the Equal Protection Clause than other state legislation classifying citizens by race. Moreover, it seems clear to us that proof sometimes will not be difficult at all. In some exceptional cases, a reapportionment plan may be so highly irregular that, on its face, it rationally cannot be understood as anything other than an effort to "segregat[e]... voters" on the basis of race. Gomillion, supra, 364 U.S., at 341 81 S.Ct., at 127. Gomillion, in which a tortured municipal boundary line was drawn to exclude black voters, was such a case. So, too, would be a case in which a State concentrated a dispersed minority population in a single district by disregarding traditional districting principles such as compactness, contiguity, and respect for political subdivisions...

The message that such districting sends to elected representatives is equally pernicious. When a district obviously is created solely to effectuate the perceived common interests of one racial group, elected officials are more likely to believe that their primary obligation is to represent only the members of that group, rather than their constituency as a whole. This is altogether antithetical to our system of representative democracy...

For these reasons, we conclude that a plaintiff challenging a reapportionment statute under the Equal Protection Clause may state a claim by alleging that the legislation, though race-neutral on its face, rationally cannot be understood as anything other than an effort to separate voters into different districts on the basis of race, and that the separation lacks sufficient justification. It is unnecessary for us to decide whether or how a reapportionment plan that, on its face, can be explained in nonracial terms successfully could be challenged. Thus, we express no view as to whether "the intentional creation of majority-minority districts, without more" always gives rise to an equal protection claim. (Citation omitted). We hold only that, on the facts of this case, plaintiffs have stated a claim sufficient to defeat the state appellees' motion to dismiss...

▶ Notes & Questions

Many observers felt that the recent decisions of the United States Supreme Court against racial re-districting would sharply curtail the number of Black legislators elected to Congress. These fears did not materialize. Despite the Court invalidating four districts in Texas and North Carolina in 1996, Blacks were elected in majority white districts. Eddie Bernie Johnson in Dallas received 55 percent of the vote. Sheila Jackson Lee in Houston received 77 percent of the vote. Cynthia McKinney of Atlanta received 58 percent.

Do these results indicate that whites have become color blind in exercising their vote? Are Blacks too sensitive on these issues? Is it irrational paranoia for some Blacks to assume that whites will not elect Blacks?

Did the election of Barack Obama mean that American voters are now color blind? Why was Obama successful when other black presidential candidates were not? Does Obama owe the following candidates gratitude for being willing to pursue the highest political office in the United States: Charlene Mitchell (1968), Shirley Chisolm (1972) and Rev. Jesse Jackson (1984, 1988)?

B.
5. *Deprivation of Voting Rights in the Bush/Gore Election*

The 2000 presidential election raised significant issues con-
cerning disenfranchisement, impartiality, and racism. As a result
of the Supreme Court giving the election to Bush, he set the nation
on a course of action both internationally and nationally that has
alienated the United States from its traditional allies and elimi-
nated from the national agenda issues such as employment, educa-
tion and health care. When the Court (Rehnquist, Scalia, Thomas,
O'Connor and Kennedy) stopped the election on December 12,
2000 and allowed Secretary of State Katherine Harris to certify
Bush the winner by 537 votes, it effectively denied at least 9,000
("undervotes") Floridians of their right to vote.

Furthermore the interference by the Court in the Florida elec-
toral process deprived blacks and other oppressed people in the
country of their choice for president. It was estimated that blacks
made up 16% of the eligible voters in Florida and 54% of the bal-
lots (automatic machines) not allowed to be reviewed manually
by the Court. Furthermore, all Americans were deprived of their
choice and instead an unelected body, the Supreme Court of the
United States chose George W. Bush as the next president. The
implications for democracy in America and the world have been
tremendous.

GEORGE W. BUSH v. ALBERT GORE, Jr.
Supreme Court of the United States
531 U.S. 98 (2000)

Per Curiam.

On December 8, 2000, the Supreme Court of Florida ordered that
the Circuit Court of Leon County tabulate by hand 9,000 ballots in
Miami-Dade County. It also ordered the inclusion in the certified
vote totals of 215 votes identified in Palm Beach County and 168
votes identified in Miami-Dade County for Vice President Albert

Gore, Jr., and Senator Joseph Lieberman, Democratic Candidates for President and Vice President. The Supreme Court noted that petitioner, Governor George W. Bush asserted that the net gain for Vice President Gore in Palm Beach County was 176 votes, and directed the Circuit Court to resolve that dispute on remand. (Citation omitted). The court further held that relief would require manual recounts in all Florida counties where so-called "undervotes" had not been subject to manual tabulation. The court ordered all manual recounts to begin at once. Governor Bush and Richard Cheney, Republican Candidates for the Presidency and Vice Presidency, filed an emergency application for a stay of this mandate. On December 9, we granted the application, treated the application as a petition for a writ of certiorari, and granted certiorari. (Citation omitted)....

On November 8, 2000, the day following the Presidential election, the Florida Division of Elections reported that petitioner, Governor Bush, had received 2,909,135 votes, and respondent, Vice President Gore, had received 2,907,351 votes, a margin of 1,784 for Governor Bush. Because Governor Bush's margin of victory was less than "one-half of a percent... of the votes cast," an automatic machine recount was conducted under §102.141(4) of the election code, the results of which showed Governor Bush still winning the race but by a diminished margin. Vice President Gore then sought manual recounts in Volusia, Palm Beach, Broward, and Miami-Dade Counties, pursuant to Florida's election protest provisions. Fla. Stat. §102.166 (2000). A dispute arose concerning the deadline for local county canvassing boards to submit their returns to the Secretary of State (Secretary). The Secretary declined to waive the November 14 deadline imposed by statute. §§102.111,102.112. The Florida Supreme Court, however, set the deadline at November 26. We granted certiorari and vacated the Florida Supreme Court's decision, finding considerable uncertainty as to the grounds on which it was based. (Citation omitted). On December 11, the Florida Supreme Court issued a decision on remand reinstating that date. (Citation omitted).

On November 26, the Florida Elections Canvassing Commission certified the results of the election and declared Governor Bush the winner of Florida's 25 electoral votes. On November 27, Vice President Gore, pursuant to Florida's contest provisions, filed a complaint in Leon County Circuit Court contesting the certification. Fla. Stat. §102.168 (2000). He sought relief pursuant to §102.168(3)(c), which provides that "[r]eceipt of a number of illegal votes or rejection of a number of legal votes sufficient to change or place in doubt the result of the election" shall be grounds for a contest. The Circuit Court denied relief, stating that Vice President Gore failed to meet his burden of proof. He appealed to the First District Court of Appeal, which certified the matter to the Florida Supreme Court.

Accepting jurisdiction, the Florida Supreme Court affirmed in part and reversed in part. (Citation omitted). The court held that the Circuit Court had been correct to reject Vice President Gore's challenge to the results certified in Nassau County and his challenge to the Palm Beach County Canvassing Board's determination that 3,300 ballots cast in that county were not, in the statutory phrase, "legal votes."

The Supreme Court held that Vice President Gore had satisfied his burden of proof under §102.168(3)(c) with respect to his challenge to Miami-Dade County's failure to tabulate, by manual count, 9,000 ballots on which the machines had failed to detect a vote for President ("undervotes"). (Citation omitted). Noting the closeness of the election, the Court explained that "[o]n this record, there can be no question that there are legal votes within the 9,000 uncounted votes sufficient to place the results of this election in doubt." (Citation omitted). A "legal vote," as determined by the Supreme Court, is "one in which there is a ' clear indication of the intent of the voter. ' " (Citation omitted). The court therefore ordered a hand recount of the 9,000 ballots in Miami-Dade County. Observing that the contest provisions vest broad discretion in the circuit judge to "provide any relief appropriate under such circumstances," Fla. Stat. §102.168(8) (2000), the Supreme Court further held that the Circuit Court could order "the Supervisor of Elections and the Canvassing Boards, as well as the necessary public officials, in all counties that have not conducted a manual recount or tabulation of the undervotes ... to do so forthwith, said tabulation to take place in the individual counties where the ballots are located." (Citation omitted).

The Supreme Court also determined that both Palm Beach County and Miami-Dade County, in their earlier manual recounts, had identified a net gain of 215 and 168 legal votes for Vice President Gore. (Citation omitted). Rejecting the Circuit Court's conclusion that Palm Beach County lacked the authority to include the 215 net votes submitted past the November 26 deadline, the Supreme Court explained that the deadline was not intended to exclude votes identified after that date through ongoing manual recounts. As to Miami-Dade County, the Court concluded that although the 168 votes identified were the result of a partial recount, they were "legal votes [that] could change the outcome of the election." (Citation omitted). The Supreme Court therefore directed the Circuit Court to include those totals in the certified results, subject to resolution of the actual vote total from the Miami-Dade partial recount.

The petition presents the following questions: whether the Florida Supreme Court established new standards for resolving Presidential election contests, thereby violating Art. II, §1, cl. 2, of the United States Constitution and failing to comply with 3 U.S.C. s.5 and whether the use of standardless manual recounts violates the Equal Protection and Due Process Clauses. With respect to the equal protection question, we find a violation of the Equal Protection Clause....

II.

A.

This case has shown that punch card balloting machines can produce an unfortunate number of ballots which are not punched in a clean, complete way by the voter. After the current counting, it is likely legislative bodies nationwide will examine ways to improve the mechanisms and machinery for voting.

B.

The individual citizen has no federal constitutional right to vote for electors for the President of the United States unless and until the state legislature chooses a statewide election as the means to implement its power to appoint members of the Electoral College. U.S. Const., Art. II, §1.... History has now favored the voter, and in each of the several States the citizens themselves vote for Presidential electors. When the state legislature vests the right to vote for President in its people, the right to vote as the legislature has prescribed is fundamental; and one source of its fundamental nature lies in the equal weight accorded to each vote and the equal dignity owed to each voter. The State, of course, after granting the franchise in the special context of Article II, can take back the power to appoint electors. (Citation omitted) ("[T]here is no doubt of the right of the legislature to resume the power at any time, for it can neither be taken away nor abdicated") (Citation omitted.).

The right to vote is protected in more than the initial allocation of the franchise. Equal protection applies as well to the manner of its exercise. Having once granted the right to vote on equal terms, the State may not, by later arbitrary and disparate treatment, value one person's vote over that of another. (Citation omitted)... It must be remembered that "the right of suffrage can be denied by a debasement or dilution of the weight of a citizen's vote just as effectively as by wholly prohibiting the free exercise of the franchise." (Citation omitted).

There is no difference between the two sides of the present controversy on these basic propositions. Respondents say that the very purpose of vindicating the right to vote justifies the recount procedures now at issue. The question before us, however, is whether the recount procedures the Florida Supreme Court has adopted are consistent with its obligation to avoid arbitrary and disparate treatment of the members of its electorate.

Much of the controversy seems to revolve around ballot cards designed to be perforated by a stylus but which, either through error or deliberate omission, have not been perforated with sufficient precision for a machine to count them. In some cases a piece of the card–a chad–is hanging, say by two corners. In other cases there is no separation at all, just an indentation.

The Florida Supreme Court has ordered that the intent of the voter be discerned from such ballots. For purposes of resolving the equal protection challenge, it is not necessary to decide whether the Florida Supreme Court had the authority under the legislative scheme for resolving election disputes to define what a legal vote is and to mandate a manual recount implementing that definition. The recount mechanisms implemented in response to the decisions of the Florida Supreme Court do not satisfy the minimum requirement for non-arbitrary treatment of voters necessary to secure the fundamental right. Florida's basic command for the count of legally cast votes is to consider the "intent of the voter." (Citation omitted). This is unobjectionable as an abstract proposition and a starting principle. The problem inheres in the absence of specific standards to ensure its equal application. The formulation of uniform rules to determine intent based on these recurring circumstances is practicable and, we conclude, necessary....

The question before the Court is not whether local entities, in the exercise of their expertise, may develop different systems for implementing elections. Instead, we are presented with a situation where a state court with the power to assure uniformity has ordered a statewide recount with minimal procedural safeguards. When a court orders a statewide remedy, there must be at least some assurance that the rudimentary requirements of equal treatment and fundamental fairness are satisfied...

None are more conscious of the vital limits on judicial authority than are the members of this Court, and none stand more in admiration of the Constitution's design to leave the selection of the President to the people, through their legislatures, and to the political sphere. When contending parties invoke the process of the courts, however, it becomes our unsought responsibility to resolve the federal and constitutional issues the judicial system has been forced to confront.

The judgment of the Supreme Court of Florida is reversed, and the case is remanded for further proceedings not inconsistent with this opinion.

Pursuant to this Court's Rule 45.2, the Clerk is directed to issue the mandate in this case forthwith.

It is so ordered.

Justice STEVENS, with whom Justice GINSBURG and Justice BREYER join, dissenting.

The Constitution assigns to the States the primary responsibility for determining the manner of selecting the Presidential electors. See Art. II, §1, cl. 2. When questions arise about the meaning of state laws, including election laws, it is our settled practice to accept the opinions of the highest courts of the States as providing the final answers. On rare occasions, however, either federal statutes or the Federal Constitution may require federal judicial intervention in state elections. This is not such an occasion.

The federal questions that ultimately emerged in this case are not substantial... Moreover, the Florida Legislature's own decision to employ a unitary code for all elections indicates that it intended the Florida Supreme Court to play the same role in Presidential elections that it has historically played in resolving electoral disputes...

In the interest of finality, however, the majority effectively orders the disenfranchisement of an unknown number of voters whose ballots reveal their intent–and are therefore legal votes under state law–but were for some reason rejected by ballot-counting machines...

What must underlie petitioners' entire federal assault on the Florida election procedures is an unstated lack of confidence in the impartiality and capacity of the state judges who would make the critical decisions if the vote count were to proceed. Otherwise, their position is wholly without merit. The endorsement of that position by the majority of this Court can only lend credence to the most cynical appraisal of the work of judges throughout the land. It is confidence in the men and women who administer the judicial system that is the true backbone of the rule of law. Time will one day heal the wound to that confidence that will be inflicted by today's decision. One thing, however, is certain. Although we may never know with complete certainty the identity of the winner of this year's Presidential election, the identity of the loser is perfectly clear. It is the Nation's confidence in the judge as an impartial guardian of the rule of law.

I respectfully dissent.

Justice SOUTER, with whom Justice BREYER joins and with whom Justice STEVENS and Justice GINSBURG join with regard to all but Part C, dissenting.

The Court should not have reviewed either Bush v. Palm Beach County Canvassing Bd., ante, (Citation omitted) (per curiam), or this case, and should not have stopped Florida's attempt to recount all undervote ballots, (Citation omitted) by issuing a stay of the Florida Supreme Court's orders during the period of this review (Citation omitted). If this Court had allowed the State to follow the course indicated by the opinions of its own Supreme Court, it is entirely possible that there would ultimately have been no issue requiring our review, and political tension could have worked itself out in the Congress following the procedure provided in 3 U.S.C. §15 The case being before us, however, its resolution by the majority is another erroneous decision....

There are three issues: whether the State Supreme Court's interpretation of the statute providing for a contest of the state election results somehow violates 3 U.S.C. s. 5; whether that court's construction of the state statutory provisions governing contests impermissibly changes a state law from what the State's legislature has provided, in violation of Article II, §1, cl. 2, of the national Constitution; and whether the manner of interpreting markings on disputed ballots failing to cause machines to register votes for President (the undervote ballots) violates the equal protection or due process guaranteed by the Fourteenth Amendment. None of these issues is difficult to describe or to resolve...

In sum, the interpretations by the Florida court raise no substantial question under Article II. That court engaged in permissible construction in determining that Gore had instituted a contest authorized by the state statute, and it proceeded to direct the trial judge to deal with that contest in the exercise of the discretionary powers generously conferred by Fla. Stat. §102.168(8) (2000), to "fashion such orders as he or she deems necessary to ensure that each allegation in the complaint is investigated, examined, or checked, to prevent or correct any alleged wrong, and to provide any relief appropriate under such circumstances."...

To recount these manually would be a tall order, but before this Court stayed the effort to do that the courts of Florida were ready to do their best to get that job done. There is no justification for denying the State the opportunity to try to count all disputed ballots now.

I respectfully dissent.

Justice GINSBURG, with whom Justice STEVENS joins, and with whom Justice SOUTER and Justice BREYER join as to Part I, dissenting.

I.

The Chief Justice acknowledges that provisions of Florida's Election Code "may well admit of more than one interpretation." (Citation omitted). But instead of respecting the state high court's province to say what the State's Election Code means, The Chief Justice maintains that Florida's Supreme Court has veered so far from the ordinary practice of judicial review that what it did cannot properly be called judging. I might join The Chief Justice were it my commission to interpret Florida law. But disagreement with the Florida court's interpretation of its own State's law does not warrant the conclusion that the justices of that court have legislated. There is no cause here to believe that the members of Florida's high court have done less than "their mortal best to discharge their oath of office," (Citation omitted), and no cause to upset their reasoned interpretation of Florida law....

Rarely has this Court rejected outright an interpretation of state law by a state high court. (Citation omitted)...

The Chief Justice's casual citation of these cases might lead one to believe they are part of a larger collection of cases in which we said that the Constitution impelled us to train a skeptical eye on a state court's portrayal of state law. But one would be hard pressed, I think, to find additional cases that fit the mold... The Florida Supreme Court concluded that counting every legal vote was the overriding concern of the Florida Legislature when it enacted the State's Election Code. The court surely should not be bracketed with state high courts of the Jim Crow South...

II.

The Court assumes that time will not permit "orderly judicial review of any disputed matters that might arise." (Citation omitted). But no one has doubted the good faith and diligence with which Florida election officials, attorneys for all sides of this controversy, and the courts of law have performed their duties. Notably, the Florida Supreme Court has produced two substantial opinions within 29 hours of oral argument. In sum, the Court's conclusion that a constitutionally adequate recount is impractical is a prophecy the Court's own judgment will not allow to be tested. Such an untested prophecy should not decide the Presidency of the United States.

I dissent.

Justice BREYER, with whom Justice STEVENS and Justice GINSBURG join except as to Part I-A-1, and with whom Justice SOUTER joins as to Part I, dissenting.

The Court was wrong to take this case. It was wrong to grant a stay. It should now vacate that stay and permit the Florida Supreme Court to decide whether the recount should resume.

I.

The political implications of this case for the country are momentous. But the federal legal questions presented, with one exception, are insubstantial…

A.

1.

Nonetheless, there is no justification for the majority's remedy, which is simply to reverse the lower court and halt the recount entirely. An appropriate remedy would be, instead, to remand this case with instructions that, even at this late date, would permit the Florida Supreme Court to require recounting all undercounted votes in Florida, including those from Broward, Volusia, Palm Beach, and Miami-Dade Counties, whether or not previously recounted prior to the end of the protest period, and to do so in accordance with a single-uniform substandard.

The majority justifies stopping the recount entirely on the ground that there is no more time… But the majority reaches this conclusion in the absence of any record evidence that the recount could not have been completed in the time allowed by the Florida Supreme Court. The majority finds facts outside of the record on matters that state courts are in a far better position to address….

By halting the manual recount, and thus ensuring that the uncounted legal votes will not be counted under any standard, this Court crafts a remedy out of proportion to the asserted harm. And that remedy harms the very fairness interests the Court is attempting to protect. The manual recount would itself redress a problem of unequal treatment of ballots… Nor do I understand why the Florida Supreme Court's recount order, which helps to redress this inequity, must be entirely prohibited based on a deficiency that could easily be remedied…

B.

II.

Of course, the selection of the President is of fundamental national importance. But that importance is political, not legal. And this Court should resist the temptation unnecessarily to resolve tangential legal disputes, where doing so threatens to determine the outcome of the election...

Given this detailed, comprehensive scheme for counting electoral votes, there is no reason to believe that federal law either foresees or requires resolution of such a political issue by this Court... Madison, at least, believed that allowing the judiciary to choose the presidential electors "was out of the question." Madison, July 25, 1787 (reprinted in 5 Elliot's Debates on the Federal Constitution 363 (2d ed. 1876)).

The decision by both the Constitution's Framers and the 1886 Congress to minimize this Court's role in resolving close federal presidential elections is as wise as it is clear. However awkward or difficult it may be for Congress to resolve difficult electoral disputes, Congress, being a political body, expresses the people's will far more accurately than does an unelected Court. And the people's will is what elections are about....

And, above all, in this highly politicized matter, the appearance of a split decision runs the risk of undermining the public's confidence in the Court itself. That confidence is a public treasure. It has been built slowly over many years, some of which were marked by a Civil War and the tragedy of segregation... But we do risk a self-inflicted wound—a wound that may harm not just the Court, but the Nation...

I respectfully dissent.

Chapter Five

AFFIRMATIVE ACTION ERA: MYTH or REALITY?

No public policy issue in America is more controversial than affirmative action. Although the vast majority of Blacks believe that these programs are necessary to remedy centuries of discrimination, the United States Supreme Court has consistently refused to recognize societal discrimination as a basis for remedial action, despite its own historical involvement in the legitimization of racism in American society. Ironically, the same court that sanctioned the belief that Blacks were property in the nineteenth century, cannot in the twentieth century acknowledge governmental complicity with racism, and therefore uphold the legality of affirmative action programs that are designed to remedy present effects of this discrimination. As a result, the court has failed to legitimize, for the most part, efforts to provide equity to Blacks and other people of color through affirmative action programs?

Fortunately, however, Black social movements of the sixties and seventies caused many employers to self-examine their employment practices in order to determine whether any of their practices or procedures discriminated against Blacks, women and other people of color. As a result of this analysis, many state and local governments developed affirmative action programs to remedy one effect of past societal discrimination, i.e. the exclusion of Blacks from employment and education.

Beginning with the *Bakke* case, the Supreme Court articulated various reasons for denying relief when institutions, both private and public, resort to voluntary affirmative action programs. The following cases analyze these rationalizations.

A.

Rationalization for Rejecting Societal Discrimination as a Justification for Affirmative Action

REGENTS OF THE UNIVERSITY OF CALIFORNIA v. BAKKE
Supreme Court of the United States
38 U.S. 265 (1978)

MR. JUSTICE POWELL announced the judgment of the Court.

This case presents a challenge to the special admissions program of the petitioner, the Medical School of the University of California at Davis, which is designed to assure the admission of a specified number of students from certain minority groups. The Superior Court of California sustained respondent's challenge, holding that petitioner's program violated the California Constitution, Title VI of the Civil Rights Act of 1964, 42 U. S. C. ' 2000d *et seq.*, and the Equal Protection Clause of the Fourteenth Amendment. The court enjoined petitioner from considering respondent's race or the race of any other applicant in making admissions decisions. It refused, however, to order respondent's admission to the Medical School, holding that he had not carried his burden of proving that he would have been admitted but for the constitutional and statutory violations. The Supreme Court of California affirmed those portions of the trial court's judgment declaring the special admissions program unlawful and enjoining petitioner from considering the race of any applicant. It modified that portion of the judgment denying respondent's requested injunction and directed the trial court to order his admission.

For the reasons stated in the following opinion, I believe that so much of the judgment of the California court as holds petitioner's special admissions program unlawful and directs that respondent be admitted to the Medical School must be affirmed. For the reasons expressed in a separate opinion, my Brothers THE CHIEF JUSTICE, MR. JUSTICE STEWART, MR. JUSTICE

REHNQUIST, and MR. JUSTICE STEVENS concur in this judgment.

I also conclude for the reasons stated in the following opinion that the portion of the court's judgment enjoining petitioner from according any consideration to race in its admissions process must be reversed. For reasons expressed in separate opinions, my Brothers MR. JUSTICE BRENNAN, MR. JUSTICE WHITE, MR. JUSTICE MARSHALL, and MR. JUSTICE BLACKMUN concur in this judgment.

Affirmed in part and reversed in part.

The Medical School of the University of California at Davis opened in 1968 with an entering class of 50 students. In 1971, the size of the entering class was increased to 100 students, a level at which it remains. No admissions program for disadvantaged or minority students existed when the school opened, and the first class contained three Asians but no blacks, no Mexican-Americans, and no American Indians. Over the next two years, the faculty devised a special admissions program to increase the representation of "disadvantaged" students in each Medical School class. (Footnote omitted). The special program consisted of a separate admissions system operating in coordination with the regular admissions process.

Under the regular admissions procedure, a candidate could submit his application to the Medical School beginning in July of the year preceding the academic year for which admission was sought. (Citation omitted.) Because of the large number of applications, (Footnote omitted) the admissions committee screened each one to select candidates for further consideration. Candidates whose overall undergraduate grade point averages fell below 2.5 on a scale of 4.0 were summarily rejected. (Citation omitted.) About one out of six applicants was invited for a personal interview. (Citation omitted.) Following the interviews, each candidate was rated on a scale of 1 to 100 by his interviewers and four other members of the admissions committee. The rating embraced the interviewers' summaries, the candidate's overall grade point average, grade point average in science courses, scores on the Medical College Admissions Test (MCAT), letters of recommendation, extracurricular activities, and other biographical data. (Citation omitted.) The ratings were added together to arrive at each candidate's "benchmark" score. Since five committee members rated each candidate in 1973, a perfect score was 500; in 1974, six members rated each candidate, so that a perfect score was 600. The full committee then reviewed the file and scores of each applicant and made offers of admission on a "rolling" basis. The chairman was responsible for placing names on the waiting list. They were not placed in strict numerical order; instead, the chairman had discretion to include persons with "special skills." (Citation omitted.).

The special admissions program operated with a separate committee, a majority of who were members of minority groups. (Citation omitted.) On the 1973 application form, candidates were asked to indicate whether they wished to be considered as "economically and/or educationally disadvantaged" applicants; on the 1974 form the question was whether they wished to be considered as members of a "minority group," which the Medical School apparently viewed as "Blacks," "Chicanos," "Asians," and "American Indians." (Citation omitted.) If these questions were answered affirmatively, the application was forwarded to the special admissions committee. No formal definition of "disadvantaged" was ever produced, (Citation omitted.) but the chairman of the special committee screened each application to see whether it reflected economic or educational deprivation. (Footnote omitted). Having passed this initial hurdle, the applications then were rated by the special committee in a fashion similar to that used by the general admissions committee, except that special candidates did not have to meet the 2.5 grade point average cutoff applied to regular applicants. About one-fifth of the total number of special applicants were invited for interviews in 1973 and 1974. (Footnote omitted). Following each interview, the special committee assigned each special applicant a benchmark score. The special committee then presented its top choices to the general admissions committee. The latter did not rate or compare the special candidates against the general applicants, (Citation omitted.), but could reject recommended special candidates for failure to meet course requirements or other specific deficiencies. (Citation omitted.). The special committee continued to recommend special applicants until a number prescribed by faculty vote were admitted. While the overall class size was still 50, the prescribed number was 8; in 1973 and 1974, when the class size had doubled to 100, the prescribed number of special admissions also doubled, to 16. (Citation omitted.)

From the year of the increase in class size, 1971 through 1974, the special program resulted in the admission of 21 black students, 30 Mexican-Americans, and 12 Asians, for a total of 63 minority students. Over the same period, the regular admissions program produced 1 black, 6 Mexican-Americans, and 37 Asians, for a total of 44 minority students". (Footnote omitted). Although disadvantaged whites applied to the special program in large numbers, (Note omitted), none received an offer of admission through that process. Indeed, in 1974, at least, the special committee explicitly considered only "disadvantaged" special applicants who were members of one of the designated minority groups. (Citation omitted.).

Allan Bakke is a white male who applied to the Davis Medical School in both 1973 and 1974. In both years Bakke's application was considered under the general admissions program, and he received an interview. His 1973 interview was with Dr. Theodore C. West, who considered Bakke "a very desirable applicant to [the] medical school." (Citation omitted). Despite a strong benchmark score of 468 out of 500, Bakke was rejected. His application had come late in the year, and no applicants in the general admissions process with scores below 470 were accepted after Bakke's application was completed. (Citation omitted). There were four special admissions slots unfilled at that time, however, for which Bakke was not considered. (Citation omitted). After his 1973 rejection, Bakke wrote to Dr. George H. Lowrey, Associate Dean and Chairman of the Admissions Committee, protesting that the special admissions program operated as a racial and ethnic quota. (Citation omitted).

Bakke's 1974 application was completed early in the year. (Citation omitted). His student interviewer gave him an overall rating of 94, finding him "friendly, well tempered, conscientious and delightful to speak with." (Citation omitted). His faculty interviewer was, by coincidence, the same Dr. Lowrey to whom he had written in protest of the special admissions program. Dr. Lowrey found Bakke "rather limited in his approach" to the problems of the medical profession and found disturbing Bakke's "very definite opinions which were based more on his personal viewpoints than upon a study of the total problem." (Citation omitted). Dr. Lowrey gave Bakke the lowest of his six ratings, an 86; his total was 549 out of 600. (Citation omitted). Again, Bakke's application was rejected. In neither year did the chairman of the admissions committee, Dr. Lowrey, exercise his discretion to place Bakke on the waiting list. (Citation omitted). In both years, applicants were admitted under the special program with grade point averages, MCAT scores, and bench-mark scores significantly lower than Bakke's. (Footnote omitted)…

III.

A.

Petitioner does not deny that decisions based on race or ethnic origin by faculties and administrations of state universities are reviewable under the Fourteenth Amendment… The parties do disagree as to the level of judicial scrutiny to be applied to the special admissions program. Petitioner argues that the court below erred in applying strict scrutiny, as this inexact term has been applied in our cases. That level of review, petitioner asserts, should be reserved for classifications that disadvantage "discrete and insular minorities." (Citation omitted). Respondent, on the other hand, contends that the California court correctly rejected the notion that the degree of judicial scrutiny accorded a particular racial or ethnic classification hinges upon membership in a discrete and insular minority and duly recognized that the "rights established [by the Fourteenth Amendment] are personal rights." (Citation omitted).

En route to this crucial battle over the scope of judicial review, (Footnote omitted), the parties fight a sharp preliminary action over the proper characterization of the special admissions program. Petitioner prefers to view it as establishing a "goal" of minority representation in the Medical School. Respondent, echoing the courts below, labels it a racial quota. (Footnote omitted).

This semantic distinction is beside the point: The special admissions program is undeniably a classification based on race and ethnic background. To the extent that there existed a pool of at least minimally qualified minority applicants to fill the 16 special admissions seats, white applicants could compete only for 84 seats in the entering class, rather than the 100 open to minority applicants. Whether this limitation is described as a quota or a goal, it is a line drawn on the basis of race and ethnic status. (Footnote omitted)... The Court has never questioned the validity of those pronouncements. Racial and ethnic distinctions of any sort are inherently suspect and thus call for the most exacting judicial examination.

B.

This perception of racial and ethnic distinctions is rooted in our Nation's constitutional and demographic history. The Court's initial view of the Fourteenth Amendment was that its "one pervading purpose" was "the freedom of the slave race, the security and firm establishment of that freedom, and the protection of the newly-made freeman and citizen from the oppressions of those who had formerly exercised dominion over him." (Citation omitted)...

Petitioner urges us to adopt for the first time a more restrictive view of the Equal Protection Clause and hold that discrimination against members of the white "majority" cannot be suspect if its purpose can be characterized as "benign." (Footnote omitted)...

IV.

We have held that in "order to justify the use of a suspect classification, a State must show that its purpose or interest is both constitutionally permissible and substantial, and that its use of the classification is 'necessary... to the accomplishment' of its purpose or the safeguarding of its interest." (Citation omitted). The special admissions program purports to serve the purposes of: (i) "reducing the historic deficit of traditionally disfavored minorities in medical schools and in the medical profession," (Citation omitted); (ii) countering the effects of societal discrimination; (Footnote omitted), (iii) increasing the number of physicians who will practice in communities currently underserved; and (iv) obtaining the educational benefits that flow from an ethnically diverse student body. It is necessary to decide which, if any, of these purposes is substantial enough to support the use of a suspect classification.

A.

If petitioner's purpose is to assure within its student body some specified percentage of a particular group merely because of its race or ethnic origin, such a preferential purpose must be rejected not as insubstantial but as facially invalid. Preferring members of any one group for no reason other than race or ethnic origin is discrimination for its own sake. This the Constitution forbids. (Citation omitted.).

B.

The State certainly has a legitimate and substantial interest in ameliorating, or eliminating where feasible, the disabling effects of identified discrimination. The line of school desegregation cases, commencing with *Brown*, attests to the importance of this state goal and the commitment of the judiciary to affirm all lawful means toward its attainment. In the school cases, the States were required by court order to redress the wrongs worked by specific instances of racial discrimination. That goal was far more focused than the remedying of the effects of "societal discrimination," an amorphous concept of injury that may be ageless in its reach into the past.

We have never approved a classification that aids persons perceived as members of relatively victimized groups at the expense of other innocent individuals in the absence of judicial, legislative, or administrative findings of constitutional or statutory violations. (Citation omitted)... Without such findings of constitutional or statutory violations, (Footnote omitted) it cannot be said that the government has any greater interest in helping one individual than in refraining from harming another. Thus, the government has no compelling justification for inflicting such harm.

Petitioner does not purport to have made, and is in no position to make, such findings. Its broad mission is education, not the formulation of any legislative policy or the adjudication of particular claims of illegality. For reasons similar to those stated in Part III of this opinion, isolated segments of our vast governmental structures are not competent to make those decisions, at least in the absence of legislative mandates and legislatively determined criteria". (Footnote omitted). (Citation omitted). Before relying upon these sorts of findings in establishing a racial classification, a governmental body must have the authority and capability to establish, in the record, that the classification is responsive to identified discrimination. (Citation omitted). Lacking this capability, petitioner has not carried its burden of justification on this issue.

Hence the purpose of helping certain groups whom the faculty of the Davis Medical School perceived as victims of "societal discrimination" does not justify a classification that imposes disadvantages upon persons like respondent, who bear no responsibility for whatever harm the beneficiaries of the special admissions program are thought to have suffered. To hold otherwise would be to convert a remedy heretofore reserved for violations of legal rights into a privilege that all institutions throughout the Nation could grant at their pleasure to whatever groups are perceived as victims of societal discrimination. That is a step we have never approved. (Citation omitted).

C.

Petitioner identifies, as another purpose of its program, improving the delivery of health-care services to communities currently underserved...

Petitioner simply has not carried its burden of demonstrating that it must prefer members of particular ethnic groups over all other individuals in order to promote better health-care delivery to deprived citizens. Indeed petitioner has not shown that its preferential classification is likely to have any significant effect on the problem. (Footnote omitted).

D.

The fourth goal asserted by petitioner is the attainment of a diverse student body. This clearly is a constitutionally permissible goal for an institution of higher education. Academic freedom though not a specifically enumerated constitutional right long has been viewed as a special concern of the First Amendment. The freedom of a university to make its own judgments as to education includes the selection of its student body. Mr. Justice Frankfurter summarized the "four essential freedoms" that constitute academic freedom:

"'It is the business of a university to provide that atmosphere which is most conducive to speculation, experiment and creation. It is an atmosphere in which there prevail "the four essential freedoms" of a university-to determine for itself on academic grounds who may teach, what may be taught, how it shall be taught, and who may be admitted to study.'" (Citation omitted).

Our national commitment to the safeguarding of these freedoms within university communities was emphasized in *Keyishian v. Board of Regents*, 385 U.S. 589, 603 (1967):

"Our Nation is deeply committed to safeguarding academic freedom which is of transcendent value to all of us and not merely to the teachers concerned. That freedom is therefore a special concern of the First Amendment... The Nation's future depends upon leaders trained through wide exposure to that robust exchange of ideas which discovers truth 'out of a multitude of tongues, [rather] than through any kind of authoritative selection.' (Citation omitted)."

The atmosphere of "speculation, experiment and creation", so essential to the quality of higher education, is widely believed to be promoted by a diverse student body. (Footnote omitted). As the Court noted in *Keyishian*, it is not too much to say that the "nation's future depends upon leaders trained through wide exposure" to the ideas and mores of students as diverse as this Nation of many peoples.

Thus in arguing that its universities must be accorded the right to select those students who will contribute the most to the "robust exchange of ideas," petitioner invokes a countervailing constitutional interest, that of the First Amendment. In this light petitioner must be viewed as seeking to achieve a goal that is of paramount importance in the fulfillment of its mission. It may be argued that there is greater force to these views at the undergraduate level than in a medical school where the training is centered primarily on professional competency. But even at the graduate level our tradition and experience lend support to the view that the contribution of diversity is substantial. In *Sweatt v. Painter*, 339 U.S., at 634, the Court made a similar point with specific reference to legal education:

"The law school, the proving ground for legal learning and practice cannot be effective in isolation from the individuals and institutions with which the law interacts. Few students and no one who has practiced law would choose to study in an academic vacuum removed from the interplay of ideas and the exchange of views with which the law is concerned."

Physicians serve a heterogeneous population. An otherwise qualified medical student with a particular background, whether it be ethnic, geographic, culturally advantaged or disadvantaged, may bring to a professional school of medicine experiences, outlooks and ideas that enrich the training of its student body and better equip its graduates to render with understanding their vital service to humanity." (Footnote omitted).

Ethnic diversity, however, is only one element in a range of factors a university properly may consider in attaining the goal of a heterogeneous student body. Although a university must have wide discretion in making the sensitive judgments as to who should be admitted, constitutional limitations protecting individual rights may not be disregarded. Respondent urges, and the courts below have held, that petitioner's dual admissions program is a racial classification that impermissibly infringes his rights under the Fourteenth Amendment. As the interest of diversity is compelling in the context of a university's admissions program, the question remains whether the program's racial classification is necessary to promote this interest. (Citation omitted).

V.

A.

It may be assumed that the reservation of a specified number of seats in each class for individuals from the preferred ethnic groups would contribute to the attainment of considerable ethnic diversity in the student body. But petitioner's argument that this is the only effective means of serving the interest of diversity is seriously flawed... The diversity that furthers a compelling state interest encompasses a far broader array of qualifications and characteristics of which racial or ethnic origin is but a single though important element. Petitioners' special admissions program, focused solely on ethnic diversity, would hinder rather than further attainment of genuine diversity. (Footnote omitted)....

B.

The fatal flaw in petitioner's preferential program is its disregard of individual rights as guaranteed by the Fourteenth Amendment. (Citation omitted). Such rights are not absolute. But when a

State's distribution of benefits or imposition of burdens hinges on ancestry or the color of a person's skin that individual is entitled to a demonstration that the challenged classification is necessary to promote a substantial state interest. Petitioner has failed to carry this burden. For this reason that portion of the California court's judgment holding petitioner's special admissions program invalid under the Fourteenth Amendment must be affirmed.

C.

In enjoining petitioner from ever considering the race of any applicant, however, the courts below failed to recognize that the State has a substantial interest that legitimately may be served by a properly devised admissions program involving the competitive consideration of race and ethnic origin. For this reason, so much of the California court's judgment as enjoins petitioner from any consideration of the race of any applicant must be reversed.

VI.

With respect to respondent's entitlement to an injunction directing his admission to the Medical School, petitioner has conceded that it could not carry its burden of proving that but for the existence of its unlawful special admissions program, respondent still would not have been admitted. Hence respondent is entitled to the injunction and that portion of the judgment must be affirmed. (Footnote omitted)…

MR. JUSTICE MARSHALL.

I agree with the judgment of the Court only insofar as it permits a university to consider the race of an applicant in making admissions decisions. I do not agree that petitioner's admissions program violates the Constitution. For it must be remembered that, during most of the past 200 years, the Constitution as interpreted by this Court did not prohibit the most ingenious and pervasive forms of discrimination against the Negro. Now, when a State acts to remedy the effects of that legacy of discrimination, I cannot believe that this same Constitution stands as a barrier.

I.

A.

Three hundred and fifty years ago, the Negro was dragged to this country in chains to be sold into slavery. Uprooted from his homeland and thrust into bondage for forced labor, the slave was deprived of all legal rights. It was unlawful to teach him to read; he could be sold away from his family and friends at the whim of his master; and killing or maiming him was not a crime. The system of slavery brutalized and dehumanized both master and slave". (Footnote omitted)... The implicit protection of slavery embodied in the Declaration of Independence was made explicit in the Constitution, which treated a slave as being equivalent to three-fifths of a person for purposes of apportioning representatives and taxes among the States. Art. I, s.2. The Constitution also contained a clause ensuring that the "Migration or Importation"of slaves into the existing States would be legal until at least 1808, Art. I, s.9, and a fugitive slave clause requiring that when a slave escaped to another State, he must be returned on the claim of the master, Art. IV, '2. In their declaration of the principles that were to provide the cornerstone of the new Nation, therefore, the Framers made it plain that "we the people,"for whose protection the Constitution was designed, did not include those whose skins were the wrong color. As Professor John Hope Franklin has observed, Americans "proudly accepted the challenge and responsibility of their new political freedom by establishing the machinery and safeguards that insured the continued enslavement of blacks." (Citation omitted).

The individual States likewise established the machinery to protect the system of slavery through the promulgation of the Slave Codes, which were designed primarily to defend the property interest of the owner in his slave. The position of the Negro slave as mere property was confirmed by this Court in *Dred Scott v. Sandford*, (Citation omitted)...

B.

The status of the Negro as property was officially erased by his emancipation at the end of the Civil War. But the long awaited emancipation, while freeing the Negro from slavery, did not bring him citizenship or equality in any meaningful way. Slavery was replaced by a system of "laws which imposed upon the colored race onerous disabilities and burdens, and curtailed their rights in the pursuit of life, liberty, and property to such an extent that their freedom was of little value." *Slaughter-House Cases*, 16 Wall. 36, 70 (1873). Despite the passage of the Thirteenth, Fourteenth, and Fifteenth Amendments, the Negro was systematically denied the rights those Amendments were supposed to secure. The combined actions and inactions of the State and Federal Governments maintained Negroes in a position of legal inferiority for another century after the Civil War.

The Southern States took the first steps to re-enslave the Negroes. Immediately following the end of the Civil War, many of the provisional legislatures passed Black Codes, similar to the Slave Codes, which, among other things, limited the rights of Negroes to own or rent property and permitted imprisonment for breach of employment contracts. Over the next several decades, the South managed to disenfranchise the Negroes in spite of the Fifteenth Amendment by various techniques, including poll taxes, deliberately complicated balloting processes, property and literacy qualifications, and finally the white primary…

…Nor were the laws restricting the rights of Negroes limited solely to the Southern States. In many of the Northern States, the Negro was denied the right to vote, prevented from serving on juries, and excluded from theaters, restaurants, hotels, and inns. Under President Wilson, the Federal Government began to require segregation in Government buildings; desks of Negro employees were curtained off; separate bathrooms and separate tables in the cafeterias were provided; and even the galleries of the Congress were segregated. When his segregationist policies were attacked, President Wilson responded that segregation was "'not humiliating but a benefit'" and that he was "'rendering [the Negroes] more safe in their possession of office and less likely to be discriminated against.'" (Citation omitted).

The enforced segregation of the races continued into the middle of the 20th century. In both World Wars, Negroes were for the most part confined to separate military units; it was not until 1948 that an end to segregation in the military was ordered by President Truman. And the history of the exclusion of Negro children from white public schools is too well known and recent to require repeating here. That Negroes were deliberately excluded from public graduate and professional schools, and thereby denied the opportunity to become doctors, lawyers, engineers, and the like, is also well established... (Citation omitted)...

II.

The position of the Negro today in America is the tragic but inevitable consequence of centuries of unequal treatment. Measured by any benchmark of comfort or achievement, meaningful equality remains a distant dream for the Negro.

A Negro child today has a life expectancy which is shorter by more than five years than that of a white child. (Footnote omitted). The Negro child's mother is over three times more likely to die of complications in childbirth, (Footnote omitted) and the infant mortality rate for Negroes is nearly twice that for whites. (Footnote omitted). The median income of the Negro family is only 60% that of the median of a white family, (Footnote omitted) and the percentage of Negroes who live in families with incomes below the poverty line is nearly four times greater than that of whites". (Footnote omitted).

When the Negro child reaches working age, he finds that America offers him significantly less than it offers his white counterpart. For Negro adults, the unemployment rate is twice that of whites, (Footnote omitted) and the unemployment rate for Negro teenagers is nearly three times that of white teenagers". (Footnote omitted). A Negro male who completes four years of college can expect a median annual income of merely $110 more than a white male who has only a high school diploma. (Footnote omitted). Although Negroes represent 11.5% of the population, (Footnote omitted), they are only 1.2% of the lawyers and judges, 2% of the physicians, 2.3% of the dentists, 1.1% of the engineers and 2.6% of the college and university professors". (Footnote omitted).

The relationship between those figures and the history of unequal treatment afforded to the Negro cannot be denied. At every point from birth to death the impact of the past is reflected in the still disfavored position of the Negro.

In light of the sorry history of discrimination and its devastating impact on the lives of Negroes, bringing the Negro into the mainstream of American life should be a state interest of the highest order. To fail to do so is to ensure that America will forever remain a divided society.

III.

I do not believe that the Fourteenth Amendment requires us to accept that fate. Neither its history nor our past cases lend any support to the conclusion that a university may not remedy the cumulative effects of society's discrimination by giving consideration to race in an effort to increase the number and percentage of Negro doctors....

A.

It is plain that the Fourteenth Amendment was not intended to prohibit measures designed to remedy the effects of the Nation's past treatment of Negroes. The Congress that passed the Fourteenth Amendment is the same Congress that passed the 1866 Freedmen's Bureau Act, an Act that provided many of its benefits only to Negroes...

IV.

While I applaud the judgment of the Court that a university may consider race in its admissions process, it is more than a little ironic that, after several hundred years of class-based discrimination against Negroes, the Court is unwilling to hold that a class-based remedy for that discrimination is permissible... It is unnecessary in 20th-century America to have individual Negroes demonstrate that they have been victims of racial discrimination; the racism of our society has been so pervasive that none, regardless of wealth or position, has managed to escape its impact. The experience of Negroes in America has been different in kind, not just in degree, from that of other ethnic groups. It is not merely the history of slavery alone but also that a whole people were marked as inferior by the law. And that mark has endured. The dream of America as the great melting pot has not been realized for the Negro; because of his skin color he never even made it to the pot...

It is because of a legacy of unequal treatment that we now must permit the institutions of this society to give consideration to race in making decisions about who will hold the positions of influence, affluence, and prestige in America. For far too long, the doors to those positions have been shut to Negroes. If we are ever to become a fully integrated society, one in which the color of a person's skin will not determine the opportunities available to him or her, we must be willing to take steps to open those doors. I do not believe that anyone can truly look into America's past and still find that a remedy for the effects of that past is impermissible...

I fear that we have come full circle. After the Civil War our Government started several "affirmative action" programs. This Court in the *Civil Rights Cases* and *Plessy v. Ferguson* destroyed the movement toward complete equality. For almost a century no action was taken, and this nonaction was with the tacit approval of the courts. Then we had *Brown v. Board of Education* and the Civil Rights Acts of Congress, followed by numerous affirmative-action programs. Now, we have this Court again stepping in, this time to stop affirmative-action programs of the type used by the University of California.

B.
Rationalization for Limited Affirmative Action in Private Employment

Should the court analyze affirmative action programs developed by private employers by the same standard it uses for public employers? If there is a difference, why? Which employer should be subject to greater legal scrutiny? Why?

UNITED STEELWORKERS OF AMERICA v. WEBER
Supreme Court of the United States
43 U.S. 193 (1979)

MR. Justice BRENNAN delivered the opinion of the Court.

Challenged here is the legality of an affirmative action plan, collectively bargained by an employer and a union, which reserves for black employees 50% of the openings in an in-plant craft-training program until the percentage of black craftworkers in the plant is commensurate with the percentage of blacks in the local labor force. The question for decision is whether Congress, in Title VII of the Civil Rights Act of 1964, 78 Stat. 253, as amended, 42 U. S. C. ' 2000e *et seq.*, left employers and unions in the private sector free to take such race-conscious steps to eliminate manifest racial imbalances in traditionally segregated job categories. We hold that Title VII does not prohibit such race-conscious affirmative action plans.

I.

In 1974, petitioner United Steelworkers of America (USWA) and petitioner Kaiser Aluminum & Chemical Corp. (Kaiser) entered into a master collective-bargaining agreement covering terms and conditions of employment at 15 Kaiser plants. The agreement contained, *inter alia*, an affirmative action plan designed to eliminate conspicuous racial imbalances in Kaiser's then almost exclusively white craftwork forces. Black craft hiring goals were set for each Kaiser plant equal to the percentage of blacks in the respective local labor forces. To enable plants to meet these goals, on-the-job training programs were established to teach unskilled production workers Cblack and white the skills necessary to become craftworkers. The plan reserved for black employees 50% of the openings in these newly created in-plant training programs.

This case arose from the operation of the plan at Kaiser's plant in Gramercy, La. Until 1974, Kaiser hired as craftworkers for that plant only persons who had prior craft experience. Because blacks had long been excluded from craft unions, (Footnote omitted), few were able to present such credentials. As a consequence, prior to 1974 only 1.83% (5 out of 273) of the skilled craftworkers at the Gramercy plant were black, even though the work force in the Gramercy area was approximately 39% black.

Pursuant to the national agreement Kaiser altered its craft hiring practice in the Gramercy plant. Rather than hiring already trained outsiders, Kaiser established a training program to train its production workers to fill craft openings. Selection of craft trainees was made on the basis of seniority, with the proviso that at least 50% of the new trainees were to be black until the percentage of black skilled craftworkers in the Gramercy plant approximated the percentage of blacks in the local labor force. (Citation omitted).

During 1974, the first year of the operation of the Kaiser-USWA affirmative action plan, 13 craft trainees were selected from Gramercy's production work force. Of these, seven were black and six white. The most senior black selected into the program had less seniority than several white production workers whose bids for admission were rejected. Thereafter one of those white production workers, respondent Brian Weber (hereafter respondent), instituted this class action in the United States District Court for the Eastern District of Louisiana. The complaint alleged that the filling of craft trainee positions at the Gramercy plant pursuant to the affirmative action program had resulted in junior black employees receiving training in preference to senior white employees, thus discriminating against respondent and other similarly situated white employees in violation of'' 703 (a) (Footnote omitted) and (d) (Footnote omitted) of Title VII. The District Court held that the plan violated Title VII, entered a judgment in favor of the plaintiff class, and granted a permanent injunction prohibiting Kaiser and the USWA "from denying plaintiffs, Brian F. Weber and all other members of the class, access to on-the-job training programs on the basis of race." (Citation omitted). A divided panel of the Court of Appeals for the Fifth Circuit affirmed, holding that all employment preferences based upon race, including those preferences incidental to bona fide affirmative action plans, violated Title VII's prohibition against racial discrimination in employment. (Citation omitted). We granted certiorari. 439 U.S. 1045 (1978).

We reverse.

II.

We emphasize at the outset the narrowness of our inquiry. Since the Kaiser-USWA plan does not involve state action, this case does not present an alleged violation of the Equal Protection Clause of the Fourteenth Amendment. Further, since the Kaiser-USWA plan was adopted voluntarily, we are not concerned with what Title VII requires or with what a court might order to remedy a past proved violation of the Act. The only question before us is the narrow statutory issue of whether Title VII forbids private employers and unions from voluntarily agreeing upon bona fide affirmative action plans that accord racial preferences in the manner and for the purpose provided in the Kaiser-USWA plan. That question was expressly left open in *McDonald v. Santa Fe Trail Transp. Co.*, 427 U. S. 273, 281 n. 8 (1976), which held, in a case not involving affirmative action, that Title VII protects whites as well as blacks from certain forms of racial discrimination.

Respondent argues that Congress intended in Title VII to prohibit all race-conscious affirmative action plans. Respondent's argument rests upon a literal interpretation of ' 703 (a) and (d) of the Act. Those sections make it unlawful to "discriminate...

because of... race" in hiring and in the selection of apprentices for training programs. Since, the argument runs, *McDonald v. Santa Fe Trail Transp. Co.*, supra, settled that Title VII forbids discrimination against whites as well as blacks, and since the Kaiser-USWA affirmative action plan operates to discriminate against white employees solely because they are white, it follows that the Kaiser-USWA plan violates Title VII.

Respondent's argument is not without force. But it overlooks the significance of the fact that the Kaiser-USWA plan is an affirmative action plan voluntarily adopted by private parties to eliminate traditional patterns of racial segregation... The prohibition against racial discrimination in ' 703 (a) and (d) of Title VII must therefore be read against the background of the legislative history of Title VII and the historical context from which the Act arose.

Congress' primary concern in enacting the prohibition against racial discrimination in Title VII of the Civil Rights Act of 1964 was with "the plight of the Negro in our economy." 110 Cong. Rec. 6548 (1964) (remarks of Sen. Humphrey). Before 1964, blacks were largely relegated to "unskilled and semi-skilled jobs." (Citation omitted). (remarks of Sen. Humphrey); (Citation omitted) (remarks of Sen. Clark); (Citation omitted) (remarks of Sen. Kennedy). Because of automation the number of such jobs was rapidly decreasing. (Citation omitted) (remarks of Sen. Humphrey); (Citation omitted) (remarks of Sen. Clark). As a consequence, "the relative position of the Negro worker [was] steadily worsening. In 1947 the nonwhite unemployment rate was only 64 percent higher than the white rate; in 1962 it was 124 percent higher." (Citation omitted) (remarks of Sen. Humphrey). See also (Citation omitted) (remarks of Sen. Clark). Congress considered this a serious social problem. As Senator Clark told the Senate:

"The rate of Negro unemployment has gone up consistently as compared with white unemployment for the past 15 years. This is a social malaise and a social situation which we should not tolerate. That is one of the principal reasons why the bill should pass." (Citation omitted).

Congress feared that the goals of the Civil Rights Act—the integration of blacks into the mainstream of American society could not be achieved unless this trend was reversed. And Congress recognized that that would not be possible unless blacks were able to secure jobs "which have a future." (Citation omitted) (remarks of Sen. Clark). See also (Citation omitted) (remarks of Sen. Kennedy). As Senator Humphrey explained to the Senate:

"What good does it do a Negro to be able to eat in a fine restaurant if he cannot afford to pay the bill? What good does it do him to be accepted in a hotel that is too expensive for his modest income? How can a Negro child be motivated to take full advantage of integrated educational facilities if he has no hope of getting a job where he can use that education?" (Citation omitted).

"Without a job, one cannot afford public convenience and accommodations. Income from employment may be necessary to further a man's education, or that of his children. If his children have no hope of getting a good job, what will motivate them to take advantage of educational opportunities?" (Citation omitted).

These remarks echoed President Kennedy's original message to Congress upon the introduction of the Civil Rights Act in 1963.

"There is little value in a Negro's obtaining the right to be admitted to hotels and restaurants if he has no cash in his pocket and no job." (Citation omitted).

Accordingly, it was clear to Congress that "[t]he crux of the problem [was] to open employment opportunities for Negroes in occupations which have been traditionally closed to them," (Citation omitted) (remarks of Sen. Humphrey), and it was to this problem that Title VII's prohibition against racial discrimination in employment was primarily addressed.

It plainly appears from the House Report accompanying the Civil Rights Act that Congress did not intend wholly to prohibit private and voluntary affirmative action efforts as one method of solving this problem...

Given this legislative history, we cannot agree with respondent that Congress intended to prohibit the private sector from taking effective steps to accomplish the goal that Congress designed Title VII to achieve. The very statutory words intended as a spur or catalyst to cause "employers and unions to self-examine and to self-evaluate their employment practices and to endeavor to eliminate, so far as possible, the last vestiges of an unfortunate and ignominious page in this country's history," (Citation omitted)...

We therefore hold that Title VII's prohibition in ' 703 (a) and (d) against racial discrimination does not condemn all private, voluntary, race-conscious affirmative action plans.

III.

We need not today define in detail the line of demarcation between permissible and impermissible affirmative action plans. It suffices to hold that the challenged Kaiser-USWA affirmative action plan falls on the permissible side of the line. The purposes of the plan mirror those of the statute. Both were designed to break down old patterns of racial segregation and hierarchy. Both were structured to "open employment opportunities for Negroes in occupations which have been traditionally closed to them." (Citation omitted) (remarks of Sen. Humphrey). (Footnote omitted).

At the same time, the plan does not unnecessarily trammel the interests of the white employees. The plan does not require the discharge of white workers and their replacement with new black hirees. (Citation omitted). Nor does the plan create an absolute bar to the advancement of white employees; half of those trained in the program will be white. Moreover, the plan is a temporary measure; it is not intended to maintain racial balance, but simply to eliminate a manifest racial imbalance. Preferential selection of craft trainees at the Gramercy plant will end as soon as the percentage of black skilled craftworkers in the Gramercy plant approximates the percentage of blacks in the local labor force. (Citation omitted).

We conclude, therefore, that the adoption of the Kaiser USWA plan for the Gramercy plant falls within the area of discretion left by Title VII to the private sector voluntarily to adopt affirmative action plans designed to eliminate conspicuous racial imbalance in traditionally segregated job categories. Accordingly, the judgment of the Court of Appeals for the Fifth Circuit is

Reversed.

C.

Rationalization for Denying Relief Negotiated Through Collective Bargaining Agreements

What if state governmental entities and collective bargaining units volunteer to remedy the effects of past discrimination on layoffs? Will the Court allow these affirmative action programs to stand?

WYGANT ET AL. v. JACKSON BOARD OF EDUCATION ET AL.
Supreme Court of the United States
476 U.S. 267 (1986)

JUSTICE POWELL announced the judgment of the Court and delivered an opinion in which the CHIEF JUSTICE and JUSTICE REHNQUIST join, and in all but Part IV of which JUSTICE O'CONNOR joins.

This case presents the question whether a school board, consistent with the Equal Protection Clause, may extend preferential protection against layoffs to some of its employees because of their race or national origin.

I.

In 1972 the Jackson Board of Education, because of racial tension in the community that extended to its schools, considered adding a layoff provision to the Collective Bargaining Agreement (CBA) between the Board and the Jackson Education Association (Union) that would protect employees who were members of certain minority groups against layoffs". (Footnote omitted)...

When layoffs became necessary in 1974, it was evident that adherence to the CBA would result in the layoff of tenured nonminority teachers while minority teachers on probationary status were retained. Rather than complying with Article XII, the Board retained the tenured teachers and laid off probationary minority teachers, thus failing to maintain the percentage of minority personnel that existed at the time of the layoff. The Union, together with two minority teachers who had been laid off, brought suit in federal court, (Citation omitted), claiming that the Board's failure to adhere to the layoff provision violated the Equal Protection Clause of the Fourteenth Amendment and Title VII of the Civil Rights Act of 1964... After dismissing the federal claims, the District Court declined to exercise pendent jurisdiction over the state-law contract claims.

Rather than taking an appeal, the plaintiffs instituted a suit in state court, *Jackson Education Assn. v. Board of Education*, No. 77-011484CZ (Jackson Cty. Cir. Ct. 1979) *(Jackson II)*, raising in essence the same claims that had been raised in Jackson I. In entering judgment for the plaintiffs, the state court found that the Board had breached its contract with the plaintiffs, and that Article XII did not violate the Michigan Teacher Tenure Act.... Nevertheless, the court held that Article XII was permissible, despite its discriminatory effect on nonminority teachers, as an attempt to remedy the effects of societal discrimination.

After *Jackson II*, the Board adhered to Article XII. As a result, during the 1976-1977 and 1981-1982 school years, nonminority teachers were laid off, while minority teachers with less seniority were retained. The displaced nonminority teachers, petitioners here, brought suit in Federal District Court, alleging violations of the Equal Protection Clause, Title VII, 42 U. S. C. ' 1983, and other federal and state statutes. On cross-motions for summary judgment, the District Court dismissed all of petitioners' claims. (Citation omitted). With respect to the equal protection claim, (Footnote omitted) the District Court held that the racial preferences granted by the Board need not be grounded on a finding of prior discrimination. Instead, the court decided that the racial preferences were permissible under the Equal Protection Clause as an attempt to remedy societal discrimination by providing "role models" for minority school children, and upheld the constitutionality of the layoff provision.

The Court of Appeals for the Sixth Circuit affirmed, largely adopting the reasoning and language of the District Court. (Citation omitted). We granted certiorari, 471 U.S. 1014 (1985), to resolve the important issue of the constitutionality of race-based layoffs by public employers.

We now reverse...

II.

We must decide whether the layoff provision is supported by a compelling state purpose and whether the means chosen to accomplish that purpose are narrowly tailored.

A.

The Court of Appeals, relying on the reasoning and language of the District Court's opinion, held that the Board's interest in providing minority role models for its minority students, as an attempt to alleviate the effects of societal discrimination, was sufficiently important to justify the racial classification embodied in the layoff provision. (Citation omitted). The court discerned a need for more minority faculty role models by finding that the percentage of minority teachers was less than the percentage of minority students. (Citation omitted).

This Court never has held that societal discrimination alone is sufficient to justify a racial classification...

Moreover, because the role model theory does not necessarily bear a relationship to the harm caused by prior discriminatory hiring practices, it actually could be used to escape the obligation to remedy such practices by justifying the small percentage of black teachers by reference to the small percentage of black students. (Citation omitted). Carried to its logical extreme, the idea that black students are better off with black teachers could lead to the very system the Court rejected in *Brown v. Board of Education*, 347 U.S. 483 (1954) *(Brown I)*.

Societal discrimination, without more, is too amorphous a basis for imposing a racially classified remedy. The role model theory announced by the District Court and the resultant holding typify this indefiniteness. There are numerous explanations for a disparity between the percentage of minority students and the percentage of minority faculty, many of them completely unrelated to discrimination of any kind. In fact, there is no apparent connection between the two groups... But as the basis for imposing discriminatory legal remedies that work against innocent people, societal discrimination is insufficient and overexpansive. In the absence of particularized findings, a court could uphold remedies that are ageless in their reach into the past, and timeless in their ability to affect the future.

B.

Respondents also now argue that their purpose in adopting the layoff provision was to remedy prior discrimination against minorities by the Jackson School District in hiring teachers. Public schools, like other public employers, operate under two interrelated constitutional duties. They are under a clear command from this Court, starting with *Brown v. Board of Education*, 349 U.S. 294 (1955), to eliminate every vestige of racial segregation and discrimination in the schools. Pursuant to that goal, race-conscious remedial action may be necessary. (Citation omitted). On the other hand, public employers, including public schools, also must act in accordance with a "core purpose of the Fourteenth Amendment" which is to "do away with all governmentally imposed discriminations based on race." (Citation omitted). These related constitutional duties are not always harmonious; reconciling them requires public employers to act with extraordinary care. In particular, a public employer like the Board must ensure that, before it embarks on an affirmative-action program, it has convincing evidence that remedial action is warranted. That is, it must have sufficient evidence to justify the conclusion that there has been prior discrimination...

IV.

As part of this Nation's dedication to eradicating racial discrimination, innocent persons may be called upon to bear some of the burden of the remedy. "When effectuating a limited and properly tailored remedy to cure the effects of prior discrimination, such a 'sharing of the burden' by innocent parties is not impermissible." (Citation omitted). In *Fullilove*, the challenged statute required at least 10 percent of federal public works funds to be used in contracts with minority-owned business enterprises. This requirement was found to be within the remedial powers of Congress in part because the "actual 'burden' shouldered by nonminority firms is relatively light." 448 U.S., at 484. (Footnote omitted).

Significantly, none of the cases discussed above involved layoffs. (Footnote omitted). Here, by contrast, the means chosen to achieve the Board's asserted purposes is that of laying off nonminority teachers with greater seniority in order to retain minority teachers with less seniority. We have previously expressed concern over the burden that a preferential-layoffs scheme imposes on innocent parties. (Citation omitted). In cases involving valid hiring goals, the burden to be borne by innocent individuals is diffused to a considerable extent among society generally. Though hiring goals may burden some innocent individuals, they simply do not impose the same kind of injury that layoffs impose. Denial of a future employment opportunity is not as intrusive as loss of an existing job.

Many of our cases involve union seniority plans with employees who are typically heavily dependent on wages for their day-to-day living. Even a temporary layoff may have adverse financial as well as psychological effects. A worker may invest many productive years in one job and one city with the expectation of earning the stability and security of seniority. "At that point, the rights and expectations surrounding seniority make up what is probably the most valuable capital asset that the worker 'owns,' worth even more than the current equity in his home." (Citation omitted). Layoffs disrupt these settled expectations in a way that general hiring goals do not.

While hiring goals impose a diffuse burden, often foreclosing only one of several opportunities, (Footnote omitted), layoffs impose the entire burden of achieving racial equality on particular individuals, often resulting in serious disruption of their lives. That burden is too intrusive. We therefore hold that, as a means of accomplishing purposes that otherwise may be legitimate, the Board's layoff plan is not sufficiently narrowly tailored". (Footnote omitted). Other, less intrusive means of accomplishing similar purposes—such as the adoption of hiring goals—are available. For these reasons, the Board's selection of layoffs as the means to accomplish even a valid purpose cannot satisfy the demands of the Equal Protection Clause. (Footnote omitted).

V.

We accordingly reverse the judgment of the Court of Appeals for the Sixth Circuit.

It is so ordered.

▶ Notes & Questions

As in Croson, the same three Justices disagreed with the majority. Justice Marshall writes that "...No-race-conscious provision that purports to serve a remedial purpose can be fairly assessed in a vacuum..." How do you reconcile the dissents' arguments of the relevancy of societal discrimination to the majority's insistence that it is too "amorphous" to be considered?

Dissenting Opinion of Justice MARSHALL

JUSTICE MARSHALL, with whom JUSTICE BRENNAN and
JUSTICE BLACKMUN join, dissenting.

...I, too, believe that layoffs are unfair. But unfairness ought
not be confused with constitutional injury. Paying no heed to the
true circumstances of petitioners' plight, the plight would nullify
years of negotiation and compromise designed to solve serious
educational problems in the public schools of Jackson, Michigan.
Because I believe that a public employer, with the full agreement
of its employees, should be permitted to preserve the benefits of
a legitimate and constitutional affirmative-action hiring plan even
while reducing its work force, I dissent....

The first black teacher in the Jackson public schools was hired
in 1954. (Footnote omitted). In 1969, when minority representation
on the faculty had risen only to 3.9%, the Jackson branch of
the NAACP filed a complaint with the Michigan Civil Rights
Commission, alleging that the Board had engaged in various
discriminatory practices, including racial discrimination in the
hiring of teachers. (Citation omitted). The Commission conducted
an investigation and concluded that each of the allegations had
merit. (Footnote omitted).

In settlement of the complaint, the Commission issued an order
of adjustment, under which the Jackson Board of Education (Board)
agreed to numerous measures designed to improve educational
opportunities for black public-school students. Among them was
a promise to "[t]ake affirmative steps to recruit, hire and promote
minority group teachers and counselors as positions bec(a)me
available..." (Citation omitted). As a result of the Board's efforts
to comply with the order over the next two years, the percentage
of minority teachers increased to 8.8%.

In 1971, however, faculty layoffs became necessary. The
contract in effect at that time, between the Board and the Jackson
Education Association (Union), provided that layoffs would be
made in reverse order of seniority. Because of the recent vintage of

the school system's efforts to hire minorities, the seniority scheme led to the layoff of a substantial number of minority teachers, "literally wip[ing] out all the gain" made toward achieving racial balance. (Citation omitted). Once again, minority teachers on the faculty were a rarity...

II.

The sole question posed by this case is whether the Constitution prohibits a union and a local school board from developing a collective-bargaining agreement that apportions layoffs between two racially determined groups as a means of preserving the effects of an affirmative hiring policy, the constitutionality of which is unchallenged. (Footnote omitted)...

► Notes & Questions

Is Justice Stevens' view that the affirmative action program should be based upon a race-neutral criteria sound? What are the advantages and disadvantages of his rationale? His review would center on the question of whether the program advances the public interest in educating children for the future. Should governments turn away from race-based rationale to race neutral ones?

Dissenting Opinion of Justice STEVENS

JUSTICE STEVENS, dissenting.

In my opinion, it is not necessary to find that the Board of Education has been guilty of racial discrimination in the past to support the conclusion that it has a legitimate interest in employing more black teachers in the future. Rather than analyzing a case of this kind by asking whether minority teachers have some sort of special entitlement to jobs as a remedy for sins that were committed in the past, I believe that we should first ask whether the Board's action advances the public interest in educating children for the future. If so, I believe we should consider whether that public interest, and the manner in which it is pursued, justifies any adverse effects on the disadvantaged group. (Footnote omitted)...

III.

Even if there is a valid purpose to the race consciousness, however, the question that remains is whether that public purpose transcends the harm to the white teachers who are disadvantaged by the special preference the Board has given to its most recently hired minority teachers. In my view, there are two important inquiries in assessing the harm to the disadvantaged teacher. The first is an assessment of the procedures that were used to adopt, and implement, the race-conscious action. (Footnote omitted). The second is an evaluation of the nature of the harm itself.

In this case, there can be no question about either the fairness of the procedures used to adopt the race-conscious provision, or the propriety of its breadth. As JUSTICE MARSHALL has demonstrated, the procedures for adopting this provision were scrupulously fair. The Union that represents petitioners negotiated the provision and agreed to it; the agreement was put to a vote of the membership, and overwhelmingly approved...

D.
Rationalization for Denying Affirmative Action Sought by Local Governments

Should local governments that develop affirmative action programs be given greater flexibility in combating the exclusion of people of color from governmental contracting programs? Shouldn't local governments take steps to insure that its public dollars are expended with individuals of all racial backgrounds? If a local governmental unit develops an aggressive affirmative action program, what are the legal pitfalls it may face?

CITY OF RICHMOND v. J.A. CROSON CO.
Supreme Court of the United States
488 U.S. 469 (1989)

JUSTICE O'CONNOR announced the judgment of the Court and delivered the opinion of the Court with respect to Parts I, III-B, and IV, an opinion with respect to Part II, in which THE CHIEF JUSTICE and JUSTICE WHITE join, and an opinion with respect to Parts III-A and V, in which THE CHIEF JUSTICE, JUSTICE WHITE, and JUSTICE KENNEDY join.

In this case, we confront once again the tension between the Fourteenth Amendment's guarantee of equal treatment to all citizens, and the use of race-based measures to ameliorate the effects of past discrimination on the opportunities enjoyed by members of minority groups in our society...

I.

On April 11, 1983, the Richmond City Council adopted the Minority Business Utilization Plan (the Plan). The Plan required prime contractors to whom the city awarded construction contracts to subcontract at least 30% of the dollar amount of the contract to one or more Minority Business Enterprises (MBE's). (Citation omitted). The 30% set-aside did not apply to city contracts awarded to minority owned prime contractors. (Citation omitted).

The Plan defined an MBE as "[a] business at least fifty-one (51) percent of which is owned and controlled... by minority group members." (Citation omitted). "Minority group members" were defined as "(c)itizens of the United States who are Blacks, Spanish-speaking, Orientals, Indians, Eskimos, or Aleuts." (Citation omitted). There was no geographic limit to the Plan; an otherwise qualified MBE from anywhere in the United States could avail itself of the 30% set-aside. The Plan declared that it was "remedial"in nature, and enacted "for the purpose of promoting wider participation by minority business enterprises in the construction of public projects."-' 12-158(a). The Plan expired on June 30, 1988, and was in effect for approximately five years. (Citation omitted).

The Plan authorized the Director of the Department of General Services to promulgate rules which "shall allow waivers in those individual situations where a contractor can prove to the satisfaction of the director that the requirements herein cannot be achieved..."

The Plan was adopted by the Richmond City Council after a public hearing. (Citation omitted). Seven members of the public spoke to the merits of the ordinance: five were in opposition, two in favor. Proponents of the set-aside provision relied on a study which indicated that, while the general population of Richmond was 50% black, only 0.67% of the city's prime construction contracts had been awarded to minority businesses in the 5-year period from 1978 to 1983. It was also established that a variety of contractors' associations, whose representatives appeared in opposition to the ordinance, had virtually no minority businesses within their membership. (Citation omitted). The city's legal counsel indicated his view that the ordinance was constitutional under this Court's decision in *Fullilove v. Klutznick*, 48 U.S. 448 (1980). (Citation omitted). Councilperson Marsh, a proponent of the ordinance, made the following statement:

"There is some information, however, that I want to make sure that we put in the record. I have been practicing law in this community since 1961, and I am familiar with the practices in the construction industry in this area, in the State, and around the nation. And I can say without equivocation, that the general conduct of the construction industry in this area, and the State, and around the nation, is one in which race discrimination and exclusion on the basis of race is widespread." (Citation omitted).

On September 6, 1983, the city of Richmond issued an invitation to bid on a project for the provision and installation of certain plumbing fixtures at the city jail. On September 30, 1983, Eugene Bonn, the regional manager of J. A. Croson Company (Croson), a mechanical plumbing and heating contractor, received the bid forms. The project involved the installation of stainless steel urinals and water closets in the city jail. Products of either of two manufacturers were specified, Acorn Engineering Company (Acorn) or Bradley Manufacturing Company (Bradley). Bonn determined that to meet the 30% set-aside requirement, a minority contractor would have to supply the fixtures. The provision of the fixtures amounted to 75% of the total contract price.

On September 30, Bonn contacted five or six MBE's that were potential suppliers of the fixtures, after contacting three local and state agencies that maintained lists of MBE's. No MBE expressed interest in the project or tendered a quote. On October 12, 1983, the day the bids were due, Bonn again telephoned a group of MBE's. This time, Melvin Brown, president of Continental Metal Hose (Continental), a local MBE, indicated that he wished to participate in the project....

On October 13, 1983, the sealed bids were opened. Croson turned out to be the only bidder, with a bid of $126,530. Brown and Bonn met personally at the bid opening, and Brown informed Bonn that his difficulty in obtaining credit approval had hindered his submission of a bid.

By October 19, 1983, Croson had still not received a bid from Continental. On that date it submitted a request for a waiver of the 30% set-aside. Croson's waiver request indicated that Continental was "unqualified" and that the other MBE's contacted had been unresponsive or unable to quote. Upon learning of Croson's waiver request, Brown contacted an agent of Acorn, the other fixture manufacturer specified by the city. Based upon his discussions with Acorn, Brown subsequently submitted a bid on the fixtures to Croson. Continental's bid was $6,183.29 higher than the price Croson had included for the fixtures in its bid to the city. This constituted a 7% increase over the market price for the fixtures. With added bonding and insurance, using Continental would have raised the cost of the project by $7,663.16. On the same day that Brown contacted Acorn, he also called city procurement officials and told them that Continental, an MBE, could supply the fixtures specified in the city jail contract. On November 2, 1983, the city denied Croson's waiver request, indicating that Croson had 10 days to submit an MBE Utilization Commitment Form, and warned that failure to do so could result in its bid being considered unresponsive....

The city denied both Croson's request for a waiver and its suggestion that the contract price be raised. The city informed Croson that it had decided to rebid the project. On December 9, 1983, counsel for Croson wrote the city asking for a review of the waiver denial. The city's attorney responded that the city had elected to rebid the project, and that there is no appeal of such a decision. Shortly thereafter Croson brought this action under 42 U. S. C. ' 1983 in the Federal District Court for the Eastern District of Virginia, arguing that the Richmond ordinance was unconstitutional on its face and as applied in this case.

The District Court upheld the Plan in all respects. (Citation omitted). In its original opinion, a divided panel of the Fourth Circuit Court of Appeals affirmed. *Croson I, 779* F. 2d. 181 (1985). Both courts applied a test derived from "the common concerns articulated by the various Supreme Court opinions"in *Fullilove v. Klutznick*, 448 U.S. 448 (1980), and *University of California Regents v. Bakke*, 438 U.S. 265 (1978). (Citation omitted). Relying on the great deference which this Court accorded Congress' findings of past discrimination in *Fullilove*, the panel majority indicated its view that the same standard should be applied to the Richmond City Council...

The majority found that national findings of discrimination in the construction industry, when considered in conjunction with the statistical study concerning the awarding of prime contracts in Richmond, rendered the city council's conclusion that low minority participation in city contracts was due to past discrimination "reasonable."...

Croson sought certiorari from this Court. We granted the writ, vacated the opinion of the Court of Appeals, and remanded the case for further consideration in light of our intervening decision in *Wygant v. Jackson Board of Education*, 476 U.S. 267 (1986). (Citation omitted).

On remand, a divided panel of the Court of Appeals struck down the Richmond set-aside program as violating both prongs of strict scrutiny under the Equal Protection Clause of the Fourteenth Amendment. (Citation omitted). The majority found that the "core" of this Court's holding in *Wygant* was that, "[t]o show that a plan is justified by a compelling governmental interest, a municipality that wishes to employ a racial preference cannot rest on broad-brush assumptions of historical discrimination." (Citation omitted). As the court read this requirement, "[f]indings of *societal* discrimination will not suffice; the findings must concern 'prior discrimination *by the government unit involved*." (Citation omitted)....

B.

We think it clear that the factual predicate offered in support of the Richmond Plan suffers from the same two defects identified as fatal in *Wygant*. The District Court found the city council's "findings sufficient to ensure that, in adopting the Plan, it was remedying the present effects of past discrimination in the construction industry." (Citation omitted). Like the "role model" theory employed in *Wygant*, a generalized assertion that there has been past discrimination in an entire industry provides no guidance for a legislative body to determine the precise scope of the injury it seeks to remedy. It "has no logical stopping point." (Citation omitted). "Relief" for such an ill-defined wrong could extend until the percentage of public contracts awarded to MBE's in Richmond mirrored the percentage of minorities in the population as a whole…

While there is no doubt that the sorry history of both private and public discrimination in this country has contributed to a lack of opportunities for black entrepreneurs, this observation, standing alone, cannot justify a rigid racial quota in the awarding of public contracts in Richmond, Virginia. Like the claim that discrimination in primary and secondary schooling justifies a rigid racial preference in medical school admissions, an amorphous claim that there has been past discrimination in a particular industry cannot justify the use of an unyielding racial quota…

Reliance on the disparity between the number of prime contracts awarded to minority firms and the minority population of the city of Richmond is similarly misplaced. There is no doubt that "[w]here gross statistical disparities can be shown, they alone in a proper case may constitute prima facie proof of a pattern or practice of discrimination" under Title VII. *Hazelwood School Dist. v. United States*, 433 U.S. 299, 307-308 (1977). But it is equally clear that "[w]hen special qualifications are required to fill particular jobs, comparisons to the general population (rather than to the smaller group of individuals who possess the necessary qualifications) may have little probative value." (Citation omitted).

In the employment context, we have recognized that for certain entry level positions or positions requiring minimal training, statistical comparisons of the racial composition of an employer's work force to the racial composition of the relevant population may be probative of a pattern of discrimination. (Citation omitted). But where special qualifications are necessary, the relevant statistical pool for purposes of demonstrating discriminatory exclusion must be the number of minorities qualified to undertake the particular task. (Citation omitted)…

In sum, none of the evidence presented by the city points to any identified discrimination in the Richmond construction industry. We, therefore, hold that the city has failed to demonstrate a compelling interest in apportioning public contracting opportunities on the basis of race. To accept Richmond's claim that past societal discrimination alone can serve as the basis for rigid racial preferences would be to open the door to competing claims for "remedial relief" for every disadvantaged group. The dream of a Nation of equal citizens in a society where race is irrelevant to personal opportunity and achievement would be lost in a mosaic of shifting preferences based on inherently unmeasurable claims of past wrongs. "Courts would be asked to evaluate the extent of the prejudice and consequent harm suffered by various minority groups. Those whose societal injury is thought to exceed some arbitrary level of tolerability then would be entitled to preferential classifications." (Citation omitted). We think such a result would be contrary to both the letter and spirit of a constitutional provision whose central command is equality.

The foregoing analysis applies only to the inclusion of blacks within the Richmond set-aside program. There is absolutely no evidence of past discrimination against Spanish speaking, Oriental, Indian, Eskimo, or Aleut persons in any aspect of the Richmond construction industry. The District Court took judicial notice of the fact that the vast majority of "minority" persons in Richmond were black. (Citation omitted). It may well be that Richmond has never had an Aleut or Eskimo citizen. The random inclusion of racial groups that, as a practical matter, may never have suffered from discrimination in the construction industry in Richmond suggests that perhaps the city's purpose was not in fact to remedy past discrimination.

If a 30% set-aside was "narrowly tailored" to compensate black contractors for past discrimination, one may legitimately ask why they are forced to share this "remedial relief" with an Aleut citizen who moves to Richmond tomorrow? The gross overinclusiveness of Richmond's racial preference strongly impugns the city's claim of remedial motivation. (Citation omitted).

▶ Notes & Questions

Why do Justice Marshall and Justices Brennan and Blackmun view the same set of facts so differently from the majority? Did the majority err in not considering the societal discrimination that Blacks have faced? Why couldn't the Court take judicial notice of the volumes of scholarly publications on slavery and the effects of slavery upon opportunities for Blacks?

Dissent of Justice MARSHALL

JUSTICE MARSHALL, with whom JUSTICE BRENNAN and
JUSTICE BLACKMUN join, dissenting.

It is a welcome symbol of racial progress when the former
capital of the Confederacy acts forthrightly to confront the effects
of racial discrimination in its midst...

...More fundamentally, today's decision marks a deliberate and
giant step backward in this Court's affirmative-action jurisprudence.
Cynical of one municipality's attempt to redress the effects of
past discrimination in a particular industry, the majority launches
a grapeshot attack on race-conscious remedies in general. The
majority's unnecessary pronouncements will inevitably discourage
or prevent governmental entities, particularly States and localities,
from acting to rectify the scourge of past discrimination. This
is the harsh reality of the majority's decision, but it is not the
Constitution's command...

A.

1.

Richmond has a second compelling interest in setting aside,
where possible, a portion of its contracting dollars. That interest is
the prospective one of preventing the city's own spending decisions
from reinforcing and perpetuating the exclusionary effects of past
discrimination. (Citation omitted)...

2.

Richmond's reliance on localized, industry-specific findings is
a far cry from the reliance on generalized "societal discrimination"
which the majority decries as a basis for remedial action. (Citation
omitted). But characterizing the plight of Richmond's minority
contractors as mere "societal discrimination" is not the only
respect in which the majority's critique shows an unwillingness
to come to grips with why construction-contracting in Richmond

is essentially a whites only enterprise. The majority also takes the disingenuous approach of disaggregating Richmond's local evidence, attacking it piecemeal, and thereby concluding that no *single* piece of evidence adduced by the city, "standing alone," (Citation omitted), suffices to prove past discrimination. But items of evidence do not, of course, "stan[d] alone" or exist in alien juxtaposition; they necessarily work together, reinforcing or contradicting each other...

The majority's perfunctory dismissal of the testimony of Richmond's appointed and elected leaders is also deeply disturbing. These officials, including councilmembers, a former mayor, and the present city manager, asserted that race discrimination in area contracting had been widespread, and that the set-aside ordinance was a sincere and necessary attempt to eradicate the effects of this discrimination. The majority, however, states that where racial classifications are concerned, "simple legislative assurances of good intention cannot suffice." (Citation omitted). It similarly discounts as minimally probative the city council's designation of its set-aside plan as remedial. "[B]lind judicial deference to legislative or executive pronouncements," the majority explains, "has no place in equal protection analysis." (Citation omitted).

No one, of course, advocates "blind judicial deference" to the findings of the city council or the testimony of city leaders. The majority's suggestion that wholesale deference is what Richmond seeks is a classic straw-man argument. But the majority's trivialization of the testimony of Richmond's leaders is dismaying in a far more serious respect. By disregarding the testimony of local leaders and the judgment of local government, the majority does violence to the very principles of comity within our federal system which this Court has long championed. Local officials, by virtue of their proximity to, and their expertise with, local affairs, are exceptionally well qualified to make determinations of public good "within their respective spheres of authority." (Citation omitted). The majority, however, leaves any traces of comity behind in its headlong rush to strike down Richmond's race conscious measure.

Had the majority paused for a moment on the facts of the Richmond experience, it would have discovered that the city's leadership is deeply familiar with what racial discrimination is. The members of the Richmond City Council have spent long years witnessing multifarious acts of discrimination, including, but not limited to, the deliberate diminution of black residents' voting rights, resistance to school desegregation, and publicly sanctioned housing discrimination. Numerous decisions of federal courts chronicle this disgraceful recent history. In *Richmond v. United States*, 422 U.S. 358 (1975), for example, this Court denounced Richmond's decision to annex part of an adjacent county at a time when the city's black population was nearing 50% because it was "infected by the impermissible purpose of denying the right to vote based on race through perpetuating white majority power to exclude Negroes from office." (Citation omitted).

When the legislatures and leaders of cities with histories of pervasive discrimination testify that past discrimination has infected one of their industries, armchair cynicism like that exercised by the majority has no place. It may well be that "the autonomy of a State is an essential component of federalism," (Citation omitted)., and that "each State is sovereign within its own domain, governing its citizens and providing for their general welfare," (Citation omitted), but apparently this is not the case when federal judges, with nothing but their impressions to go on, choose to disbelieve the explanations of these local governments and officials. Disbelief is particularly inappropriate here in light of the fact that appellee Croson, which had the burden of proving unconstitutionality at trial, (Citation omitted), has at no point come forward with any direct evidence that the city council's motives were anything other than sincere. Footnote omitted)...

A.

Today, for the first time, a majority of this Court has adopted strict scrutiny as its standard of Equal Protection Clause review of race-conscious remedial measures. (Citation omitted). This is an unwelcome development. A profound difference separates governmental actions that themselves are racist, and governmental actions that seek to remedy the effects of prior racism or to prevent neutral governmental activity from perpetuating the effects of such racism. (Citations omitted)...

In concluding that remedial classifications warrant no different standard of review under the Constitution than the most brutal and repugnant forms of state-sponsored racism, a majority of this Court signals that it regards racial discrimination as largely a phenomenon of the past, and that government bodies need no longer preoccupy themselves with rectifying racial injustice. I, however, do not believe this Nation is anywhere close to eradicating racial discrimination or its vestiges. In constitutionalizing its wishful thinking, the majority today does a grave disservice not only to those victims of past and present racial discrimination in this Nation whom government has sought to assist, but also to this Court's long tradition of approaching issues of race with the utmost sensitivity.

B.

I am also troubled by the majority's assertion that, even if it did not believe generally in strict scrutiny of race-based remedial measures, "the circumstances of this case" require this Court to look upon the Richmond City Council's measure with the strictest scrutiny. (Citation omitted). The sole such circumstance which the majority cites, however, is the fact that blacks in Richmond are a "dominant racial grou[p]" in the city. (Citation omitted). In support of this characterization of dominance, the majority observes that "blacks constitute approximately 50% of the population of the city of Richmond" and that "[f]ive of the nine seats on the City Council are held by blacks." (Citation omitted). It cannot seriously be suggested that nonminorities in Richmond have any "history of purposeful unequal treatment." (Citation omitted). If the majority really believes that groups like Richmond's nonminorities, which constitute approximately half the population but which are outnumbered even marginally in political fora, are deserving of suspect class status for these reasons alone, this Court's decisions denying suspect status to women, (Citation omitted), and to persons with below-average incomes, (Citation omitted), stand on extremely shaky ground. (Citation omitted).

In my view, the "circumstances of this case," (Citation omitted) underscore the importance of not subjecting to a strict scrutiny straitjacket the increasing number of cities which have recently come under minority leadership and are eager to rectify, or at least prevent the perpetuation of, past racial discrimination. In many cases, these cities will be the ones with the most in the way of prior discrimination to rectify. Richmond's leaders had just witnessed decades of publicly sanctioned racial discrimination in virtually all walks of life-discrimination amply documented in the decisions of the federal judiciary. (Citation omitted). This history of "purposefully unequal treatment" forced upon minorities, not imposed by them, should raise an inference that minorities in Richmond had much to remedy-and that the 1983 set-aside was undertaken with sincere remedial goals in mind, not "simple racial politics." (Citation omitted).

Richmond's own recent political history underscores the facile nature of the majority's assumption that elected officials' voting decisions are based on the color of their skins. In recent years, white and black councilmembers in Richmond have increasingly joined hands on controversial matters. When the Richmond City Council elected a black man mayor in 1982, for example, his victory was won with the support of the city council's four white members. (Citation omitted). The vote on the set-aside plan a year later also was not purely along racial lines. Of the four white councilmembers, one voted for the measure and another abstained. (Citation omitted). The majority's view that remedial measures undertaken by municipalities with black leadership must face a stiffer test of Equal Protection Clause scrutiny than remedial measures undertaken by municipalities with white leadership implies a lack of political maturity on the part of this Nation's elected minority officials that is totally unwarranted. Such insulting judgments have no place in constitutional jurisprudence....

JUSTICE BLACKMUN, with whom JUSTICE BRENNAN joins, dissenting.

I join JUSTICE MARSHALL's perceptive and incisive opinion revealing great sensitivity toward those who have suffered the pains of economic discrimination in the construction trades for so long.

I never thought that I would live to see the day when the city of Richmond, Virginia, the cradle of the Old Confederacy, sought on its own, within a narrow confine, to lessen the stark impact of persistent discrimination. But Richmond, to its great credit, acted. Yet this Court, the supposed bastion of equality, strikes down Richmond's efforts as though discrimination had never existed or was not demonstrated in this particular litigation. JUSTICE MARSHALL convincingly discloses the fallacy and the shallowness of that approach. History is irrefutable, even though one might sympathize with those who-though possibly innocent in themselves- benefit from the wrongs of past decades...

So the Court today regresses. I am confident, however, that, given time, it one day again will do its best to fulfill the great promises of the Constitution's Preamble and of the guarantees embodied in the Bill of Rights—a fulfillment that would make this Nation very special.

E.

The Bakke Case Rationale Revisited in the Supreme Court's University of Michigan Decisions

Since Justice Powell's plurality decision in Bakke, universities have felt that their affirmative action admission policies would survive judicial scrutiny because of Powell's ruling which upheld diversity of perspective as a compelling state interest. A university, Powell wrote, through academic freedom has the right to determine who should be admitted, a right which is closely tied to the First Amendment to speak on campuses.

By a 5-4 decision, the Supreme Court of the United States upheld recently the University of Michigan Law School's admission program, relying heavily upon the rationale in Bakke. This case has insured that in law school and other admissions programs affirmative action can pass constitutional scrutiny if properly constructed.

GRUTTER v. BOLLINGER
Supreme Court of the United States
539 U.S. 306 (2003)

Justice O'CONNOR delivered the opinion of the Court.

This case requires us to decide whether the use of race as a factor in student admissions by the University of Michigan Law School (Law School) is unlawful.

A.

The Law School ranks among the Nation's top law schools. It receives more than 3,500 applications each year for a class of around 350 students. Seeking to "admit a group of students who individually and collectively are among the most capable," the Law School looks for individuals with "substantial promise for success in law school" and "a strong likelihood of succeeding in the practice of law and contributing in diverse ways to the well-being of others." (Citation omitted). More broadly, the Law School seeks "a mix of students with varying backgrounds and experiences who will respect and learn from each other." (Citation omitted). In 1992, the dean of the Law School charged a faculty committee with crafting a written admissions policy to implement these goals. In particular, the Law School sought to ensure that its efforts to achieve student body diversity complied with this Court's most recent ruling on the use of race in university admissions. See *Regents of Univ. of Cal. v. Bakke*, 438 U.S. 265 (1978). Upon the unanimous adoption of the committee's report by the Law School faculty, it became the Law School's official admissions policy.

The hallmark of that policy is its focus on academic ability coupled with a flexible assessment of applicants' talents, experiences, and potential "to contribute to the learning of those around them." (Citation omitted). The policy requires admissions officials to evaluate each applicant based on all the information available in the file, including a personal statement, letters of recommendation, and an essay describing the ways in which the applicant will contribute to the life and diversity of the Law School. (Citation omitted). In reviewing an applicant's file, admissions officials must consider the applicant's undergraduate grade point average (GPA) and Law School Admissions Test (LSAT) score because they are important (if imperfect) predictors of academic success in law school. (Citation omitted). The policy stresses that "no applicant should be admitted unless we expect that applicant to do well enough to graduate with no serious academic problems." (Citation omitted).

The policy makes clear, however, that even the highest possible score does not guarantee admission to the Law School. (Citation omitted). Nor does a low score automatically disqualify an applicant. (Citation omitted). Rather, the policy requires admissions officials to look beyond grades and test scores to other criteria that are important to the Law School's educational objectives. (Citation omitted). So-called "soft variables" such as "the enthusiasm of recommenders, the quality of the undergraduate institution, the quality of the applicant's essay, and the areas and difficulty of undergraduate course selection" are all brought to bear in assessing an "applicant's likely contributions to the intellectual and social life of the institution." (Citation omitted).

The policy aspires to "achieve that diversity which has the potential to enrich everyone's education and thus make a law school class stronger than the sum of its parts." (Citation omitted). The policy does not restrict the types of diversity contributions eligible for "substantial weight" in the admissions process, but instead recognizes "many possible bases for diversity admissions." (Citation omitted). The policy does, however, reaffirm the Law School's longstanding commitment to "one particular type of diversity," that is, "racial and ethnic diversity with special reference to the inclusion of students from groups which have been historically discriminated against, like African-Americans, Hispanics and Native Americans, who without this commitment might not be represented in our student body in meaningful numbers." (Citation omitted). By enrolling a "'critical mass' of [underrepresented] minority students," the Law School seeks to "ensur[e] their ability to make unique contributions to the character of the Law School." (Citation omitted.).

The policy does not define diversity "solely in terms of racial and ethnic status." (Citation omitted). Nor is the policy "insensitive to the competition among all students for admission to the [L]aw [S]chool." (Citation omitted). Rather, the policy seeks to guide admissions officers in "producing classes both diverse and academically outstanding, classes made up of students who promise to continue the tradition of outstanding contribution by Michigan Graduates to the legal profession." (Citation omitted).

B.

Petitioner Barbara Grutter is a white Michigan resident who applied to the Law School in 1996 with a 3.8 grade point average and 161 LSAT score. The Law School initially placed petitioner on a waiting list, but subsequently rejected her application. In December 1997, petitioner filed suit in the United States District Court for the Eastern District of Michigan against the Law School, the Regents of the University of Michigan, Lee Bollinger (Dean of the Law School from 1987 to 1994, and President of the University of Michigan from 1996 to 2002), Jeffrey Lehman (Dean of the Law School), and Dennis Shields (Director of Admissions at the Law School from 1991 until 1998). Petitioner alleged that respondents discriminated against her on the basis of race in violation of the Fourteenth Amendment; Title VI of the Civil Rights Act of 1964, 78 Stat. 252, 42 U. S. C. §2000d; and Rev. Stat. §1977, as amended, 42 U. S. C. §1981.

Petitioner further alleged that her application was rejected because the Law School uses race as a "predominant" factor, giving applicants who belong to certain minority groups "a significantly greater chance of admission than students with similar credentials from disfavored racial groups." (Citation omitted). Petitioner also alleged that respondents "had no compelling interest to justify their use of race in the admissions process." (Citation omitted). Petitioner requested compensatory and punitive damages, an order requiring the Law School to offer her admission, and an injunction prohibiting the Law School from continuing to discriminate on the basis of race. (Citation omitted). Petitioner clearly has standing to bring this lawsuit. *Northeastern Fla. Chapter, Associated Gen. Contractors of America v. Jacksonville*, 508 U.S. 656, 666 (1993).

The District Court granted petitioner's motion for class certification and for bifurcation of the trial into liability and damages phases. The class was defined as "'all persons who (A) applied for and were not granted admission to the University of Michigan Law School for the academic years since (and including) 1995 until the time that judgment is entered herein; and (B) were members of those racial or ethnic groups, including Caucasian, that Defendants treated less favorably in considering their applications for admission to the Law School.'" (Citation omitted).

The District Court heard oral argument on the parties' cross-motions for summary judgment on December 22, 2000. Taking the motions under advisement, the District Court indicated that it would decide as a matter of law whether the Law School's asserted interest in obtaining the educational benefits that flow from a diverse student body was compelling. The District Court also indicated that it would conduct a bench trial on the extent to which race was a factor in the Law School's admissions decisions, and whether the Law School's consideration of race in admissions decisions constituted a race-based double standard.

During the 15-day bench trial, the parties introduced extensive evidence concerning the Law School's use of race in the admissions process. Dennis Shields, Director of Admissions when petitioner applied to the Law School, testified that he did not direct his staff to admit a particular percentage or number of minority students, but rather to consider an applicant's race along with all other factors. (Citation omitted). Shields testified that at the height of the admissions season, he would frequently consult the so-called "daily reports" that kept track of the racial and ethnic composition of the class (along with other information such as residency status and gender). (Citation omitted). This was done, Shields testified, to ensure that a critical mass of underrepresented minority students would be reached so as to realize the educational benefits of a diverse student body. (Citation omitted). Shields stressed, however, that he did not seek to admit any particular number or percentage of underrepresented minority students. (Citation omitted).

Erica Munzel, who succeeded Shields as Director of Admissions, testified that "critical mass" means "meaningful numbers" or "meaningful representation," which she understood to mean a number that encourages underrepresented minority students to participate in the classroom and not feel isolated. (Citation omitted). Munzel stated there is no number, percentage, or range of numbers or percentages that constitute critical mass. (Citation omitted). Munzel also asserted that she must consider the race of applicants because a critical mass of underrepresented minority students could not be enrolled if admissions decisions were based primarily on undergraduate GPAs and LSAT scores. (Citation omitted).

The current Dean of the Law School, Jeffrey Lehman, also testified. Like the other Law School witnesses, Lehman did not quantify critical mass in terms of numbers or percentages. (Citation omitted). He indicated that critical mass means numbers such that underrepresented minority students do not feel isolated or like spokespersons for their race. (Citation omitted). When asked about the extent to which race is considered in admissions, Lehman testified that it varies from one applicant to another. (Citation omitted). In some cases, according to Lehman's testimony, an applicant's race may play no role, while in others it may be a "determinative" factor. (Citation omitted).

The District Court heard extensive testimony from Professor Richard Lempert, who chaired the faculty committee that drafted the 1992 policy. Lempert emphasized that the Law School seeks students with diverse interests and backgrounds to enhance classroom discussion and the educational experience both inside and outside the classroom. (Citation omitted). When asked about the policy's "commitment to racial and ethnic diversity with special reference to the inclusion of students from groups which have been historically discriminated against," Lempert explained that this language did not purport to remedy past discrimination, but rather to include students who may bring to the Law School a perspective different from that of members of groups which have not been the victims of such discrimination. (Citation omitted). Lempert acknowledged that other groups, such as Asians and Jews, have experienced discrimination, but explained they were not mentioned in the policy because individuals who are members of those groups were already being admitted to the Law School in significant numbers. (Citation omitted).

Kent Syverud was the final witness to testify about the Law School's use of race in admissions decisions. Syverud was a professor at the Law School when the 1992 admissions policy was adopted and is now Dean of Vanderbilt Law School. In addition to his testimony at trial, Syverud submitted several expert reports on the educational benefits of diversity. Syverud's testimony indicated that when a critical mass of underrepresented minority students is present, racial stereotypes lose their force because nonminority students learn there is no "minority viewpoint" but rather a variety of viewpoints among minority students. (Citation omitted).

In an attempt to quantify the extent to which the Law School actually considers race in making admissions decisions, the parties introduced voluminous evidence at trial. Relying on data obtained from the Law School, petitioner's expert, Dr. Kinley Larntz, generated and analyzed "admissions grids" for the years in question (1995-2000). These grids show the number of applicants and the number of admittees for all combinations of GPAs and LSAT scores. Dr. Larntz made "cell-by-cell" comparisons between applicants of different races to determine whether a statistically significant relationship existed between race and admission rates. He concluded that membership in certain minority groups "is an extremely strong factor in the decision for acceptance," and that applicants from these minority groups "are given an extremely large allowance for admission" as compared to applicants who are members of nonfavored groups. (Citation omitted). Dr. Larntz conceded, however, that race is not the predominant factor in the Law School's admissions calculus. (Citation omitted). Dr. Stephen Raudenbush, the Law School's expert, focused on the predicted effect of eliminating race as a factor in the Law School's admission process. In Dr. Raudenbush's view, a race-blind admissions system would have a "very dramatic," negative effect on underrepresented minority admissions. (Citation omitted). He testified that in 2000, 35 percent of underrepresented minority applicants were admitted. (Citation omitted). Dr. Raudenbush predicted that if race were not considered, only 10 percent of those applicants would have been admitted. (Citation omitted). Under this scenario, underrepresented minority students would have comprised 4 percent of the entering class in 2000 instead of the actual figure of 14.5 percent. (Citation omitted).

In the end, the District Court concluded that the Law School's use of race as a factor in admissions decisions was unlawful. Applying strict scrutiny, the District Court determined that the Law School's asserted interest in assembling a diverse student body was not compelling because "the attainment of a racially diverse class ... was not recognized as such by *Bakke* and is not a remedy for past discrimination." (Citation omitted). The District Court went on to hold that even if diversity were compelling, the Law School had not narrowly tailored its use of race to further that interest. The District Court granted petitioner's request for declaratory relief and enjoined the Law School from using race as a factor in its admissions decisions. The Court of Appeals entered a stay of the injunction pending appeal.

Sitting en banc, the Court of Appeals reversed the District Court's judgment and vacated the injunction. The Court of Appeals first held that Justice Powell's opinion in *Bakke* was binding precedent establishing diversity as a compelling state interest. According to the Court of Appeals, Justice Powell's opinion with respect to diversity comprised the controlling rationale for the judgment of this Court under the analysis set forth in *Marks v. United States*, 430 U.S. 188 (1977). The Court of Appeals also held that the Law School's use of race was narrowly tailored because race was merely a "potential 'plus' factor" and because the Law School's program was "virtually identical" to the Harvard admissions program described approvingly by Justice Powell and appended to his *Bakke* opinion. 288 F. 3d 732, 746, 749 (CA6 2002)...

We granted certiorari, 537 U.S. 1043 (2002), to resolve the disagreement among the Courts of Appeals on a question of national importance: Whether diversity is a compelling interest that can justify the narrowly tailored use of race in selecting applicants for admission to public universities. Compare *Hopwood v. Texas*, 78 F. 3d 932 (CA5 1996) (Hopwood I) (holding that diversity is not a compelling state interest), with *Smith v. University of Wash. Law School*, 233 F. 3d 1188 (CA9 2000) (holding that it is).

II.
A.

We last addressed the use of race in public higher education over 25 years ago. In the landmark *Bakke* case, we reviewed a racial set-aside program that reserved 16 out of 100 seats in a medical school class for members of certain minority groups. (Citation omitted)...

Since this Court's splintered decision in *Bakke*, Justice Powell's opinion announcing the judgment of the Court has served as the touchstone for constitutional analysis of race-conscious admissions policies. Public and private universities across the Nation have modeled their own admissions programs on Justice Powell's views on permissible race-conscious policies. See, e.g., Brief for Judith Areen et al. as Amici Curiae 12-13 (law school admissions programs employ "methods designed from and based on Justice Powell's opinion in *Bakke*"); Brief for Amherst College et al. as Amici Curiae 27 ("After *Bakke*, each of the amici (and undoubtedly other selective colleges and universities as well) reviewed their admissions procedures in light of Justice Powell's opinion… and set sail accordingly"). We therefore discuss Justice Powell's opinion in some detail.

Justice Powell began by stating that "[t]he guarantee of equal protection cannot mean one thing when applied to one individual and something else when applied to a person of another color. If both are not accorded the same protection, then it is not equal. (Citation omitted). In Justice Powell's view, when governmental decisions "touch upon an individual's race or ethnic background, he is entitled to a judicial determination that the burden he is asked to bear on that basis is precisely tailored to serve a compelling governmental interest." (Citation omitted). Under this exacting standard, only one of the interests asserted by the university survived Justice Powell's scrutiny… More important, for the reasons set out below, today we endorse Justice Powell's view that student body diversity is a compelling state interest that can justify the use of race in university admissions.

B.

The Equal Protection Clause provides that no State shall "deny to any person within its jurisdiction the equal protection of the laws." U.S. Const., Amdt. 14, §2. Because the Fourteenth Amendment "protect[s] persons, not groups," all "governmental action based on race—a group classification long recognized as in most circumstances irrelevant and therefore prohibited—should be subjected to detailed judicial inquiry to ensure that the personal right to equal protection of the laws has not been infringed.", 515 U.S. 200, 227 (1995) (emphasis in original; internal quotation marks and citation omitted). We are a "free people whose institutions are founded upon the doctrine of equality." *Loving v. Virginia*, 388 U.S. 1, 11 (1967) (internal quotation marks and citation omitted). It follows from that principle that "government may treat people differently because of their race only for the most compelling reasons." *Adarand Constructors, Inc. v. Peña*, 515 U.S., at 227. We have held that all racial classifications imposed by government" must be analyzed by a reviewing court under strict scrutiny." (Citation omitted). This means that such classifications are constitutional only if they are narrowly tailored to further compelling governmental interests. "Absent searching judicial inquiry into the justification for such race-based measures," we have no way to determine what "classifications are 'benign' or 'remedial' and what classifications are in fact motivated by illegitimate notions of racial inferiority or simple racial politics." *Richmond v. J. A. Croson Co.*, 488 U.S. 469, 493 (1989) (plurality opinion). We apply strict scrutiny to all racial classifications to "'smoke out' illegitimate uses of race by assuring that [government] is pursuing a goal important enough to warrant use of a highly suspect tool." (Citation omitted).

Strict scrutiny is not "strict in theory, but fatal in fact." *Adarand Constructors, Inc. v. Peña*, supra, at 237 (internal quotation marks and citation omitted). Although all governmental uses of race are subject to strict scrutiny, not all are invalidated by it… When race-based action is necessary to further a compelling governmental interest, such action does not violate the constitutional guarantee of equal protection so long as the narrow-tailoring requirement is also satisfied.

Context matters when reviewing race-based governmental action under the Equal Protection Clause. See *Gomillion v. Lightfoot*, 364 U.S. 339, 343-344 (1960) (admonishing that, "in dealing with claims under broad provisions of the Constitution, which derive content by an interpretive process of inclusion and exclusion, it is imperative that generalizations, based on and qualified by the concrete situations that gave rise to them, must not be applied out of context in disregard of variant controlling facts"). In *Adarand Constructors, Inc. v. Peña*, we made clear that strict scrutiny must take "'relevant differences' into account." (Citation omitted). Indeed, as we explained, that is its "fundamental purpose." (Citation omitted). Not every decision influenced by race is equally objectionable and strict scrutiny is designed to provide a framework for carefully examining the importance and the sincerity of the reasons advanced by the governmental decisionmaker for the use of race in that particular context.

III.

A.

With these principles in mind, we turn to the question whether the Law School's use of race is justified by a compelling state interest. Before this Court, as they have throughout this litigation, respondents assert only one justification for their use of race in the admissions process: obtaining "the educational benefits that flow from a diverse student body" (Citation omitted). In other words, the Law School asks us to recognize, in the context of higher education, a compelling state interest in student body diversity.

We first wish to dispel the notion that the Law School's argument has been foreclosed, either expressly or implicitly, by our affirmative-action cases decided since *Bakke*. It is true that some language in those opinions might be read to suggest that remedying past discrimination is the only permissible justification for race-based governmental action. See, e.g., *Richmond v. J. A. Croson Co.*, supra, at 493 (plurality opinion) (stating that unless classifications based on race are "strictly reserved for remedial settings, they may in fact promote notions of racial inferiority and lead to a politics of racial hostility"). But we have never held that the only governmental use of race that can survive strict scrutiny is remedying past discrimination. Nor, since *Bakke*, have we directly addressed the use of race in the context of public higher education. Today, we hold that the Law School has a compelling interest in attaining a diverse student body.

The Law School's educational judgment that such diversity is essential to its educational mission is one to which we defer. The Law School's assessment that diversity will, in fact, yield educational benefits is substantiated by respondents and their amici. Our scrutiny of the interest asserted by the Law School is no less strict for taking into account complex educational judgments in an area that lies primarily within the expertise of the university. Our holding today is in keeping with our tradition of giving a degree of deference to a university's academic decisions, within constitutionally prescribed limits. (Citation omitted)...

We have repeatedly acknowledged the overriding importance of preparing students for work and citizenship, describing education as pivotal to "sustaining our political and cultural heritage" with a fundamental role in maintaining the fabric of society. *Plyler v. Doe*, 457 U.S. 202, 221 (1982). This Court has long recognized that "education… is the very foundation of good citizenship." *Brown v. Board of Education*, 347 U.S. 483, 493 (1954). For this reason, the diffusion of knowledge and opportunity through public institutions of higher education must be accessible to all individuals regardless of race or ethnicity. The United States, as amicus curiae, affirms that "[e]nsuring that public institutions are open and available to all segments of American society, including people of all races and ethnicities, represents a paramount government objective." Brief for United States as Amicus Curiae 13. And, "[n]owhere is the importance of such openness more acute than in the context of higher education." (Citation omitted). Effective participation by members of all racial and ethnic groups in the civic life of our Nation is essential if the dream of one Nation, indivisible, is to be realized.

Moreover, universities, and in particular, law schools, represent the training ground for a large number of our Nation's leaders. *Sweatt v. Painter*, 339 U.S. 629, 634 (1950) (describing law school as a "proving ground for legal learning and practice"). Individuals with law degrees occupy roughly half the state governorships, more than half the seats in the United States Senate, and more than a third of the seats in the United States House of Representatives. See Brief for Association of American Law Schools as Amicus Curiae 5-6. The pattern is even more striking when it comes to highly selective law schools. A handful of these schools accounts for 25 of the 100 United States Senators, 74 United States Courts of Appeals judges, and nearly 200 of the more than 600 United States District Court judges. (Citation omitted).

In order to cultivate a set of leaders with legitimacy in the eyes of the citizenry, it is necessary that the path to leadership be visibly open to talented and qualified individuals of every race and ethnicity. All members of our heterogeneous society must have confidence in the openness and integrity of the educational institutions that provide this training. As we have recognized, law schools "cannot be effective in isolation from the individuals and institutions with which the law interacts." See *Sweatt v. Painter*, supra, at 634. Access to legal education (and thus the legal profession) must be inclusive of talented and qualified individuals of every race and ethnicity, so that all members of our heterogeneous society may participate in the educational institutions that provide the training and education necessary to succeed in America...

We find that the Law School's admissions program bears the hallmarks of a narrowly tailored plan. As Justice Powell made clear in *Bakke*, truly individualized consideration demands that race be used in a flexible, nonmechanical way. It follows from this mandate that universities cannot establish quotas for members of certain racial groups or put members of those groups on separate admissions tracks. See id., at 315-316. Nor can universities insulate applicants who belong to certain racial or ethnic groups from the competition for admission. Ibid. Universities can, however, consider race or ethnicity more flexibly as a 'plus' factor in the context of individualized consideration of each and every applicant. (Citation omitted).

We are satisfied that the Law School's admissions program, like the Harvard plan described by Justice Powell, does not operate as a quota. Properly understood, a 'quota' is a program in which a certain fixed number or proportion of opportunities are "reserved exclusively for certain minority groups." *Richmond v. J. A. Croson Co.*, supra, at 496 (plurality opinion). Quotas "impose a fixed number or percentage which must be attained, or which cannot be exceeded," *Sheet Metal Workers v. EEOC*, 478 U.S. 421, 495 (1986) (O'Connor, J., concurring in part and dissenting in part), and "insulate the individual from comparison with all other candidates for the available seats." *Bakke*, supra, at 317 (opinion of Powell, J.). In contrast, "a permissible goal... require[s] only a good-faith effort... to come within a range demarcated by the goal itself," *Sheet Metal Workers v. EEOC*, supra, at 495, and permits consideration of race as a "plus" factor in any given case while still ensuring that each candidate "compete[s] with all other qualified applicants," *Johnson v. Transportation Agency, Santa Clara Cty.*, 480 U.S. 616, 638 (1987)...

The Law School's current admissions program considers race as one factor among many, in an effort to assemble a student body that is diverse in ways broader than race. Because a lottery would make that kind of nuanced judgment impossible, it would effectively sacrifice all other educational values, not to mention every other kind of diversity. So too with the suggestion that the Law School simply lower admissions standards for all students, a drastic remedy that would require the Law School to become a much different institution and sacrifice a vital component of its educational mission. The United States advocates "percentage plans," recently adopted by public undergraduate institutions in Texas, Florida, and California to guarantee admission to all students above a certain class-rank threshold in every high school in the State. Brief for United States as Amicus Curiae 14-18. The United States does not, however, explain how such plans could work for graduate and professional schools. Moreover, even assuming such plans are race-neutral, they may preclude the university from conducting the individualized assessments necessary to assemble a student body that is not just racially diverse, but diverse along all the qualities valued by the university. We are satisfied that the Law School adequately considered race-neutral alternatives currently capable of producing a critical mass without forcing the Law School to abandon the academic selectivity that is the cornerstone of its educational mission...

IV.

In summary, the Equal Protection Clause does not prohibit the Law School's narrowly tailored use of race in admissions decisions to further a compelling interest in obtaining the educational benefits that flow from a diverse student body. Consequently, petitioner's statutory claims based on Title VI and 42 U. S. C. §1981 also fail. See *Bakke*, supra, at 287 (opinion of Powell, J.) ("Title VI

...proscribe[s] only those racial classifications that would violate the Equal Protection Clause or the Fifth Amendment"); *General Building Contractors Assn., Inc. v. Pennsylvania*, 458 U.S. 375, 389-391 (1982) (the prohibition against discrimination in §1981 is co-extensive with the Equal Protection Clause). The judgment of the Court of Appeals for the Sixth Circuit, accordingly, is affirmed.

It is so ordered.

Justice GINSBURG, with whom Justice BREYER joins, concurring.

The Court's observation that race-conscious programs "must have a logical end point," (Citation omitted), accords with the international understanding of the office of affirmative action. The International Convention on the Elimination of All Forms of Racial Discrimination, ratified by the United States in 1994, see State Dept., Treaties in Force 422-423 (June 1996), endorses "special and concrete measures to ensure the adequate development and protection of certain racial groups or individuals belonging to them, for the purpose of guaranteeing them the full and equal enjoyment of human rights and fundamental freedoms." Annex to G. A. Res. 2106, 20 U. N. GAOR Res. Supp. (No. 14) 47, U. N. Doc. A/6014, Art. 2(2) (1965). But such measures, the Convention instructs, "shall in no case entail as a consequence the maintenance of unequal or separate rights for different racial groups after the objectives for which they were taken have been achieved." (Citation omitted). *See also Art.* 1(4) (similarly providing for temporally limited affirmative action); Convention on the Elimination of All Forms of Discrimination against Women, Annex to G. A. Res. 34/180, 34 U. N. GAOR Res. Supp. (No. 46) 194, U. N. Doc. A/34/46, Art. 4(1) (1979) (authorizing "temporary special measures aimed at accelerating de facto equality"that "shall be discontinued when the objectives of equality of opportunity and treatment have been achieved")...

It is well documented that conscious and unconscious race bias, even rank discrimination based on race, remain alive in our land, impeding realization of our highest values and ideals. See, e.g., *Gratz v. Bollinger*, ante, at 1-4 (Ginsburg, J., dissenting); *Adarand Constructors, Inc. v. Peña*, 515 U.S. 200, 272-274 (1995) (Ginsburg, J., dissenting); Krieger, Civil Rights Perestroika: Intergroup Relations after Affirmative Action, 86 Calif. L. Rev. 1251, 1276-1291, 1303 (1998). As to public education, data for the years 2000-2001 show that 71.6% of African-American children and 76.3% of Hispanic children attended a school in which minorities made up a majority of the student body. See E. Frankenberg, C. Lee, & G. Orfield, A Multiracial Society with Segregated Schools: Are We Losing the Dream? (Citation omitted). And schools in predominantly minority communities lag far behind others measured by the educational resources available to them. (Citation omitted).

However strong the public's desire for improved education systems may be, see P. Hart & R. Teeter, A National Priority: Americans Speak on Teacher Quality 2, 11 (2002) (public opinion research conducted for Educational Testing Service); The No Child Left Behind Act of 2001, Pub. L. 107-110, 115 Stat. 1425, 20 U. S. C. A. §7231 (2003 Supp. Pamphlet), it remains the current reality that many minority students encounter markedly inadequate and unequal educational opportunities. Despite these inequalities, some minority students are able to meet the high threshold requirements set for admission to the country's finest undergraduate and graduate educational institutions. As lower school education in minority communities improves, an increase in the number of such students may be anticipated. From today's vantage point, one may hope, but not firmly forecast, that over the next generation's span, progress toward nondiscrimination and genuinely equal opportunity will make it safe to sunset affirmative action.

Justice THOMAS, with whom Justice SCALIA joins as to Parts I-VII, concurring in part and dissenting in part.

Frederick Douglass, speaking to a group of abolitionists almost 140 years ago, delivered a message lost on today's majority:

> "[I]n regard to the colored people, there is always more that is benevolent, I perceive, than just, manifested towards us. What I ask for the negro is not benevolence, not pity, not sympathy, but simply justice. The American people have always been anxious to know what they shall do with us.... I have had but one answer from the beginning. Do nothing with us! Your doing with us has already played the mischief with us. Do nothing with us! If the apples will not remain on the tree of their own strength, if they are worm-eaten at the core, if they are early ripe and disposed to fall, let them fall! ... And if the negro cannot stand on his own legs, let him fall also. All I ask is, give him a chance to stand on his own legs! Let him alone! ... [Y]our interference is doing him positive injury."What the Black Man Wants: An Address Delivered in Boston, Massachusetts, on 26 January 1865, reprinted in 4 The Frederick Douglass Papers 59, 68 (J. Blassingame & J. McKivigan eds. 1991) (emphasis in original).

Like Douglass, I believe blacks can achieve in every avenue of American life without the meddling of university administrators. Because I wish to see all students succeed whatever their color, I share, in some respect, the sympathies of those who sponsor the type of discrimination advanced by the University of Michigan Law School (Law School). The Constitution does not, however, tolerate institutional devotion to the status quo in admissions policies when such devotion ripens into racial discrimination. Nor does the Constitution countenance the unprecedented deference the Court gives to the Law School, an approach inconsistent with the very concept of "strict scrutiny."

No one would argue that a university could set up a lower general admission standard and then impose heightened requirements only on black applicants. Similarly, a university may not maintain a high admission standard and grant exemptions to favored races. The Law School, of its own choosing, and for its own purposes, maintains an exclusionary admissions system that it knows produces racially disproportionate results. Racial discrimination is not a permissible solution to the self-inflicted wounds of this elitist admissions policy.

The majority upholds the Law School's racial discrimination not by interpreting the people's Constitution, but by responding to a faddish slogan of the cognoscenti. Nevertheless, I concur in part in the Court's opinion. First, I agree with the Court insofar as its decision, which approves of only one racial classification, confirms that further use of race in admissions remains unlawful. Second, I agree with the Court's holding that racial discrimination in higher education admissions will be illegal in 25 years. (Citation omitted). (stating that racial discrimination will no longer be narrowly tailored, or "necessary to further" a compelling state interest, in 25 years). I respectfully dissent from the remainder of the Court's opinion and the judgment, however, because I believe that the Law School's current use of race violates the Equal Protection Clause and that the Constitution means the same thing today as it will in 300 months....

II.

The proffered interest that the majority vindicates today, then, is not simply "diversity." Instead the Court upholds the use of racial discrimination as a tool to advance the Law School's interest in offering a marginally superior education while maintaining an elite institution. Unless each constituent part of this state interest is of pressing public necessity, the Law School's use of race is unconstitutional. I find each of them to fall far short of this standard...

III.

As the foregoing makes clear, Michigan has no compelling interest in having a law school at all, much less an elite one. Still, even assuming that a State may, under appropriate circumstances, demonstrate a cognizable interest in having an elite law school, Michigan has failed to do so here...

Similarly no modern law school can claim ignorance of the poor performance of blacks, relatively speaking, on the Law School Admissions Test (LSAT). Nevertheless, law schools continue to use the test and then attempt to "correct" for black underperformance by using racial discrimination in admissions so as to obtain their aesthetic student body. The Law School's continued adherence to measures it knows produce racially skewed results is not entitled to deference by this Court. (Citation omitted)...

Having decided to use the LSAT, the Law School must accept the constitutional burdens that come with this decision. The Law School may freely continue to employ the LSAT and other allegedly merit-based standards in whatever fashion it likes. What the Equal Protection Clause forbids, but the Court today allows, is the use of these standards hand-in-hand with racial discrimination. An infinite variety of admissions methods are available to the Law School. Considering all of the radical thinking that has historically occurred at this country's universities, the Law School's intractable approach toward admissions is striking...

It is uncontested that each year, the Law School admits a handful of blacks who would be admitted in the absence of racial discrimination. (Citation omitted). Who can differentiate between those who belong and those who do not? The majority of blacks are admitted to the Law School because of discrimination, and because of this policy all are tarred as undeserving. This problem of stigma does not depend on determinacy as to whether those stigmatized are actually the "beneficiaries" of racial discrimination. When blacks take positions in the highest places of government, industry, or academia, it is an open question today whether their skin color played a part in their advancement. The question itself is the stigma—because either racial discrimination did play a role, in which case the person may be deemed "otherwise unqualified," or it did not, in which case asking the question itself unfairly marks those blacks who would succeed without discrimination. Is this what the Court means by "visibly open"? (Citation omitted)...

In the companion case to Grutter, the Supreme Court ruled that the assignment of admission points in University of Michigan's undergraduate colleges that were based upon underrepresented minority status, violated the 14th Amendment to the United States Constitution.

GRATZ AND HAMACHER v. BOLLINGER
Supreme Court of the United States
539 U.S. 244 (2003)

Chief Justice REHNQUIST delivered the opinion of the Court.

We granted certiorari in this case to decide whether "the University of Michigan's use of racial preferences in undergraduate admissions violate[s] the Equal Protection Clause of the Fourteenth Amendment, Title VI of the Civil Rights Act of 1964 (42 U.S.C. § 2000d), or 42 U.S.C. § 1981." (Citation omitted). Because we find that the manner in which the University considers the race of applicants in its undergraduate admissions guidelines violates these constitutional and statutory provisions, we reverse that portion of the District Court's decision upholding the guidelines.

A.

Petitioners Jennifer Gratz and Patrick Hamacher both applied for admission to the University of Michigan's (University) College of Literature, Science, and the Arts (LSA) as residents of the State of Michigan. Both petitioners are Caucasian. Gratz, who applied for admission for the fall of 1995, was notified in January of that year that a final decision regarding her admission had been delayed until April. This delay was based upon the University's determination that, although Gratz was "well qualified," she was "less competitive than the students who ha[d] been admitted on first review." (Citation omitted). Gratz was notified in April that the LSA was unable to offer her admission. She enrolled in the University of Michigan at Dearborn, from which she graduated in the spring of 1999.

Hamacher applied for admission to the LSA for the fall of 1997. A final decision as to his application was also postponed because, though his "academic credentials [were] in the qualified range, they [were] not at the level needed for first review admission." (Citation omitted). Hamacher's application was subsequently denied in April 1997, and he enrolled at Michigan State University. (Citation omitted).

In October 1997, Gratz and Hamacher filed a lawsuit in the United States District Court for the Eastern District of Michigan against the University of Michigan, the LSA, (Citation omitted). James Duderstadt, and Lee Bollinger. (Citation omitted). Petitioners' complaint was a class-action suit alleging "violations and threatened violations of the rights of the plaintiffs and the class they represent to equal protection of the laws under the Fourteenth Amendment... and for racial discrimination in violation of 42 U.S.C. § 1981 1983, and 2000d *et seq.*" (Citation omitted). Petitioners sought, *inter alia*, compensatory and punitive damages for past violations, declaratory relief finding that respondents violated petitioners' "rights to nondiscriminatory treatment," an injunction prohibiting respondents from "continuing to discriminate on the basis of race in violation of the Fourteenth Amendment," and an order requiring the LSA to offer Hamacher admission as a transfer student. (Citation omitted).

The District Court granted petitioners' motion for class certification after determining that a class action was appropriate pursuant to Federal Rule of Civil Procedure 23(b)(2). The certified class consisted of "those individuals who applied for and were not granted admission to the College of Literature, Science and the Arts of the University of Michigan for all academic years from 1995 forward and who are members of those racial or ethnic groups, including Caucasian, that defendants treated less favorably on the basis of race in considering their application for admission." (Citation omitted). And Hamacher, whose claim the District Court found to challenge a "practice of racial discrimination pervasively applied on a classwide basis," was designated as the class representative. (Citation omitted)...

B.

The University has changed its admissions guidelines a number of times during the period relevant to this litigation, and we summarize the most significant of these changes briefly. The University's Office of Undergraduate Admissions (OUA) oversees the LSA admissions process. (Citation omitted). In order to promote consistency in the review of the large number of applications received, the OUA uses written guidelines for each academic year. Admissions counselors make admissions decisions in accordance with these guidelines.

OUA considers a number of factors in making admissions decisions, including high school grades, standardized test scores, high school quality, curriculum strength, geography, alumni relationships, and leadership. OUA also considers race. During all periods relevant to this litigation, the University has considered African-Americans, Hispanics, and Native Americans to be "underrepresented minorities," and it is undisputed that the University admits "virtually every qualified... applicant" from these groups. (Citation omitted).

During 1995 and 1996, OUA counselors evaluated applications according to grade point average combined with what were referred to as the "SCUGA" factors...

In both years, applicants with the same GPA 2 score and ACT/ SAT score were subject to different admissions outcomes based upon their racial or ethnic status. (Citation omitted). For example, as a Caucasian in-state applicant, Gratz's GPA 2 score and ACT score placed her within a cell calling for a postponed decision on her application. An in-state or out-of-state minority applicant with Gratz's scores would have fallen within a cell calling for admission. In 1997, the University modified its admissions procedure... Under this new system, applicants could receive points for underrepresented minority status, socioeconomic disadvantage, or attendance at a high school with a predominantly underrepresented minority population, or underrepresentation in the unit to which the student was applying (for example, men who sought to pursue a career in nursing)...

Beginning with the 1998 academic year, the OUA dispensed with the Guidelines tables and the SCUGA point system in favor of a "selection index," on which an applicant could score a maximum of 150 points... Of particular significance here, under a "miscellaneous" category, an applicant was entitled to 20 points based upon his or her membership in an underrepresented racial or ethnic minority group. The University explained that the "development of the selection index for admissions in 1998 changed only the mechanics, not the substance of how race and ethnicity were considered in admissions." (Citation omitted).

In all application years from 1995 to 1998, the guidelines provided that qualified applicants from underrepresented minority groups be admitted as soon as possible in light of the University's belief that such applicants were more likely to enroll if promptly notified of their admission. Also from 1995 through 1998, the University carefully managed its rolling admissions system to permit consideration of certain applications submitted later in the academic year through the use of "protected seats." Specific groups-including athletes, foreign students, ROTC candidates, and underrepresented minorities-were "protected categories" eligible for these seats. A committee called the Enrollment Working Group (EWG) projected how many applicants from each of these protected categories the University was likely to receive after a given date and then paced admissions decisions to permit full consideration of expected applications from these groups. If this space was not filled by qualified candidates from the designated groups toward the end of the admissions season, it was then used to admit qualified candidates remaining in the applicant pool, including those on the waiting list.

During 1999 and 2000, the OUA used the selection index, under which every applicant from an underrepresented racial or ethnic minority group was awarded 20 points. Starting in 1999, however, the University established an Admissions Review Committee (ARC), to provide an additional level of consideration for some applications. Under the new system, counselors may, in their discretion, "flag" an application for the ARC to review after determining that the applicant (1) is academically prepared to succeed at the University, (Citation omitted). (2) has achieved a minimum selection index score, and (3) possesses a quality or characteristic important to the University's composition of its freshman class, such as high class rank, unique life experiences, challenges, circumstances, interests or talents, socioeconomic disadvantage, and underrepresented race, ethnicity, or geography. After reviewing "flagged" applications, the ARC determines whether to admit, defer, or deny each applicant.

C.

The parties filed cross-motions for summary judgment with respect to liability. Petitioners asserted that the LSA's use of race as a factor in admissions violates Title VI of the Civil Rights Act of 1964, 78 Stat. 252, 42 U.S.C. § 2000d and the Equal Protection Clause of the Fourteenth Amendment. Respondents relied on Justice Powell's opinion in *Regents of Univ. of Cal. v. Bakke*, 438 U.S. 265 (1978), to respond to petitioners' arguments. As discussed in greater detail in the Court's opinion in *Grutter v. Bollinger, post*, at 10-13, Justice Powell, in *Bakke*, expressed the view that the consideration of race as a factor in admissions might in some cases serve a compelling government interest. See 438 U.S., at 317. Respondents contended that the LSA has just such an interest in the educational benefits that result from having a racially and ethnically diverse student body and that its program is narrowly tailored to serve that interest. Respondent-intervenors asserted that the LSA had a compelling interest in remedying the University's past and current discrimination against minorities. (Citation omitted)…

It is by now well established that "all racial classifications reviewable under the Equal Protection Clause must be strictly scrutinized." *Adarand Constructors, Inc. v. Peña*, 515 U.S. 200, 224 (1995). This "standard of review... is not dependent on the race of those burdened or benefited by a particular classification." Ibid. (quoting *Richmond v. J. A. Croson Co.*, 488 U.S. 469, 494 (1989) (plurality opinion)). Thus, "any person, of whatever race, has the right to demand that any governmental actor subject to the Constitution justify any racial classification subjecting that person to unequal treatment under the strictest of judicial scrutiny." *Adarand*, 515 U.S., at 224. To withstand our strict scrutiny analysis, respondents must demonstrate that the University's use of race in its current admission program employs "narrowly tailored measures that further compelling governmental interests." (Citation omitted). Because "[r]acial classifications are simply too pernicious to permit any but the most exact connection between justification and classification," *Fullilove v. Klutznick*, 448 U.S. 448, 537 (1980) (Stevens, J., dissenting), our review of whether such requirements have been met must entail "a most searching examination." *Adarand, supra*, at 223 (quoting *Wygant v. Jackson Bd. of Ed.*, 476 U.S. 267, 273 (1986) (plurality opinion of Powell, J.). We find that the University's policy, which automatically distributes 20 points, or one-fifth of the points needed to guarantee admission, to every single "underrepresented minority" applicant solely because of race, is not narrowly tailored to achieve the interest in educational diversity that respondents claim justifies their program... Also instructive in our consideration of the LSA's system is the example provided in the description of the Harvard College Admissions Program, which Justice Powell both discussed in, and attached to, his opinion in *Bakke*. The example was included to "illustrate the kind of significance attached to race" under the Harvard College program. *Id.*, at 324. It provided as follows:

"The Admissions Committee, with only a few places left to fill, might find itself forced to choose between A, the child of a successful black physician in an academic community with promise of superior academic performance, and B, a black who grew up in an inner-city ghetto of semi-literate parents whose academic achievement was lower but who had demonstrated energy and leadership as well as an apparently abiding interest in black power. If a good number of black students much like A but few like B had already been admitted, the Committee might prefer B; and vice versa. If C, a white student with extraordinary artistic talent, were also seeking one of the remaining places, his unique quality might give him an edge over both A and B. Thus, the critical criteria are often individual qualities or experience *not dependent upon race but sometimes associated with it." Ibid.* (emphasis added).

This example further demonstrates the problematic nature of the LSA's admissions system. Even if student C's "extraordinary artistic talent" rivaled that of Monet or Picasso, the applicant would receive, at most, five points under the LSA's system. (Citation omitted). At the same time, every single underrepresented minority applicant, including students A and B, would automatically receive 20 points for submitting an application. Clearly, the LSA's system does not offer applicants the individualized selection process described in Harvard's example. Instead of considering how the differing backgrounds, experiences, and characteristics of students A, B, and C might benefit the University, admissions counselors reviewing LSA applications would simply award both A and B 20 points because their applications indicate that they are African-American, and student C would receive up to 5 points for his "extraordinary talent." (Citation omitted)....

We conclude, therefore, that because the University's use of race in its current freshman admissions policy is not narrowly tailored to achieve respondents' asserted compelling interest in diversity, the admissions policy violates the Equal Protection Clause of the Fourteenth Amendment. (Citation omitted). We further find that the admissions policy also violates Title VI and 42 U.S.C. § 1981. Accordingly, we reverse that portion of the District Court's decision granting respondents summary judgment with respect to liability and remand the case for proceedings consistent with this opinion.

It is so ordered.

pearl harbor—Order 9066—korematsu refuses—convicted

1862 Cali, 88 chinese-americans murdered by

1877 Cali,

Key Claim= "this claim supports"
  ↳ EVIDENCE
      • examples
      • images
      • other cases?
        • ALL CITED
        • CITE JOHNSON OR LARSON ONLY

x2
Key concepts

Chapter Six

BEYOND AFFIRMATIVE ACTION:
The Case for Reparations

Given the extent that Blacks, through their labor, contributed to the making of the western world, should they be given remuneration for this unjust treatment? Is the treatment afforded Blacks unjust? If not, why not? If yes, why shouldn't they be afforded reparations? Shouldn't Blacks receive compensation for the psychological and economic damages flowing from the dehumanization of a people? Have Blacks, as a class, suffered such peculiar and extraordinary discrimination, to warrant such an extraordinary remedy? The Japanese Americans have received monetary compensation for their internment in concentration camps during World War II. Shouldn't Blacks receive compensation for their internment on southern plantations? Millions of dollars have been paid to the State of Israel as compensation for lost of approximately six million Jews during the holocaust. Shouldn't Blacks receive compensation for the loss of at least fifteen million Africans during the "middle passage," i.e. the trip from Africa to the Americas? Given the mounting demand for reparations, should Blacks continue to struggle for affirmative action? If not, why not?

Is there no restitution for a class of people who have suffered such action at the hands of both private individuals and governmental institutions? For over four hundred years the western world in general, the American colonies and the United States of America in particular, benefitted from this exploitation of Black labor. The exploitation of this human labor had a direct and substantial impact upon the development of American colonies and the Republic. The enslavement of Black people was morally unjust and lead to the enrichment of large segments of the western world, including America. Wouldn't it therefore follow that some form of restitution should be given to the descendants of American slaves?

One could also argue that those Blacks, who can not directly trace their ancestry to slavery, still should be entitled to restitution for damages caused by governmentally sanctioned racism. De jure segregation, which was the supreme law of the land until 1954, crippled the minds of Black people and denied them essential services and opportunities because of race.

In this context, are the sporadic affirmative action programs that require limited benefits for Blacks sufficient? Do the programs developed by public and private entities adequately compensate for the legacies of slavery and racism? Should the Federal Government raise the issue of reparations for Blacks and develop a plan similar to the Marshall Plan and the compensation schemes for Japanese Americans? Should Congress conduct national hearings on the issue of reparations and therefore create the legislative history of slavery and pervasive racism, that could serve as a justification for race-based programs? What is the state of the Congressional record at the present time? When and under what circumstances should reparations become a political issue raised by the national political parties or independent parties?

Can the Rosewood, Florida legislation be considered a model for future legislation, perhaps on the national level? Shouldn't state governments, particularly in the South, pass similar legislation as reparations for slavery and overt and debilitating racism?

What has been the precedent for restitution and reparations in America? An examination of the restitution programs formulated as a result of the incarceration of Japanese-Americans, and the destruction of Jews in Europe, provide some examples of means that have been developed to provide reparations.

A.

Legal Redress Due to the Incarceration of Japanese-Americans in Concentration Camps

At the time that the United States was involved in a war to prevent the spread of fascism, Japanese-Americans were being deprived of their rights, by being placed in concentration camps. American law upheld such detention of a race of people who had demonstrated no disloyalty to America. Sure, the United States had been bombed by the Japanese at Pearl Harbor on December 7, 1941, but there was no evidence that Japanese-Americans were involved with the bombings. Despite constitutional guarantees of equal protection, the United States Supreme Court sanctioned the detention of these American citizens.

The legal institutions of the United States were quick to curtail rights of the Japanese-Americans. On February 19, 1942, President Franklin Roosevelt issued Executive Order 9066, which authorized the Secretary of War to exclude individuals from "military areas." Congress later issued Public Law No. 503, making it a crime to disobey a military order.

The end result of the internment was that approximately 110,000 individuals were deprived of their liberty and property as a result of governmental action. The response of the government to the claims of unjust deprivation of rights was immediate, compared to those of African-Americans. In 1948, Congress passed the-Japanese-American Evacuation Claims Act. The government ultimately paid out $37 million dollars to claimants.[1] This payment was the result of a report filed by the Commission on Wartime Relocation and Internment of Civilians in 1982. The Commission recommended that $20,000 be paid to every survivor of the concentration camps. In 1988 Congress passed legislation authorizing the payments, which began in 1990.

The government sweep of Japanese-Americans was not limited solely to those who lived in California. The American initiative

---

1 Charles McClain, *Asian Americans and the Law*, "Historical and Contemporary Perspectives," (New York: Garland Publishing, 1994), p. xii.

involved citizens who lived in California, and the western portions of Washington and Oregon, including southern Arizona. The Canadians developed a similar legal posture toward the Japanese-Americans that led to the incarceration of a number of individuals.

Although many challenged their incarceration and deprivation of rights, none of them were successful. In one case, Korematsu, who was born in California, and had never left the United States, challenged his conviction for refusing to vacate his home. He had remained in his home because of a relationship with a woman who was not Japanese. He also indicated that he was willing to render service against Japan if requested by the United States government.[2]

Despite these factual predicates, the United States Supreme Court found that Korematsu had violated the law and that his rights under the constitution were not violated. The Court based its decision upon a precedent established in an earlier case that upheld a curfew against Japanese-Americans.[3]

Civil Rights advocates had hoped that the Korematsu case would be decided differently from *Hirabayashi*, given that the deprivation of rights was more profound and extensive. Such was not the case. The Court upheld the incarceration of Korematsu on a theory of "military necessity." The former case involved a curfew, the latter involved over 100,000 Americans of Japanese heritage. Could the government's claim of military necessity withstand constitutional scrutiny? Can a citizen's constitutional rights be suspended in time of war? Why were the Japanese the only group to be singled out? What role did racism play in the decision of the government? Was Korematsu justified in disobeying the Exclusion Order?

The entire governmental establishment supported the detention of Japanese Americans. The entire west coast Congressional delegation

---

2 "Racial Discrimination and the Military Judgment: the Supreme Court's Korematsu and Endo Decisions," by Nanette Dembitz, *The Mass Internment of Japanese Americans and Their Quest for Legal Redress* (New York: Garland Publishing, 1994), p. 182.

3 *Hirabayashi v. United States*, 320 U.S. 81 (1943).

supported the detention.[4] While the President of the United States was most responsible, Congress, through its ratifying Act of March 21, 1942, gave support as well. These governmental decisions found support among the private sector, especially the media. On January 28, 1942, the *Los Angeles Times* urged the detention of Japanese Americans, who were subsequently taken from Assembly Centers to Detention Centers. These centers were created pursuant to Executive Order No. 9102 issued March 18, 1942. They were built and administered by the War Relocation Authority. Once the relocation had been completed by November, 1942, General De Witt issued an order which prohibited the Japanese Americans from leaving the centers except by written authorization. Some individuals, however, were allowed to leave the centers to engage in agricultural labor, but the special permits were rarely given.[5]

Soon after the *Endo* decision, on December 17, 1944, General De Witt announced the end of the ban on returning to one's residence. Those individuals, who were deemed dangerous, were not released from the ban. Many Japanese-Americans, however, did not return to their residences because of lack of employment opportunities, and fear of racial reprisals. The detention of Endo and others for over three years in barbed wire compounds caused many to suffer psychological damage, resulting in irrational fears of the outside world. What effect did this incarceration have upon the Japanese-Americans? The most significant negative impact was the denial and deprivation of civil rights. American citizens were imprisoned

4   Dembitz, p. 207.

5   A challenge to the military authority to deny permits was brought by Mitsuye Endo in the District Court for the Northern District of California in July, 1942. In her petition she alleged that she was a loyal civil servant of the State of California and that she could not apply for a leave because she could not get permission to go to Sacramento. She was denied relief of habeas corpus in the District Court. She was eventually granted leave clearance, but the Circuit Court of Appeals asked the Supreme Court to rule on the question of whether the military could detain a loyal citizen because she failed to satisfy the requirements of the War Relocation Authority with respect to her prospective employment and residence? The court ruled that Endo was entitled to her freedom, that the War Relocation Authority had no right to subject loyal citizens to its leave procedure. 65 Sup. Ct. 208, 216, 218-219 (1944).

without an indictment. They were placed in relatively small quarters surrounded by barbed wire. They were forcibly taken from their homes, their property sold and their families separated.[6] Some people were even forced to live in horse stalls.

More importantly, it caused a segment of the American population to believe that their rights could be arbitrarily taken away by government. One Japanese- American wrote:

"It was really sort of unbelievable. You know, when you go to college you have very high ideals of democracy, and when you have your rights taken away, it is really a shock. I kept saying all along, we're American citizens and the government couldn't possibly put us into camps. I really didn't believe it would happen until it did."[7] His experience was typical of many. He was born in San Diego, graduated from UCLA, passed the civil service examination and was working for the city. A model citizen, without any prior criminal record or any evidence of disloyalty to the United States. Other individuals, such as Fred Korematsu, Gordon Hirabayashi and Minoru Yasui challenged their deprivation of rights, but failed to get legal redress, even from the United States Supreme Court.[8] These cases were subsequently overturned as a result of public pressure and continued legal challenge. In November, 1983, Korematsu was cleared of the conviction on the grounds that his conviction was obtained by faulty government evidence.

---

6   Philip Tajitsu Nash, "Moving for Redress,"Charles McClain, Editor, *The Internment of Japanese Americans and the Quest for Legal Redress* (New York, Garland Publishing, 1994), p.744.

7   Nash, p. 177. This article was originally published in *The Yale Law Journal* Vol. 94:743 (1985).

8   *Hirabayashi v. United States*, 320 U.S. 81 (1943), *Yasui v. United States*,320 U.S. 115 (1943), and *Korematsu v. United States*, 323 U.S. 214 (1944) Social Security Amendments of 1972, Pub. L. No. 92-603, s142, 86 Stat. 1367(codified at 42 U.S.C. s431); Act of Sept. 22, 1978, Pub. L. No. 95-382,92 Stat. 727.

1. Legal Reparations

It took the Congress of the United States and private citizens, who were outraged by this mass denial of civil rights, to initiate legal redress. One of the leaders in this movement was Eugene V. Rostow, Professor and Dean of Yale Law School. He was one of the first individuals to advocate reparations for the Japanese-Americans.[9] He pressed the federal government to enforce the Civil Rights Act of 1870. Many Japanese Americans faced blatant racial discrimination in housing, jobs and education. This enforcement would help them overcome prejudice that was heightened as a result of the war. He also argued that the government should provide financial compensation for the lost of private property.

In 1948, Congress passed the Japanese American Evacuation Claims Act, Pub. L. No. 80-886, 62 Stat. 1231. This statute gave Japanese Americans the right to file claims for property losses, both real and personal. It did not allow claims for loss of income or pain and suffering. As a result of this statute, approximately $37 million dollars was paid to claimants.[10] Other legislative victories were the repeal of Title II of the Internal Security Act of 1950 Pub. L. No 81-831, 64 Stat. 1019 (1950), repealed by Act of September 25, 1971, Pub. L. No. 92-128, s2(a); an Amendment to the Social Security Act and the federal civil service retirement act.[11]

In 1979, several pieces of legislation were introduced into Congress. In the House, H.R. 5499 was introduced and in the Senate, S. 1647.[12] These bills established a commission to determine whether any wrongs had been committed against Japanese Americans as a result of Executive Order 9066. The

---

9   Rostow, "The Japanese American Cases-A Disaster," 54 *Yale Law Journal* 489, 490 (1945).

10   Nash, p. 179

11   Social Security Amendments of 1972, Pub. L. No. 92-603, s142, 86 Stat. 1367 (codified at 42 U.S. C. s431); Act of Sept. 22, 1978, Pub. L. No. 95-382, 92 Stat. 727 (codified at 5 U.S.C. s8332(k) (1982)

12   H.R. 5499, 96th Cong., 1st Sess., 125 Cong. Rec. 26,884 (1979); S. 1647, 96th Cong., 1st Sess., 125 Cong. Rec. 22,333 (1979)

commission would make appropriate recommendations to Congress. A more ambitious bill was introduced by Representative Michael Lowry of Washington, which directed the Justice Department to locate internees, pay each $15,000.00 and $15 for each day of incarceration.[13]

On July 31, 1980, the bill was passed that established the commission.[14] The commission heard testimony for twenty days and issued a report, *Personal Justice Denied*.[15] On February 24, 1983 the commission recommended to Congress the following:

1. Passage of a joint resolution recognizing the injustice and offering an apology;
2. A presidential pardon of persons convicted of violating curfews and refusing to obey discriminatory orders;
3. Insure that federal agencies review applications of Japanese Americans for restitution of positions that were lost between December 1941 and 1945;
4. Establish a foundation to sponsor research and educational activities related to the incarceration;
5. Appropriate $1.5 billion to provide compensatory payments of $20,000.00 to each surviving victim and to fund the research.[16]

---

13   Nash, p. 180. The bill was titled "World War II Japanese American Human Rights Violation Redress Act." H.R. 5977, 96th Cong., 1st Sess., 125 Cong. Rec. 33,966 (1979)

14   Commission on Wartime Relocation and Internment of Civilians Act, Pub. L. No. 96-317, 94 Stat. 964 (1980)

15   Nash, p. 181

16   Nash, p. 181. In the same year nineteen Japanese Americans filed suit in *Hohri v. United States*, 586 F. Supp. 769 (D.D.C. 1984), appeal docketed, No. 83-0750 (D.C. Cir. August 15, 1984). Judge Louis Opberdorfer dismissed the suit on grounds of statute of limitations. Earlier noteworthy legal challenges to these discriminatory and unfair conditions were lodged by Attorney Wayne Collins in the case of *Abo v. Clark*, 77 F. Supp. 806 (1948). Tadayasu Abo was born an American citizen in 1911. In 1940, he registered for the draft. In 1942, Abo and his family were relocated to a detention center. He was then told that he had been re-classified as "4C" or enemy alien. In 1943, the government created an all Japanese combat unit and required all men to swear

2. Legal Reforms

As Americans awakened to the nature of the pervasive injustices, incremental legal adjustments were developed. A major turning point was the creation of the Japanese American Citizens League in July, 1974 and its position on redress. A direct result of its political lobbying efforts was the decision by President Gerald Ford to rescind Executive Order 9066 on February 19, 1976. Following this event the JACL garnered support from other Asian elected officials, such as Senators Daniel Inouye and Spark Matsunaga, and Congressman Norman Mineta and Robert Matsui. This political involvement led to substantive changes in the law. On July 31, 1980, President Jimmy Carter signed into law the Commission on Wartime Relocation and Internment of Civilians (CWRIC) Act. Nine years later President Ronald Reagan signed into law the Civil Liberties Act of 1988. On September 27, 1989, the Senate approved an appropriation of $17.3 billion for the Departments of Commerce, Justice and State to be used to redress the wrongs committed against Japanese Americans and Aleutian Islanders. The latter group was added to provide redress to a group of people located primarily in Alaska. The Aleuts were removed from their home and placed in camps until 1944. After Japan bombed the Islands on June 3, 1942, the United States burned

---

"unqualified allegiance to the United States." Because of his bitterness, Abo answered "no" to the questions of loyalty. He was therefore transferred to Tule Lake Segregation Center. In December, 1944, Abo applied for denunciation of his citizenship. On August 26, 1945, he learned that his application had been granted. In the meantime the war had ended. Suddenly the 5,000 individuals, who had renounced their citizenship, tried to recant their denunciation on the grounds that they had been coerced and out of fear of reprisal. On September 27, 1948, a federal district court canceled the renunciations because they were obtained by duress and intimidation. On April 12, 1949, the court issued its final order. On January 17, 1951, the trial judge's order was partially reversed in *Abo v. McGrath* 186 F. 2nd 766 (1950). After the Department of Justice accepted Abo's affidavit explaining why he had denounced his citizenship, the District Court issued an order restoring his citizenship on February 7, 1957. The vast majority of the original plaintiffs received their citizenship back. (See Nash, p. 374)

the Aleut village on the island of Atka.[17] Once the Aleuts were returned, their homes had been destroyed and they received little support from the Federal Government. Although the inclusion of the Aleuts provision affected only 400 people, it helped get the bill through the Governmental Affairs Committee, which was chaired by Senator Stevens, a ranking member from Alaska. President Bush signed H.R. 2991 which established an entitlement program on November 21, 1989. On October 9, 1990, the first nine checks were issued to former internees. On September 27, 1992, President Bush signed H.R. 4551 which expanded the amount of coverage and those eligible to receive such payments.

B.

Legal Redress Due to Violations of International Law

1. <u>Nuremberg Trials</u>

What lesson can African-Americans learn from the Nuremberg trials? Are the principles from these trials only applicable for violations of international law during periods of declared war? To what extent can reparations be claimed and proven in this international forum?

The trials that resulted from the atrocities in Germany during World War II evolved in two parts. The International Military Tribunal (IMT), which completed its deliberations in 1946, was followed by the trials of twelve other defendants. The IMT was used to prosecute major war criminals. These trials were held from November 20, 1945 until October 1, 1946. Personnel serving in this court came from the United States, United Kingdom, France and the Soviet Union. The latter trials were conducted from 1946 to 1949 by American judges. A total of 177 individuals were placed on trial.

After the surrender of Germany on May 8, 1945, it was clear to the allies that the war criminals had to be punished. Agreements,

---

17   Leslie T. Hatamiya, *Righting a Wrong*, "Japanese Americans and the Passage of the Civil Liberties Act of 1988" (Stanford, Stanford University Press, 1993), p. 121.

such as that at Potsdam, guaranteed that the atrocities would be avenged. Control Council Law No. 10, adopted by the International Control Council, was based upon the IMT charter and formed the legal basis for the subsequent cases. Article II set forth the substantive provisions of the law which the defendants had been charged with violating. They were:[18]

1. "... Crimes against Peace. Initiation of invasions of other countries and wars of aggression in violation of international laws and treaties, including but not limited to, planning, preparation, initiation or waging a war of aggression, or a war of violation of international treaties, agreements or assurances, or participation in a common plan or conspiracy for the accomplishment of any of the foregoing.

2. "War Crimes. Atrocities or offenses against persons or property constituting violations of the laws or customs of war, including, but not limited to, murder, ill-treatment or deportation to slave labor or for any other purpose, of civilian population from occupied territory, murder or ill-treatment of prisoners of war or persons on the seas, killing of hostages, plunder of public or private property, wanton destruction of cities, towns or villages or devastation not justified by military necessity.

3. "Crimes against Humanity. Atrocities and offenses, including, but not limited to, murder, extermination, enslavement, deportation, imprisonment, torture, rape or other inhumane acts committed against any civilian population or persecutions on political, racial or religious grounds whether or not in violation of the domestic laws of the country where perpetrated..."

These legal pronouncements caused considerable discussion among legal scholars over whether Control Council Law No. 10 was an ex post facto law, or one that was passed after a specific event had occurred that would be applied retroactively. In other words, some legal scholars argued that one could not be tried for violating a law that did not exist at the time of the alleged infraction.

18   August Von Knieriem, *The Nuremberg Trials* (Chicago: Henry Regnery Company, 1959), pp. 4-5.

Other legal issues related to the question of whether the defendants should be punished under national law. Which national law should be applied? If the criminal act occurred in Argentina, the defendant was Brazilian and the victim Chilean, which law should apply?

Despite the imperfections of the legal proceedings, the world was resolute that it had to address the massive wrongs perpetrated upon the Jewish people. It would be morally wrong for the world not to punish those individuals responsible for the crimes against humanity. The rise of the Third Reich led to blatant racism and the attempted extermination of a people.

Racism formed the basis of the military assault upon the Jewish people. These anti-semitic views were manifested extensively in Adolf Hitler's *Mein Kampf.* When he came to power in 1933, his views became manifest through governmental institutions. Governmental power was therefore used to remove Jews from private jobs and prevent them from holding certain public jobs.[19] By 1935, the Jews had been totally segregated in public life, and were not allowed to join the German army. By 1938 Hitler had openly begun to speak of the extermination of Jews. Increasingly, laws were developed that were designed to take economic power away from them. They were forbidden to operate "...retail stores, mail order houses, goods or sales agencies..." Neither could they offer for sale goods or services. Any establishment that violated these ordinances would be shut down by the police. By the beginning of World War II Jews were subject to forced labor. The social and economic condition of the Jews continued to deteriorate, particularly when the Germans entered Austria. In Vienna, Eichmann began plans to forcibly emigrate the Jewish people. On July 4, 1939, a law was passed that required all Jews to be classified as belonging to the Reichsvereinigung. This new organization ran all Jewish schools, to which all Jews were allowed to attend. It provided all social welfare programs that was needed

---

19   Yitzhak Arad, Yisrael Gutman, Abraham Margaliot, *Documents on the Holocaust* "Selected Sources on the Destruction of the Jews of Germany, Austria, Poland, and the Soviet Union," (Oxford, Pergamon Press, 1981), p. 8.

for Jewish people. By October 23, 1941, the emigration of Jews was ordered stopped. They were then placed under the jurisdiction of the Gestapo and the SS.[20]

The occupation of Poland, beginning in September, 1939, marked a crucial turning point in the German assault against the Jewish people. It was here that the Germans engaged in a systematic policy of placing Jews in concentration and extermination camps. There was also a government policy of placing Jews in ghettoes and attempting to starve them by preventing foodstuff from entering. The extermination camp, however, represented the highest form of Hitler's racist violence. In 1941 one of the first camps was established at Chelmno and in 1942 at Auschwitz, Belzec, Treblinka and Sobibor.[21] At these camps the German policy took on the form of mass murders, as unsuspecting individuals were put to death in showers and gas chambers. Those who were not put to death could not freely leave the camps. If they did so without prior authorization, they could be put to death. Anyone who gave shelter to Jews could also be put to death. This Third Regulation for Restrictions of Residence in the Government-General, October 15, 1941, was similar to the Fugitive Slave Act of 1850, which made it a crime for anyone to aid a runaway slave.

Another obvious parallel between the Third Reich and the United States is the extent of hatred that was directed at the Jew and the Black. The hatred was irrational, not based upon objective realities. Chaim A. Kaplan describes the hatred he experienced in the Warsaw Ghetto on March 10, 1940:[22]

The gigantic catastrophe which has descended on Polish Jewry has no parallel, even in the darkest periods of Jewish history. Firstly, the depth of the hatred. This is not hatred whose source is some psychotic disease. In its outward manifestation it appears as physiological hatred, which sees the object of its hatred as tainted in body, as lepers who have no place in society.

---

20   Arad, p. 11.

21   Arad, p.170.

22   Arad, p. 201.

The masses have accepted this sort of objective hatred. Their limited understanding does not grasp ideological hatred; psychology is beyond them, and they are incapable of understanding it. They have absorbed their master's teaching in a concrete bodily form. The Jew is filthy; the Jew is a swindler and evil; the Jew is the enemy of Germany and undermines its existence; the Jew was the prime mover in the Versailles Treaty, which reduced Germany to a shambles; the Jew is Satan, who sows dissension between the nations, arousing them to bloodshed in order to profit from their destruction. These are easily understood concepts whose effect on day-to-day life can be felt immediately...

Starvation was another weapon employed in the camps. The numbers of deaths in the year 1941 were particularly revealing of the plan to starve the Jews to death:[23]

January	898
February	1,023
March	1,608
April	2,061
May	3,821
June	4,290
July	5,550
August	5,560

The total number of Jews in the Warsaw ghetto in 1941 was 480,000.

As with all oppressed people, a movement developed to oppose the brutal tactic of the Nazi. In January, 1943 the Jewish Fighting Organization in the Warsaw Ghetto issued the following call for resistance:

"...Today we must understand that the Nazi murderers have let us live only because they want to make use of our capacity to work to our last drop

23   Arad, p. 245.

of blood and sweat, to our last breath. We are slaves. And when the slaves are no longer profitable, they are killed. Everyone among us must understand that, and everyone among us must remember it always..."[24]

Another group called the Jewish Military Organization wrote in the same year:

"...We are rising up for war! We are of those who have set themselves the aim of awakening the people. Our wish is to take this watchword to our people: Awake and fight! Do not despair of the road to escape! Know that escape is not to be found by walking to your death passively, like sheep to the slaughter. It is to be found in something much greater: in war! Whoever defends himself has a chance of being saved! Whoever gives up self-defense from the outset, he has lost already! Nothing awaits him except only a hideous death in the suffocation-machine of Treblinka..

Let the people awaken to war! Find the courage in your soul for desperate action! Put an end to our terrible acceptance of such phrases as: We are all under the sentence of death! It is a lie!!! We also were destined to live! We too have a right to life! One only needs to know how to fight for it!..."[25]

The end result of these exhortations was that the people did rise up in revolt to the oppression that they experienced in the Warsaw ghetto. Many believed that they were being taken from one ghetto to another, when in reality they were being taken to death camps. Near the end, when only 40,000 remained alive in the ghetto, many decided to resist their deportation through violence.

---

24 Arad, p.302.

25 Arad, p. 303.

Some, as in the camp at Belzec, were not as lucky. Through deception many rode trains from their holding camps to their death. An SS engineer described the path to death for many Jews:[26]

> ...Next morning, a few minutes before 7 o'clock, I was told that the first train would arrive in 10 minutes. And in fact the first train from Lvov arrived a few minutes later. There were 45 carriages with 6,700 persons, of whom 1,450 were already dead on arrival. Through small openings closed with barbed wire one could see yellow, frightened children, men and women. The train stopped, and 200 Ukrainians, who were forced to perform this service, tore open the doors and chased the people through a large loud-speaker: The people are to take off all their clothes out of doors—and a few of them in the barracks—including artificial limbs and glasses. Shoes must be tied in pairs with a little piece of string handed out by a small fourteen year-old Jewish boy. All valuables and money are to be handed in at the window marked "Valuables," without any document or receipt being given. The women and girls must then go to the barber, who cuts off their hair with one or two snips. The hair disappears into large potato sacks, "to make something special for the submarines, to seal them and so on," the duty SS Unterscharfuhrer explained to me.
>
> Then the march starts: Barbed wire to the right and left and two dozen Ukrainians with rifles at the rear. They came on, led by an exceptionally pretty girl. I myself was standing with Police Captain Wirth in front of the death chambers. Men, women, children, infants, people with amputated legs, all naked, completely naked, moved past us. In one

---

26   Arad, p. 349-350.

corner there is a whimsical SS man who tells these poor people in an unctuous voice, "Nothing at all will happen to you. You must just breathe deeply, that strengthens the lungs; this inhalation is necessary because of the infectious diseases, it is good disinfection!" When somebody asks what their fate will be, he explains that the men will of course have to work, building streets and houses. But the women will not have to work. If they want to, they can help in the house or the kitchen. A little glimmer of hope flickers once more in some of these poor people, enough to make them march unresisting into the death chambers. But most of them understand what is happening; the smell reveals their fate! Then they climb up a little staircase and see the truth. Nursing mothers with an infant at the breast, naked; many children of all ages, naked. They hesitate, but they enter the death chambers, most of them silent, forced on by those behind them, who are driven by the whip lashes of the SS men. A Jewish woman of about 40, with flaming eyes, calls down (revenge) for the blood of her children on the head of the murderers. Police Captain Wirth in person strikes her in the face 5 times with his whip, and she disappears into the gas chamber...

Similar acts of violence and murder were perpetrated against the Jews in Russia as well.

World War brought to an end this sad chapter in European history. The price of this war was staggering, both in human and monetary terms. The destruction of Europe, particularly France, was extensive. What would be the response of the United States? Should it get involved in rebuilding Europe? Was there a moral or legal obligation for this country to get involved in rebuilding Europe?

2. The Marshall Plan

At the close of the war European nations had to take inventory of their human losses. They were staggering. Russia lost close to 20 million, Poland 4.3 million, Yugoslavia 1.7 million, Japan 1.2 million, France 600,000, Italy 410,000, America 400,000 and Britain 390,000. In addition, approximately six million Jews were killed.[27] Although the loss was pervasive, the four major powers realized that Germany had to be rebuilt. Britain was in no financial shape to contribute, the French were reluctant and the Russians had hoped to get $10 billion dollars in reparations from Germany. The United States had worries about the conflict between Greece and Turkey and the possible spread of communism in that region.

The key concern of the western world, however, was to resurrect the economy of Germany. The survival of its economy was viewed as essential to the survival of the European economy. The United States, of course, had a vested interest in the revival of the European economy. The framework of the American plan was presented by Secretary of State George C. Marshall at a Harvard University Commencement Address on June 5, 1947:

> I need not tell you gentlemen that the world situation is very serious. That must be apparent to all intelligent people. I think one difficulty is that the problem is one of such enormous complexity that the very mass of facts presented to the public by press and radio make it exceedingly difficult for the man in the street to reach a clear appraisement of the situation. Furthermore, the people of this country are distant from the troubled areas of the earth and it is hard for them to comprehend the plight and consequent reactions of the long-suffering peoples, and the effect of those reactions on their governments in connection with our efforts to promote peace in the world.

27   Charles L. Mee, Jr. *The Marshall Plan* "The Launching of the Pax Americana" (New York: Simon and Schuster, 1984), p.17.

In considering the requirements for the rehabilitation of Europe, the physical loss of life, the visible destruction of cities, factories, mines, and railroads was correctly estimated, but it has become obvious during recent months that this visible destruction was probably less serious than the dislocation of the entire fabric of European economy. For the past 10 years conditions have been highly abnormal. The feverish preparation for war and the more feverish maintenance of the war effort engulfed all aspects of national economies. Machinery has fallen into disrepair or is entirely obsolete. Under the arbitrary and destructive Nazi rule, virtually every possible enterprise was geared into the German war machine... The breakdown of the business structure of Europe during the war was complete...

There is a phase of this matter which is both interesting and serious. The farmer has always produced the foodstuffs to exchange with the city dweller for the other necessities of life. This division of labor is the basis of modern civilization. At the present time it is threatened with breakdown... So the governments are forced to use their foreign money and credits to procure these necessities abroad. This process exhausts funds which are urgently needed for reconstruction...

The truth of the matter is that Europe's requirements for the next three or four years of foreign food and other essential products, principally from America, are so much greater than her present ability to pay that she must have substantial additional help or face economic, social, and political deterioration of a very grave character...

Aside from the demoralizing effect on the world at large and the possibilities of disturbances arising as a result of the desperation of the people concerned, the consequences to the economy of the United States should be apparent to all. Our policy is directed not against any country or doctrine but against hunger, poverty, desperation, and chaos. Its purpose should be the revival of a working economy in the world so as to permit the emergence of political and social conditions in which free institutions can exist...

It is already evident that, before the United States Government can proceed much further in its efforts to alleviate the situation and help start the European world on its way to recovery, there must be some agreement among the countries of Europe as to the requirements of the situation and the part those countries themselves will take in order to give proper effect to whatever action might be undertaken by this Government. It would be neither fitting nor efficacious for this Government to undertake to draw up unilaterally a program designed to place Europe on its feet economically... The initiative, I think, must come from Europe...

An essential part of any successful action on the part of the United States is an understanding on the part of the people of America of the character of the problem and the remedies to be applied. Political passion and prejudice should have no part. With foresight, and a willingness on the part of our people to face up to the vast responsibility which history has clearly placed upon our country, the difficulties I have outlined can and will be overcome.

The formal plan that was ultimately presented to Congress was the European Recovery Program. The program was termed a plan to fight communism, to revive the economy of Europe and to preserve American economic interests. The administration was seeking authorization of $17 billion to be spent over four years. After a difficult fight, the legislation was passed.

The impact of the aid to Europe was immediate. Steel factories in Lisle, France were kept open. The world's largest textile mills were kept open in Rabbis. French harbors were restored within two years: 70% of the harbors had been destroyed during the war.[28] The total amount of money contributed to the recovery of Europe was $13,015,000,000.[29] Some scholars have argued that this expenditure of tax payer funds reduced the amounts in reparations that Germany would have had to pay to France, Great Britain and Russia.[30] From 1945-1949, Germany had been occupied by the United States, Soviet Union, Britain and France. Each of these nations had differing ideas about how Germany would pay for the tremendous cost of the war.

3. Restitution as Reparations

An essential part of the bargaining process that went on among the Allies after the end of the war was restitution. It was clear to all parties that Germany would not be able to walk away without paying for the tremendous damage it had inflicted upon the economies of Europe. France, for example, wanted full restitution for items taken from France during the occupation.[31] The Allied Commission on Reparations was charged with setting policy for the removal of plants and equipment not necessary to maintain a peace economy in Germany. The end result of all of the activity was to focus the energies of the major European industrial economies and the United States upon the issues of restitution and reparation.

---

28   Mee, p. 252.

29   Mee, p. 258.

30   John Gamble, *The Origins of the Marshall Plan* (Stanford, Stanford University Press, 1976), p. 5.

31   Gamble, p. 61.

C.
Legal Redress Due to Destruction
of African-American Property and Lives

Throughout their history in the United States, Blacks have been subjected to destruction of both their lives and property. This destruction originated in slavery and manifests itself in the present day. Unlike the other governmental programs designed to remedy the effects of past wrongs, a systematic effort has never been developed, specifically to remedy wrongs to Blacks, with the exception of the Freedmen's Bureau in the nineteenth century. Is the present condition of Blacks a consequence of slavery and overt discrimination? If so, should there be a remedy for such wrongs? What should be the nature of this remedy? Is affirmative action a remedy or should a more massive effort be required? Dr. Robert S. Brown, director of the Black Economic Resource Center, wrote in 1974 that "a massive capital transfer of a sizeable chunk of America's wealth to the black community" is required.[32] Is it realistic to think of reparations as a transfer of capital? As a minimum, should the government recognize the legacy of injustice and develop a comprehensive rationale as a justification for remedial programs?

The first step is to recognize and admit the legacy of discrimination and violence perpetrated against Black people. Some states have begun this process and the result has been mixed. In the case of Tulsa, Oklahoma there has been recognition, but no compensation. In Rosewood, Florida the Black victims received compensation.

1. The Tulsa Race Riots

On June 1, 1921, a race riot erupted in Tulsa, Oklahoma that led to as many as 300 Black deaths and a total destruction of Black Greenwood section of the city. A total of 40 city blocks were looted

---

32   William Darity, Jr. "Forty Acres and a Mule: Placing a Price Tag on Oppression," Richard F. America, Editor, *The Wealth of Races* "The Present Value of Benefits for Past Injustices" (New York, Greenwood Press, 1990), p. 3.

and destroyed by fire. A total of 23 churches and 1000 homes were destroyed by whites.[33]

Despite a service at Mount Zion Baptist Church on June 1, 1996, a monument raised by the city, no compensation was ever offered to the victims of this violence. One of the survivors, LaVerne Davis stated: "I wouldn't say it's too late, but it shouldn't have taken this long. You're not suppose to cover up history. The only way you're going to know history is to talk about it."[34]

The Tulsa 1921 Race Riot Commission recommended to the Oklahoma Legislature in February, 2000 that it pay reparations to 80 survivors, amounting to as much as $33 million. To date, nothing has been done to implement the report.

2. Elaine Race Riot of 1919

In Elaine, Arkansas a February, 2000 conference on its race riot of 1919, where hundreds of Blacks were killed, brought the matter to the public for the first time. The riot occurred on the night of September 30, 1919 when black sharecroppers gathered for a union meeting and a gun fight broke out between two deputies and the Blacks. Soon white vigilantes joined the fight which resulted in from 80-800 Blacks being killed. The conference went on without incident, and no initiatives to seek reparations materialized.

3. The Rosewood Violence and Massacre

Approximately two years after the racist violence in Tulsa, a similar riot occurred in Rosewood, Florida. This riot started as a result of a similar incident. On June 1, 1923, Fannie Taylor, a white woman in the Town of Sumner stated that she had been assaulted by a Black man. She claimed that the man broke into her house while her husband was away at work. Many Blacks believed that her story was fabricated to cover up a relationship Ms. Taylor was having with a white lover. Sarrah Carrier, a Black maid to Ms. Taylor stated that she was present at the Taylor house, washing clothing with her

---

33   *New York Times*, "75 Years Later, Tulsa Confronts Its Race Riot," May 31, 1996.

34   Ibid.

granddaughter, Philomena. Both of these women indicated that a white man, who was not Ms. Taylor's husband, entered the house through the rear door and had visited the house frequently in the past. The two heard Ms. Taylor and the man arguing. Philomena stated that shortly after the man left, Ms. Taylor ran out of the house yelling that a Black man had assaulted her.

As a result of the allegations, a white mob killed eight Blacks and burned the Black hamlet to the ground. The mob first tortured Sam Carter, by hanging him from a tree. When he refused to confess as to who had assaulted Ms. Taylor; he was shot once in the head. Another person singled out for mob violence was Sylvester Carrier, who was a proud man who refused to give whites the deference many felt they deserved from Blacks. Three nights after the alleged assault, the mob arrived at the Carrier house. They shot his barking dog. Sylvester's mother, Sarah, went to a window and asked the men to leave. One of the men shot her in the head. Sylvester waited downstairs with his shotgun. One of the men, Polly Wilkerson, kicked open the front door, and stepped into the house. Sylvester shot him. Henry Andrews entered the house and was shot as well. The men then retreated to the woods and continued to fire at the house. Later that night Sylvester's sisters escaped into the woods. He remained in the house and was killed the next day.

Governmental officials did nothing to stop the violence. Cary Hardee, Governor of Florida was aware of the violence, but did nothing. He was in contact with county sheriff Robert Walker, but he did not intercede by sending in the National Guard.

Many Blacks fled to the woods where they had to sleep in the cold until some sympathetic whites helped them escape. These individuals managed to arrange for a train to stop in the woods for a quick pick up. The train arrived at midnight and took the Blacks to Gainesville. By the end of the week approximately 150 white men burned the entire town to the ground. The grand jury failed to indict anyone for the violence.

After seventy years of silence, the State of Florida eventually admitted that a wrong had been perpetrated. A journalist, Gary Moore, brought the story to light. While on the staff of the St.

Petersburg Times, he was asked to go to Gulf Hammock and write a story about the area. When he arrived, he realized that no Blacks lived there. He was told by an old lady about the massacre, and he began to research the issue. He contacted twenty witnesses. In 1991, a movie producer, Michael O' McCarthy bought the rights to the life stories of Lee Ruth Davis and Minnie Langley. He was also able to get Stephen Hanlon of the firm of Holland and Knight to take on the case pro-bono. The case that was developed was modeled upon the Japanese internment cases.[35]

Attorney Hanlon approached the state legislature for redress. The Speaker of Florida's House commissioned five historians to study the issues. Once the report was in, the court authorized the appointment of a special master. After considering the report and hearing from survivors, the House passed legislation granting reparations. Wilson Hall, one of the survivors of the riot, stated "We was drove off like dogs." He was speaking about being driven into the swamps. Mr. Hall had to abandon his two story house and eighty acres of land.

When the issue of the massacre came before the state legislature, many legislators were unsure of what to do for the surviving victims. Should today's taxpayers be responsible for the acts of individuals in 1923? Some feared that the precedent would cause other victims of lynching to bring similar claims. Still others felt that a park should be erected. After six days of hearings before a special master, a bill was passed which granted each survivor $150,000.00. The vote was 71 in favor, 40 against. The bill was based upon a recommendation from Special Master Richard Hixson, who heard testimony from survivors and descendants of victims. He wrote: "A moral obligation exists to redress their injuries." A $7 million dollar trust fund was to be established for 11 survivors and 45 descendants.[36] This Florida Act is a first step in recognizing past racial wrongs.

---

35   Much of this information was abstracted from a report issued by the Hearst Corporation 1994, Electronic Collection: A15467090.

36   *The Legal Intelligencer*, March 23, 1994.

<u>The Legal Response</u>

From the first day that Blacks arrived in this country, they suffered physical and mental assault by some whites and governmental institutions. Florida is one of the first states to respond to the violence within its borders. Thousands of Blacks have been lynched throughout the South and in some Northern states as well. Reparations as a legal response to this violence may provide a remedy for many of these individual acts.

CHAPTER 94-359

"An act relating to Rosewood, Florida; directing the Florida Department of Law Enforcement to conduct investigations; requiring a report to the Legislature; appropriating funds to compensate Rosewood families for property damage; appropriating funds to compensate former students, including Arnett T. Goins, Minnie L. Langley, Willie Evans, and Wilson Hall; providing for the establishment of a state university scholarship fund for Rosewood families; continue the Rosewood research and development of materials; providing an effective date.

"WHEREAS, during the month of January 1923, the African-American community of Rosewood, Florida, was destroyed, and

"WHEREAS, the African-American residents of Rosewood, Florida, sustained personal and property damages, and

"WHEREAS, The Rosewood Massacre was a unique tragedy in Florida's history in that the State and local government officials were on notice of the serious racial conflict in Rosewood during the entire week of January 1, 1923, and had sufficient time and opportunity to act to prevent the tragedy, and nonetheless failed to act to prevent the tragedy; an entire town was destroyed and its residents killed or fled, never to return; and the State and local government officials thereafter failed to reasonably investigate the matter, failed to bring the perpetrators to justice and failed to secure the area for the safe return of the displaced residents; and

"WHEREAS, a hearing was held by the Special Master of the House of Representatives, and Arnett T. Goins, Minnie Lee Langley, Willie Evans, and Wilson Hall have shown by a preponderance of the evidence that they were present and directly affected by the violence that took place at Rosewood in January, 1923, and that they each suffered compensable damages of at least $150,000.

"WHEREAS, the State of Florida recognizes an equitable obligation to redress the injuries sustained as a result of the destruction of Rosewood, Florida,

"NOW, THEREFORE,

"Be It Enacted by the Legislature of the State of Florida:

"Section 1. The facts stated in the preamble of this act are found and declared to be true.

"Section 2. The Florida Department of Law Enforcement is hereby directed to investigate the crimes committed in and around Rosewood, Florida, in 1923, to determine if any criminal prosecutions may be pursued, and to report its findings to the Legislature.

"Section 3. The amount of $500,000 is appropriated from the General Revenue Fund to the Office of the Attorney General for the purpose of compensating the African-American families of Rosewood, Florida, who demonstrate real property and personal property damages sustained as a result of the destruction of Rosewood, Florida in 1923. The Attorney General is authorized to compensate each eligible family in the amount of $20,000 and, upon a finding by the Attorney General that the present-day value of real and personal property loss exceeds $20,000; the Attorney General may settle such property claims up to the amount of $100,000.

"Section 4. Any African-American resident from Rosewood, Florida, living upon the effective date of this act, who was present and affected by the violence that took place at Rosewood in January, 1923, and was evacuated the week of January 1, 1923, shall be eligible for a payment of compensation from the State of Florida of up to $150,000. The Attorney General shall identify and locate eligible individuals by using records already in possession of the State of Florida and by giving notice in the newspaper as provided in Chapter 50. The identification and location of all eligible individuals shall be completed within 6 months of the effective date of this act or December 31, 1994, whichever is later. Failure to be identified and located by the end of the designated time period shall preclude an eligible individual from receiving payment under this section. The individual seeking compensation must provide the Attorney General with reasonable proof of eligibility and the extent of their damages. Upon receipt of reasonable proof of the individual's eligibility and extent of damages, the Attorney General shall notify the Comptroller of the individual's name, eligibility, and amount of compensation not to exceed $150,000. There is hereby appropriated $1.5 million from the General Revenue Fund to implement this section. If funds are insufficient to provide maximum compensation to each eligible individual the comptroller may pro-rate available funds and make a partial award to each eligible individual. Any unused appropriations in this section shall revert to the Working Capital Fund.

"Section 5. (1) There is created a Rosewood Family Scholarship Fund for minority persons with preference given to the direct descendants of the Rosewood families, not to exceed 25 scholarships per year.

" (2) The Rosewood Family Scholarship Fund shall be administered by the Department of Education. The State Board of Education shall adopt rules for administering this program which shall at a minimum provide for the following:

" (a) The annual award to a student shall be up to $4,000 but should not exceed an amount in excess of tuition and registration fees.

" (b) If funds are insufficient to provide a full scholarship to each eligible applicant, the department may prorate available funds and make a partial award to each eligible applicant.

" (c) The department shall rank eligible initial applicants for the purposes of awarding scholarships with preference being given to the direct descendants of the Rosewood families. The remaining applicants shall be ranked based on need as determined by the Department of Education.

" (d) Payment of an award shall be transmitted in advance of the registration period each semester on behalf of the student to the president of the university or community college, or his representative, or to the director of the area vocational-technical school which the recipient is attending.

" (3) Beginning with the 1994-95 academic year, the department is authorized to make awards for undergraduate study to students who:

" (a) Meets the general requirements for students eligibility as provided in s.240.404, except as otherwise provided in this section;

" (b) Files an application for the scholarship within the established time limits;

" (c) Enrolls as a certificate-seeking or degree-seeking student at a public university, community college or area vocational-technical school authorized by law.

"Section 6. The state university system shall continue the research of the Rosewood incident and the history of race relations in Florida and develop materials for the educational instruction of these events."

"Section 7. This act shall take effect upon becoming a law.

Approved by the Governor May 4, 1994

Filed in Office Secretary of State May 4, 1994"

4. Reparations and Public Policy

Should the United States Congress establish a commission to study the extent to which Blacks have been systematically murdered, raped and maimed for no other reason than the color of their skin and their condition of servitude? The history is replete with evidence of discrimination and deprivation. Frederick Douglass left literary evidence of the brutality of slavery. His description of the murder of Demby provides some evidence of these atrocities:(57) [37]

"...His savage barbarity was equalled only by the consummate coolness with which he committed the grossest and most savage deed upon the slaves under his charge. Mr. Gore once undertook to whip one of Colonel Lloyd's slaves, by the name of Demby. He had given Demby but few stripes, when, to get rid of scourging, he ran and plunged himself into a creek, and stood there at the depth of his shoulders, refusing to come out. Mr. Gore told him that he would give him three calls, and that, if he did not come out at the third call, he would shoot him. The first call was given. Demby made no response, but stood his ground. The second and third calls were given with the same result. Mr. Gore then, without consultation or deliberation with any one, not even giving Demby an additional call, raised his musket to his face, taking deadly aim at his standing victim, and in an instant poor Demby was no more. His mangled body sank out of sight, and blood and brains marked the water where he had stood..."

---

37   Frederick Douglass, *Narrative of the Life of Frederick Douglass: An American Slave* (Cambridge, Belknap Press, 1960), p. 47.

5. The Legislative Response

The concept of reparations in American public policy has a long history. The first major initiative developed at the end of the Civil War through the 1867 Slave Reparations Bill introduced by Congressman Thaddeus Stevens.

REPARATIONS BILL FOR THE AFRICAN SLAVES IN THE UNITED STATES THE FIRST SESSION FORTIETH CONGRESS March 11, 1867 Thaddeus Stevens of Pennsylvania H.R. 29 Whereas it is due to justice, as an example to future times, that some future punishment should be inflicted on the people who constituted the "confederate States of America," both because they, declaring an unjust war against the United States for the purpose of destroying republican liberty and permanently establishing slavery, as well as, for the cruel and barbarous manner in which they conducted said war, in violation of all the laws of civilized warfare, and also to compel them to make some compensation for the damages and expenditures caused by the said war: Therefore, Be it enacted by the Senate and House of Representatives of the United States of America in Congress assembled. That all the public lands belonging to the ten States that formed the government of the so-called confederate States of America shall be forfeited by said States and become forthwith vested in the United States. SEC. 2. And be it further enacted. That the President shall forthwith proceed to cause the seizure of such of the property belonging to the belligerent enemy as is deemed forfeited by the act of July 17, A. D. 1862, and hold and appropriate the same as enemy's property, and to proceed to condemnation with that already seized. SEC. 3. And be it further enacted, that in lieu of the proceeding to condemn the property thus seized enemy's property as is provided by the act of July A. D. 1862, two commissions or more, as by him may be deemed necessary. shall be appointed by the President for each of the said "confederate states," to consist of three persons each, one of whom shall be an officer of the late or present Army, and two shall be civilians, neither of whom shall be citizens of the State for which he shall be appointed; that the said commissions shall proceed

adjudicate and condemn the property foresaid, under such forms
and proceedings it shall be prescribed by the Attorney General of
the United States, whereupon the title to said property shall become
vested in the United States. SEC. 4. And be it further enacted. That
out of the lands thus seized and confiscated the slaves who have
been liberated by the operations of the war and the amendment
to the constitution or otherwise, who resided in said "confederate
States" on the 4th day of March, A. D. 1861, or since, shall have
distributed to them as follows, namely: to each male person who
is the head of a family, forty acres; to each adult male, whether the
head of a family or not, forty acres, to each widow who is the head
of a family, forty acres-to be held by them in fee-simple, but to be
inalienable for the next ten years after they become seized thereof.
For the purpose of distributing and allotting said land the Secretary
of War shall appoint as many commissions in each State as he shall
deem necessary, to consist of three members each, two of whom
at least shall not be citizens of the State for which he is appointed.
Each of said commissioners shall receive a salary of $3,000
annually and all his necessary expenses. Each commission shall be
allowed one clerk, whose salary shall be $2,000 per annum. The
title to the homestead aforesaid shall be vested in trustees for the
use of the liberated persons aforesaid. Trustees shall be appointed
by the Secretary of War, and shall receive such salary as he shall
direct, not exceeding $3,000 per annum. At the end of ten years the,
absolute title to said homesteads shall be conveyed to said owners
or to the heirs of such as are then dead. SEC. 5. And be it further
enacted, That out of the balance of the property thus seized and
confiscated there shall be raised, in the manner hereinafter provided,
a sum equal to fifty dollars, for each homestead, to be applied by
the trustees hereinafter mentioned toward the erection of buildings
on the said homesteads for the use of said slaves; and the further
sum of $500,000,000, which shall be appropriated as follows, to
wit: $200,000,000 shall be invested in United States six per cent,
securities; and the interest thereof shall be semi-annually added
to the pensions allowed by law to pensioners who have become
so by reason of the late war; $300,000,000, or so much thereof as

may be needed, shall be appropriated to pay damages done to loyal citizens by the civil or military operations of the government lately called the "confederate States of America."

6. Rep. John Conyers Bill- HR 40

The attempt to establish a public policy response to slavery, segregation and discrimination continued into the twentieth century. As in 1867, the initiative developed out of the House of Representatives, but this time through an African-American legislator who filed a thoughtful reparations bill in 1989, and every year thereafter.

105th CONGRESS

1st Session

H. R. 40

IN THE HOUSE OF REPRESENTATIVES

January 7, 1997

Mr. CONYERS (for himself, Mr. FATTAH, Mr. FOGLIETTA, Mr. HASTINGS of Florida, Mr. HILLIARD, Mr. JEFFERSON, Ms. EDDIE BERNICE JOHNSON of Texas, Mrs. MEEK of Florida, Mr. OWENS, Mr. RUSH, and Mr. TOWNS) introduced the following bill; which was referred to the Committee on the Judiciary

A BILL

To acknowledge the fundamental injustice, cruelty, brutality, and inhumanity of slavery in the United States and the 13 American colonies between 1619 and 1865 and to establish a commission to examine the institution of slavery, subsequently de jure and de facto racial and economic discrimination against African-Americans, and the impact of these forces on living African-Americans, to make recommendations to the Congress on appropriate remedies, and for other purposes.

Be it enacted by the Senate and House of Representatives of the United States of America in Congress assembled,

SECTION 1. SHORT TITLE.
This Act may be cited as the 'Commission to Study Reparation Proposals for African-Americans Act'.

SEC. 2. FINDINGS AND PURPOSE.
(a) FINDINGS- The Congress finds that—
(1) approximately 4,000,000 Africans and their descendants were enslaved in the United States and the colonies that became the United States from 1619 to 1865;
(2) the institution of slavery was constitutionally and statutorily sanctioned by the Government of the United States from 1789 through 1865;
(3) the slavery that flourished in the United States constituted an immoral and inhumane deprivation of Africans' life, liberty, African citizenship rights, and cultural heritage, and denied them the fruits of their own labor; and
(4) sufficient inquiry has not been made into the effects of the institution of slavery on living African-Americans and society in the United States.

(b) PURPOSE- The purpose of this Act is to establish a commission to—
(1) examine the institution of slavery which existed from 1619 through 1865 within the United States and the colonies that became the United States, including the extent to which the Federal and State Governments constitutionally and statutorily supported the institution of slavery;
(2) examine de jure and de facto discrimination against freed slaves and their descendants from the end of the Civil War to the present, including economic, political, and social discrimination;

(3) examine the lingering negative effects of the institution of slavery and the discrimination described in paragraph (2) on living African-Americans and on society in the United States;

(4) recommend appropriate ways to educate the American public of the Commission's findings;

(5) recommend appropriate remedies in consideration of the Commission's findings on the matters described in paragraphs (1) and (2); and

(6) submit to the Congress the results of such examination, together with such recommendations.

SEC. 3. ESTABLISHMENT AND DUTIES.

(a) ESTABLISHMENT- There is established the Commission to Study Reparation Proposals for African Americans (hereinafter in this Act referred to as the `Commission').

(b) DUTIES- The Commission shall perform the following duties:

(1) Examine the institution of slavery which existed within the United States and the colonies that became the United States from 1619 through 1865. The Commission's examination shall include an examination of:

(A) the capture and procurement of Africans;

(B) the transport of Africans to the United States and the colonies that became the United States for the purpose of enslavement, including their treatment during transport;

(C) the sale and acquisition of Africans as chattel property in interstate and intrastate commerce; and

(D) the treatment of African slaves in the colonies and the United States, including the deprivation of their freedom, exploitation of their labor, and destruction of their culture, language, religion, and families.

(2) Examine the extent to which the Federal and State governments of the United States supported the institution of slavery in constitutional and statutory provisions, including the extent to which such governments prevented, opposed, or restricted efforts

of freed African slaves to repatriate to their home land.

(3) Examine Federal and State laws that discriminated against freed African slaves and their descendants during the period between the end of the Civil War and the present.

(4) Examine other forms of discrimination in the public and private sectors against freed African slaves and their descendants during the period between the end of the Civil War and the present.

(5) Examine the lingering negative effects of the institution of slavery and the matters described in paragraphs (1), (2), (3), and (4) on living African-Americans and on society in the United States.

(6) Recommend appropriate ways to educate the American public of the Commission's findings.

(7) Recommend appropriate remedies in consideration of the Commission's findings on the matters described in paragraphs (1), (2), (3), and (4). In making such recommendations, the Commission shall address, among other issues, the following questions:

(A) Whether the Government of the United States should offer a formal apology on behalf of the people of the United States for the perpetration of gross human rights violations on African slaves and their descendants.

(B) Whether African-Americans still suffer from the lingering affects of the matters described in paragraphs (1), (2), (3), and (4).

(C) Whether, in consideration of the Commission's findings, any form of compensation to the descendants of African slaves is warranted.

(D) If the Commission finds that such compensation is warranted, what should be the amount of compensation, what form of compensation should be awarded, and who should be eligible for such compensation.

(c) REPORT TO CONGRESS- The Commission shall submit a written report of its findings and recommendations to the Congress not later than the date which is one year after the date of the first meeting of the Commission held pursuant to section 4(c).

SEC. 4. MEMBERSHIP.

(a) NUMBER AND APPOINTMENT- (1) The Commission shall be composed of 7 members, who shall be appointed, within 90 days after the date of enactment of this Act, as follows:

(A) Three members shall be appointed by the President.

(B) Three members shall be appointed by the Speaker of the House of Representatives.

(C) One member shall be appointed by the President pro tempore of the Senate.

(2) All members of the Commission shall be persons who are especially qualified to serve on the Commission by virtue of their education, training, or experience, particularly in the field of African-American studies.

(b) TERMS- The term of office for members shall be for the life of the Commission. A vacancy in the Commission shall not affect the powers of the Commission, and shall be filled in the same manner in which the original appointment was made.

(c) FIRST MEETING- The President shall call the first meeting of the Commission within 120 days after the date of the enactment of this Act, or within 30 days after the date on which legislation is enacted making appropriations to carry out this Act, whichever date is later.

(d) QUORUM- Four members of the Commission shall constitute a quorum, but a lesser number may hold hearings.

(e) CHAIR AND VICE CHAIR- The Commission shall elect a Chair and Vice Chair from among its members. The term of office of each shall be for the life of the Commission.

(f) COMPENSATION- (1) Except as provided in paragraph (2), each member of the Commission shall receive compensation at the daily equivalent of the annual rate of basic pay payable for GS-18 of the General Schedule under section 5332 of title 5, United

States Code, for each day, including travel time, during which he or she is engaged in the actual performance of duties vested in the Commission.

(2) A member of the Commission who is a full-time officer or employee of the United States or a Member of Congress shall receive no additional pay, allowances, or benefits by reason of his or her service on the Commission.

(3) All members of the Commission shall be reimbursed for travel, subsistence, and other necessary expenses incurred by them in the performance of their duties to the extent authorized by chapter 57 of title 5, United States Code.

SEC. 5. POWERS OF THE COMMISSION.

(a) HEARINGS AND SESSIONS- The Commission may, for the purpose of carrying out the provisions of this Act, hold such hearings and sit and act at such times and at such places in the United States, and request the attendance and testimony of such witnesses and the production of such books, records, correspondence, memoranda, papers, and documents, as the Commission considers appropriate. The Commission may request the Attorney General to invoke the aid of an appropriate United States district court to require, by subpoena or otherwise, such attendance, testimony, or production.

(b) POWERS OF SUBCOMMITTEES AND MEMBERS- Any subcommittee or member of the Commission may, if authorized by the Commission, take any action which the Commission is authorized to take by this section.

(c) OBTAINING OFFICIAL DATA- The Commission may acquire directly from the head of any department, agency, or instrumentality of the executive branch of the Government, available information which the Commission considers useful in the discharge of its duties. All departments, agencies, and instrumentalities of the executive branch of the Government shall cooperate with the Commission with respect to such information and shall furnish all information requested by the Commission to the extent permitted by law.

SEC. 6. ADMINISTRATIVE PROVISIONS.

(a) STAFF- The Commission may, without regard to section 5311(b) of title 5, United States Code, appoint and fix the compensation of such personnel as the Commission considers appropriate.

(b) APPLICABILITY OF CERTAIN CIVIL SERVICE LAWS- The staff of the Commission may be appointed without regard to the provisions of title 5, United States Code, governing appointments in the competitive service, and without regard to the provisions of chapter 51 and subchapter III of chapter 53 of such title relating to classification and General Schedule pay rates, except that the compensation of any employee of the Commission may not exceed a rate equal to the annual rate of basic pay payable for GS-18 of the General Schedule under section 5332 of title 5, United States Code.

(c) EXPERTS AND CONSULTANTS- The Commission may procure the services of experts and consultants in accordance with the provisions of section 3109(b) of title 5, United States Code, but at rates for individuals not to exceed the daily equivalent of the highest rate payable under section 5332 of such title.

(d) ADMINISTRATIVE SUPPORT SERVICES- The Commission may enter into agreements with the Administrator of General Services for procurement of financial and administrative services necessary for the discharge of the duties of the Commission. Payment for such services shall be made by reimbursement from funds of the Commission in such amounts as may be agreed upon by the Chairman of the Commission and the Administrator.

(e) CONTRACTS- The Commission may—
(1) procure supplies, services, and property by contract in accordance with applicable laws and regulations and to the extent or in such amounts as are provided in appropriations Acts; and
(2) enter into contracts with departments, agencies, and instrumentalities of the Federal Government, State agencies, and

private firms, institutions, and agencies, for the conduct of research or surveys, the preparation of reports, and other activities necessary for the discharge of the duties of the Commission, to the extent or in such amounts as are provided in appropriations Acts.

SEC. 7. TERMINATION.

The Commission shall terminate 90 days after the date on which the Commission submits its report to the Congress under section 3(c).

SEC. 8. AUTHORIZATION OF APPROPRIATIONS.

To carry out the provisions of this Act, there are authorized to be appropriated $8,000,000.
END

► Notes & Questions

1. Would money be enough compensation for an entire race of people? Perhaps the key to an appropriate legal redress of these historical wrongs against Blacks would be an apology and admission on the part of Congress and the Presidency. This admission could form the legal justification for the continued development and implementation of remedial programs, such as affirmative action.

2. As with Rosewood, questions of eligibility and authenticity of records would have to be addressed. Would Blacks who pass for white be eligible? How would the government determine if some whites with Blacks in their lineage are eligible?

3. What about those Blacks who betrayed their own people and worked in conjunction with the slavers? What about the Black slaver? Should they be excluded from any remedial programs?

4. Some Blacks have achieved substantial wealth and power in America. Should remedial programs be strictly based upon one's racial and class status? Should individuals such as Colin Powell, Michael Jordan, and Bill Cosby be eligible for remedial programs? Despite the impediments of the past, these individuals have achieved beyond most Americans of any race. Have middle class Blacks suffered from segregation and discrimination, despite their economic status?

5. Would remedial programs have an effect upon racism in our society? Would they cause more racial division among the American population?

▶ Notes & Questions

6. Would these programs be fair to poor and working class whites who claim that they and their ancestors played no role in slavery, and its subsequent segregation and discrimination? Would remedial programs cause white backlash?

7. Should repatriation to Africa be raised as an option for Blacks? The Nation of Islam for the past 70 years has called for land, tax relief and other forms of reparations from the United States. Shouldn't the issue of land be at the top of the agenda? Isn't national sovereignty one of the major problems facing African-Americans?

8. Professor Charles Ogletree, Co-Chair of The Reparations Coordinating Committee, wrote the following in *The New York Times* (3/31/02): "The legacy of slavery and racial discrimination in America is seen in well-documented racial disparities in access to education, health care, housing, insurance, employment and other social goods."

   Should the remedial focus of the reparations initiative be upon provision of social services, rather than upon monetary compensation?

9. On May 4, 1969, activist James Forman brought the reparations issue before one of New York's largest, white congregations. In his speech he demanded $500,000.00 in reparations for slavery. What role should religious congregations play in the reparations debate? To what extent did the Islamic and Christian faiths play a role in slavery? Should they be required to apologize and/or compensate victims for their loss of culture and financial resources?

► Notes & Questions

10. In July, 2001, the *New York Amsterdam News* reported that a bill had been introduced in New York State legislature to create a commission to study the reparations issue. The leader of the New York initiative was Assemblyman Roger Green, president of the Black and Puerto Rican Legislative Caucus. The following cities have already set up study commissions: Dallas, Nashville, Detroit and Chicago.

    Should state and city commissions be set up to study this problem? In 1790, only 22,000 African-American slaves lived in New York State. Is that a sufficient number to warrant a study of this magnitude?

11. An African-American woman, Deadria Farmer-Paellmann, has recently (March 2, 2002) joined with others to file a class action lawsuit against Fleet-Boston, Aetna, CSX and other to be named defendants. The lead attorney in the suit filed in United States District Court in Brooklyn, New York is Edward Fagan, who obtained $8 billion dollars in settlement from European companies who did business with the Nazis.

    Does this type of lawsuit give more credence to the reparations movement? If lawyers see the possibility of substantial legal fees, will this help the cause?

12. On September 8, 2000, the Bureau of Indian Affairs celebrated its 175th anniversary. It was founded in 1824. Kevin Gover, head of the bureau, said that celebration was inappropriate, that it was time "for sorrowful truths to be spoken, a time of contrition." He went further to say "This agency participated in the ethnic cleansing that befell the western tribes."

► Notes & Questions

Should the reparations debate include Native-Americans? What are some steps that the nation can take to remedy this legacy of genocide?

Chapter Seven

LEGAL RESPONSE
TO URBAN CRIME

Many Blacks believe that the law has been applied more severely against them. The notion that justice is blind is one that many do not believe is true. Much of this mistrust and outright paranoia comes from concrete experiences with police officers in urban communities. The assaults of police officers against Blacks have been documented from Rodney King to Robert Davis. The most frightening assaults, however, have come from governmental institutions, such as the judiciary and the executive branch. Many of these governmental policies and decisions have been directed at urban crime, particularly against Black people who operate in the lower echelons of the massive American criminal enterprise.

Needless to say, there has been a steady increase in the level of violent crime in the United States since 1975. This increase has varied directly with the mounting availability of drugs in the inner city. The response of politicians has been more and longer jail sentences and the death penalty. Many people support this demand, even though the death penalty is applied to the poor and to people of color in a disproportionate manner. Furthermore, it is usually applied to Blacks killing Whites, rather than Whites killing Blacks or Blacks killing Blacks.

Amnesty International has concluded from its research that since 1972, 60 percent of the individuals on death row were unemployed at the time of their crime.[1] It found that since 1930, 90 percent of the men executed for rape were Black.[2]

---

1   Amnesty International U.S.A., *The Death Penalty: Cruel and Inhuman Punishment* (322 Eighth Avenue, New York, 10001)

2   Ibid.

Therefore, it has issued the following recommendations on the death penalty:

"The right to life and the right not to be subjected to cruel, inhuman or degrading treatment or punishment are enshrined in the Universal Declaration of Human Rights and other international human rights documents. The death penalty is a denial of those rights and its use in the USA has resulted in violations of human rights throughout that country. Amnesty International is calling on the USA to join the growing number of nations all over the world who have abolished the death penalty or are working towards abolition... Amnesty International believes that the evidence of racial discrimination in the application of the death penalty is a matter of urgent concern and recommends that the executive or legislative branch of the federal government commission a thorough, impartial inquiry into the question..."[3]

Is the death penalty the appropriate response to urban violence? Should a more reasoned approach prevail? Is the death penalty a deterrent to violent crime? If the government executed the rich executives who bring the ship loads of drugs into the country, would you support the penalty? If you oppose it, why? If you support it, why?

A.
Restraining Black Mobility in Neighborhoods

What should be the role of law in protecting the liberty of individuals? Should people, who are perceived by some to be undesirable or a threat, be able to walk the streets of America without unreasonable interference by the police? To what extent should Black youth, for example, be subject to arbitrary stops and frisks in their own neighborhoods? Are these stops by the police lingering legacies of slavery? How have the courts responded to these governmental infringements on constitutional rights?

---

3   Amnesty International, *United States of America: The Death Penalty: Briefing*, October, 1987 (322 Eighth Avenue, New York), page 19

KOLENDER, CHIEF OF POLICE
OF SAN DIEGO, ET AL. v. LAWSON
Supreme Court of the United States
461 U.S. 352 (1983)

JUSTICE O'CONNOR delivered the opinion of the Court.

This appeal presents a facial challenge to a criminal statute that requires persons who loiter or wander on the streets to provide a "credible and reliable" identification and to account for their presence when requested by a peace officer under circumstances that would justify a stop under the standards of *Terry v. Ohio*, 392 U.S. 1 (1968). (Footnote omitted). We conclude that the statute as it has been construed is unconstitutionally vague within the meaning of the Due Process Clause of the Fourteenth Amendment by failing to clarify what is contemplated by the requirement that a suspect provide a "credible and reliable" identification. Accordingly, we affirm the judgment of the court below.

I.

Appellee Edward Lawson was detained or arrested on approximately 15 occasions between March 1975 and January 1977 pursuant to Cal. Penal Code Ann. s.647(e)(West 1970).(Footnote omitted). Lawson was prosecuted only twice, and was convicted once. The second charge was dismissed.

Lawson then brought a civil action in the District Court for the Southern District of California seeking a declaratory judgment that s.647(e) is unconstitutional, a mandatory injunction to restrain enforcement of the statute, and compensatory and punitive damages against the various officers who detained him. The District Court found that s.647(e) was overbroad because "a person who is stopped on less than probable cause cannot be punished for failing to identify himself." ...The District Court enjoined enforcement of the statute, but held that Lawson could not recover damages because the officers involved acted in the good-faith belief that each detention or arrest was lawful...

The Court of Appeals affirmed the District Court determination as to the unconstitutionality of s.647 (e)…The appellate court determined that the statute was unconstitutional in that it violates the Fourth Amendment's proscription against unreasonable searches and seizures, it contains a vague enforcement standard that is susceptible to arbitrary enforcement, and it fails to give fair and adequate notice of the type of conduct prohibited. Finally, the Court of Appeals reversed the District Court as to its holding that Lawson was not entitled to a jury trial to determine the good faith of the officers in his damages action against them, and remanded the case to the District Court for trial…

III.

Our constitution is designed to maximize individual freedoms within a framework of ordered liberty. Statutory limitations on those freedoms are examined for substantive authority and content as well as for definiteness or certainty of expression…

As generally stated, the void-for-vagueness doctrine requires that a penal statute define the criminal offense with sufficient definiteness that ordinary people can understand what conduct is prohibited and in a manner that does not encourage arbitrary and discriminatory enforcement. (Citations omitted). Although the doctrine focuses both on actual notice to citizens and arbitrary enforcement, we have recognized recently that the more important aspect of the vagueness doctrine "is not actual notice, but the other principal element of the doctrine-the requirement that a legislature establish minimal guidelines to govern law enforcement." (Citation omitted). Where the legislature fails to provide such minimal guidelines, a criminal statute may permit a standardless sweep [that] allows policemen, prosecutors, and juries to pursue their personal predilections." (Citation and footnote omitted).

Section 647(e), as presently drafted and as construed by the state courts, contains no standard for determining what a suspect has to do in order to satisfy the requirement to provide a "credible and reliable" identification. As such, the statute vests virtually complete discretion in the hands of the police to determine whether the suspect has satisfied the statute and must be permitted to go on his way in the absence of probable cause to arrest. An individual, whom police may think is suspicious but do not have probable cause to believe has committed a crime, is entitled to continue to walk the public streets "only at the whim of any police officer" who happens to stop that individual under s.647(e). *Shuttlesworth v. City of Birmingham*, 382 U.S. 87, 90 (1965). Our concern here is based upon the "potential for arbitrarily suppressing First Amendment liberties..." Id., at 91. In addition, s.647(e) implicates consideration of the constitutional right to freedom of movement. See *Kent v. Dulles*, 357 U.S. 116, 126 (1958); *Aptheker v. Secretary of State*, 378 U.S. 500, 505-506 (1964). (Footnote omitted)...Appellants stress the need for strengthened law enforcement tools to combat the epidemic of crime that plagues our Nation. The concern of our citizens with curbing criminal activity is certainly a matter requiring the attention of all branches of government. As weighty as this concern is, however, it cannot justify legislation that would otherwise fail to meet constitutional standards for definiteness and clarity. See *Lanzetta v. New Jersey*, 306 U.S. 451 (1939). Action as presently construed, requires that "suspicious" persons satisfy some undefined identification requirement, or face criminal punishment. Although due process does not require "impossible standards" of clarity, see *United States v. Petrillo*, 332 U.S. 1, 7-8 (1947), this is not a case where further precision in the statutory language is either impossible or impractical.

IV.

We conclude ' 647(e) is unconstitutionally vague on its face because it encourages arbitrary enforcement by failing to de-scribe with sufficient particularity what a suspect must do in order to satisfy the statutes. Accordingly, the judgment of the Court of Appeals is affirmed, and the case is remanded for further proceedings consistent with this opinion.

It is so ordered.

JUSTICE BRENNAN, concurring.

I join the Court's opinion; it demonstrates convincingly that the California statute at issue in this case, Cal. Penal Code Ann. ' 647(e) (West 1970), as interpreted by California courts, is unconstitutionally vague. Even if the defect iden-tified by the Court were cured, however, I would hold that this statute violates the Fourth Amendment. (Footnote omitted). Merely to facilitate the general law enforcement objectives of investigating and preventing unspecified crimes, States may not authorize the arrest and criminal prosecution of an individ-ual for failing to produce identification or further information on demand by a police officer.

It has long been settled that the Fourth Amendment prohibits the seizure and detention or search of an individual's person unless there is probable cause to believe that he has committed a crime, except under certain conditions strictly defined by the legitimate requirements of law enforcement and by the limited extent of the resulting intrusion on individual liberty and privacy. See *Davis v. Mississippi*, 394 U.S. 721, 726-727 (1969). The scope of that exception to the probable-cause requirement for seizures of the person has been defined by a series of cases, beginning with *Terry v. Ohio*, 392 U.S. 1 (1968), holding that a police officer with reasonable suspicion of criminal activity, based on articulable facts, may detain a suspect briefly for purposes of limited questioning and, in so doing, may conduct a brief "frisk" of the suspect to protect himself from concealed weapons. See, e. g., United States v. Brignoni-Ponce, 422 U.S. 873, 880-884 (1975); *Adams v. Williams*, 407 U.S. 143, 145-146 (1972). Where probable cause is lacking, we have expressly declined to allow significantly more intrusive detentions or searches on the Terry rationale, despite the assertion of compelling law enforcement interests. "For all but those narrowly defined intrusions, the requisite 'balancing' has been performed in centuries of precedent and is embodied in the principle that seizures are 'reasonable' only if supported by probable cause." *Dunaway v. New York*, 442 U.S. 200, 214 (1979)". (Footnote omitted)…

▶ Notes & Questions

1. In *Kolender* the Court struck down a statute that allowed police to stop and seek identification from individuals pursuant to a statute that was unconstitutionally vague. Do you agree with the court's decision? Should police officers be allowed greater latitude to stop and question individuals in order to fight criminal activity? Should the public trust the judgment of police officers and therefore grant them greater discretion on the streets?

2. What about teenagers in high crime areas? Should the police be allowed to stop them to determine whether they are engaged in criminal activity? If police were allowed to have this authority in high crime, inner city neighborhoods, should they have similar authority in affluent and predominantly white ones?

B.
Restraining Access of Blacks to Jury Service

Should race play a role in limiting a person's right to a fair trial? Historically, why were Blacks eliminated from service on juries? Isn't the attempt to bar Blacks from juries or to eliminate them through challenges by lawyers a continuing legacy of slavery? Should the Thirteenth Amendment be used to combat these types of racial discrimination?

BATSON v. KENTUCKY
Supreme Court of the United States
476 U.S. 79 (1986)

JUSTICE POWELL delivered the opinion of the Court.

This case requires us to reexamine that portion of *Swain v. Alabama*, 380 U.S. 202 (1965), concerning the evidentiary burden placed on a criminal defendant who claims that he has been denied equal protection through the State's use of peremptory challenges to exclude members of his race from the petit jury. (Footnote omitted).

I.

Petitioner, a black man, was indicted in Kentucky on charges of second-degree burglary and receipt of stolen goods. On the first day of trial in Jefferson Circuit Court, the judge conducted *voir dire* examination of the venire, excused certain jurors for cause, and permitted the parties to exercise peremptory challenges. (Footnote omitted). The prosecutor used his peremptory challenges to strike all four black persons on the venire, and a jury composed only of white persons was selected. Defense counsel moved to discharge the jury before it was sworn on the ground that the prosecutor's removal of the black veniremen violated petitioner's rights under the Sixth and Fourteenth Amendments to a jury drawn from a cross section of the community, and under the Fourteenth Amendment to equal protection of the laws. Counsel requested a hearing on his motion. Without expressly ruling on the request for a hearing, the trial judge observed that the parties were entitled to use their peremptory challenges to "strike anybody they want to." The judge then denied petitioner's motion, reasoning that the cross-section requirement applies only to selection of the venire and not to selection of the petit jury itself.

The jury convicted petitioner on both counts. On appeal to the Supreme Court of Kentucky, petitioner pressed, among other claims, the argument concerning the prosecutor's use of peremptory challenges. Conceding that *Swain v. Alabama*, supra, apparently foreclosed an equal protection claim based solely on the prosecutor's conduct in this case, petitioner urged the court to follow decisions of other States, (Citation omitted), and to hold that such conduct violated his rights under the Sixth Amendment and ' 11 of the Kentucky Constitution to a jury drawn from a cross section of the community. Petitioner also contended that the facts showed that the prosecutor had engaged in a "pattern" of discriminatory challenges in this case and established an equal protection violation under *Swain*.

The Supreme Court of Kentucky affirmed. In a single paragraph, the court declined petitioner's invitation to adopt the reasoning of *People v. Wheeler, supra*, and *Commonwealth v. Soares, supra*. The court observed that it recently had reaffirmed its reliance on *Swain*, and had held that a defendant alleging lack of a fair cross section must demonstrate systematic exclusion of a group of jurors from the venire. (Citation omitted). We granted certiorari, (Citation omitted), and now reverse.

II.

In *Swain v. Alabama*, this Court recognized that a "State's purposeful or deliberate denial to Negroes on account of race of participation as jurors in the administration of justice violates the Equal Protection Clause." (Citation omitted). This principle has been "consistently and repeatedly" reaffirmed, (Citation omitted), in numerous decisions of this Court both preceding and following *Swain*". (Footnote omitted). We re-affirm the principle today". (Footnote omitted).

A.

More than a century ago, the Court decided that the State denies a black defendant equal protection of the laws when it puts him on trial before a jury from which members of his race have been purposefully excluded. *Strauder v. West Virginia*, 100 U.S. 303 (1880). That decision laid the foundation for the Court's unceasing efforts to eradicate racial discrimination in the procedures used to select the venire from which individual jurors are drawn. In *Strauder*, the Court explained that the central concern of the recently rati-fied Fourteenth Amendment was to put an end to governmental discrimination on account of race. (Citation omitted). Exclusion of black citizens from service as jurors constitutes a primary example of the evil the Fourteenth Amendment was designed to cure.

In holding that racial discrimination in jury selection offends the Equal Protection Clause, the Court in *Strauder* recognized, however, that a defendant has no right to a "petit jury composed in whole or in part of persons of his own race." (Footnote omitted). "The number of our races and nationalities stands in the way of evolution of such a conception of the demand of equal protection". (Footnote omitted). But the defendant does have the right to be tried by a jury whose members are selected pursuant to non-discriminatory criteria. (Citation omitted). The Equal Protection Clause guarantees the defendant that the State will not exclude members of his race from the jury venire on account of race, (Footnote omitted) or on the false assumption that members of his race as a group are not qualified to serve as jurors, (Citation omitted).

Purposeful racial discrimination in selection of the venire violates a defendant's right to equal protection because it denies him the protection that a trial by jury is intended to secure...

(Footnote omitted). Those on the venire must be "indifferently chosen," (Footnote omitted) to secure the defendant's right under the Fourteenth Amendment to "protection of life and liberty against race or color prejudice." (Citation omitted).

Racial discrimination in selection of jurors harms not only the accused whose life or liberty they are summoned to try. Competence to serve as a juror ultimately depends on an assessment of individual qualifications and ability impartially to consider evidence presented at a trial. (Citation omitted). As long ago as *Strauder*, therefore, the Court recognized that by denying a person participation in jury service on account of his race, the State unconstitutionally discriminated against the excluded juror. (Citation omitted). The harm from discriminatory jury selection extends beyond that inflicted on the defendant and the excluded juror to touch the entire community. Selection procedures that purposefully exclude black persons from juries undermine public confidence in the fairness of our system of justice. (Citation omitted). Discrimination within the judicial system is most pernicious because it is "a stimulant to that race prejudice which is an impediment to securing to [black citizens] that equal justice which the law aims to secure to all others." (Citation omitted).

A.

In *Strauder*, the Court invalidated a state statute that provided that only white men could serve as jurors. *Id.*, at 305. We can be confident that no State now has such a law...

Accordingly, the component of the jury selection process at issue here, the State's privilege to strike individual jurors through peremptory challenges, is subject to the commands of the Equal Protection Clause. Although a prosecutor ordinarily is entitled to exercise permitted peremptory challenges (Citation omitted), the Equal Protection Clause forbids the prosecutor to challenge potential jurors solely on account of their race or on the assumption that black jurors as a group will be unable impartially to consider the State's case against a black defendant...

B.

Moreover, since *Swain*, we have recognized that a black defendant alleging that members of his race have been impermissibly excluded from the venire may make out a prima facie case of purposeful discrimination by showing that the totality of the relevant facts gives rise to an inference of discriminatory purpose. (Citation omitted). Once the defendant makes the requisite showing, the burden shifts to the State to explain adequately the racial exclusion. (Citation omitted). The State cannot meet this burden on mere general assertions that its officials did not discriminate or that they properly performed their official duties. (Citation omitted). Rather, the State must demonstrate that "permissible racially neutral selection criteria and procedures have produced the monochromatic result." (Citation omitted). (Footnote omitted)...

Since the ultimate issue is whether the State has discriminated in selecting the defendant's venire, however, the defendant may establish a prima facie case "in other ways than by evidence of long-continued unexplained absence" of members of his race "from many panels." (Citation omitted). In cases involving the venire, this Court has found a prima facie case on proof that members of the defendant's race were substantially underrepresented on the venire from which his jury was drawn, and that the venire was selected under a practice providing "the opportunity for discrimination." (Citation omitted). This combination of factors raises the necessary inference of purposeful discrimination because the Court has declined to attribute to chance the absence of black citizens on a particular jury array where the selection mechanism is subject to abuse. When circumstances suggest the need, the trial court must undertake a "factual inquiry," that "takes into account all possible explanatory factors" in the particular case. (Citation omitted).

Thus, since the decision in *Swain*, this Court has recognized that a defendant may make a prima facie showing of purposeful racial discrimination in selection of the venire by relying solely on the facts concerning its selection in his case. These decisions are in accordance with the proposition, articulated in *Arlington Heights v. Metropolitan Housing Development Corp.*, that "a consistent pattern of official racial discrimination" is not "a necessary predicate to a violation of the Equal Protection Clause. A single invidiously discriminatory governmental act" is not "immunized by the absence of such discrimination in the making of other comparable decisions." (Citation omitted)....

C.

The standards for assessing a prima facie case in the context of discriminatory selection of the venire have been fully articulated since *Swain*. (Citation omitted). These principles support our conclusion that a defendant may establish a prima facie case of purposeful discrimination in selection of the petit jury solely on evidence concerning the prosecutor's exercise of peremptory challenges at the defendant's trial. To establish such a case, the defendant first must show that he is a member of a cognizable racial group, (Citation omitted), and that the prosecutor has exercised peremptory challenges to remove from the venire members of the defendant's race. Second, the defendant is entitled to rely on the fact, as to which there can be no dispute, that peremptory challenges constitute a jury selection practice that permits "those to discriminate who are of a mind to discriminate." (Citation omitted). Finally, the defendant must show that these facts and any other relevant circumstances raise an inference that the prosecutor use that practice to exclude the veniremen from the petit jury on account of their race. This combination of factors in the empaneling of the petit jury, as in the selection of the venire, raises the necessary inference of purposeful discrimination.

In deciding whether the defendant has made the requisite showing, the trial court should consider all relevant circumstances. For example, a "pattern" of strikes against black jurors included in the particular venire might give rise to an inference of discrimination. Similarly, the prosecutor's questions and statements during *voir dire* examination and in exercising his challenges may support or refute an inference of discriminatory purpose. These examples are merely illustrative. We have confidence that trial judges, experienced in supervising *voir dire,* will be able to decide if the circumstances concerning the prosecutor's use of peremptory challenges creates a prima facie case of discrimination against black jurors.

Once the defendant makes a prima facie showing, the burden shifts to the State to come forward with a neutral explanation for challenging black jurors. Though this requirement imposes a limitation in some cases on the full peremptory character of the historic challenge, we emphasize that the prosecutor's explanation need not rise to the level justifying exercise of a challenge for cause. (Citation omitted). The prosecutor therefore must articulate a neutral explanation related to the particular case to be tried." (Footnote omitted). The trial court then will have the duty to determine if the defendant has established purposeful discrimination. (Footnote omitted)...

V.

In this case, petitioner made a timely objection to the prosecutor's removal of all black persons on the venire. Because the trial court flatly rejected the objection without requiring the prosecutor to give an explanation for his action, we remand this case for further proceedings. If the trial court decides that the facts establish, prima facie, purposeful discrimination and the prosecutor does not come forward with a neutral explanation for his action, our precedents require that petitioner's conviction be reversed. (Footnote omitted).

It is so ordered.

▶ Notes & Questions

1. What's wrong with a prosecutor eliminating Blacks from a jury pool when he suspects that a Black jury might be sympathetic to a Black defendant?

2. Given the history of exclusion of Blacks from juries, shouldn't affirmative steps be taken to include them on juries?

3. Can a Black person get a fair trial from an all white jury? The initial Rodney King trial in a California court resulted in the police officers, accused of assaulting him, being acquitted. Does this indicate that racism was a factor, or that the verdict was appropriate under the circumstances?

4. Given that Blacks in inner cities are often victimized by Black defendants, wouldn't Black juries be harder on Black defendants?

The United States Supreme Court has decided the appeal of Thomas Miller-El, a Texas death row inmate, who alleged that the prosecutors in his 1986 trial purposefully excluded 10 of 11 prospective Black jurors. Miller-El was scheduled to be executed on February 21, 2002, but the Court issued a stay. At issue was whether evidence of an official Dallas policy of excluding Blacks from juries of black defendants was constitutional? How far back in the history of a particular jurisdiction should a defendant be able to go in his attempt to prove unlawful exclusion from a jury?

THOMAS JOE MILLER-EL v. DRETKE
SUPREME COURT OF THE UNITED STATES
545 U.S. 1 (2005)

Justice SOUTER delivered the opinion of the Court.

Two years ago, we ordered that a certificate of appealability, under 28 U.S.C. § 2253(c), be issued to habeas petitioner Miller-El, affording review of the District Court's rejection of the claim that prosecutors in his capital murder trial made peremptory strikes of potential jurors based on race. Today we find Miller-El entitled to prevail on that claim and order relief under §2254.

I.

In the course of robbing a Holiday Inn in Dallas, Texas in late 1985, Miller-El and his accomplices bound and gagged two hotel employees, whom Miller-El then shot, killing one and severely injuring the other. During jury selection in Miller-El's trial for capital murder, prosecutors used peremptory strikes against 10 qualified black venire members. Miller-El objected that the strikes were based on race and could not be presumed legitimate, given a history of excluding black members from criminal juries by the Dallas County District Attorney's Office. The trial court received evidence of the practice alleged but found no "systematic exclusion of blacks as a matter of policy" by that office, (Citation omitted), and therefore no entitlement to relief under *Swain v. Alabama*, 380 U.S. 202 (1965), the case then defining and marking the limits of relief from racially biased jury selection. The court denied Miller-El's request to pick a new jury, and the trial ended with his death sentence for capital murder.

While an appeal was pending, this Court decided *Batson v. Kentucky*, 476 U.S. 79 (1986), which replaced *Swain*'s threshold requirement to prove systemic discrimination under a Fourteenth Amendment jury claim, with the rule that discrimination by the prosecutor in selecting the defendant's jury sufficed to establish the constitutional violation. The Texas Court of Criminal Appeals then remanded the matter to the trial court to determine whether Miller-El could show that prosecutors in his case peremptorily struck prospective black jurors because of race. (Citation omitted).

The trial court found no such demonstration. After reviewing the *voir dire* record of the explanations given for some of the challenged strikes, and after hearing one of the prosecutors, Paul Macaluso, give his justification for those previously unexplained, the trial court accepted the stated race-neutral reasons for the strikes, which the judge called "completely credible [and] sufficient" as the grounds for a finding of "no purposeful discrimination." (Citation omitted). The Court of Criminal Appeals affirmed, stating it found "ample support" in the *voir dire* record for the race-neutral explanations offered by prosecutors for the peremptory strikes. (Citation omitted).

Miller-El then sought habeas relief under 28 U.S.C. § 2254 again pressing his *Batson* claim, among others not now before us. The District Court denied relief, (Citation omitted), and the Court of Appeals for the Fifth Circuit precluded appeal by denying a certificate of appealability, (Citation omitted). We granted certiorari to consider whether Miller-El was entitled to review on the *Batson* claim, (Citation omitted), and reversed the Court of Appeals. After examining the record of Miller-El's extensive evidence of purposeful discrimination by the Dallas County District Attorney's Office before and during his trial, we found an appeal was in order, since the merits of the *Batson* claim were, at the least, debatable by jurists of reason. (Citation omitted). After granting a certificate of appealability, the Fifth Circuit rejected Miller-El's *Batson* claim on the merits. (Citation omitted). We again granted certiorari, (Citation omitted), and again we reverse.

II.
A.

"It is well known that prejudices often exist against particular classes in the community, which sway the judgment of jurors, and which, therefore, operate in some cases to deny to persons of those classes the full enjoyment of that protection which others enjoy." *Strauder v. West Virginia*, 100 U.S. 303, 309 (1880); see also *Batson v. Kentucky, supra*, at 86. Defendants are harmed, of course, when racial discrimination in jury selection compromises the right of trial by impartial jury, *Strauder v. West Virginia, supra*, at 308, but racial minorities are harmed more generally, for prosecutors drawing racial lines in picking juries establish "state-sponsored group stereotypes rooted in, and reflective of, historical prejudice," *J. E. B. v. Alabama ex rel. T. B.*, 511 U.S. 127, 128 (1994).

Nor is the harm confined to minorities. When the government's choice of jurors is tainted with racial bias, that "overt wrong ... casts doubt over the obligation of the parties, the jury, and indeed the court to adhere to the law throughout the trial..." *Powers v. Ohio*, 499 U.S. 400, 412 (1991). That is, the very integrity of the courts is jeopardized when a prosecutor's discrimination "invites cynicism respecting the jury's neutrality," (Citation omitted), and undermines public confidence in adjudication, (Citation omitted). So, "[f]or more than a century, this Court consistently and repeatedly has reaffirmed that racial discrimination by the State in jury selection offends the Equal Protection Clause." (Citation omitted).

The rub has been the practical difficulty of ferreting out discrimination in selections discretionary by nature, and choices subject to myriad legitimate influences, whatever the race of the individuals on the panel from which jurors are selected. In *Swain v. Alabama,* we tackled the problem of "the quantum of proof necessary" to show purposeful discrimination, (Citation omitted), with an eye to preserving each side's historical prerogative to make a peremptory strike or challenge, the very nature of which is traditionally "without a reason stated," (Citation omitted). The *Swain* Court tried to relate peremptory challenge to equal protection by presuming the legitimacy of prosecutors' strikes except in the face of a longstanding pattern of discrimination: when "in case after case, whatever the circumstances," no blacks served on juries, then "giving even the widest leeway to the operation of irrational but trial-related suspicions and antagonisms, it would appear that the purposes of the peremptory challenge [were] being perverted." (Citation omitted).

Swain's demand to make out a continuity of discrimination over time, however, turned out to be difficult to the point of unworkable, and in *Batson v. Kentucky,* we recognized that this requirement to show an extended pattern imposed a "crippling burden of proof" that left prosecutors' use of peremptories "largely immune from constitutional scrutiny." (Citation omitted). By *Batson*'s day, the law implementing equal protection elsewhere had evolved into less discouraging standards for assessing a claim of purposeful discrimination, (Citation omitted) and we accordingly held that a defendant could make out a prima facie case of discriminatory jury selection by "the totality of the relevant facts" about a prosecutor's conduct during the defendant's own trial. *Batson v. Kentucky,* 476 U.S., at 94, 96. "Once the defendant makes a prima facie showing, the burden shifts to the State to come forward with a neutral explanation for challenging…jurors" within an arguably targeted class. (Citation omitted). Although there may be "any number of bases on which a prosecutor reasonably [might] believe that it is desirable to strike a juror who is not excusable for cause…, the prosecutor must give a clear and reasonably specific explanation of his legitimate reasons for exercising the challeng[e]." (Citation omitted) (internal quotation marks omitted). "The trial court then will have the duty to determine if the defendant has established purposeful discrimination." (Citation omitted).

Although the move from *Swain* to *Batson* left a defendant free to challenge the prosecution without having to cast *Swain*'s wide net, the net was not entirely consigned to history, for *Batson*'s individualized focus came with a weakness of its own owing to its very emphasis on the particular reasons a prosecutor might give. If any facially neutral reason sufficed to answer a *Batson* challenge, then *Batson* would not amount to much more than *Swain*. Some stated reasons are false, and although some false reasons are shown up within the four corners of a given case, sometimes a court may not be sure unless it looks beyond the case at hand. Hence *Batson*'s explanation that a defendant may rely on "all relevant circumstances" to raise an inference of purposeful discrimination. (Citation omitted).

B.

This case comes to us on review of a denial of habeas relief sought under 28 U.S.C. § 2254 following the Texas trial court's prior determination of fact that the State's race-neutral explanations were true (Citation omitted).

Under the Antiterrorism and Effective Death Penalty Act of 1996, Miller-El may obtain relief only by showing the Texas conclusion to be "an unreasonable determination of the facts in light of the evidence presented in the State court proceeding." 28 U.S.C. § 2254(d)(2). Thus we presume the Texas court's factual findings to be sound unless Miller-El rebuts the "presumption of correctness by clear and convincing evidence." (Citation omitted). The standard is demanding but not insatiable; as we said the last time this case was here, "[d]eference does not by definition preclude relief." (Citation omitted).

III.
A.

The numbers describing the prosecution's use of peremptories are remarkable. Out of 20 black members of the 108-person venire panel for Miller-El's trial, only 1 served. Although 9 were excused for cause or by agreement, 10 were peremptorily struck by the prosecution. (Citation omitted). "The prosecutors used their peremptory strikes to exclude 91% of the eligible African-American venire members... Happenstance is unlikely to produce this disparity." (Citation omitted).

More powerful than these bare statistics, however, are side-by-side comparisons of some black venire panelists who were struck and white panelists allowed to serve. If a prosecutor's proffered reason for striking a black panelist applies just as well to an otherwise-similar nonblack who is permitted to serve, that is evidence tending to prove purposeful discrimination to be considered at *Batson*'s third step. (Citation omitted). In employment discrimination cases, "[p]roof that the defendant's explanation is unworthy of credence is simply one form of circumstantial evidence that is probative of intentional discrimination, and it may be quite persuasive"). While we did not develop a comparative juror analysis last time, we did note that the prosecution's reasons for exercising peremptory strikes against some black panel members appeared equally on point as to some white jurors who served. (Citation omitted). The details of two panel member comparisons bear this out.

The prosecution used its second peremptory strike to exclude Billy Jean Fields, a black man who expressed unwavering support for the death penalty. On the questionnaire filled out by all panel members before individual examination on the stand, Fields said that he believed in capital punishment, (Citation omitted), and during questioning he disclosed his belief that the State acts on God's behalf when it imposes the death penalty. "Therefore, if the State exacts death, then that's what it should be." (Citation omitted). He testified that he had no religious or philosophical reservations about the death penalty and that the death penalty deterred crime. (Citation omitted). He twice averred, without apparent hesitation, that he could sit on Miller-El's jury and make a decision to impose this penalty. (Citation omitted).

Although at one point in the questioning, Fields indicated that the possibility of rehabilitation might be relevant to the likelihood that a defendant would commit future acts of violence, (Citation omitted), he responded to ensuing questions by saying that although he believed anyone could be rehabilitated, this belief would not stand in the way of a decision to impose the death penalty:

"[B]ased on what you [the prosecutor] said as far as the crime goes, there are only two things that could be rendered, death or life in prison. If for some reason the testimony didn't warrant death, then life imprisonment would give an individual an opportunity to rehabilitate. But, you know, you said that the jurors didn't have the opportunity to make a personal decision in the matter with reference to what I thought or felt, but it was just based on the questions according to the way the law has been handed down." (Citation omitted).

Fields also noted on his questionnaire that his brother had a criminal history. (Citation omitted). During questioning, the prosecution went into this, too:

"Q. Could you tell me a little bit about that?

"A. He was arrested and convicted on [a] number of occasions for possession of a controlled substance.

"Q. Was that here in Dallas?

"A. Yes.

"Q. Was he involved in any trials or anything like that?

"A. I suppose of sorts. I don't really know too much about it.

"Q. Was he ever convicted?

"A. Yeah, he served time.

"Q. Do you feel that that would in any way interfere with your service on this jury at all?

"A. No." App. 190.

Fields was struck peremptorily by the prosecution, with prosecutor James Nelson offering a race-neutral reason:

"[W]e...have concern with reference to some of his statements as to the death penalty in that he said that he could only give death if he thought a person could not be rehabilitated and he later made the comment that any person could be rehabilitated if they find God or are introduced to God and the fact that we have a concern that his religious feelings may affect his jury service in this case." (Citation omitted).

Thus, Nelson simply mischaracterized Fields's testimony. He represented that Fields said he would not vote for death if rehabilitation was possible, whereas Fields unequivocally stated that he could impose the death penalty regardless of the possibility of rehabilitation. Perhaps Nelson misunderstood, but unless he had an ulterior reason for keeping Fields off the jury we think he would have proceeded differently. In light of Fields's outspoken support for the death penalty, we expect the prosecutor would have cleared up any misunderstanding by asking further questions before getting to the point of exercising a strike.

If, indeed, Fields's thoughts on rehabilitation did make the prosecutor uneasy, he should have worried about a number of white panel members he accepted with no evident reservations. Sandra Hearn said that she believed in the death penalty "if a criminal cannot be rehabilitated and continues to commit the same type of crime." (Citation omitted). Hearn went so far as to express doubt that at the penalty phase of a capital case she could conclude that a convicted murderer "would probably commit some criminal acts of violence in the future." (Citation omitted). "People change," she said, making it hard to assess the risk of someone's future dangerousness. "[T]he evidence would have to be awful strong." (Citation omitted). But the prosecution did not respond to Hearn the way it did to Fields, and without delving into her views about rehabilitation with any further question, it raised no objection to her serving on the jury. White panelist Mary Witt said she would take the possibility of rehabilitation into account in deciding at the penalty phase of the trial about a defendant's probability of future dangerousness, (Citation omitted), but the prosecutors asked her no further question about her views on reformation, and they accepted her as a juror. (Citation omitted) Latino venireman Fernando Gutierrez, who served on the jury, said that he would consider the death penalty for someone who could not be rehabilitated, (Citation omitted), but the prosecutors did not question him further about this view. In sum, nonblack jurors whose remarks on rehabilitation could well have signaled a limit on their willingness to impose a death sentence were not questioned further and drew no objection, but the prosecution expressed apprehension about a black juror's belief in the possibility of reformation even though he repeatedly stated his approval of the death penalty and testified that he could impose it according to state legal standards even when the alternative sentence of life imprisonment would give a defendant (like everyone else in the world) the opportunity to reform.

The unlikelihood that his position on rehabilitation had anything to do with the peremptory strike of Fields is underscored by the prosecution's response after Miller-El's lawyer pointed out that the prosecutor had misrepresented Fields's responses on the subject. A moment earlier the prosecutor had finished his misdescription of Fields's views on potential rehabilitation with the words, "Those are our reasons for exercising our…strike at this time." (Citation omitted). When defense counsel called him on his misstatement, he neither defended what he said nor withdrew the strike. (Citation omitted). Instead, he suddenly came up with Fields's brother's prior conviction as another reason for the strike. (Citation omitted)…

The prosecution's proffered reasons for striking Joe Warren, another black venireman, are comparably unlikely. Warren gave this answer when he was asked what the death penalty accomplished:

"I don't know. It's really hard to say because I know sometimes you feel that it might help to deter crime and then you feel that the person is not really suffering. You're taking the suffering away from him. So it's like I said, sometimes you have mixed feelings about whether or not this is punishment or, you know, you're relieving personal punishment." (Citation omitted). The prosecution said nothing about these remarks when it struck Warren from the panel, but prosecutor Paul Macaluso referred to this answer as the first of his reasons when he testified at the later *Batson* hearing:

"I thought [Warren's statements on *voir dire*] were inconsistent responses. At one point he says, you know, on a case-by-case basis and at another point he said, well, I think- I got the impression, at least, that he suggested that the death penalty was an easy way out, that they should be made to suffer more." (Citation omitted).

On the face of it, the explanation is reasonable from the State's point of view, but its plausibility is severely undercut by the prosecution's failure to object to other panel members who expressed views much like Warren's. Kevin Duke, who served on the jury, said, "sometimes death would be better to me than-being in prison would be like dying every day and, if you were in prison for life with no hope of parole, I'd just as soon have it over with than be in prison for the rest of your life." (Citation omitted). Troy Woods, the one black panelist to serve as juror, said that capital punishment "is too easy. I think that's a quick relief... I feel like [hard labor is] more of a punishment than putting them to sleep." (Citation omitted). Sandra Jenkins, whom the State accepted (but who was then struck by the defense) testified that she thought "a harsher treatment is life imprisonment with no parole." (Citation omitted). Leta Girard, accepted by the State (but also struck by the defense) gave her opinion that "living sometimes is a worse-is worse to me than dying would be." (Citation omitted). The fact that Macaluso's reason also applied to these other panel members, most of them white, none of them struck, is evidence of pretext.

The suggestion of pretext is not, moreover, mitigated much by Macaluso's explanation that Warren was struck when the State had 10 peremptory challenges left and could afford to be liberal in using them. (Citation omitted). If that were the explanation for striking Warren and later accepting panel members who thought death would be too easy, the prosecutors should have struck Sandra Jenkins, whom they examined and accepted before Warren. Indeed, the disparate treatment is the more remarkable for the fact that the prosecutors repeatedly questioned Warren on his capacity and willingness to impose a sentence of death and elicited statements of his ability to do so if the evidence supported that result and the answer to each special question was yes, (Citation omitted), whereas the record before us discloses no attempt to determine whether Jenkins would be able to vote for death in spite of her view that it was easy on the convict, (Citation omitted). Yet the prosecutors accepted the white panel member Jenkins and struck the black venireman Warren.

Macaluso's explanation that the prosecutors grew more sparing with peremptory challenges as the jury selection wore on does, however, weaken any suggestion that the State's acceptance of

Woods, the one black juror, shows that race was not in play. Woods was the eighth juror, qualified in the fifth week of jury selection. (Citation omitted). When the State accepted him, 11 of its 15 peremptory strikes were gone, 7 of them used to strike black panel members. (Citation omitted). The juror questionnaires show that at least three members of the venire panel yet to be questioned on the stand were opposed to capital punishment,... (Citation omitted). With at least three remaining panel members highly undesirable to the State, the prosecutors had to exercise prudent restraint in using strikes. This late-stage decision to accept a black panel member willing to impose a death sentence does not, therefore, neutralize the early-stage decision to challenge a comparable venireman, Warren. In fact, if the prosecutors were going to accept any black juror to obscure the otherwise consistent pattern of opposition to seating one, the time to do so was getting late…

B.

The case for discrimination goes beyond these comparisons to include broader patterns of practice during the jury selection. The prosecution's shuffling of the venire panel, its enquiry into views on the death penalty, it's questioning about minimum acceptable sentences: all indicate decisions probably based on race. Finally, the appearance of discrimination is confirmed by widely known evidence of the general policy of the Dallas County District Attorney's Office to exclude black venire members from juries at the time Miller-El's jury was selected.

The first clue to the prosecutors' intentions, distinct from the peremptory challenges themselves, is their resort during *voir dire* to a procedure known in Texas as the jury shuffle. In the State's criminal practice, either side may literally reshuffle the cards bearing panel members' names, thus rearranging the order in which members of a venire panel are seated and reached for questioning. Once the order is established, the panel members seated at the back are likely to escape *voir dire* altogether, for those not questioned by the end of the week are dismissed. As we previously explained, "the prosecution's decision to seek a jury shuffle when a predominant number of African-Americans were seated in the front of the panel, along with its decision to delay a formal objection to the defense's shuffle until after the new racial composition was revealed, raise a suspicion that the State sought to exclude African-Americans from the jury. Our concerns are amplified by the fact that the state court also had before it, and apparently ignored, testimony demonstrating that the Dallas County District Attorney's Office had, by its own admission, used this process to manipulate the racial composition of the jury in the past." (Citation omitted).

In this case, the prosecution and then the defense shuffled the cards at the beginning of the first week of *voir dire*; the record does not reflect the changes in order. (Citation omitted). At the beginning of the second week, when a number of black members were seated at the front of the panel, the prosecution shuffled. (Citation omitted). At the beginning of the third week, the first four panel members were black. The prosecution shuffled, and these black panel members ended up at the back. Then the defense shuffled, and the black panel members again appeared at the front. The prosecution requested another shuffle, but the trial court refused. (Citation omitted). Finally, the defense shuffled at the beginning of the fourth and fifth weeks of *voir dire*; the record does not reflect the panel's racial composition before or after those shuffles. (Citation omitted)...

The next body of evidence that the State was trying to avoid black jurors is the contrasting *voir dire* questions posed respectively to black and nonblack panel members, on two different subjects. First, there were the prosecutors' statements preceding questions about a potential juror's thoughts on capital punishment. Some of these prefatory statements were cast in general terms, but some followed the so-called graphic script, describing the method of execution in rhetorical and clinical detail. It is intended, Miller-El contends, to prompt some expression of hesitation to consider the death penalty and thus to elicit plausibly neutral grounds for a peremptory strike of a potential juror subjected to it, if not a strike for cause. If the graphic script is given to a higher proportion of blacks than whites, this is evidence that prosecutors more often wanted blacks off the jury, absent some neutral and extenuating explanation.

As we pointed out last time, for 94% of white venire panel members, prosecutors gave a bland description of the death penalty before asking about the individual's feelings on the subject. Miller-El v. Cockrell, 537 U.S., at 332. The abstract account went something like this:

"I feel like it [is] only fair that we tell you our position in this case. The State of Texas…is actively seeking the death penalty in this case for Thomas Joe Miller-El. We anticipate that we will be able to present to a jury the quantity and type of evidence necessary to convict him of capital murder and the quantity and type of evidence sufficient to allow a jury to answer these three questions over here in the affirmative. A yes answer to each of those questions results in an automatic death penalty from Judge McDowell." (Citation omitted).

Only 6% of white venire panelists, but 53% of those who were black, heard a different description of the death penalty before being asked their feelings about it. This is an example of the graphic script:

"I feel like you have a right to know right up front what our position is. Mr. Kinne, Mr. Macaluso and myself, representing the people of Dallas County and the state of Texas, are actively seeking the death penalty for Thomas Joe Miller-El…

"We do that with the anticipation that, when the death penalty is assessed, at some point Mr. Thomas Joe Miller-El-the man sitting right down there-will be taken to Huntsville and will be put on death row and at some point taken to the death house and placed on a gurney and injected with a lethal substance until he is dead as a result of the proceedings that we have in this court on this case. So that's basically our position going into this thing." (Citation omitted)…

The State's purported rationale fails again if we look only to the treatment of ambivalent panel members, ambivalent black individuals having been more likely to receive the graphic description than ambivalent nonblacks. Three nonblack members of the venire indicated ambivalence to the death penalty on their questionnaires; only one of them, Fernando Gutierrez, received the graphic script. But of the four black panel members who expressed ambivalence, all got the graphic treatment...

There is a final body of evidence that confirms this conclusion. We know that for decades leading up to the time this case was tried prosecutors in the Dallas County office had followed a specific policy of systematically excluding blacks from juries, as we explained the last time the case was here.

"Although most of the witnesses [presented at the *Swain* hearing in 1986] denied the existence of a systematic policy to exclude African-Americans, others disagreed. A Dallas County district judge testified that, when he had served in the District Attorney's Office from the late-1950's to early-1960's, his superior warned him that he would be fired if he permitted any African-Americans to serve on a jury. Similarly, another Dallas County district judge and former assistant district attorney from 1976 to 1978 testified that he believed the office had a systematic policy of excluding African-Americans from juries.

"Of more importance, the defense presented evidence that the District Attorney's Office had adopted a formal policy to exclude minorities from jury service.... A manual entitled 'Jury Selection in a Criminal Case' [sometimes known as the Sparling Manual] was distributed to prosecutors. It contained an article authored by a former prosecutor (and later a judge) under the direction of his superiors in the District Attorney's Office, outlining the reasoning for excluding minorities from jury service. Although the manual was written in 1968, it remained in circulation until 1976, if not later, and was available at least to one of the prosecutors in Miller-El's trial." (Citation omitted).

Prosecutors here "marked the race of each prospective juror on their juror cards." (Citation omitted)...

In the course of drawing a jury to try a black defendant, 10 of the 11 qualified black venire panel members were peremptorily struck. At least two of them, Fields and Warren, were ostensibly acceptable to prosecutors seeking a death verdict, and Fields was ideal. The prosecutors' chosen race-neutral reasons for the strikes do not hold up and are so far at odds with the evidence that pretext is the fair conclusion, indicating the very discrimination the explanations were meant to deny....

If anything more is needed for an undeniable explanation of what was going on, history supplies it. The prosecutors took their cues from a 20-year old manual of tips on jury selection, as shown by their notes of the race of each potential juror. By the time a jury was chosen, the State had peremptorily challenged 12% of qualified nonblack panel members, but eliminated 91% of the black ones.

It blinks reality to deny that the State struck Fields and Warren, included in that 91%, because they were black. The strikes correlate with no fact as well as they correlate with race, and they occurred during a selection infected by shuffling and disparate questioning that race explains better than any race-neutral reason advanced by the State. The State's pretextual positions confirm Miller-El's claim, and the prosecutors' own notes proclaim that the Sparling Manual's emphasis on race was on their minds when they considered every potential juror....

The judgment of the Court of Appeals is reversed, and the case is remanded for entry of judgment for petitioner together with orders of appropriate relief.

It is so ordered.

C.
Imposition of the Death Penalty and the Eighth Amendment

When does the State have the right to kill it's citizens? In the slavery era police knew that their law did not protect blacks and that they had the right to keep blacks in their place. Ironically, this was the situation in Mississippi in the mid 1960's. Three Mississippi law men and fifteen individuals set out to kill three civil rights workers: James Chaney, Andrew Goodman and Michael Schwerner. The three workers were held in police custody, released and followed by a group of police and private citizens down a dark Mississippi road. The civil rights workers were then taken out into a wooded area and brutally slain. The officers were charged with criminal offenses, but the District Court dismissed the charges against the remaining fifteen private citizens. The appeals to this case were heard by the United States Supreme Court. The opinion delivered by Justice Fortas was that the decision of the lower court must be reversed and the case remanded.

This case did not end the practice of the police taking the law into their own hands in the name of justice, as was the situation in Los Angeles in 1992 in the Rodney King case. Rodney King was a black man who was caught speeding and then resisted police arrest. Because he resisted, the police used excessive physical force to apprehend him. Fortunately, the entire event was captured on videotape. As their defense, police claimed that in an effort to make an arrest of an unruly and dangerous individual, they had to subdue him with force. The police were acquitted by a lower district court, but after public outcry through riots and talk shows, the case was then tried in a federal court. The final outcome was that two of the four defendants were found guilty. The question remains; how often do police abuse their authority and exhibit racial prejudice in the name of justice? Could such unlawful, official conduct cause an innocent person to be charged and convicted of a capital offense?

Some people may argue that the police are only upholding the law. Has the law purged itself of racism borne from the slavery era? Are black men stigmatized by their color and their prior condition of servitude? What safeguards should be developed to protect black men in the sentencing process? Can inequities occur not only during the time of a trial, but also at the time of sentencing? In the case of Furman v. Georgia, the Supreme Court struck down the death penalty. Using the Eighth Amendment as a basis they declared the use of the death penalty to be cruel and unusual punishment. In the 1976 case of Gregg v. Georgia the high court reversed itself and allowed the decision to administer the death penalty to be left up to the individual states. In the case of McCleskey v. Kemp, the defense presented striking evidence and documentation that the death penalty was unfairly administered to black men. Although, the Supreme Court acknowledged that discrimination does occur in the sentencing process, it felt that there was insufficient evidence to rule in favor of McCleskey. Should the court have decided McCleskey differently given the history of slavery and the statistical evidence presented in the Baldus Study? Is the death penalty fair?

FURMAN v. GEORGIA
Supreme Court of the United States
476 U.S. 79 (1972)

PER CURIAM.

Petitioner in No. 69-5003 was convicted of murder in Georgia and was sentenced to death pursuant to Ga. Code Ann. ' 26-1005 (Supp. 1971) (effective prior to July 1,1969). 225 Ga. 253, 167 S. E. 2d 628 (1969). Petitioner in No. 69-5030 was convicted of rape in Georgia and was sentenced to death pursuant to Ga. Code Ann. ' 26-1302(Supp. 1971) (effective prior to July 1, 1969). 225 Ga.790, 171 S. 13. 2d 501 (1969). Petitioner in No. 69-5031 was convicted of rape in Texas and was sentenced to death pursuant to Tex. Penal Code, Art. 1189 (1961).447 S. W. 2d 932 (Ct. Crim. App. 1969). Certiorari was granted limited to the following question: "Does the imposition and carrying out of the death penalty in[these cases] constitute cruel and unusual punishment in violation of the Eighth and Fourteenth Amendments?"403 U.S. 952 (1971). The Court holds that the imposition and carrying out of the death penalty in these cases constitute cruel and unusual punishment in violation of the Eighth and Fourteenth Amendments. The judgment in each case is therefore reversed insofar as it leaves un-disturbed the death sentence imposed, and the cases are remanded for further proceedings.

So ordered.

MR. JUSTICE DOUGLAS, MR. JUSTICE BRENNAN, MR. JUSTICE STEWART, MR. JUSTICE WHITE, and MR. JUSTICE MARSHALL have filed separate opinions in support of the judgments. THE CHIEF JUSTICE, MR. JUSTICE BLACKMUN, MR. JUSTICE POWELL, and MR. JUSTICE REHNQUIST have filed separate dissenting opinions.

MR. JUSTICE DOUGLAS, concurring.

In these three cases the death penalty was imposed, one of them for murder, and two for rape. In each the determination of whether the penalty should be death or a lighter punishment was left by the State to the discretion of the judge or of the jury. In each of the three cases the trial was to a jury. They are here on petitions for certiorari which we granted limited to the question whether the imposition and execution of the death penalty constitute "cruel and unusual punishment" within the meaning of the Eighth Amendment as applied to the States by the Fourteenth". (Footnote omitted). I vote to vacate each judgment, believing that the exaction of the death penalty does violate the Eighth and Fourteenth Amendments. That the requirements of due process ban cruel and unusual punishment is now settled. (Citation omitted). It is also settled that the proscription of cruel and unusual punishments forbids the judicial imposition of them as well as their imposition by the legislature. (Citation omitted).

Congressman Bingham, in proposing the Fourteenth Amendment, maintained that "the privileges or immunities of citizens of the United States" as protected by the Fourteenth Amendment included protection against "cruel and unusual punishments:

[M]any instances of State injustice and oppression have already occurred in the State legislation of this Union, of flagrant violations of the guaranteed privileges of citizens of the United States, for which the national Government furnished and could furnish by law no remedy whatever. Contrary to the express letter of your Constitution, 'cruel and unusual punishments' have been inflicted under State laws within this Union upon citizens, not only for crimes committed, but for sacred duty one, for which and against which the Government of the United States had provided no remedy and could provide none." Cong. Globe, 39th Cong., 1st Sess., 2542. Whether the privileges and immunities route is followed, or the due process route, the result is the same. It has been assumed in our decisions that punishment by death is not cruel, unless the manner of execution can be said to be inhuman and barbarous. In *re Kemmler*, 136 U.S. 436, 447. It is also said in our opinions that the proscription of cruel and unusual punishments "is not fastened to the obsolete but may acquire meaning as public opinion becomes enlightened by a humane justice." (Citation omitted). A like statement was made in *Trop v. Dulles*, 356 U.S. 86, 101, that the Eighth Amendment "must draw its meaning from the evolving standards of decency that mark the progress of a maturing society."…

Mr. Justice Field, dissenting in *O'Neil v. Vermont*, 144 U.S. 323, 340, said, "The State may, indeed, make the drinking of one drop of liquor an offence to be punished by imprisonment, but it would be an unheard-of cruelty if it should count the drops in a single glass and make thereby a thousand offenses, and thus extend the punishment for drinking the single glass of liquor to an imprisonment of almost indefinite duration." What the legislature may not do for all classes uniformly and systematically, a judge or jury may not do for a class that prejudice sets apart from the community.

There is increasing recognition of the fact that the basic theme of equal protection is implicit in "cruel and unusual" punishments. "A penalty... should be considered 'unusually' imposed if it is administered arbitrarily or discriminatorily." (Footnote omitted). The same authors add that "[t]he extreme rarity with which applicable death penalty provisions are put to use raises a strong inference of arbitrariness." (Footnote omitted). The President's Commission on Law Enforcement and Administration of Justice recently concluded: (Footnote omitted).

"Finally there is evidence that the imposition of the death sentence and the exercise of dispensing power by the courts and the executive follow discriminatory patterns. The death sentence is disproportionately imposed and carried out on the poor, the Negro, and the members of unpopular groups."

A study of capital cases in Texas from 1924 to 1968 reached the following conclusions: (Footnote omitted).

"Application of the death penalty is unequal: most of those executed were poor, young, and ignorant. Seventy-five of the 460 cases involved co-defendants, who, under Texas law, were given separate trials. In several instances where a white and a Negro were co-defendants, the white was sentenced to life imprisonment or a term of years, and the Negro was given the death penalty. Another ethnic disparity is found in the type of sentence imposed for rape. The Negro convicted of rape is far more likely to get the death penalty than a term sentence, whereas whites and Latins are far more likely to get a term sentence than the death penalty."

Warden Lewis E. Lawes of Sing Sing said: (Footnote omitted).

"Not only does capital punishment fail in its justification, but no punishment could be invented with so many inherent defects. It is an unequal punishment in the way it is applied to the rich and to the poor. The defendant of wealth and position never goes to the electric chair or to the gallows. Juries do not intentionally favour the rich, the law is theoretically impartial, but the defendant with ample means is able to have his case presented with every favourable aspect, while the poor defendant often has a lawyer assigned by the court. Sometimes such assignment is considered part of political patronage; usually the lawyer assigned has had no experience whatever in a capital case."

Former Attorney General Ramsey Clark has said, "It is the poor, the sick, the ignorant, the powerless and the hated who are executed." (Footnote omitted). One searches our chronicles in vain for the execution of any member of the affluent strata of this society. The Leopolds and Loebs are given prison terms, not sentenced to death.

Jackson, a black, convicted of the rape of a white woman, was 21 years old. A court-appointed psychiatrist said that Jackson was of average education and average intelligence, that he was not an imbecile, or schizophrenic, or psychotic, that his traits were the product of environmental influences, and that he was competent to stand trial. Jackson had entered the house after the husband left for work. He held scissors against the neck of the wife, demanding money. She could find none and a struggle ensued for the scissors, a battle which she lost; and she was then raped, Jackson keeping the scissors pressed against her neck. While there did not appear to be any long-term traumatic impact on the victim, she was bruised and abrased in the struggle but was not hospitalized. Jackson was a convict who had escaped from a work gang in the area, a result of a three-year sentence for auto theft. He was at large for three days and during that time had committed several other offenses-burglary, auto theft, and assault and battery. *Furman*, a black, killed a householder while seeking to enter the home at night. *Furman* shot the deceased through a closed door. He was 26 years old and had finished the sixth grade in school. Pending trial, he was committed to the Georgia Central State Hospital for a psychiatric examination on his plea of insanity tendered by court-appointed counsel. The superintendent reported that a unanimous staff diagnostic conference had concluded "that this patient should retain his present diagnosis of Mental Deficiency, Mild to Moderate, with Psychotic Episodes associated with Convulsive Disorder." The physicians agreed that "at present the patient is not psychotic, but he is not capable of cooperating with his counsel in the preparation of his defense"; and the staff believed "that he is in need of further psychiatric hospitalization and treatment."

Later, the superintendent reported that the staff diagnosis was Mental Deficiency, Mild to Moderate, with Psychotic Episodes associated with Convulsive Disorder. He concluded, however, that *Furman* was "not psychotic at present, knows right from wrong and is able to cooperate with his counsel in preparing his defense."

Branch, a black, entered the rural home of a 65 year-old widow, a white, while she slept and raped her, holding his arm against her throat. Thereupon he demanded money and for 30 minutes or more the widow searched for money, finding little. As he left, Jackson said if the widow told anyone what happened, he would return and kill her. The record is barren of any medical or psychiatric evidence showing injury to her as a result of Branch's attack.

He had previously been convicted of felony theft and found to be a borderline mental deficient and well below the average IQ of Texas prison inmates. He had the equivalent of five and a half years of grade school education. He had a "dull intelligence" and was in the lowest fourth percentile of his class.

We cannot say from facts disclosed in these records that these defendants were sentenced to death because they were black. Yet our task is not restricted to an effort to divine what motives impelled these death penalties. Rather, we deal with a system of law and of justice that leaves to the uncontrolled discretion of judges or juries the determination whether defendants committing these crimes should die or be imprisoned. Under these laws no standards govern the selection of the penalty. People live or die, dependent on the whim of one man or of 12...

Any law which is nondiscriminatory on its face may be applied in such a way as to violate the Equal Protection Clause of the Fourteenth Amendment. (Citation omitted). Such conceivably might be the fate of a mandatory death penalty, where equal or lesser sentences were imposed on the elite, a harsher one on the minorities or members of the lower castes. Whether a mandatory death penalty would otherwise be constitutional is a question I do not reach.

I concur in the judgments of the Court.

MR. JUSTICE MARSHALL, Concurring.
These three cases present the question whether the death penalty is a cruel and unusual punishment prohibited by the Eighth Amendment Constitution". (Footnote omitted)...

The criminal acts with which we are confronted are ugly, vicious, reprehensible acts. Their sheer brutality cannot and should not be minimized. But, we are not called upon to condone the penalized conduct; we are asked only to examine the penalty imposed on each of the petitioners and to determine whether or not it violates the Eighth Amendment. The question then is not whether we condone rape or murder, for surely we do not; it is whether capital punishment is "a punishment no longer consistent with our own self-respect" (Footnote omitted) and, therefore, violative of the Eighth Amendment...

V.

In order to assess whether or not death is an excessive or unnecessary penalty, it is necessary to consider the reasons why a legislature might select it as punishment for one or more offenses, and examine whether less severe penalties would satisfy the legitimate legislative wants as well as capital punishment. If they would, then the death penalty is unnecessary cruelty, and, therefore, unconstitutional.

There are six purposes conceivably served by capital punishment: retribution, deterrence, prevention of repetitive criminal acts, encouragement of guilty pleas and confessions, eugenics, and economy. These are considered *seriatim* below.

A. The concept of retribution is one of the most misunderstood in all of our criminal jurisprudence. The principal source of confusion derives from the fact that, in dealing with the concept, most people confuse the question "why do men in fact punish?" with the question "what justifies men in punishing?" (Footnote omitted). Men may punish for any number of reasons, but the one reason that punishment is morally good or morally justifiable is that someone has broken the law. Thus, it can correctly be said that breaking the law is the *sine qua non* of punishment, or, in other words, that we only tolerate punishment as it is imposed on one who deviates from the norm established by the criminal law... Punishment as retribution has been condemned by scholars for centuries, (Footnote omitted) and the Eighth Amendment itself was adopted to prevent punishment from becoming synonymous with vengeance...

To preserve the integrity of the Eighth Amendment, the Court has consistently denigrated retribution as a permissible goal of punishment. (Footnote omitted). It is undoubtedly correct that there is a demand for vengeance on the part of many persons in a community against one who is convicted of a particularly offensive act. At times a cry is heard that morality requires vengeance to evidence society's abhorrence of the act. (Footnote omitted). But the Eighth Amendment is our insulation from our baser selves. The "cruel and unusual" language limits the avenues through which vengeance can be channeled. Were this not so, the language would be empty and a return to the rack and other tortures would be possible in a given case....

The history of the Eighth Amendment supports only the conclusion that retribution for its own sake is improper.

B. The most hotly contested issue regarding capital punishment is whether it is better than life imprisonment as a deterrent to crime. (Footnote omitted).

While the contrary position has been argued, (Footnote omitted) it is my firm opinion that the death penalty is a more severe sanction than life imprisonment. Admittedly, there are some persons—who would rather die than languish in prison for a lifetime. But, whether or not they should be able to choose death as an alternative is a far different question from that presented here i.e., whether the State can impose death as a punishment. Death is irrevocable; life imprisonment is not. Death, of course, makes rehabilitation impossible; life imprisonment does not. In short, death has always been viewed as the ultimate sanction and it seems perfectly reasonable to continue to view it as such. (Footnote omitted).

It must be kept in mind, then, that the question to be considered is not simply whether capital punishment is a deterrent, but whether it is a better deterrent than life imprisonment. (Footnote omitted).

There is no more complex problem than determining the deterrent efficacy of the death penalty. "Capital punishment has obviously failed as a deterrent when a murder is committed. We can number its failures. But we cannot number its successes. No one can ever know how many people have refrained from murder because of the fear of being hanged." (Footnote omitted). This is the nub of the problem and it is exacerbated by the paucity of useful data... (Footnote omitted)...

Statistics also show that the deterrent effect of capital punishment is no greater in those communities where executions take place than in other communities. (Footnote omitted). In fact, there is some evidence that imposition of capital punishment may actually encourage crime, rather than deter it. (Footnote omitted). And, while police and law enforcement officers are the strongest advocates of capital punishment, (Footnote omitted) the evidence is overwhelming that police are no safer in communities that retain the sanction than in those that have abolished it. (Footnote omitted)...

The United Nations Committee that studied capital punishment found that "[i]t is generally agreed between the retentionists and abolitionists, whatever their opinions about the validity of comparative studies of deterrence, that the data which now exist show no correlation between the existence of capital punishment and lower rates of capital crime." (Footnote omitted)...

As for the argument that it is cheaper to execute capital offender than to imprison him for life, even assuming that such an argument, if true, would support a capital sanction, it is simply incorrect. A disproportionate amount of money spent on prisons is attributable to death row. (Footnote omitted) Condemned men are not productive members of the prison community, although they could be, (Footnote omitted) and executions are expensive. (Footnote omitted) Appeals are often automatic, and courts admittedly spend more time with death cases. (Footnote omitted)...

When all is said and done, there can be no doubt that it costs more to execute a man than to keep him in prison for life." (Footnote omitted). ...There is no rationale basis for concluding that capital punishment is not excessive. It therefore violates the Eighth Amendment. (Footnote omitted)...

VI.

In addition, even if capital punishment is not excessive, it nonetheless violates the Eighth Amendment because it is morally unacceptable to the people of the United States at this time in their history…

► Notes & Questions

1. The Court seemed to base its decision upon the fact that the states had not developed standards to govern the imposition of the death penalty. In the absence of standards would it be more likely that the death penalty would be imposed in a discriminatory manner?

2. In *Gregg v. Georgia*, 428 U.S. 153 (1976), the Court reversed the *Furman* ruling and found the death penalty constitutional. Troy Gregg shot and killed two men who had picked him up as a hitchhiker. The Court based its decision upon the fact that Georgia had established standards to govern the imposition of the death penalty.

3. What problem is there with discretion in the criminal justice system? The police and the prosecution can make judgments concerning who they will arrest and prosecute, how vigorous they will prosecute and what penalties they will seek upon conviction. Would the limiting of discretion be one way to control inequality in sentencing and the death penalty?

4. Is waiting on death row for twenty years a violation of the 8th Amendment?

D.
Is the Death Penalty Applied in a Discriminatory Manner?

Does racism, a legacy of slavery, prevent blacks from receiving a fair and impartial trial? One of the important issues raised in a review of death penalty cases is whether black life is of less value than white life? Is there a greater likelihood that a black person will be put to death than a white person? When statistical evidence of disparity in imposition of the death penalty is presented, shouldn't the Court strike down the death penalty as cruel and unusual punishment?

MCCLESKEY v. KEMP, SUPERINTENDENT, GEORGIA DIAGNOSTIC and CLASSIFICATION CENTER
Supreme Court of the United States
481 U.S. 279 (1987)

JUSTICE POWELL delivered the opinion of the Court.

This case presents the question whether a complex statistical study that indicates a risk that racial considerations enter into capital sentencing determinations proves that petitioner *McCleskey*'s capital sentence is unconstitutional under the Eighth or Fourteenth Amendment.

I.

McCleskey, a black man, was convicted of two counts of armed robbery and one count of murder in the Superior Court of Fulton County, Georgia, on October 12, 1978. *McCleskey*'s convictions arose out of the robbery of a furniture store and the killing of a white police officer during the course of the robbery. The evidence at trial indicated that *McCleskey* and three accomplices planned and carried out the robbery. All four were armed. *McCleskey* entered the front of the store while the other three entered the rear. *McCleskey* secured the front of the store by rounding up the customers and forcing them to lie face down on the floor. The other three rounded up the employees in the rear and tied them up with tape. The manager was forced at gunpoint to turn over the store receipts, his watch, and $6. During the course of the robbery, a police officer, answering a silent alarm, entered the store through the front door. As he was walking down the center aisle of the store, two shots were fired. Both struck the officer. One hit him in the face and killed him.

Several weeks later, *McCleskey* was arrested in connection with an unrelated offense. He confessed that he had participated in the furniture store robbery, but denied that he had shot the police officer. At trial, the State introduced evidence that at least one of the bullets that struck the officer was fired from a .38 caliber Rossi revolver. This description matched the description of the gun that *McCleskey* had carried during the robbery. The State also introduced the testimony of two witnesses who had heard *McCleskey* admit to the shooting.

The jury convicted *McCleskey* of murder. (Footnote omitted). At the penalty hearings, (Footnote omitted) the jury heard arguments as to the appropriate sentence. Under Georgia law, the jury could not consider imposing the death penalty unless it found beyond a reasonable doubt that the murder was accompanied by one of the statutory aggravating circumstances. Ga. Code Ann.' 17-10-30(c) (1982). (Footnote omitted). The jury in this case found two aggravating circumstances to exist beyond a reasonable doubt: the murder was committed during the course of an armed robbery, ' 17-10-30(b)(2); and the murder was committed upon a peace officer engaged in the performance of his duties, ' 17-10-30(b)(8). In making its decision whether to impose the death sentence, the jury considered the mitigating and aggravating circumstances of *McCleskey*'s conduct. 117-10- 2(c). *McCleskey* offered no mitigating evidence. The jury recommended that he be sentenced to death on the murder charge and to consecutive life sentences on the armed robbery charges. The court followed the jury's recommendation and sentenced *McCleskey* to death. (Footnote omitted).

On appeal, the Supreme Court of Georgia affirmed the convictions and the sentences. (Citation omitted). This Court denied a petition for a writ of certiorari. (Citation omitted). The Superior Court of Fulton County denied *McCleskey*'s extraordinary motion for a new trial. *McCleskey* then filed a petition for a writ of habeas corpus in the Superior Court of Butts County. After holding an evidentiary hearing, the Superior Court denied relief. (Citation omitted). The Supreme Court of Georgia denied *McCleskey*'s application for a certificate of probable cause to appeal the Superior Court's denial of his petition, No. 81-5523, and this Court again denied certiorari (Citation omitted).

McCleskey next filed a petition for a writ of habeas corpus in the Federal District Court for the Northern District of Georgia. His petition raised 18 claims, one of which was that the Georgia capital sentencing process is administered in a racially discriminatory manner in violation of the Eighth and Fourteenth Amendments to the United States Constitution. In support of his claim, *McCleskey* proffered a statistical study performed by Professors David C. Baldus, Charles Pulaski, and George Woodworth (the Baldus study) that purports to show a disparity in the imposition of the death sentence in Georgia based on the race of the murder victim and, to a lesser extent, the race of the defendant. The Baldus study is actually two sophisticated statistical studies that examine over 2,000 murder cases that occurred in Georgia during the 1970's. The raw numbers collected by Professor Baldus indicate that defendants charged with killing white persons received the death penalty in 11% of the cases, but defendants charged with killing blacks received the death penalty in only 1% of the cases. The raw numbers also indicate a reverse racial disparity according to the race of the defendant: 4% of the black defendants received the death penalty, as opposed to 7% of the white defendants.

Baldus also divided the cases according to the combination of the race of the defendant and the race of the victim. He found that the death penalty was assessed in 22% of the cases involving black defendants and white victims; 8% of the cases involving white defendants and white victims; 1% of the cases involving black defendants and black victims; and 3% of the cases involving white defendants and black victims.

Similarly, Baldus found that prosecutors sought the death penalty in 70% of the cases involving black defendants and white victims; 32% of the cases involving white defendants and white victims; 15% of the cases involving black defendants and black victims; and 19% of the cases involving white defendants and black victims... The Court of Appeals affirmed the denial by the District Court of *McCleskey*'s petition for a writ of habeas corpus insofar as the petition was based upon the Baldus study, with three judges dissenting as to *McCleskey*'s claims based on the Baldus study. We granted certiorari, 478 U.S. 1019 (1986), and now affirm.

II.

McCleskey's first claim is that the Georgia capital punishment statute violates the Equal Protection Clause of the Fourteenth Amendment. (Footnote omitted). He argues that race has infected the administration of Georgia's statute in two ways: persons who murder whites are more likely to be sentenced to death than persons who murder blacks, and black murderers are more likely to be sentenced to death than white murderers. (Footnote omitted).

As a black defendant who killed a white victim, *McCleskey* claims that the Baldus study demonstrates that he was discriminated against because of his race and because of the race of his victim. In its broadest form, *McCleskey*'s claim of discrimination extends to every actor in the Georgia capital sentencing process, from the prosecutor who sought the death penalty and the jury that imposed the sentence, to the State itself that enacted the capital punishment statute and allows it to remain in effect despite its allegedly discriminatory application. We agree with the Court of Appeals, and every other court that has considered such a challenge, (Footnote omitted) that this claim must fail.

A.

Our analysis begins with the basic principle that a defendant who alleges an equal protection violation has the burden of proving "the existence of purposeful discrimination." Whitus v. Georgia, 385 U.S. 545, 550 (1967). (Footnote omitted). A corollary to this principle is that a criminal defendant must prove that the purposeful discrimination "had a discriminatory effect" on him. (Citation omitted). Thus, to prevail under the Equal Protection Clause, *McCleskey* must prove that the decisionmakers in his case acted with discriminatory purpose. He offers no evidence specific to his own case that would support an inference that racial considerations played a part in his sentence. Instead, he relies solely on the Baldus study. (Footnote omitted). *McCleskey* argues that the Baldus study compels an inference that his sentence rests on purposeful discrimination. *McCleskey*'s claim that these statistics are sufficient proof of discrimination, without regard to the facts of a particular case, would extend to all capital cases in Georgia, at least where the victim was white and the defendant is black...

But the nature of the capital sentencing decision, and the relationship of the statistics to that decision, are fundamentally different from the corresponding elements in the venire selection or Title VII cases. Most importantly, each particular decision to impose the death penalty is made by a petit jury selected from a properly constituted venire. Each jury is unique in its composition, and the Constitution requires that its decision rest on consideration of innumerable factors that vary according to the characteristics of the individual defendant and the facts of the particular capital offense. (Citation omitted). Thus, the application of an inference drawn from the general statistics to a specific decision in a trial and sentencing simply is not comparable to the application of an inference drawn from general statistics to a specific venire-selection or Title VII case. In those cases, the statistics relate to fewer entities, (Footnote omitted) and fewer variables are relevant to the challenged decisions". (Footnote omitted)

Another important difference between the cases in which we have accepted statistics as proof of discriminatory intent and this case is that, in the venire-selection and Title VII contexts, the decisionmaker has an opportunity to explain the statistical disparity. (Citation omitted). Here, the State has no practical opportunity to rebut the Baldus study. (Citation omitted). Similarly, the policy considerations behind a prosecutor's traditionally "wide discretion" (Footnote omitted) suggest the impropriety of our requiring prosecutors to defend their decisions to seek death penalties, "often years after they were made." (Footnote omitted). Moreover, absent far stronger proof, it is unnecessary to seek such a rebuttal, because a legitimate and unchallenged explanation for the decision is apparent from the record: *McCleskey* committed an act for which the United States Constitution and Georgia laws permit imposition of the death penalty. (Footnote omitted).

Finally, *McCleskey*'s statistical proffer must be viewed in the context of his challenge. *McCleskey* challenges decisions at the heart of the State's criminal justice system. "[O]ne of society's most basic tasks is that of protecting the lives of its citizens and one of the most basic ways in which it achieves the task is through criminal laws against murder." *Gregg v. Georgia*, 428 U.S. 153, 226 (1976) (WHITE, J., concurring). Implementation of these laws necessarily requires discretionary judgments. Because discretion is essential to the criminal justice process, we would demand exceptionally clear proof before we would infer that the discretion has been abused. The unique nature of the decisions at issue in this case also counsels against adopting such an inference from the disparities indicated by the Baldus study. Accordingly, we hold that the Baldus study is clearly insufficient to support an inference that any of the decisionmakers in *McCleskey*'s case acted with discriminatory purpose.

B.

McCleskey also suggests that the Baldus study proves that thetate as a whole has acted with a discriminatory purpose. He appears to argue that the State has violated the Equal Protection Clause by adopting the capital punishment statute and allowing it to remain in force despite its allegedly discriminatory application.

But "'[d]iscriminatory purpose'... implies more than intent as volition or intent as awareness of consequences. It implies that the decisionmaker, in this case a state legislature, selected or reaffirmed a particular course of action at least in part 'because of,' not merely 'in spite of,' its adverse effects upon an identifiable group." *Personnel Administrator of Massachusetts v. Feeney*, 442 U.S. 256, 279 (1979) (Footnote and citation omitted). (Citation omitted). For this claim to prevail, *McCleskey* would have to prove that the Georgia Legislature enacted or maintained the death penalty statute because of an anticipated racially discriminatory effect... (Citation omitted). There was no evidence then, and there is none now, that the Georgia Legislature enacted the capital punishment statute to further a racially discriminatory purpose. (Footnote omitted).

Nor has *McCleskey* demonstrated that the legislature maintains the capital punishment statute because of the racially disproportionate impact suggested by the Baldus study. As legislatures necessarily have wide discretion in the choice of criminal laws and penalties, and as there were legitimate reasons for the Georgia Legislature to adopt and maintain capital punishment, (Citation omitted), we will not infer a discriminatory purpose on the part of the State of Georgia. (Footnote omitted). Accordingly, we reject *McCleskey*'s equal protection claims.

II.

McCleskey also argues that the Baldus study demonstrates that the Georgia capital sentencing system violates the Eighth Amendment. (Footnote omitted). We begin our analysis of this claim by reviewing the restrictions on death sentences established by our prior decisions under that Amendment...

D.

In sum, our decisions since *Furman* have identified a constitutionally permissible range of discretion in imposing the death penalty. First, there is a required threshold below which the death penalty cannot be imposed. In this context, the State must establish rational criteria that narrow the decisionmaker's judgment as to whether the circumstances of a particular defendant's case meet the threshold. Moreover, a societal consensus that the death penalty is disproportionate to a particular offense prevents a State from imposing the death penalty for that offense. Second, States cannot limit the sentencer's consideration of any relevant circumstance that could cause it to decline to impose the penalty. In this respect, the State cannot channel the sentencer's discretion, but must allow it to consider any relevant information offered by the defendant...

B.

Although our decision in Gregg as to the facial validity of the Georgia capital punishment statute appears to foreclose *McCleskey*'s disproportionality argument, he further contends that the Georgia capital punishment system is arbitrary and capricious in application, and therefore his sentence is excessive, because racial considerations may influence capital sentencing decisions in Georgia. We now address this claim.

To evaluate *McCleskey*'s challenge, we must examine exactly what the Baldus study may show. Even Professor Baldus does not contend that his statistics prove that race enters into any capital sentencing decisions or that race was a factor in *McCleskey*'s particular case". (Footnote omitted). Statistics at most may show only a likelihood that a particular factor entered into some decisions. There is, of course, some risk of racial prejudice influencing a jury's decision in a criminal case. There are similar risks that other kinds of prejudice will influence other criminal trials. (Citation omitted)). *McCleskey* asks us to accept the likelihood allegedly shown by the Baldus study as the constitutional measure of an unacceptable risk of racial prejudice influencing capital sentencing decisions. This we decline to do...

McCleskey's argument that the Constitution condemns the discretion allowed decisionmakers in the Georgia capital sentencing system is antithetical to the fundamental role of discretion in our criminal justice system. Discretion in the criminal justice system offers substantial benefits to the criminal defendant. Not only can a jury decline to impose the death sentence, it can decline to convict or choose to convict of a lesser offense. Whereas decisions against a defendant's interest may be reversed by the trial judge or on appeal, these discretionary exercises of leniency are final and unreviewable. (Footnote omitted). Similarly, the capacity of prosecutorial discretion to provide individualized justice is firmly entrenched in American law." (Citation omitted). As we have noted, a prosecutor can decline to charge, offer a plea bargain, (Footnote omitted) or decline to seek a death sentence in any particular case… (Citation omitted).

C.

At most, the Baldus study indicates a discrepancy that appears to correlate with race. Apparent disparities in sentencing are an inevitable part of our criminal justice system. (Footnote omitted). The discrepancy indicated by the Baldus study is "a far cry from the major systemic defects identified in *Furman*," (Footnote omitted). As this Court has recognized, any mode for determining guilt or punishment "has its weaknesses and the potential for misuse." (Citation omitted). Specifically, "there can be 'no perfect procedure for deciding in which cases governmental authority should be used to impose death.'" (Citation omitted). Despite these imperfections, our consistent rule has been that constitutional guarantees are met when "the mode [for determining guilt or punishment] itself has been surrounded with safeguards to make it as fair as possible." Citation omitted). Where the discretion that is fundamental to our criminal process is involved, we decline to assume that what is unexplained is invidious. In light of the safeguards designed to minimize racial bias in the process, the fundamental value of jury trial in our criminal justice system, and the benefits that discretion provides to criminal defendants, we hold that the Baldus study does not demonstrate a constitutionally significant risk of racial bias affecting the Georgia capital sentencing process.

V.

Two additional concerns inform our decision in this case.... The Constitution does not require that a State eliminate any demonstrable disparity that correlates with a potentially irrelevant factor in order to operate a criminal justice system that includes capital punishment. As we have stated specifically in the context of capital punishment, the Constitution does not "plac[e] totally unrealistic conditions on its use." *Gregg v. Georgia*, 428 U.S., at 199, n. 50.

Second, *McCleskey*'s arguments are best presented to the legislative bodies. It is not the responsibility or indeed even the right of this Court to determine the appropriate punishment for particular crimes. It is the legislatures, the elected representatives of the people, that are "constituted to respond to the will and consequently the moral values of the people." (Citation omitted). Legislatures also are better qualified to weigh and "evaluate the results of statistical studies in terms of their own local conditions and with a flexibility of approach that is not available to the courts," (Citation omitted). Capital punishment is now the law in more than two-thirds of our States. It is the ultimate duty of courts to determine on a case-by-case basis whether these laws are applied consistently with the Constitution. Despite *McCleskey*'s wide-ranging arguments that basically challenge the validity of capital punishment in our multiracial society, the only question before us is whether in his case, (Citation omitted), the law of Georgia was properly applied. We agree with the District Court and the Court of Appeals for the Eleventh Circuit that this was carefully and correctly done in this case.

► Notes & Questions

1. In this decision the Court recognizes the importance of discretion in the criminal justice system. Do you agree with the Court's assessment of the importance of discretion?

2. Did the Court give the proper credence to the Baldus Study? Does the data raise an inference of discriminatory application?

3. Shouldn't the Court have considered the Baldus data in the context of Georgia's past practice of racial discrimination?

4. Why are so many members of society pressing for the death penalty? If the alarm stems from the sharp rise in violent crime, what other approaches can be utilized to combat the rise in crime?

5. Should the State be involved in the business of death?

6. Should there be a mandatory death penalty for killing a police officer? What about for terrorism or rape? The United States Supreme Court has ruled in *Coker v. Georgia* 433 U.S. 485 (1977) that the death penalty for rape is "…grossly disproportionate and excessive punishment…" Do you agree with the court's decision on rape? What arguments can you advance to justify the court's decision? Why would the death penalty be excessive for rape?

7. Since *McCleskey* there have been a number of cases that have raised similar issues. In *Fuller v. Georgia State Board of Pardons and Paroles*, 851 F.2d 1307 (1988), the United States Court of Appeals for the Eleventh Circuit denied claim that race was a factor in their denial of parole. In *United States v. Walker*, 910 F. Supp. 837 (1995) several Blacks unsuccessfully

▶ Notes & Questions

argued that the Department of Justice engaged in systematic racial discrimination in their policies and procedures relating to capital punishment. A white death row inmate's claim of economic discrimination was rejected on *McCleskey* grounds in *State of Arizona v. Stokkey*, 482 P.2d 505. Another white death row inmate unsuccessfully argued that he was more likely to receive a death sentence because his victim was white. Again the argument was rejected on *McCleskey* grounds, *Gerlaugh v. Lewis, 898 F. Supp.* 1388.

8. Should the death penalty be imposed for drug dealers? Are drug dealers a threat to American society? Should drug dealers be held responsible for drug deaths? Would the quantity of the drugs influence your decision concerning the death penalty for drug dealers?

9. As a result of the United States Supreme Court decision making the death penalty lawful, the number of executions has increased to a thirty-eight year high. In 1995 fifty-six men were executed, with 3,054 waiting in death row. The executed prisoners had been on death row for an average of 11 years and two months.[4] Of the 56 men executed, thirty-three were white (58.9%), two Hispanic, twenty-two black (39.3%) and one Asian. Even though blacks are approximately twelve (12) percent of the United States population, they were close to forty (40) percent of those executed in 1995. In the future blacks will continue to be disproportionately represented on death row, given that of the 3,054 individuals remaining on death row, 1,262 are black (41.3%) and 1,513 are white (49.5%). The remaining individuals were 22 Native Americans, 19 Asians and 2 other.

---

4   *The Boston Globe*, December 5, 1996

► Notes & Questions

10. Mumia Abu-Jamal— In 1981, Mumia Abu-Jamal was elected as President of the Philadelphia Association of Black Journalists. *Philadelphia Magazine* named him as a person to watch in 1981. He was a journalist who wrote about police brutality in Philadelphia and drove a cab at night. One night in 1981, at 4 a.m., he came upon a police officer who was beating a black man. It turned out that the man was his brother. Soon thereafter Mumia was shot in the stomach and the police officer was killed. Mumia was charged with killing the police officer. He was charged even though a police ballistics expert could not match the bullet killing the police officer with the gun that was legally registered to Mumia. Four individuals at the scene had reported seeing a man flee after the shooting. The police did not investigate these reports. At the trial the prosecution excluded 11 of 16 potential black jurors. The prosecution introduced into evidence the fact that as a youth, Mumia was a member of the Black Panther Party. He was convicted by a jury of ten whites and two blacks and sentenced to death. On death row in Pennsylvania, blacks make up 61% of the inmates, even though they are 9% of the state population. Is this disparity probative of discrimination? Many prominent individuals have come to the defense of Mumia, including American Civil Liberties Union, Amnesty International, U.S. Representative Ron Dellums, Southern Christian Leadership Conference, Ossie Davis, Whoopi Goldberg, Harry Belafonte, Ed Asner and Alice Walker. On June 15, 1995, Governor Thomas Ridge signed the death warrant for Mumia. He was scheduled to be executed on August 17, 1995. The execution has been delayed due to public outcry and appeals. Should Mumia receive a new trial? Should a potentially innocent man be sentenced to death, given the irregularities in his trial? On December 19, 2001,

► Notes & Questions

Judge William Yohn, a federal judge overturned the 1982 death sentence of Mumia. The United States Circuit Court of Appeals for the Third Circuit recently ruled that Mumia is entitled to another hearing on the sentencing portion of his case, but the Court upheld his conviction.

11. The question of whether the criminal justice system is fair to blacks has been raised many times as a reason why capital punishment should be outlawed. The most clarion argument has been that an innocent person may be sent to his death by the state. The following example adds credence to the argument. On May 11, 1978, a white couple in Chicago was murdered after being abducted from a Chicago gas station. The woman was raped and then shot in the head twice. Her fiance was also shot in the head. Four black men were apprehended the next day as a result of an anonymous tip. After a trial they were convicted of the murders. Two of the men were sentenced to death and the other two to life imprisonment. On June 15, 1996, three of the men, Kenneth Adams, William Rainge and Dennis Williams were released from prison, pending further review of their cases. Verneal Jimerson was released on bond after the Illinois Supreme Court overturned his conviction. The men were released due to new DNA evidence. The DNA tests proved that the semen found on the dead woman could not be that of the convicted men. In an interview with the New York Times, Dennis Williams said "It's like if you see a ghost. You believe it, but you don't. I had no doubt the state would murder me for a crime I did not commit. I just didn't think anybody cared." Another inmate, Ira Johnson, confessed to the killings. After he and three others killed Carol Schmal and Lawrence Lionberg, Mr. Johnson killed another woman. He is serving 74 years

▶ Notes & Questions

for that murder. Was it racism that caused the Chicago Police to arrest the four defendants without conducting a thorough investigation? Why would police officers do such?

12. Texas has executed more men and women than any other state (380) followed by Virginia (98).

13. Thirty seven states permit the death penalty. Yet, in 2007 New Jersey, through legislative action, outlawed the penalty.

14. In Connecticut, seven of nine inmates on death row have had their challenges bolstered by a Yale Law School study that concluded among other things the following: "Black Defendants receive death sentences at three times the rate of white defendants in cases where the victims are white. Killers of white victims are treated more severely than people who kill minorities, when it comes time to decide the charges. Minorities who kill whites receive death sentences at higher rates than minorities who kill minorities." (Dave Collins, "Yale Study: Race bias mars Conn. Death penalty cases" *Bay State Banner*, December 20, 2007.)

E.
Is the Death Penalty Fundamentally Unfair?

Two cases out of Tennessee reveal the extent to which the legal system puts innocent or undeserving people on death row and to death. The first case involves Ndume (Erskine Leroy Johnson) who has maintained that at the time of a Memphis robbery and murder, for which he was convicted, he was in St. Louis, Missouri with family members celebrating his mother's birthday. He had been on death row for twenty-two years before the Supreme Court of Tennessee ordered a new sentencing hearing on the grounds that the police withheld material information at the original hearing that would have shown that he had not fired a weapon in the direction of a sixteen year old girl and therefore did not deserve the sentence of death. As a result of this litigation, his death sentence was reduced to life imprisonment While on death row he became an accomplished painter and had 30 of his works displayed at Middle Tennessee State University in 2001. He has also become a model prisoner, and remains confident that his innocence will be established.

Ndume Olatushani Fights for his Dignity and Freedom

ERSKINE LEROY JOHNSON v. STATE OF TENNESSEE
Supreme Court of Tennessee, Western Section, at Jackson
38 S.W.3d 52
January 19, 2001

WILLIAM M. BARKER, J., delivered the opinion of the court:

This case comes before this Court on an appeal from a post-conviction petition filed by the appellee, Erskine Leroy Johnson, who was convicted of felony murder and sentenced to death by a jury in Shelby County in 1985. The events giving rise to this case occurred in early October of 1983 when the appellee and two other persons robbed a Food Rite Grocery Store in Memphis. Upon entering the store, the appellee approached the manager, who was working at the checkout counter, and the other two persons headed for the office where the safe was located. The appellee placed his pistol to the manager's head, and the manager turned around and threw up his hands. Witnesses testified that the manager hit or bumped into the appellee's pistol, causing it to fire a bullet into the ceiling of the store. After this shot was fired, the appellee shot the store manager twice, mortally wounding him. The appellee then went to the next open register, where he put his pistol close to the face of the manager's wife and demanded money. Meanwhile, the other two co-felons apprehended the security guard on the other side of the store, and one of them placed a pistol to his head. At some point during this episode, someone fired a bullet, known as the "Pac-Man" bullet, which went through a Pac-Man video-game machine and grazed a sixteen-year-old girl across her chest.

The appellee was tried and convicted of felony murder in December of 1985, and a jury sentenced him to die by electrocution. The jury found that the following three aggravating circumstances outweighed any mitigating circumstances: (1) that the defendant was previously convicted of one or more felonies that involved the use or threat of violence to the person. (Citations excluded)); (2) that the defendant knowingly created a great risk of death to two or more persons, other than the victim murdered, during his act of murder, (Citations excluded); and (3) that the murder was committed while the defendant was engaged in the commission of a robbery, (Citations excluded). The appellee's conviction and sentence were later affirmed by this Court in *State v. Johnson*, 762 S.W.2d 110 (Tenn. 1988).

On October 3, 1991, the appellee filed a pro se petition for post-conviction relief, and his appointed counsel later filed an amended petition in December of 1991. Eventually, additional attorneys were appointed to represent the appellee, and these attorneys filed a second amended petition in August of 1996. (Note excluded). The trial court held a hearing lasting seven days between December 1996 and February 1997. During this hearing, the appellee introduced, among other things, proof showing that the

State improperly withheld a police report at the sentencing hearing in violation of *Brady v. Maryland*, 373 U.S. 83, 83 S. Ct. 1194, 10 L. Ed. 2d 215 (1963). This police report, which was completed within days of the armed robbery, concluded that the "Pac-Man" bullet could not have been fired from the cash register area where the appellant was standing, due to the angle of the bullet entry into the machine. Moreover, photographs attached to the report showed that solid obstructions were between the cash register area and the Pac-Man machine. The appellee then argued that because he did not fire the bullet that grazed the sixteen-year-old girl, the proof was insufficient to establish the (i)(3) "great risk of death" aggravating circumstance. (Note excluded). On April 22, 1997, the trial judge dismissed the appellee's petition, finding that "the petition for post conviction relief as amended is without merit." Although the trial court found the felony murder aggravating circumstance inapplicable after this Court's decision in *State v. Middlebrooks*, 840 S.W.2d 317 (Tenn. 1992), the court found that the error was harmless given "the strong case supporting the other two aggravating circumstances found by the jury..." The trial court made no specific written findings with respect to the alleged Brady violation concerning the withheld police report.

The Court of Criminal Appeals reversed the dismissal of the petition and remanded the case for a new capital sentencing hearing. The intermediate court found that the withheld police report was material exculpatory evidence within the meaning of *Brady v. Maryland*, 373 U.S. 83, 10 L. Ed. 2d 215, 83 S. Ct. 1194 (1963), and therefore, the report should have been disclosed to the appellee. This failure to disclose the police report, the court stated, resulted in an arguable misapplication of the (i)(3) aggravating circumstance. Viewing the withheld report in combination with the unconstitutional application of the felony murder aggravating circumstance, the court stated that it was "unable to conclude that the jury would have sentenced the Defendant to death based solely on the prior violent felonies aggravator." Accordingly, while the Court of Criminal Appeals affirmed the judgment of the trial court in all other respects, it remanded the case for a new capital sentencing hearing.

The State then requested, and this Court granted, permission to appeal on the sole issue of whether the withheld police report was "material" as applied to the (i)(3) "great risk of death" aggravating circumstance. After reviewing the extensive record in this case, we conclude that the police report was both "evidence favorable to the accused" and "material" within the meaning of *Brady v. Maryland*. We therefore hold that the report should have been disclosed to the appellee prior to his sentencing hearing, and because the State's failure to disclose this police report severely undermines our confidence in the jury's sentence of death, we remand this case to the Shelby County Criminal Court for a new capital sentencing hearing.

ALLEGED BRADY VIOLATION DURING THE APPELLEE'S CAPITAL SENTENCING HEARING

Every criminal defendant is guaranteed the right to a fair trial under the Due Process Clause of the Fourteenth Amendment to the United States Constitution and the "Law of the Land" Clause of Article I, section 8 of the Tennessee Constitution. (Citations excluded). "To facilitate this right, a defendant has a constitutionally protected privilege to request and obtain from the prosecution evidence that is either material to guilt or relevant to punishment." (Citation excluded) This fundamental principle of law is derived from the landmark case, *Brady v. Maryland*, 373 U.S. 83, 10 L. Ed. 2d 215, 83 S. Ct. 1194 (1963), in which the United States Supreme Court held that "suppression by the prosecution of evidence favorable to an accused upon request violates due process where the evidence is material either to guilt or to punishment, irrespective of the good faith or bad faith of the prosecution," (Citation excluded)" favorable to an accused" includes evidence deemed to be exculpatory in nature and evidence that could be used to impeach the state's witnesses. (Citation excluded)…

…In this case, there is no question that the first two requirements have been met. Before the appellee's trial in 1985, defense counsel made a general Brady request seeking "copies of and the right to inspect any written statements given to the prosecution and/

or any investigatory agencies which in whole or in part support the innocence of the accused and/or is exculpatory in nature..." Moreover, it is clear that the State has suppressed this police report given that it has had this report in its possession since its completion on October 8, 1983. (Note excluded).

We also conclude that the police report is information favorable to the accused... (Citation omitted). As we view the police report in the context of the State's theory supporting the death penalty at the sentencing hearing, we conclude that this third factor is easily met.

The State's principal theory as to the application of the (i)(3) aggravating circumstance was that the appellee fired the "Pac-Man" bullet that grazed a sixteen-year-old girl, Melinda Jordan, (Note excluded) and the State made clear that it believed that the appellee alone fired the shots from the cash register area during the robbery...

When viewed in light of the State's theory, the withheld police report clearly tends to "corroborate the accused's position in asserting his innocence [in firing the "Pac-Man" bullet]." (Citation excluded). Moreover, because the report calls into question a key "element of the prosecution's version of events," i.e., that the appellee fired the "Pac-Man" bullet, (Citation omitted), this report constitutes "evidence favorable to the accused" within the meaning of Brady, and it should have been disclosed by the State. Accordingly, we conclude that the appellee has successfully established the third element needed to assert a constitutional violation under Brady.

The only remaining issue, then, is whether the failure of the State to disclose the police report was "material" as to the sentence of death. Evidence is deemed to be material when "there is a reasonable probability that, had the evidence been disclosed to the defense, the result of the proceeding would have been different." (Citation omitted)... Instead, a reviewing court must determine whether the defendant has shown that "the favorable evidence could reasonably be taken to put the whole case in such a different light as to undermine the confidence of the verdict." (Citation omitted). In other words, evidence is material when, because of its absence, the defendant failed to receive a fair trial, "understood as a trial resulting in a verdict worthy of confidence." (Citation omitted)...

After carefully reviewing the extensive record in this appeal, including the record of the original trial, we believe that the withheld police report "could reasonably be taken to put the whole case in such a different light as to undermine confidence in the [sentencing] verdict." As in Kyles, 514 U.S. at 445, the "likely damage" from the State's suppression of the police report in this case "is best understood by taking the word of the prosecutor" during his arguments to the jury. As the State concedes in its brief before this Court, "the prosecutor did rely heavily upon the Pac-Man bullet in closing argument to establish the great risk aggravator," and the emphasis placed upon this critical factor by the State can first be seen from its opening statement to the jury at the sentencing phase:...

From these statements, it is clear that the State relied heavily—if not almost exclusively—upon the shooting of this one sixteen-year-old girl to justify finding the (i)(3) aggravating circumstance, and also to support the finding that this aggravating circumstance, when considered with the others, outweighed any mitigating circumstances...

We conclude that the disproportionate amount of attention devoted to showing that the appellee fired the infamous "Pac-Man" bullet, combined with the fact that the withheld police report seems to indicate that the appellee was never in a position to fire this bullet, certainly undermines confidence in the jury's sentence of death, as it significantly weakens confidence in the jury's finding and weighing of this particular aggravating circumstance... Under these circumstances, we cannot be reasonably confident that every single member of the jury, after considering the withheld report, would have applied this aggravating circumstance or that every member of the jury would have assigned it the same weight in relation to the other aggravating and mitigating circumstances. Accordingly, we hold that the withheld police report is "material" within the meaning of Brady...

From our review of the original trial transcript, we did find testimony that the appellee, after shooting the manager, held his pistol to the head of the store manager's wife and demanded money. While this fact could help provide a basis for finding the (i)(3)aggravating circumstance, we note that the great-risk-of-death aggravator requires that two or more people, other than the victim murdered, be placed in great risk of death. (Note and citation omitted). From our examination of the record, we cannot conclude that the State proved beyond a reasonable doubt that another person was placed in great risk of death by the appellee without the "Pac-Man" bullet, and we decline to adopt a per se rule that would automatically allow this aggravating circumstance in all felony murder cases where the defendant is armed with a pistol and others are present. Such a per se rule would not adequately provide for individualized sentencing, and it would unnecessarily broaden the (i)(3) aggravating circumstance to a point that it would fail in its essential function of narrowing the death-eligible class. (Citation omitted)...

Having found that all four elements necessary to establish a Brady violation are present, including that the withheld police report reasonably undermines confidence in the jury's verdict, we must remand this case for a new capital sentencing hearing... The appellee's sentence, therefore, is vacated, and this case is remanded to the Shelby County Criminal Court for a new capital sentencing hearing....

Ndume's Letter to the Public

It takes an extraordinary person to maintain his dignity in the face of unjust state oppression. In the above case there was mounting and overwhelming evidence that Ndume had been unlawfully on death row for twenty-two years. Many, such as Rev. Joseph Ingle, who have visited him over the years, have organized and fought for his freedom. Ndume, on the other hand, has had to struggle alone, to reach deep inside his soul to keep his real self alive. He gives us a glimpse of his life on Tennessee death row in the following essay written in June, 2002:

To those of whom my pain may concern:

If you could see my face, my smile would belie the pain of my suffering. We've often been told that our eyes are the windows to our souls. Sometime, I wonder when I stand before my little tin mirror straining to see my eyes clearly, if the pain of my soul can be told.

I think of myself as being fortunate than a lot of people and the fact that I have been given this opportunity to share my story is a testament of this. However, as fortunate as I think of myself, I am still forced every day to scan the recesses of my mind only to relive moments of personal pain and suffering as I search for illusive thoughts of joy. I have even wished many days that, "I could just lie down and never have to wake up to this hellish reality again." But then I find myself thinking, if I were to lie down and never get back up my captors will have won. And I refuse to let this instrument of death devour my mind, body, and soul or my will to fight for life over death.

As I sit here trying to think of the words to convey to you what life on death row has been like for me, I am quickly reminded that words are so grossly inadequate to express this reality.

Imagine if you had to live for 19 years in your bathroom without all of your personal things. Replace your bathtub with a cold steel slab with a two-inch foam cushion which serves as your mattress. Imagine that you are locked in your death cell for twenty-two hours of each day. The only light of day you get comes from a two-inch wide by three-foot high slit in the wall. The window is so small that you can only look out of it with one eye at a time, unless you stand several feet away from it.

Imagine that the air and heat circulating in your death cell is so stale and laden with secondhand smoke and dust particles from being recycled through the system that your mucous membranes bleed from the slightest blow of your nose, because your nose is so dried out from the stale recycled air. Imagine being cold and not having sufficient bed coverings, so that you have to sleep in two pair of socks, sweat pants, and shirt. Not so much because it is extremely cold outside, but because, instead of getting heat, cool air is being pumped into your death cell. And when you complain about it, you are told by the administration, "There is nothing we can do about it, because it is being controlled by computers hundreds of miles away."

Imagine trying to maintain a sense of sanity when you come out of your death cell to shower, and you know that by the time you get soaped up good, the guard will be coming to tell you that your time is up. Or when you go to the "yard" for fresh air and exercise, it turns out to be nothing more than a 20x20 foot cage which no caring individual would confine a cat or dog to. Perhaps, if you are lucky, you might experience a non-life threatening medical emergency, which would allow you to leave this death house to go to the infirmary. Even then, the entire time you are out of your cell, you must be shackled like an imaginary monster from some horror movie. But at least you get to feel the sun on your face and see the sky unobstructed by the many wires and fences that confine you when you are in the "yard."

How would you respond when a fellow prisoner, whom you have been having intelligent conversations with for years, suddenly changes? One day you try to engage him in a conversation and share your thoughts, and he looks as if he is seeing you for the very first time in his life. And instead of him responding to your approach, he begins to talk to himself. Do you search his eyes, hoping to find your own salvation? Or do you resign yourself to the unfortunate reality that another one has succumbed to the pressures of this devilish hell hole and its many mental deprivations?

Imagine being given enough food to keep you from starving, but never enough to get you full. And as bad as the food is, you find yourself looking forward to it. Imagine yourself being fed the same stuff over and over constantly. You know the days of the week by what you are fed. Even if you wanted to try escape this ordeal, distract yourself, and forget about the routine existence, you cannot because the smell of the food snaps you back to reality and reminds you of what day it is. For example, on a Tuesday or Saturday, the smell of powdered eggs and pork sausages, cooked two days prior to you getting them, tells you what day of the week it is.

In spite of my conditions and circumstances, I decided long ago that I had to make the best of what I have to work with. I would be lying if I told you that I never was a bitter man. Or that I never asked, "why me?" But after time, I realized that if I were going to raise myself up from the smoldering ashes of this hell hole intact, I had to turn my negative energy into some positive directions. Unfortunately, it is the suffering of my misfortune that has made me realize our existence here on earth has much more to do with our contributions to the betterment of all living creatures great and small. And little at all to do with our limited imagination beyond that of ourselves and those individuals immediately around us.

Now I want you to imagine that everything that I have said was happening to you for a crime that you did not commit. The death penalty has always served as the pretext for victory of injustice, by virtue of passive toleration. The only effective guarantee against the victory of injustice is an indivisible mass movement which refuses to allow the status quo to thrive. It is imperative that those who believe in justice for all become conscious of the fact that passive and silent approval of the oppression of others only makes themselves more vulnerable to those same oppressive forces of injustice. Can you imagine that?

Written by
Ndume Olatushani

Philip Workman: Was He Put to Death Unfairly?

In 2001 the second Tennessee inmate, Philip Workman came extremely close to being put to death by the state. In Nashville, friends and relatives had already begun a death vigil when just 42 minutes before he was scheduled to die, the Supreme Court of Tennessee stayed his execution and ruled that he was entitled to a hearing on the grounds that new information had come to the defense's attention that cast doubt on guilt. The new information was the following:

1. A prime prosecution witness in the trial, Harold Davis, recanted his testimony and said that the police had coerced him to point the finger at Workman. In a video tape confession in November, 1999, Davis stated that the Memphis police and prosecutors coached him to lie at the trial. He now says that he did not see Workman shoot Lt. Ronald Oliver on August 5, 1981.

2. The police and state medical examiner withheld X ray reports that showed that the officer had been shot by a caliber bullet other than the 45 caliber that Workman was alleged to have when he and others robbed a Wendy's Restaurant. The defense was told of the X rays in March, 2000.

3. The Chairman of the jury that convicted Workman and two other jurors have stated in sworn testimony that if they had the above information at trial they would not have convicted Workman.

4. The state Probation and Parole Board, equipped with this new evidence and testimony from two jurors that if they had this evidence they would not have convicted Workman, still refused to recommend clemency to Governor Don Sundquist. On March 30, 42 minutes from execution, the Tennessee high court in a 3 to 2 decision stayed the execution and ordered a hearing on the new evidence in the case.

On May 9, 2007, Philip Workman, a poor white man, was put to death despite lingering concerns over his innocence.

PHILIP R. WORKMAN v. STATE OF TENNESSEE
Supreme Court of Tennessee
Middle Section, at Nashville
41 S.W.3d 100
March 29, 2001

FRANK F. DROWOTA, III, ADOLPHO A. BIRCH, JR., and JANICE M. HOLDER, JJ., delivered the opinion of the court.

In this case, the trial court held that Workman's petition for a writ of error coram nobis is barred because he failed to file it timely within the statute of limitations. See Tenn. Code Ann. @ 40-26-105. The trial court rejected Workman's claim that the due process considerations discussed in *Burford v. State*, 845 S.W.2d 204 (Tenn. 1992) require tolling of the statute of limitations. For the reasons that follow, we reverse the decision of the trial court and order a hearing on Workman's petition for writ of error coram nobis. In our view, the due process considerations discussed in *Burford*, and more recently in *Seals v. State*, 23 S.W.3d 272 (Tenn. 2000) and *Williams v. State*, S.W.3d (Tenn. 2001), released just today, apply with even greater force when the statute of limitations is being applied in a capital case to bar a claim that newly discovered evidence may prove that the defendant is actually innocent of the capital crime of which he was convicted. (Note excluded)...

Clearly, in a variety of contexts, due process may require tolling of an applicable statute of limitations. As in *Burford*, to determine whether due process requires tolling in this case, we must consider the governmental interests involved and the private interests affected by the official action. In this case, as in *Burford*, the governmental interest in asserting the statute of limitations is the prevention of stale and groundless claims. The private interest involved here is the petitioner's opportunity to have a hearing on the grounds of newly discovered evidence which may have resulted in a different verdict if heard by the jury at trial. If the procedural time bar is applied, Workman will be put to death without being given any opportunity to have the merits of his claim evaluated by a court of this State.

Weighing these competing interests in the context of this case, we have no hesitation in concluding that due process precludes application of the statute of limitations to bar consideration of the writ of error coram nobis in this case. Workman's interest in obtaining a hearing to present newly discovered evidence that may establish actual innocence of a capital offense far outweighs any governmental interest in preventing the litigation stale claims. Workman has raised serious questions regarding whether he fired the shot that killed Memphis Police Lieutenant Ronald Oliver. If he did not fire that shot, he is not guilty of the crime for which he is scheduled to be put to death. These claims are based upon evidence obtained from the Shelby County Medical Examiner's Office long after the conclusion of the state post-conviction proceedings. The delay in obtaining this evidence is not attributable to the fault of Workman or his attorneys. In fact, Workman previously had filed a subpoena requesting an x-ray of this type, but it was not provided. No court in this State has actually held a hearing to fully evaluate the strength of these claims. Under such circumstances, Workman's interest in obtaining a hearing on these claims clearly outweighs the governmental interest embodied in the statute of limitations. Accordingly, due process precludes summary dismissal of this claim based upon a statutory time bar.

The fact that this petition for writ of error coram nobis was filed approximately thirteen months after discovery of the evidence at issue does not change the foregoing conclusion... Upon consideration of the circumstances of this case, we conclude that the time within which this petition was filed does not exceed the reasonable opportunity afforded by due process. Indeed, "the magnitude and gravity of the penalty of death persuades us that the important values which justify limits on untimely... petitions are outweighed" by Workman's interest having a court evaluate newly discovered evidence that may show actual innocence of the capital offense. (Citation omitted).

For the foregoing reasons, we conclude that the decision of the trial court dismissing the writ of error coram nobis should be reversed and the case remanded for a hearing. At the hearing, Workman will have the opportunity to establish that newly discovered evidence may have resulted in a different judgment if the evidence had been admitted at the previous trial. (Citation omitted). If he makes this showing, and if he also establishes that he "was without fault" in failing to present the newly discovered evidence at the appropriate time, he will be entitled to a new trial...

▶ Notes & Questions

1. Maryland Governor's Moratorium on Death Penalty
On May 9, 2002 the Governor of the State of Maryland issued a stay of execution for Wesley Eugene Baker on death row. The Governor wrote:

"The most difficult decision that a Governor must make is to determine whether or not the State should impose the death penalty. I continue to believe that there are certain crimes that are so brutal and so vile that they call for society to impose the ultimate punishment. However, reasonable questions have been raised in Maryland and across the country about the application of the death penalty.

It is imperative that I, as well as our citizens, have complete confidence that the legal process involved in capital cases is fair and impartial. An extensive two-year study by the University of Maryland examining the effects of racial and jurisdictional factors on the imposition of the death penalty is nearing completion. Given that the study will be released soon, and the critical need to be absolutely sure of the integrity of the process, I am issuing a stay for this case and I will stay any others that come before me, pending completion of the study.

In effect, I am issuing a moratorium until the study has been released and thoroughly reviewed by the Governor, the legislature and the public. It is important to note that the decision to issue these stays is in no way based on the specifics of these cases. While I have not conducted a full and comprehensive review of each case, I do know that the crimes for which the death row inmates were convicted and sentenced were vicious. They are precisely the type of terrible murders that call for the ultimate sanction.

We must have absolute confidence in the integrity of the process. I envision the stay remaining in place until the study is

▶ Notes & Questions

reviewed and acted upon by the legislature which I expect to take about a year. The next Governor will have the authority to adjust that timetable.

This was a difficult decision. My heart goes out to the families of the victims of these horrible crimes. But I must honor the responsibility I have to be absolutely certain of both the guilt of the criminal and the fairness and impartiality of the process."

2. Since the Governor has sought the death penalty for John Muhammad in the sniper cases of October, 2002, is this action consistent with his statement on the moratorium? Do you agree with his modified view?

3. Between September 5, 2002 and October 23, 2002 the Beltway Snipers, John Muhammad and Lee Malvo, age 17, shot and killed ten individuals. Both were convicted and John Muhammad was sentenced to death. Lee Malvo was sentenced to life without parole. It is clear that individuals under the age of 18 cannot be sentenced to death as a result of the 2005 Supreme Court decision in *Roper v. Simmons* 543 U.S. 551 (2005). Should juveniles be subject to the death penalty?

4. Is there a sign of hope that the Court will ban capital punishment given that a majority of the justices ruled recently that it was unconstitutional to execute mentally retarded prisoners? See *Atkins v. Virginia*, 536 U.S. 304(2002).

F.
Unequal Sentencing for Criminal Offenses
(Crack vs. Powder Cocaine)

The Reverend Jesse Jackson and other civil rights leaders have raised issues concerning unequal sentencing with respect to possession and sale of cocaine. They have alleged that the federal criminal statutes are unequal with respect to powder versus crack cocaine. It is believed that convictions for white powder cocaine tends to fall primarily upon white, more affluent individuals, while crack cocaine affects primarily black and poor people. Was the federal statute drafted deliberately to have this impact? Nevertheless, given this impact, should Congress change the law to equalize the penalities? What public purpose is served, if any, by the disparity in sentencing? Should prosecutorial discretion be limited?

UNITED STATES v. ARMSTRONG
Supreme Court of the United States
116 S. Ct. 1480 (1996)

Chief Justice Rehnquist delivered the opinion

In this case, we consider the showing necessary for a defendant to be entitled to discovery on a claim that the prosecuting attorney singled him out for prosecution on the basis of his race. We conclude that respondents failed to satisfy the threshold showing: They failed to show that the Government declined to prosecute similarly situated suspects of other races.

In April 1992, respondents were indicted in the United States District Court for the Central District of California on charges of conspiring to possess with intent to distribute more than 50 grams of cocaine base (crack) and conspiring to distribute the same, in violation of 21 USC '' 841 and 846 (1988 ed. and Supp. IV) [21 USCS '' 841 and 846], and federal firearms offenses. For three months prior to the indictment, agents of the Federal Bureau of

Alcohol, Tobacco and Firearms and the Narcotics Division of the Inglewood, California, Police Department had infiltrated a suspected crack distribution ring by using three confidential informants. On seven separate occasions during this period, the informants had bought a total of 124.3 grams of crack from respondents and witnessed respondents carrying firearms during the sales. The agents searched the hotel room in which the sales were transacted, arrested respondents Armstrong and Hampton in the room, and found more crack and a loaded gun. The agents later arrested the other respondents as part of the ring.

In response to the indictment, respondents filed a motion for discovery or for dismissal of the indictment, alleging that they were selected for federal prosecution because they are black. In support of their motion they offered only an affidavit by a "Paralegal Specialist," employed by the Office of the Federal Public Defender representing one of the respondents. The only allegation in the affidavit was that, in every one of the 24 841 or 846 cases closed by the office during 1991, the defendant was black. Accompanying the affidavit was a "study" listing the 24 defendants, their race, whether they were prosecuted for dealing cocaine as well as crack, and the status of each case. (Footnote omitted).

The Government opposed the discovery motion, arguing, among other things, that there was no evidence or allegation "that the Government has acted unfairly or has prosecuted nonblack defendants or failed to prosecute them." (Citation omitted). The District Court granted the motion. It ordered the Government (1) to provide a list of all cases from the last three years in which the Government charged both cocaine and firearms offenses, (2) to identify the race of the defendants in those cases, (3) to identify what levels of law enforcement were involved in the investigations of those cases, and

(4) to explain its criteria for deciding to prosecute those defendants for federal cocaine offenses. (Citation omitted)…

The Government moved for reconsideration of the District Court's discovery order…

The District Court denied the motion for reconsideration.

When the Government indicated it would not comply with the court's discovery order, the court dismissed the case". (Footnote omitted).

A divided three judge panel of the Court of Appeals for the Ninth Circuit reversed, holding that, because of the proof requirements for a selective-prosecution claim, defendants must "provide a colorable basis for believing that 'others similarly situated have not been prosecuted' to obtain discovery. (Citation omitted). The Court of Appeals voted to rehear the case en banc, and the en banc panel affirmed the District Court's order of dismissal, holding that a defendant is not required to demonstrate that the government has failed to prosecute others who are similarly situated." (Citation omitted) (emphasis deleted). We granted certiorari to determine the appropriate standard for discovery for a selective prosecution claim. (Citation omitted).

A selective prosecution claim asks a court to exercise judicial power over a "special province" of the Executive. (Citation omitted). The Attorney General and United States Attorneys retain broad discretion to enforce the Nation's criminal laws. (Citation omitted). They have this latitude because they are designated by statute as the President's delegates to help him discharge his constitutional responsibility to "take Care that the Laws be faithfully executed." (Citation omitted). As a result, "[t]he presumption of regularity supports" their prosecutorial decisions and "in the absence of clear evidence to the contrary, courts presume that they have properly discharged their official duties." (Citation omitted). In the ordinary case, "so long as the prosecutor has probable cause to believe that the accused committed an offense defined by statute, the decision whether or not to prosecute, and what charge to file or bring before a grand jury, generally rests entirely in his discretion." (Citation omitted).

Of course, a prosecutor's discretion is "subject to constitutional constraints." (Citation omitted). One of these constraints, imposed by the equal protection component of the Due Process Clause of the Fifth Amendment, *Bolling v Sharpe*, 347 US 497, 500, 98 L Ed 884, 74 S Ct 693 (1954), is that the decision whether to prosecute may not be based on "an unjustifiable standard such as race, religion, or other arbitrary classification,"... (Citation omitted).

In order to dispel the presumption that a prosecutor has not violated equal protection, a criminal defendant must present "clear evidence to the contrary." (Citation omitted). Judicial deference to the decisions of these executive officers rests in part on an assessment of the relative competence of prosecutors and courts. (Citation omitted)... The requirements for a selective-prosecution claim draw on "ordinary equal protection standards." (Citation omitted). The claimant must demonstrate that the federal prosecutorial policy "had a discriminatory effect and that it was motivated by a discriminatory purpose." (Citation omitted). To establish a discriminatory effect in a race case, the claimant must show that similarly situated individuals of a different race were not prosecuted.

The similarly situated requirement does not make a selective prosecution claim impossible to prove. Twenty years before Ah Sin, we invalidated an ordinance, also adopted by San Francisco, which prohibited the operation of laundries in wooden buildings. Yick Wo, 118 US, at 374, 30 L Ed 220, 6 S Ct 1064. The plaintiff in error successfully demonstrated that the ordinance was applied against Chinese nationals but not against other laundry- shop operators. The authorities had denied the applications of 200 Chinese subjects for permits to operate shops in wooden buildings, but granted the applications of 80 individuals who were not Chinese subjects to operate laundries in wooden buildings "under similar conditions."...

(Citation omitted)... The judgment of the Court of Appeals is therefore reversed, and the case is remanded for proceedings consistent with this opinion. It is so ordered.

Having reviewed the requirements to prove a selective prosecution claim, we turn to the showing necessary to obtain discovery in support of such a claim. If discovery is ordered, the Government must assemble from its own files documents which might corroborate or refute the defendant's claim. Discovery thus imposes many of the costs present when the Government must respond to a prima facie case of selective prosecution. It will divert prosecutors' resources and may disclose the Government's prosecutorial strategy. The justifications for a rigorous standard for the elements of a selective-prosecution claim thus require a correspondingly rigorous standard for discovery in aid of such a claim.

The Court of Appeals reached its decision in part because it started "with the presumption that people of all races commit all types of crimes not with the premise that any type of crime is the exclusive province of any particular racial or ethnic group." (Citation omitted). It cited no authority for this proposition, which seems contradicted by the most recent statistics of the United States Sentencing Commission. Those statistics show that: More than 90% of the persons sentenced in 1994 for crack cocaine trafficking were black, United States Sentencing Comm'n, 3...

JUSTICE STEVENS, dissenting.

Federal prosecutors are respected members of a respected profession. Despite an occasional misstep, the excellence of their work abundantly justifies the presumption that "they have properly discharged their official duties." (Citation omitted). Nevertheless, the possibility that political or racial animosity may infect a decision to institute criminal proceedings cannot be ignored. (Citation omitted). For that reason, it has long been settled that the prosecutor's broad discretion to determine when criminal charges should be filed is not completely unbridled. As the Court notes, however, the scope of judicial review of particular exercises of that discretion is not fully defined. (Citation omitted).

The Court correctly concludes that in this case the facts presented to the District Court in support of respondents' claim that they had been singled out for prosecution because of their race were not sufficient to prove that defense. Moreover, I agree with the Court that their showing was not strong enough to give them a right to discovery, either under Rule 16 or under the District Court's inherent power to order discovery in appropriate circumstances.

Like Chief Judge Wallace of the Court of Appeals, however, I am persuaded that the District Judge did not abuse her discretion when she concluded that the factual showing was sufficiently disturbing to *require* some response from the United States Attorney's Office. (Citation omitted). Perhaps the discovery order was broader than necessary, but I cannot agree with the Court's apparent conclusion that no inquiry was permissible.

The District Judge's order should be evaluated in light of three circumstances that underscore the need for judicial vigilance over certain types of drug prosecutions. First, the AntiDrug Abuse Act of 1986 and subsequent legislation established a regime of extremely high penalties for the possession and distribution of so-called "crack" cocaine. (Citation omitted). Those provisions treat one gram of crack as the equivalent of 100 grams of powder cocaine. The distribution of 50 grams of crack is thus punishable by the same mandatory minimum sentence of 10 years in prison that applies to the distribution of 5,000 grams of powder cocaine. The Sentencing Guidelines extend this ratio to penalty levels above the mandatory minimums: for any given quantity of crack, the guideline range is the same as if the offense had involved 100 times that amount in powder cocaine. (Footnote omitted). These penalties result in sentences for crack offenders that average three to eight times longer than sentences for comparable powder offenders.' (Citation omitted).

Second, the disparity between the treatment of crack cocaine and powder cocaine is matched by the disparity between the severity of the punishment imposed by federal law and that imposed by state law for the same conduct. For a variety of reasons, often including the absence of mandatory minimums, the existence of parole, and lower baseline penalties, terms of imprisonment for drug offenses tend to be substantially lower in state systems than in the federal system. The difference is especially marked in the case of crack offenses. The majority of States draw no distinction between types of cocaine in their penalty schemes; of those that do, none has established as stark a differential as the Federal Government. (Citation omitted). For example, if respondent Hampton is found guilty, his federal sentence might be as long as a mandatory life term. Had he been tried in state court, his sentence could have been as short as 12 years, less worktime credits of half that amount. (Footnote omitted).

Finally, it is undisputed that the brunt of the elevated federal penalties falls heavily on blacks. While 65% of the persons who have used crack are white, in 1993 they represented only 4% of the federal offenders convicted of trafficking in crack. Eighty-eight percent of such defendants were black. (Citation omitted). During the first 18 months of full guideline implementation, the sentencing disparity between black and white defendants grew from pre-guideline levels: blacks on average received sentences over 40% longer than whites. (Citation omitted).

The extraordinary severity of the imposed penalties and the troubling racial patterns of enforcement give rise to a special concern about the fairness of charging practices for crack offenses. Evidence tending to prove that black defendants charged with distribution of crack in the Central District of California are prosecuted in federal court, whereas members of other races charged with similar offenses are prosecuted in state court, warrants close scrutiny by the federal judges in that District. In my view, the District Judge, who has sat on both the federal and the state benches in Los Angeles, acted well within her discretion to call for the development of facts that would demonstrate what standards, if any, governed the choice of forum where similarly situated offenders are prosecuted.

Respondents submitted a study showing that of all cases involving crack offenses that were closed by the Federal Public Defender's Office in 1991, 24 out of 24 involved black defendants. To supplement this evidence, they submitted affidavits from two of the attorneys in the defense team. The first reported a statement from an intake coordinator at a local drug treatment center that, in his experience, an equal number of crack users and dealers were caucasian as belonged to minorities. (Citation omitted). The second was from David R. Reed, counsel for respondent Armstrong. Reed was both an active court-appointed attorney in the Central District of California and one of the directors of the leading association of criminal defense lawyers who practice before the Los Angeles County courts. Reed stated that he did not recall "ever handling a [crack] cocaine case involving non-black defendants" in federal court, nor had he even heard of one. Id., at 140. He further stated that "[t]here are many crack cocaine sales cases prosecuted in state court that do involve racial groups other than blacks." (Citation omitted).

The majority discounts the probative value of the affidavits, claiming that they recounted "hearsay" and reported "personal conclusions based on anecdotal evidence." (Citation omitted). But the Reed affidavit plainly contained more than mere hearsay; Reed offered information based on his own extensive experience in both federal and state courts. Given the breadth of his background, he was well qualified to compare the practices of federal and state prosecutors. In any event, the Government never objected to the admission of either affidavit on hearsay or any other grounds. (Citation omitted). It was certainly within the District Court's discretion to credit the affidavits of two members of the bar of that Court, at least one of whom had presumably acquired a reputation by his frequent appearances there, and both of whose statements were made on pains of perjury.

The criticism that the affidavits were based on "anecdotal evidence" is also unpersuasive. I thought it was agreed that defendants do not need to prepare sophisticated statistical studies in order to receive mere discovery in cases like this one. Certainly evidence based on a drug counselor's personal observations or on an attorney's practice in two sets of courts, state and federal, can "ten[d] to show the existence" of a selective prosecution. (Citation omitted).

Even if respondents failed to carry their burden of showing that there were individuals who were not black but who could have been prosecuted in federal court for the same offenses, it does not follow that the District Court abused its discretion in ordering discovery. There can be no doubt that such individuals exist, and indeed the Government has never denied the same. In those circumstances, I fail to see why the District Court was unable to take judicial notice of this obvious fact and demand information from the Government's files to support or refute respondents' evidence… (Citation omitted). In this case, the evidence was sufficiently disturbing to persuade the District Judge to order discovery that might help explain the conspicuous racial pattern of cases before her Court. I cannot accept the majority's conclusion that the District Judge either exceeded her power or abused her discretion when she did so. I therefore respectfully dissent.

► Notes & Questions

1. Was it a coincidence that the entire 24 defendants in the public defenders study were black? If whites were involved in the possession and sale of crack cocaine, why weren't any of them indicted in federal court?

2. The possession of white powder cocaine does not carry as severe penalties as crack cocaine. Should the penalties be equal? What steps should be taken to equalize the penalties? Is it a coincidence that possession of crack cocaine is penalized more severely than possession of white powder cocaine? What would be some public policy arguments to justify this disparity in sentencing?

3. In 1994, California passed a new law which advanced the proposition "Three Strikes and You're Out." The new law recently came under attack by Franklin Zimring, Director of the Earl Warren Legal Institute at the University of California at Berkeley. Professor Zimring cited a study conducted by the Center on Juvenile and Criminal Justice in San Francisco which found that blacks were sent to prison under the new statute 13 times more often than whites. The law requires double the normal sentencing for a second felony and life for a third felony. Blacks, the critics argued make up 7% of the population in California, and 31% of the state's prison population. In addition, the critics argue that more people are being convicted of marijuana possession (192), than murder (40), rape (25) and kidnaping (24). Why is there this disparity in sentencing under this California statute? Should the public be concerned about this type of disparity?

▶ Notes & Questions

4. In New York State a study was released by the Pataki administration in the fall of 1995 that concluded that blacks and Hispanics were sentenced more severely for minor infractions than were whites. The study focused upon sentences issued between 1990 and 1992. The study found that 1/3 of black and Hispanic defendants would have been given less jail time, if they were white. The disparity led to 4,000 extra jail sentences per year for black and Hispanic defendants. The study was conducted by the Division of Criminal Justice Services of New York State. The study raises inferences of discrimination in the criminal justice system of New York State. What role doe race play in the criminal justice system? How much weight should be given to the data released in the New York State Study? Do blacks and Hispanics receive longer sentences because they are poor, rather than because of race? Poor people do not have resources to hire private attorneys or investigators and therefore, may receive longer and more frequent sentences. What public policies and procedures should be implemented to prevent these types of injustices?

5. In the November, 1996 issue of the Journal of the American Medical Association, Dorothy K. Hatsykami from the University of Minnesota and Marian W. Fischman from Columbia University, determined that the effects of different forms of cocaine are similar. They further argued that the disparities in sentences for crack and powder cocaine are not justified, given the similar effects upon people. The Federal Government, however, stood by its sentencing guidelines, despite the discriminatory effect because of its belief that crack creates more violent addicts.

▶ Notes & Questions

In 1995, the United States Sentencing Commission, a group of experts who advise the Federal courts on sentencing, urged the elimination of sentencing disparities. Their recommendation was based upon compelling data. In 1993, 80.3 percent of those convicted in Federal courts for selling crack cocaine were black. Blacks represented only 27 percent of those convicted for selling powder cocaine.

6. The Black community has raised a very controversial issue with respect to the alleged role of the Federal government in allowing crack cocaine to enter the black community. The allegation is that during the 1980's the leaders of CIA-backed Nicaraguan regime sold crack cocaine to Los Angeles gangs. The profits from the sales, it is alleged, were used to pay for the war against the Sandinista regime. Specifically, it has been alleged by articles in the San Jose Mercury News that the Nicaraguan Democratic Force ("Contra"), which was created and supported by the Central Intelligence Agency (CIA) ignited the explosion of the crack cocaine epidemic in the United States. Many leaders, particularly the Congressional Black Caucus, have called for Congressional investigations into the role of the Federal government in supporting an organization that may have been directly responsible for the destruction of American citizens. Officials in the Drug Enforcement Administration (DEA) have indicated that some Contra officials may have flown into the United States massive amounts of cocaine.

Not only are the allegations of a CIA connection to the crack explosion being raised in the black communities, but also by white criminal defendants. In 1996, Ricky Ross, a convicted cocaine dealer attempted to get his conviction overturned in a United States District Court in San Diego, California. He was

► **Notes & Questions**

facing a mandatory life sentence for buying 220 pounds of cocaine from Oscar Danilo Blandon. Ross alleged that because Blandon was a Federal drug informant and a civilian leader of a CIA backed guerilla group, he should not be sentenced to life imprisonment. Judge Marilyn L. Huff rejected these arguments and refused to overturn Ross' conviction.

7. Judge Nancy Gertner of the United States District Court in Boston ignored the federal sentencing guidelines in a case involving a black crack cocaine dealer. In making her ruling she said "Isn't it time for us to say that there is on the one hand the impact of the drug trafficking and on the other hand the impact of mass incarceration of African-Americans from crack cocaine?" Speaking of the defendant's 8 year old son in the courtroom, the judge continued: "Indeed, when I see your son, I think that public safety requires that you be with your son so that he doesn't follow in your footsteps." (Jonathan Suzman, "Judge skips guidelines, releases man in crack case," *The Boston Globe*, November 21, 2007.

8. After the favorable decision in the *Kimbrough* case, the U.S. Sentencing Commission voted to make the new guidelines retroactive which would make 19,500 priosners eligible for early release. Hillary Clinton was the only Democractic candidate who opposed this early release. ("Hillary's Indiscretion," Editorial, *Boston Banner*, December 20, 2007.)

F.
KIMBROUGH v. UNITED STATES
SUPREME COURT OF THE UNITED STATES
552 U.S. 85 (2007)

Under the statute criminalizing the manufacture and distribution of cocaine, 21 U.S. C. §841, and the relevant Federal Sentencing Guidelines, a drug trafficker dealing in crack cocaine is subject to the same sentence as one dealing in 100 times more powder cocaine. Petitioner Kimbrough pleaded guilty to four offenses: conspiracy to distribute crack and powder; possession with intent to distribute more than 50 grams of crack; possession with intent to distribute powder; and possession of a firearm in furtherance of a drug-trafficking offense. Under the relevant statutes, Kimbrough's plea subjected him to a minimum prison term of 15 years and a maximum of life. The applicable advisory Guidelines range was 228 to 270 months, or 19 to 22.5 years. The District Court found, however, that a sentence in this range would have been greater than necessary to accomplish the purposes of sentencing set forth in 18 U.S. C. §3553(a). In making that determination, the court relied in part on its view that Kimbrough's case exemplified the "disproportionate and unjust effect that crack cocaine guidelines have in sentencing." The court noted that if Kimbrough had possessed only powder cocaine, his Guidelines range would have been far lower: 97 to 106 months. Concluding that the statutory minimum sentence was long enough to accomplish §3553(a)'s objectives, the court sentenced Kimbrough to 15 years, or 180 months, in prison. The Fourth Circuit vacated the sentence, finding that a sentence outside the Guidelines range is per se unreasonable when it is based on a disagreement with the sentencing disparity for crack and powder offenses.

Held:

Under *United States v. Booker*, 543 U.S. 220, the cocaine Guidelines, like all other Guidelines, are advisory only, and the Fourth Circuit erred in holding the crack/powder disparity effectively mandatory. A district judge must include the Guidelines range in the array of factors warranting consideration, but the judge may determine that, in the particular case, a within-Guidelines sentence is "greater than necessary" to serve the objectives of sentencing, §3553(a). In making that determination, the judge may consider the disparity between the Guidelines' treatment of crack and powder offenses. (Citation omitted). (a) Crack and powder cocaine have the same physiological and psychotropic effects, but are handled very differently for sentencing purposes. The relevant statutes and Guidelines employ a 100-to-1 ratio that yields sentences for crack offenses three to six times longer than those for offenses involving equal amounts of powder. Thus, a major supplier of powder may receive a shorter sentence than a low-level dealer who buys powder and converts it to crack. (Citation omitted).

(1) The crack/powder disparity originated in the Anti-Drug Abuse Act of 1986 (1986 Act), which created a two-tiered scheme of five-and ten-year mandatory minimum sentences for drug manufacturing and distribution offenses. Congress apparently adopted the 100-to-1 ratio because it believed that crack, a relatively new drug in 1986, was significantly more dangerous than powder. Thus, the 1986 Act's five-year mandatory minimum applies to any defendant accountable for 5 grams of crack or 500 grams of powder, and its ten-year mandatory minimum applies to any defendant accountable for 50 grams of crack or 5,000 grams of powder. In developing Guidelines sentences for cocaine offenses, the Sentencing Commission employed the statute's weight-driven scheme, rather than its usual empirical approach based on past sentencing practices. The statute itself specifies only two quantities of each drug, but the Guidelines used the 100-to-1 ratio to set sentences for a full range of drug quantities. (Citation omitted).

(2) Based on additional research and experience with the 100-to-1 ratio, the Commission later determined that the crack/ powder differential does not meet the objectives of the Sentencing Reform Act and the 1986 Act. The Commission also found the disparity inconsistent with the 1986 Act's goal of punishing major drug traffickers more severely than low-level dealers, and furthermore observed that the differential fosters a lack of confidence in the criminal justice system because of a perception that it promotes an unwarranted divergence based on race. (Citation omitted).

(3) The Commission has several times sought to achieve a reduction in the crack/powder ratio. Congress rejected a 1995 amendment to the Guidelines that would have replaced the 100-to-1 ratio with a 1-to-1 ratio, but directed the Commission to propose revision of the ratio under the relevant statutes and Guidelines. Congress took no action after the Commission's 1997 and 2002 reports recommended changing the ratio. The Commission's 2007 report again urged Congress to amend the 1986 Act, but the Commission also adopted an ameliorating change in the Guidelines. The modest amendment, which became effective on November 1, 2007, yields sentences for crack offenses between two and five times longer than sentences for equal amounts of powder. The Commission thus noted that it is only a partial remedy to the problems generated by the crack/powder disparity. (Citation omitted).

(b) The federal sentencing statute, as modified by Booker, requires a court to give respectful consideration to the Guidelines, but "permits the court to tailor the sentence in light of other [§3553(a)] concerns as well," (Citation omitted). The Government contends that the Guidelines adopting the 100-to-1 ratio are an exception to this general freedom and offers three arguments in support of its position, each of which this Court rejects. (Citation omitted).

(1) The Government argues that the 1986 Act itself prohibits the Commission and sentencing courts from disagreeing with the 100-to-1 ratio. This position lacks grounding in the statute, which,

by its terms, mandates only maximum and minimum sentences: A person convicted of possession with intent to distribute 5 grams or more of crack must be sentenced to a minimum of 5 years and a maximum of 40. A person with 50 grams or more of crack must be sentenced to a minimum of 10 years and a maximum of life. The statute says nothing about appropriate sentences within these brackets, and this Court declines to read any implicit directive into the congressional silence. (Citation omitted)... (2) The Government also argues that Congress made clear, in disapproving the Commission's 1995 proposed Guidelines amendment, that the 1986 Act required the Commission and courts to respect the 100-to-1 ratio. But nothing in Congress' 1995 action suggested that crack sentences must exceed powder sentences by a ratio of 100 to 1. To the contrary, Congress required the Commission to recommend a revision of the ratio. The Government argues that, by calling for recommendations to change both the statute and the Guidelines, Congress meant to bar any Guidelines alteration in advance of congressional action. But the more likely reading is that Congress sought proposals to amend both the statute and the Guidelines because the Commission's criticisms of the 100-to-1 ratio concerned the exorbitance of the crack/powder disparity in both contexts. Moreover, as a result of the 2007 amendment, which Congress did not disapprove or modify, the Guidelines now deviate from the statute's 100-to-1 ratio, advancing a ratio that varies (at different offense levels) between 25 to 1 and 80 to 1. (Citation omitted)....

2. The 180-month sentence imposed on Kimbrough should survive appellate inspection. The District Court began by properly calculating and considering the advisory Guidelines range. It then addressed the relevant §3553(a) factors, including the Sentencing Commission's reports criticizing the 100-to-1 ratio. Finally, the court did not purport to establish a ratio of its own, but appropriately framed its final determination in line with §3553(a)'s overarching instruction to "impose a sentence sufficient, but not greater than necessary" to accomplish the sentencing goals advanced in §3553(a)(2). The court thus rested its sentence on the appropriate

considerations and "committed no procedural error," *Gall, ante*, at 17. Kimbrough's sentence was 4.5 years below the bottom of the Guidelines range. But in determining that 15 years was the appropriate prison term, the District Court properly homed in on the particular circumstances of Kimbrough's case and accorded weight to the Sentencing Commission's consistent and emphatic position that the crack/powder disparity is at odds with §3553(a). Giving due respect to the District Court's reasoned appraisal, a reviewing court could not rationally conclude that the 4.5-year sentence reduction Kimbrough received qualified as an abuse of discretion. (Citation omitted).

Reversed and remanded.

GINSBURG, J., delivered the opinion of the Court, in which ROBERTS, C. J., and STEVENS, SCALIA, KENNEDY, SOUTER, and BREYER, JJ., joined. SCALIA, J., filed a concurring opinion. THOMAS, J., and ALITO, J., filed dissenting opinions.

G.
Stop and Frisk: Black Youth and Police Harassment

CITY OF CHICAGO, PETITIONER
v. JESUS MORALES ET AL.
Supreme Court of the United States
527 U.S. 41 (1999)

JUSTICE STEVENS announced the judgment of the Court and delivered the opinion of the Court with respect to Parts I, II, and V, and an opinion with respect to Parts III, IV, and VI, in which JUSTICE SOUTER and JUSTICE GINSBURG join.

In 1992, the Chicago City Council enacted the Gang Congregation Ordinance, which prohibits "criminal street gang members" from "loitering" with one another or with other persons in any public place. The question presented is whether the Supreme

Court of Illinois correctly held that the ordinance violates the Due Process Clause of the Fourteenth Amendment to the Federal Constitution.

I.

Before the ordinance was adopted, the city council's Committee on Police and Fire conducted hearings to explore the problems created by the city's street gangs, and more particularly, the consequences of public loitering by gang members. Witnesses included residents of the neighborhoods where gang members are most active, as well as some of the aldermen who represent those areas. Based on that evidence, the council made a series of findings that are included in the text of the ordinance and explain the reasons for its enactment. (Note omitted). The council found that a continuing increase in criminal street gang activity was largely responsible for the city's rising murder rate, as well as an escalation of violent and drug related crimes. It noted that in many neighborhoods throughout the city, "the burgeoning presence of street gang members in public places has intimidated many law abiding citizens." (Citation omitted). Furthermore, the council stated that gang members "establish control over identifiable areas ... by loitering in those areas and intimidating others from entering those areas; and... members of criminal street gangs avoid arrest by committing no offense punishable under existing laws when they know the police are present..." (Citation omitted). It further found that "loitering in public places by criminal street gang members creates a justifiable fear for the safety of persons and property in the area" and that "aggressive action is necessary to preserve the city's streets and other public places so that the public may use such places without fear." Moreover, the council concluded that the city "has an interest in discouraging all persons from loitering in public places with criminal gang members." (Citation omitted).

The ordinance creates a criminal offense punishable by a fine of up to $500, imprisonment for not more than six months, and a requirement to perform up to 120 hours of community service.

Commission of the offense involves four predicates. First, the police officer must reasonably believe that at least one of the two or more persons present in a "public place" is a "criminal street gang member." Second, the persons must be "loitering," which the ordinance defines as "remaining in any one place with no apparent purpose." Third, the officer must then order "all" of the persons to disperse and remove themselves "from the area." Fourth, a person must disobey the officer's order. If any person, whether a gang member or not, disobeys the officer's order, that person is guilty of violating the ordinance. (Citation and note omitted)...

II.

During the three years of its enforcement, (Note omitted) the police issued over 89,000 dispersal orders and arrested over 42,000 people for violating the ordinance (Note omitted). In the ensuing enforcement proceedings, two trial judges upheld the constitutionality of the ordinance, but eleven others ruled that it was invalid (Note omitted). In respondent Youkhana's case, the trial judge held that the "ordinance fails to notify individuals what conduct is prohibited, and it encourages arbitrary and capricious enforcement by police." (Note omitted).

The Illinois Appellate Court affirmed the trial court's ruling in the Youkhana case, (Note omitted) consolidated and affirmed other pending appeals in accordance with Youkhana, (Note omitted) and reversed the convictions of respondents Gutierrez, Morales, and others.(Note omitted). The Appellate Court was persuaded that the ordinance impaired the freedom of assembly of non-gang members in violation of the First Amendment to the Federal Constitution and Article I of the Illinois Constitution, that it was unconstitutionally vague, that it improperly criminalized status rather than conduct, and that it jeopardized rights guaranteed under the Fourth Amendment. (Note omitted)

We granted certiorari, 523 U.S. ___ (1998), and now affirm. Like the Illinois Supreme Court, we conclude that the ordinance enacted by the city of Chicago is unconstitutionally vague.

III.

The basic factual predicate for the city's ordinance is not in dispute. As the city argues in its brief, "the very presence of a large collection of obviously brazen, insistent, and lawless gang members and hangers-on on the public ways intimidates residents, who become afraid even to leave their homes and go about their business. That, in turn, imperils community residents' sense of safety and security, detracts from property values, and can ultimately destabilize entire neighborhoods." (Note omitted). The findings in the ordinance explain that it was motivated by these concerns. We have no doubt that a law that directly prohibited such intimidating conduct would be constitutional, (Note omitted) but this ordinance broadly covers a significant amount of additional activity. Uncertainty about the scope of that additional coverage provides the basis for respondents' claim that the ordinance is too vague…

While we, like the Illinois courts, conclude that the ordinance is invalid on its face, we do not rely on the overbreadth doctrine. We agree with the city's submission that the law does not have a sufficiently substantial impact on conduct protected by the First Amendment to render it unconstitutional. The ordinance does not prohibit speech. Because the term "loiter" is defined as remaining in one place "with no apparent purpose," it is also clear that it does not prohibit any form of conduct that is apparently intended to convey a message. By its terms, the ordinance is inapplicable to assemblies that are designed to demonstrate a group's support of, or opposition to, a particular point of view. (Citations omitted). Its impact on the social contact between gang members and others does not impair the First Amendment "right of association" that our cases have recognized.

On the other hand, as the United States recognizes, the freedom to loiter for innocent purposes is part of the "liberty" protected by the Due Process Clause of the Fourteenth Amendment. (Note omitted). We have expressly identified this "right to remove from one place to another according to inclination" as "an attribute of personal liberty" protected by the Constitution. (Citations omitted).

Indeed, it is apparent that an individual's decision to remain in a public place of his choice is as much a part of his liberty as the freedom of movement inside frontiers that is "a part of our heritage" (Citation omitted), or the right to move "to whatsoever place one's own inclination may direct" identified in Blackstone's Commentaries. 1 W. Blackstone, Commentaries on the Laws of England 130 (1765). (Note omitted).

There is no need, however, to decide whether the impact of the Chicago ordinance on constitutionally protected liberty alone would suffice to support a facial challenge under the overbreadth doctrine. (Citations and notes omitted). For it is clear that the vagueness of this enactment makes a facial challenge appropriate. This is not an ordinance that "simply regulates business behavior and contains a scienter requirement." (Citation omitted). It is a criminal law that contains no mens rea requirement, (Citation omitted), and infringes on constitutionally protected rights (Citation omitted). When vagueness permeates the text of such a law, it is subject to facial attack. (Note omitted).

Vagueness may invalidate a criminal law for either of two independent reasons. First, it may fail to provide the kind of notice that will enable ordinary people to understand what conduct it prohibits; second, it may authorize and even encourage arbitrary and discriminatory enforcement. (Citation omitted). Accordingly, we first consider whether the ordinance provides fair notice to the citizen and then discuss its potential for arbitrary enforcement.

IV.

"It is established that a law fails to meet the requirements of the Due Process Clause if it is so vague and standardless that it leaves the public uncertain as to the conduct it prohibits... " (Citation omitted). The Illinois Supreme Court recognized that the term "loiter" may have a common and accepted meaning, (Citation omitted), but the definition of that term in this ordinance -- "to remain in any one place with no apparent purpose"-- does not. It is difficult to imagine how any citizen of the city of Chicago standing in a public place with a group of people would know if he or she had an "apparent purpose." If she were talking to another person, would she have an apparent purpose? If she were frequently checking her watch and looking expectantly down the street, would she have an apparent purpose? (Note omitted)...

First, the purpose of the fair notice requirement is to enable the ordinary citizen to conform his or her conduct to the law. "No one may be required at peril of life, liberty or property to speculate as to the meaning of penal statutes." (Citation omitted). Although it is true that a loiterer is not subject to criminal sanctions unless he or she disobeys a dispersal order, the loitering is the conduct that the ordinance is designed to prohibit. (Note omitted) If the loitering is in fact harmless and innocent, the dispersal order itself is an unjustified impairment of liberty. If the police are able to decide arbitrarily which members of the public they will order to disperse, then the Chicago ordinance becomes indistinguishable from the law we held invalid in Shuttlesworth v. Birmingham, 382 U.S. 87, 90, 15 L. Ed. 2d 176, 86 S. Ct.(1965). (Note omitted)...

Second, the terms of the dispersal order compound the inadequacy of the notice afforded by the ordinance. It provides that the officer "shall order all such persons to disperse and remove themselves from the area." (Citation omitted). This vague phrasing raises a host of questions. After such an order issues, how long must the loiterers remain apart? How far must they move? If each loiterer walks around the block and they meet again at the same location, are they subject to arrest or merely to being ordered to disperse again? As we do here, we have found vagueness in a criminal statute exacerbated by the use of the standards of "neighborhood" and "locality." (Citation omitted)...

V.

The broad sweep of the ordinance also violates "the requirement that a legislature establish minimal guidelines to govern law enforcement." (Citation omitted). There are no such guidelines in the ordinance. In any public place in the city of Chicago, persons who stand or sit in the company of a gang member may be ordered to disperse unless their purpose is apparent. The mandatory language in the enactment directs the police to issue an order without first making any inquiry about their possible purposes. It matters not whether the reason that a gang member and his father, for example, might loiter near Wrigley Field is to rob an unsuspecting fan or just to get a glimpse of Sammy Sosa leaving the ballpark; in either event, if their purpose is not apparent to a nearby police officer, she may —indeed, she "shall"—order them to disperse....

VI.

In our judgment, the Illinois Supreme Court correctly concluded that the ordinance does not provide sufficiently specific limits on the enforcement discretion of the police "to meet constitutional standards for definiteness and clarity." (Note and citation omitted). We recognize the serious and difficult problems testified to by the citizens of Chicago that led to the enactment of this ordinance. "We are mindful that the preservation of liberty depends in part on the maintenance of social order." (Citation omitted). However, in this instance the city has enacted an ordinance that affords too much discretion to the police and too little notice to citizens who wish to use the public streets.

Accordingly, the judgment of the Supreme Court of Illinois is Affirmed.

JUSTICE THOMAS, with whom THE CHIEF JUSTICE and JUSTICE SCALIA join, dissenting.

The duly elected members of the Chicago City Council enacted the ordinance at issue as part of a larger effort to prevent gangs from establishing dominion over the public streets. By invalidating Chicago's ordinance, I fear that the Court has unnecessarily sentenced law-abiding citizens to lives of terror and misery. The ordinance is not vague. (Citation omitted). Nor does it violate the

Due Process Clause. The asserted "freedom to loiter for innocent purposes," (Citation omitted), is in no way "deeply rooted in this Nation's history and tradition," (Citation omitted). I dissent.

I.

The human costs exacted by criminal street gangs are inestimable. In many of our Nation's cities, gangs have "virtually overtaken certain neighborhoods, contributing to the economic and social decline of these areas and causing fear and lifestyle changes among law-abiding residents." (Citation omitted). Gangs fill the daily lives of many of our poorest and most vulnerable citizens with a terror that the Court does not give sufficient consideration, often relegating them to the status of prisoners in their own homes. (Citation omitted).

The city of Chicago has suffered the devastation wrought by this national tragedy. Last year, in an effort to curb plummeting attendance, the Chicago Public Schools hired dozens of adults to escort children to school. The youngsters had become too terrified of gang violence to leave their homes alone. (Citation omitted). The children's fears were not unfounded. In 1996, the Chicago Police Department estimated that there were 132 criminal street gangs in the city. (Citation omitted). Between 1987 and 1994, these gangs were involved in 63,141 criminal incidents, including 21,689 nonlethal violent crimes and 894 homicides. (Citation and note omitted). Many of these criminal incidents and homicides result from gang "turf battles," which take place on the public streets and place innocent residents in grave danger.

Before enacting its ordinance, the Chicago City Council held extensive hearings on the problems of gang loitering. Concerned citizens appeared to testify poignantly as to how gangs disrupt their daily lives. Ordinary citizens like Ms. D'Ivory Gordon explained that she struggled just to walk to work:

"When I walk out my door, these guys are out there...

"They watch you... They know where you live. They know what time you leave, what time you come home. I am afraid of them. I have even come to the point now that I carry a meat cleaver to work with me...

"...I don't want to hurt anyone, and I don't want to be hurt. We need to clean these corners up. Clean these communities up and take it back from them." (Citation omitted).

Eighty-eight-year-old Susan Mary Jackson echoed her sentiments, testifying, "We used to have a nice neighborhood. We don't have it anymore... I am scared to go out in the daytime... you can't pass because they are standing. I am afraid to go to the store. I don't go to the store because I am afraid. At my age if they look at me real hard, I be ready to holler." (Citation omitted). Another long-time resident testified:

"I have never had the terror that I feel everyday when I walk down the streets of Chicago... I have had my windows broken out. I have had guns pulled on me. I have been threatened. I get intimidated on a daily basis, and it's come to the point where I say, well, do I go out today. Do I put my ax in my briefcase. Do I walk around dressed like a bum so I am not looking rich or got any money or anything like that." (Citation omitted)...

II.

As part of its ongoing effort to curb the deleterious effects of criminal street gangs, the citizens of Chicago sensibly decided to return to basics. The ordinance does nothing more than confirm the well-established principle that the police have the duty and the power to maintain the public peace, and, when necessary, to disperse groups of individuals who threaten it...

B.

The Court concludes that the ordinance is also unconstitutionally vague because it fails to provide adequate standards to guide police discretion and because, in the plurality's view, it does not give residents adequate notice of how to conform their conduct to the confines of the law. I disagree on both counts.

At the outset, it is important to note that the ordinance does not criminalize loitering per se. Rather, it penalizes loiterers' failure to obey a police officer's order to move along...

In their role as peace officers, the police long have had the authority and the duty to order groups of individuals who threaten the public peace to disperse...

In order to perform their peace-keeping responsibilities satisfactorily, the police inevitably must exercise discretion. Indeed, by empowering them to act as peace officers, the law assumes that the police will exercise that discretion responsibly and with sound judgment... Just as we trust officers to rely on their experience and expertise in order to make spur-of-the-moment determinations about amorphous legal standards such as "probable cause" and "reasonable suspicion," so we must trust them to determine whether a group of loiterers contains individuals (in this case members of criminal street gangs) whom the city has determined threaten the public peace...

2.

The plurality's conclusion that the ordinance "fails to give the ordinary citizen adequate notice of what is forbidden and what is permitted," (Citation omitted), is similarly untenable. There is nothing "vague" about an order to disperse...

Today, the Court focuses extensively on the "rights" of gang members and their companions. It can safely do so -- the people who will have to live with the consequences of today's opinion do not live in our neighborhoods. Rather, the people who will suffer from our lofty pronouncements are people like Ms. Susan Mary Jackson; people who have seen their neighborhoods literally destroyed by gangs and violence and drugs. They are good, decent people who must struggle to overcome their desperate situation, against all odds, in order to raise their families, earn a living, and remain good citizens. As one resident described, "There is only about maybe one or two percent of the people in the city causing these problems maybe, but it's keeping 98 percent of us in our houses and off the streets and afraid to shop." (Citation omitted). By focusing exclusively on the imagined "rights" of the two percent, the Court today has denied our most vulnerable citizens the very thing that JUSTICE

STEVENS, (Citation omitted) elevates above all else--the "freedom of movement." And that is a shame. I respectfully dissent.

H.
Is the War on Drugs a War Against the Wrong People?

DEPARTMENT OF HOUSING AND URBAN DEVELOPMENT, PETITIONER v. PEARLIE RUCKER ET AL., OAKLAND HOUSING AUTHORITY, ET AL.
Supreme Court of the United States
122 S. Ct. 1230 (2002)

JUDGES: REHNQUIST, C. J., delivered the opinion of the Court, in which all other Members joined, except BREYER, J., who took no part in the consideration or decision of the cases.

With drug dealers "increasingly imposing a reign of terror on public and other federally assisted low-income housing tenants," Congress passed the Anti-Drug Abuse Act of 1988. ' 5122, 102 Stat. 4301, 42 U.S.C. ' 11901(3) (1994 ed.). The Act, as later amended, provides that each "public housing agency shall utilize leases which... provide that any criminal activity that threatens the health, safety, or right to peaceful enjoyment of the premises by other tenants or any drug-related criminal activity on or off such premises, engaged in by a public housing tenant, any member of the tenant's household, or any guest or other person under the tenant's control, shall be cause for termination of tenancy." 42 U.S.C. ' 1437d (l)(6) (1994 ed., Supp. V). Petitioners say that this statute requires lease terms that allow a local public housing authority to evict a tenant when a member of the tenant's household or a guest engages in drug-related criminal activity, regardless of whether the tenant knew, or had reason to know, of that activity. Respondents say it does not. We agree with petitioners.

Respondents are four public housing tenants of the Oakland Housing Authority (OHA). Paragraph 9(m) of respondents' leases, tracking the language of '1437d(l)(6), obligates the tenants to "assure that the tenant, any member of the household, a guest, or another person under the tenant's control, shall not engage in . . . any drug-related criminal activity on or near the premises." (Citation omitted). Respondents also signed an agreement stating that the tenant "understands that if I or any member of my household or guests should violate this lease provision, my tenancy may be terminated and I may be evicted." Id., (Citation omitted).

In late 1997 and early 1998, OHA instituted eviction proceedings in state court against respondents, alleging violations of this lease provision. The complaint alleged: (1) that the respective grandsons of respondents William Lee and Barbara Hill, both of whom were listed as residents on the leases, were caught in the apartment complex parking lot smoking marijuana; (2) that the daughter of respondent Pearlie Rucker, who resides with her and is listed on the lease as a resident, was found with cocaine and a crack cocaine pipe three blocks from Rucker's apartment; (Note omitted) and (3) that on three instances within a 2-month period, respondent Herman Walker's caregiver and two others were found with cocaine in Walker's apartment. OHA had issued Walker notices of a lease violation on the first two occasions, before initiating the eviction action after the third violation.

After OHA initiated the eviction proceedings in state court, respondents commenced actions against HUD, OHA, and OHA's director in United States District Court. They challenged HUD's interpretation of the statute under the Administrative Procedure Act, (Citation omitted), arguing that 42 U.S.C. ' 1437d(l)(6) does not require lease terms authorizing the eviction of so-called "innocent" tenants, and, in the alternative, that if it does, then the statute is unconstitutional. (Note omitted). The District Court issued a preliminary injunction, enjoining OHA from "terminating the leases of tenants pursuant to paragraph 9(m) of the ' Tenant Lease' for drug-related criminal activity that does not occur within the tenant's apartment unit when the tenant did not know of and had no reason to know of, the drug-related criminal activity." (Citation omitted).

A panel of the Court of Appeals reversed, holding that ' 1437d(l)(6) unambiguously permits the eviction of tenants who violate the lease provision, regardless of whether the tenant was personally aware of the drug activity, and that the statute is constitutional. (Citation omitted)…

The en banc Court of Appeals thought the statute did not address "the level of personal knowledge or fault that is required for eviction." (Citation omitted)…

The en banc Court of Appeals also thought it possible that "under the tenant's control" modifies not just "other person," but also "member of the tenant's household" and "guest." (Citation omitted). The court ultimately adopted this reading, concluding that the statute prohibits eviction where the tenant "for a lack of knowledge or other reason, could not realistically exercise control over the conduct of a household member or guest." (Citation omitted). But this interpretation runs counter to basic rules of grammar. The disjunctive "or" means that the qualification applies only to "other person." Indeed, the view that "under the tenant's control" modifies everything coming before it in the sentence would result in the nonsensical reading that the statute applies to "a public housing tenant… under the tenant's control." HUD offers a convincing explanation for the grammatical imperative that "under the tenant's control" modifies only "other person": "by 'control,' the statute means control in the sense that the tenant has permitted access to the premises." (Citation omitted). Implicit in the terms "household member" or "guest" is that access to the premises has been granted by the tenant. Thus, the plain language of ' 1437d(l)(6) requires leases that grant public housing authorities the discretion to terminate tenancy without regard to the tenant's knowledge of the drug-related criminal activity…

The en banc Court of Appeals next resorted to legislative history. The Court of Appeals correctly recognized that reference to legislative history is inappropriate when the text of the statute is unambiguous. (Citation omitted). Given that the en banc Court of Appeals' finding of textual ambiguity is wrong, (Citation omitted), there is no need to consult legislative history. (Note omitted).

Nor was the en banc Court of Appeals correct in concluding that this plain reading of the statute leads to absurd results. (Note omitted). The statute does not require the eviction of any tenant who violated the lease provision. Instead, it entrusts that decision to the local public housing authorities, who are in the best position to take account of, among other things, the degree to which the housing project suffers from "rampant drug-related or violent crime," (Citation omitted), "the seriousness of the offending action," (Citation omitted), and "the extent to which the leaseholder has . . . taken all reasonable steps to prevent or mitigate the offending action," (Citation omitted). It is not "absurd" that a local housing authority may sometimes evict a tenant who had no knowledge of the drug-related activity. Such "no-fault" eviction is a common "incident of tenant responsibility under normal landlord-tenant law and practice." (Citation omitted). Strict liability maximizes deterrence and eases enforcement difficulties. (Citation omitted).

And, of course, there is an obvious reason why Congress would have permitted local public housing authorities to conduct no-fault evictions: Regardless of knowledge, a tenant who "cannot control drug crime, or other criminal activities by a household member which threaten health or safety of other residents, is a threat to other residents and the project." (Citation omitted). With drugs leading to "murders, muggings, and other forms of violence against tenants," and to the "deterioration of the physical environment that requires substantial governmental expenditures," (Citation omitted), it was reasonable for Congress to permit no-fault evictions in order to "provide public and other federally assisted low-income housing that is decent, safe, and free from illegal drugs," (Citation omitted).

We hold that "Congress has directly spoken to the precise question at issue." (Citation omitted). Section 1437d(1)(6) requires lease terms that give local public housing authorities the discretion to terminate the lease of a tenant when a member of the household or a guest engages in drug-related activity, regardless of whether the tenant knew, or should have known, of the drug-related activity.

Accordingly, the judgment of the Court of Appeals is reversed, and the cases are remanded for further proceedings consistent with this opinion.

It is so ordered.

▶ Notes & Questions

1. According to the Sentencing Project, a non-profit criminal justice research organization, between 1986 and 1991, the rate of African-American women incarcerated in state prisons for drug offenses increased 828 percent.[5] For example, Kemba Smith, age 26, a former student at Hampton University in Virginia is serving a 24 year sentence because of her association with a drug dealer. What impact will these types of laws have upon African-American children who are left without both mothers and fathers? The problem is the mandatory sentencing laws that leave judges with very little discretion. Is it more cost effective for the public to support these women in prison and their children in foster care, than to provide short term incarceration and intensive counseling and job training?

2. The following will provide a glimpse at some recent cases that concerned searches of automobiles and Fourth Amendment rights: *Ohio v. Robinette*, 519 U.S. 33 (1996) (Consent to search cars, drivers' freedom to leave); *Maryland v. Wilson*, 519 U.S. 408 (1997) (Police can order passengers out of cars); Wyoming v. Houghton, 526 U.S. 295 (1999) (Once driver is arrested, police can search purses of drivers); *Whren v. United States*, 792 A.2d 256 (2000) (Police can stop and frisk because of traffic stops).

---

5   Zachary R. Dowdy, They speak for the fallen in war on drugs, the *Boston Globe*, July 2, 1998.

Chapter Eight

LEGAL RESPONSE TO RACIST VIOLENCE

A.
The Murder of Emmett Till

Many individuals consider the murder of Emmett Till to be a crucial turning point in the black struggle for equality in America. Not only did the murder symbolize the gross brutality that some whites in the South were capable of inflicting upon blacks, but it also confirmed that racism was prevalent in the Southern judicial system. Could a white jury in Mississippi hear the evidence in a case involving two white defendants and a dead black teenager, and deliver a fair and just verdict? The Till case indicated that fairness and justice was but a dream for the vast majority of blacks in Mississippi.

For many blacks in the South, controversies between them and whites were not resolved in a court of law, but rather in the backwoods. However, for blacks, there was no fundamental difference between a lynching and a court trial? Stephen J. Whitfield, in his book *A Death in the Delta:* "The Story of Emmett Till," indicated that 4,743 persons were lynched between 1882 and 1968, of whom 3,446 were black. These individuals were denied due process of law and equal protection and instead subjected to mob violence. If you were a black defendant, you were presumed to be guilty. If you were a black victim, the white defendant was presumed innocent. A presumed guilty black defendant's punishment was swift and sure: death.

The case of Emmett Till was, therefore, a classic one of racism in the law. Even when the evidence against the white defendants was overwhelming, justice was denied to young Till and his family.

Facts

Emmett Till was born near Chicago in July 25, 1941. His mother, Mamie Till Bradley was born in Tallahatchie County, Mississippi and later moved to Chicago. In the summer of 1955 Mamie decided to send her son back home to spend a few weeks with a relative, Moses "Preacher" Wright and his wife, Elizabeth. Emmett made the trip to Mississippi with a cousin, Curtis Jones.

On August 24, Emmett decided to visit the Town of Money with some friends. He was fourteen at the time. The young people drove to Bryant's Grocery and Meat Market, owned by Roy Bryant and Carolyn Bryant. The store was frequented by blacks who would buy sodas and other provisions. In fact, when Emmett and his party arrived, there were many other young people already sitting in the front of the store. [1] Roy Bryant was not present at the time. Carolyn Bryant and Juanita Milam were tending the store alone.

What exactly happened next is subject to dispute, but not much. It is clear that outside the store young Till began to brag about having white girl friends in Chicago. He even showed a picture of a white girl to the group of teenagers. Someone then told him that two white women were in the store and dared him to go in and ask for a date. Emmett immediately met the challenge by going into the store and asking Carolyn Bryant for a date. At trial she testified that Emmett grabbed her waist and said "Don't be afraid of me, baby. I ain't gonna hurt you. I been with white girls before."[2] She testified that she went to the Milam car and obtained a pistol and reentered the store, whereupon Emmett said "Bye Baby" and "wolf-whistled" at her. Curtis Jones disputed her testimony, by saying that Emmett only said "Bye, Baby."

1   Stephen J. Whitfield, *A Death in the Delta*, "The Story of Emmett Till" (Baltimore, The Johns Hopkins University Press, 1992) p. 16

2   Whitfield, p.17

By August 26, Roy Bryant had become so incensed by what had occurred that he decided to punish the young boy from Chicago. That night he asked J.W. Milam to drive him over to "Preacher" Wright, where Emmett was staying. They took with them their Colt 45's. When they arrived, Moses Wright came to the door. After he was told that they wanted Emmett, Moses told them that he had already chastised the boy. His wife, Elizabeth also said that they would pay for any damage done.[3] The men rejected the pleas and took the young boy and put him in the bed of the truck. One of the men told Moses when they left "If you cause any trouble, you'll never live to be-sixty-five."[4]

The two men then drove around with Emmett in the back of Milam's Chevy truck, before going to Milam's house in Glendora. They took Emmett into a shed and pistol whipped him. The whipping did not break Emmett's spirit. The men stated that Emmett pulled out a picture of a white girl and said that he had been with her. This statement was recounted by Bryant in a subsequent magazine article. Therefore, it is impossible to verify the validity of this assertion. Nevertheless, it was at that point that the men decided to kill Emmett. They put Emmett back into the bed of the truck and drove near Boyle where they picked up a cotton gin fan. They then drove back to the vicinity of Glendora, where Emmett was told to strip. Milam said to Emmett "Nigger, you still as good as I am? You still done it to white girls and you gonna keep on doin' it?"[5] Milam then fired a bullet into Emmett's head. Bryant tied the fan around his neck. The body was then dropped into the Tallahatchie River.

Soon after the disappearance of Emmett, Moses and Elizabeth Wright drove to Sumner and asked Crosby Smith to help them. A call was also made to Mamie Till Bradley in Chicago, Emmett's mother. Later that day, Sunday, Milam and Bryant were arrested on suspicion of murder. They admitted that they had taken Emmett, but denied that they had murdered him.

---

3   Whitfield, p. 20.

4   Whitfield, p.20.

5   Whitfield, p.21.

A few days later the body was found. The left side of his head was detached, his tongue had swollen to eight times its normal size and an eye dangled from its socket. The body had a bullet hole above the right ear. A ring bearing the initials of "L.T." was on a finger.

The sheriff of Tallahatchie County wanted to bury the body right away, but Mamie Till Bradley objected, and demanded that the body be sent to Chicago. Upon arrival in Chicago, she identified the body and stated that she would have an open casket funeral. She wanted the world to see what Mississippi had done to her child. On September 3, Emmett was buried in Chicago.

Legal Proceedings

Bryant and Milam were indicted in Tallahatchie County for kidnapping and murder. The prosecuting attorney was Hamilton Caldwell. Because Emmett was taken from Leflore County, the kidnapping charges would have to be brought in that county. The only charges they faced in Tallahatchie County were the murder charges.

Five lawyers from Sumner agreed to represent Milam and Bryant pro bono. Sheriff Strider changed his earlier statements that blood had been found on the bridge, from which the body had been dropped. He subsequently testified that the body found was not that of Emmett Till, but that of an adult. He refused to cooperate with the prosecution and became a defense witness.[6] This was not an unusual occurrence in the South, given that local and state officials systematically aligned themselves with racist forces within their counties.

The Trial

The jury in the case was all white, despite blacks representing over 60% of the population in Tallahatchie County. Neither were white women on the jury because jury service was limited to white males. This pattern of exclusion from jury service was not limited to Mississippi, but, was practiced throughout the South. Through

---

6   Whitfield, p. 30.

devices such as poll taxes, grandfather clauses, tests and other devices, Southern states were able to effectively eliminate blacks from the political process.

Blacks were prevented from voting or participating in the criminal justice system by threats of physical violence. Threats could not, however, keep Moses Wright from testifying against the two defendants. He had to be kept, however, in hiding from the date of the kidnapping until the trial because of the threats to his life. He was the first witness called by the prosecution. He testified that the "two white men came to his house and asked for the boy from Chicago-the one that did the talking at Money."[7] "Preacher" Wright made a positive identification of the men who came to take Emmett by pointing them out in the courtroom.

Another major witness was Ms. Bradley. She testified about the warnings she had given her son when he came to Mississippi. She testified that he had a bad stutter and would sometimes whistle in his attempt to pronounce words. She raised this as a possible explanation for the defense claim that he whistled at Carolyn Bryant. The most important aspect of her testimony was her identification of the body of her son when it arrived in Chicago. The defense would mount a claim that the body was not Emmetts, and that he was, in fact, still alive.

Two other prosecution witnesses put J. W. Milam at the barn where Emmett was beaten. Willie Reed, age nineteen, testified that he saw Emmett in a 1955 Chevrolet pickup truck, that was then parked in front of the barn. He then testified that he heard someone being beaten and screams. He later testified that he saw Milam exit the barn. His aunt, Amanda Bailey, testified that she heard the beatings as well.[8]

---

7   Whitfield, p. 38.

8   Whitfield, p.40.

After hearing from defense witnesses, who included the sheriff of Tallahatchie County, and Carolyn Bryant, the jury started its deliberations on September 23. After deliberating a little over one hour, the defendants were found not guilty of murder. Two months later a Grand Jury, sitting in Greenwood, refused to indict the men on kidnapping charges. After these proceedings in Greenwood, Moses Wright and his wife, Elizabeth left Mississippi for Chicago.

The Confessions

In the January 24, 1956 issue of *Look magazine* the defendants talked about how they had abducted Emmett Till and murdered him. Since they could not be tried twice for the same offense, they could not be prosecuted for their admissions.

B.

The Murder of Medgar Evers

Throughout their history in America, blacks have been subjected to violence at the hands of whites. In slavery, the violence took physical forms, such as lynchings. Later, the violence took on more subtle forms, such as insults and disparate treatment. In both forms of violence, the law responded much slower than it did when whites were the victims of black violence. One of the more telling examples of the slow approach the law took in the face of white racist violence was the case of Byron De La Beckwith. The setting is Mississippi. The victim of this violence was Medgar Evers, who was killed on June 12, 1963. A year later, three civil rights workers were murdered in Neshoba County, Mississippi. On June 23, 1963, Beckwith was arrested. He was subsequently released. On July 2, 1963, he was arrested again. On February 7, 1964, a mistrial was declared. On April 17, 1964, another mistrial was entered in the case. On March 10, 1969, the murder charge was dismissed.

From 1969 until 1990, De La Beckwith remained a free man until he was indicted on December 14, 1990. On October 8, 1991, he pled not guilty. The new indictments were challenged *before the Mississippi Supreme Court, but the Court upheld the indictments. On December 23, 1992, De La Beckwith was released on $100,000.00 bond. De La Beckwith appealed to the United States Supreme Court, which refused to hear his claim of double-jeopardy. The Court's decision was rendered on October 4, 1993. Later in 1994, De La Beckwith was convicted of the murder of Medgar Evers and began serving a life sentence. He was finally forced to pay for the murder of a civil rights leader more than thirty years after the crime was committed.*

BYRON De La BECKWITH
v.
STATE of MISSISSIPPI
Supreme Court of Mississippi
1992.

HAWKINS, Presiding Justice, for the Court:

Medgar Evers, a black civil rights activist and leader in the turbulent 1950s-1960s civil rights struggles, was murdered at his home in Jackson June 12, 1963. Byron De La Beckwith, a vocal pro-segregationist and white supremacist in this State, was arrested June 23 and indicted for Evers' murder at the July, 1963, term of the grand jury of Hinds County. He stood trial in February, 1964, and following a hung jury, a mistrial was ordered by the circuit judge February 7. He again stood trial in April, and following another hung jury, the circuit judge declared a mistrial on April 17, 1964. Until his second trial, Beckwith had been incarcerated without bail.

Following his second trial Beckwith was released on $10,000 bail. He ran a markedly unsuccessful campaign for Lieutenant Governor in 1967. The district attorney prosecuting the case did not seek re-election, and his successor on March 10, 1969, moved the court to enter a *nolle prosequi* of the indictment. The three circuit judges of the Seventh Circuit Court District signed the order granting a *nolle prosequi*. There was no objection by the defense to the entry of the *nolle prosequi*.

Over the years this case has received considerable public attention by the press, but no further effort was made by the State to initiate criminal proceedings against Beckwith until the December, 1990, term of the Hinds County grand jury when he again was indicted for murder. Beckwith, then living in Tennessee, following an extradition contest in the Tennessee courts, was extradited to Mississippi and incarcerated in a Hinds County jail.

His request for bail was denied by the circuit judge, and affirmed on appeal by this Court's order of March 25, 1992. He has been in jail in this State since October, 1991.

In April 1992, he sought dismissal of the indictment against him on three constitutional grounds. The circuit court on August 4, 1992, denied his motion, and Beckwith then petitioned this Court for an interlocutory appeal, pursuant to our Rule 5, Mississippi Supreme Court Rules. This Court by August 26, 1992, Order granted an interlocutory appeal. (Footnote omitted)...

[2] On his appeal Beckwith seeks the dismissal of the indictment and his discharge from custody on three grounds:

(1) Denial of a speedy trial. "In all criminal prosecutions, the accused shall enjoy the right to a speedy and public trial, by an impartial jury of the State and district wherein the crime shall have been committed...." Amendment 6, U.S. Constitution. "In all criminal prosecutions the accused shall have a right to a . . . speedy and public trial by an impartial jury of the county where the offense was committed.... "Art. 3, §26, Mississippi Constitution.

(2) Denial of due process. "No person shall be . . . deprived of life, liberty or property, without due process of law.... "Amendment 5, U.S. Constitution.

(3) Double jeopardy. [N]or shall any person be subject for the same offense to be twice put in jeopardy of life or limb.... "Amendment 5, U.S. Constitution...

After mature consideration we have concluded that the first two grounds asserted by Beckwith afford no basis for an interlocutory appeal, and decline to address them...

ROY NOBLE LEE, Chief Justice, dissenting:

In my view, the majority opinion does violence to the United States Constitution, the Mississippi Constitution and established law and precedent of the United States and the State of Mississippi. I believe it to be erroneous and the worst pronouncement of the law during my tenure on the Mississippi Supreme Court bench, and that it is an egregious miscarriage of justice. Therefore, I emphatically dissent!...

A.

DENIAL OF A SPEEDY TRIAL

The Sixth Amendment to the U.S. Constitution provides that "in all criminal prosecutions the accused shall have a right to a ... speedy and public trial..." Article 3, Section 26 of the Mississippi Constitution of 1890 provides that "in all criminal prosecutions the accused shall have a right to a ...speedy and public trial..." On March 10, 1969, the State of Mississippi requested a *nolle prosequi* of the indictment, which request was approved by all three circuit judges of the Seventh Circuit Court District. The effect of the *nolle prosequi* was to conclude and dismiss the murder charge against Beckwith.

The time lapse from April 17, 1964, the date of the second mistrial, until March 10 1969, the date of the *nolle prosequi,* was five years, lacking one month. The cases are legion that the prosecution at that point was in egregious violation of Beckwith's federal and state constitutional rights to a speedy trial after five years delay. Instead of acknowledging and facing those facts, the prosecution simply filed a motion requesting that the indictment be dismissed on a *nolle prosequi* order. The Latin phrase *nolle prosequi* means that the State was "unwilling to prosecute"; "unwilling to follow (in its prosecution)"; "cannot prosecute."

At the December, 1990, term of Hinds County Circuit Court, Second Judicial District, the grand jury again indicted Beckwith for the murder of Evers. The indictment was exactly the same as the 1963 indictment, as if it had been pulled from the 1963 court record. For all purposes, it was a revival of the 1963 case against Beckwith. This Court should vindicate his speedy trial rights for that period of time, and grant him the relief sought in this appeal.

B.

SPEEDY TRIAL AND RIGHT TO DUE PROCESS UNDER THE LAW

The Fifth Amendment to the U.S. Constitution and Article 3, Section 26, of the Mississippi Constitution of 1890, provide that no person shall be deprived of life, liberty or property, without due process of law. Due process of law commands that a person shall not be denied anything under the law that adversely affects his life, liberty or property. This includes his right to a speedy trial, his right to be confronted with witnesses, even though in the meantime they may have died, his right to enjoyment of life and liberty and other things related thereto...

The three questions of constitutional law, which we have before us today, were thoroughly presented to the trial court in exhaustive hearings. There was a complete record made of all the facts surrounding those issues, including anything that could have been presented or developed in a jury trial of the case. The facts developed on those issues are undisputed. They reflect that the long delay of twenty-nine years for a third trial of Beckwith has highly prejudiced him in his defense of the 1990 charge against him:

(1) The bullet fragments from the deceased, the unspent shells from the rifle found at the scene and fifty-three test shells were sought for an independent examination by Beckwith's counsel. The prosecution advised the items of evidence are unavailable. (2) Witnesses testifying at the second trial are no longer available, since they are deceased or their memories are extinct. (3) Two of Beckwith's

prior attorneys are deceased and their files no longer are in existence. The only other defense attorney is eighty-three years of age and his file has been lost due to the passage of time. (4) The prosecution intends to use transcripts of dead prosecution witnesses, who cannot now be impeached and Beckwith will be denied confrontation for cross-examination of those witnesses. (5) The crucial alibi of a witness for Beckwith, Roy Jones, is deceased. (6) Mr. and Mrs. B.L. Pittman; Chief of Detectives M.B. Pierce; John Goza; Lee S. Prosperer; Sheriff J.R. Gilfoy; Sam Allen, Jr.; and Warren, Bullock, Cunningham, Sanders and Speights, witnesses or potential witness, are deceased. (7) Beckwith is now seventy-one years of age and in poor health. He does not have the ability to concentrate; he has been unable to recall events essential to his defense; and he has been unable to recall his whereabouts on June 7 or June 11, 1963, in order to rebut probable testimony of the prosecution's witnesses...

The finality of the proceedings against Beckwith in 1969 are indicated by the facts that the murder rifle ended up in the closet of one of the circuit judges; and, after his death, the closet of a prosecutor; the fragmented murder bullet was missing; the court file was missing and other items of evidence and important documents were missing.

Further indication of the finality of the Judgment of *nolle prosequi is* when the district attorney for the Seventh Circuit Court District, of which Hinds County is a part, Honorable Edward J. Peters, was being pressed to indict and try Beckwith, on August 17, 1987, gave the following statement to the *Clarion Ledger* newspaper:

"There is no way under any stretch of the law that this case could be tried again. Anyone having the first class in law school ought to know that..."

C.

DOUBLE JEOPARDY

The Fifth Amendment to the State's Constitution guarantees that Beckwith will not be twice put in jeopardy of a trial for the murder of Medger Evers. That same guarantee provides that no state can diminish or lessen that right by its constitution or law. States may grant more relief in their interpretation of the state constitution, but not less than the relief provided by the U.S. Constitution. With this principle in mind, we apply it to the Beckwith case now being considered on that issue.

Jeopardy attaches in a criminal trial when the jury is empaneled, which includes an oath by the jury to well and truly try the accused and a true verdict give. A conviction, or an acquittal, a voluntary dismissal by the state, an act by the state violative of due process (taking unfair advantage of the defendant), which requires a mistrial, terminates jeopardy incurred by the defendant. Of course, a mistrial which is declared by the Court because of the inability of a jury to agree upon a verdict does not terminate jeopardy and the ability of the prosecution to continue its efforts to try and convict the defendant. Also, where an incident occurs during the trial for which the state is not responsible or accountable, arising to a manifest necessity for mistrial, the entry of such a mistrial by the trial judge does not terminate the jeopardy which has attached.

Applying that principle and reasoning to Beckwith, jeopardy attached in his trial when he was tried in February, 1964. It was not terminated when that trial resulted in a mistrial because the jury could not agree upon a verdict. At the second trial in April, 1964, the attachment of jeopardy was carried over and still existed from the first trial because it had not been terminated. There was no double jeopardy. Likewise, the second trial in April, 1964, resulted in a hung jury and the trial court entered a mistrial. Jeopardy still had not been terminated. That jeopardy continued for five years until, at the motion of the prosecution and the approval of all trial judges of the district, a *nolle prosequi* judgment was entered.

That judgment ended the case against Beckwith, which had been pending for five years. The jeopardy which had attached with the first trial was then terminated. All the scrubbing and washing from the adoption of the United States Constitution cannot erase that red blotch of former jeopardy which Beckwith had incurred. Reams of paper and volumes of law books cannot change or sweeten it where it would be palatable to the U.S. Constitution.

When Beckwith was indicted in December, 1990, on an indictment charging, in the same words and manner, the crime for which Beckwith had already been tried twice; when jeopardy had been terminated and when he was brought before the same court on the same charge, double jeopardy reared its two pronged head and tried to strike again in violation of the Fifth Amendment to the U.S. Constitution, the shield and sword against double prosecution.

Since *Benton v. Maryland,* 395 U.S. 784, 89 S.Ct. 2056, 23 L.Ed.2d 707 (1969), holding that double jeopardy under the U.S. Constitution applies to the states, Mississippi and all other states have been bound by it, without question...

The prosecution concedes that Beckwith has been in its sights for twenty-nine years; that twenty-eight years ago it shot at him twice and missed after full trials on the merits; that it then quit, having nothing additional to support the case or to proceed with; and, finally, that when time removed and eroded the files, evidence and Beckwith's witnesses, and he became old and infirm, the prosecution takes advantage of those facts and again cocks and aims its gun at him...

I think the majority has erred grievously and has disregarded and obfuscated the meaning of that great document and Gibraltar of human and civil rights...

I dissent to the majority opinion!

▶ Notes & Questions

1. The dissenting opinions suggest that De La Beckwith was being deprived of his constitutional rights by being tried for a third time. What are the arguments that, despite his conviction, he has benefitted by the system, instead of being victimized?

2. Has justice been accomplished in this case? Why has it taken Mississippi so long to practice equal justice under the law?

3. In December, 1997, the Mississippi Supreme Court upheld the murder conviction of Byron De La Beckwith. At the age of 77 he finally had his fate determined by the highest court in the state.

C.

The Murders of Schwerner, Chaney and Goodman

One of the most outrageous acts during the civil rights movement was the murder of three civil rights workers in Mississippi. The murder of the two white and one black worker in 1964 shocked the nation. Many could not believe that one hundred years after the Emancipation Proclamation, blacks and those who joined in their struggle for civil and human rights were still the object of racial violence and murder.

In June 1964, racial violence in Mississippi had reached an all time high. On June 16, White Knights burned the Mount Zion Methodist Church and beat many of the civil rights workers. On June 21, Michey Schwerner, James Chaney and Andy Goodman left Meridian to visit the workers in Longdale. On their way back from Longdale, they were arrested by Meridian Deputy Sheriff Cecil Price. They were taken to Neshoba County jail in Philadelphia. Later that night Chaney, the driver, paid a fine and the three were released. Price intercepted them again, and turned them over to a white mob. The three were killed by a group of Klansmen. Their bodies were discovered in July as a result of a tip from an informant, who was paid $30,000.00 by the Federal Bureau of Investigation. Another informant, Delmar Dennis provided information that ultimately led to the arrest of the individuals responsible for the murders.

The United States Justice Department brought the indictments under U.S. Code and the defendants were charged with conspiracy to deprive the civil rights workers of their civil rights.

UNITED STATES v. PRICE ET AL.
Supreme Court of the United States
383 U.S. 787 (1966)

MR. JUSTICE FORTAS delivered the opinion of the Court.

These are direct appeals from the dismissal in part of two indictments returned by the United States Grand Jury for the Southern District of Mississippi. The indictments allege assaults by the accused persons upon the rights of the asserted victims to due process of law under the Fourteenth Amendment. The indictment in No. 59 charges 18 persons (Footnote omitted) with violations of 18 U.S. C. §241 (1964 ed.). In No. 60, the same 18 persons are charged with offenses based upon 18 U. S. C. §242 (1964 ed.). These are among the so-called civil rights statutes which have come to us from Reconstruction days, the period in our history which also produced the Thirteenth, Fourteenth, and Fifteenth Amendments to the Constitution.

The sole question presented in these appeals is whether the specified statutes make criminal the conduct for which the individuals were indicted...

The events upon which the charges are based, as alleged in the indictments, are as follows: On June 21, 1964, Cecil Ray Price, the Deputy Sheriff of Neshoba County, Mississippi, detained Michael Henry Schwerner, James Earl Chaney and Andrew Goodman in the Neshoba County jail located in Philadelphia, Mississippi. He released them in the dark of that night. He then proceeded by automobile on Highway 19 to intercept his erstwhile wards. He removed the three men from their automobile, placed them in an official automobile of the Neshoba County Sheriff's office, and transported them to a place on an unpaved road.

These acts, it is alleged, were part of a plan and conspiracy whereby the three men were intercepted by the 18 defendants, including Deputy Sheriff Price, Sheriff Rainey and Patrolman Willis of the Philadelphia, Mississippi, Police Department. The purpose and intent of the release from custody and the interception, according to the charge, were to "punish" the three men. The defendants, it is alleged, "did wilfully assault, shoot and kill"each of the three. And, the charge continues, the bodies of the three victims were transported by one of the defendants from the rendezvous on the unpaved road to the vicinity of the construction site of an earthen dam approximately five miles southwest of Philadelphia, Mississippi.

These are federal and not state indictments. They do not charge as crimes the alleged assaults or murders. The indictments are framed to fit the stated federal statutes, and the question before us is whether the attempt of the draftsman for the Grand Jury in Mississippi has been successful: whether the indictments charge offenses against the various defendants which may be prosecuted under the designated federal statutes.

We shall deal first with the indictment in No. 60, based on §242 of the Criminal Code, and then with the indictment in No. 59, under §241. We do this for ease of exposition and because §242 was enacted by the Congress about four years prior to §241.3 Section 242 was enacted in 1866; §241 in 1870.

I. No. 60.

Section 242 defines a misdemeanor, punishable by fine of not more than $1,000 or imprisonment for not more than one year, or both. So far as here significant, it provides punishment for "Whoever, under color of any law, statute, ordinance, regulation, or custom, willfully subjects any inhabitant of any State...to the deprivation of any rights, privileges, or immunities protected by the Constitution or laws of the United States..."

The indictment in No. 60 contains four counts, each of which names as defendants the three officials and 15 nonofficial persons. The First Count charges, on the basis of allegations substantially as set forth above, that all of the defendants conspired "to wilfully subject" Schwerner, Chaney and Goodman "to the deprivation of their right, privilege and immunity secured and protected by the Fourteenth Amendment to the Constitution of the United States not to be summarily punished without due process of law by persons acting under color of the laws of the State of Mississippi." This is said to constitute a conspiracy to violate §242, and therefore an offense under 18 U.S.C. §371 (1964 ed.). The latter section, the general conspiracy statute, makes it a crime to conspire to commit any offense against the United States. The penalty for violation is the same as for direct violation of §242 - that is, it is a misdemeanor". (Footnote omitted)...

The Second, Third and Fourth Counts of the indictment in No. 60 charge all of the defendants, not with conspiracy, but with substantive violations of §242. Each of these counts charges that the defendants, acting "under color of the laws of the State of Mississippi," "did willfully assault, shoot and kill" Schwerner, Chaney and Goodman, respectively, "for the purpose and with the intent" of punishing each of the three and that the defendant "did thereby wilfully deprive" each "of rights, privileges and immunities secured and protected by the Constitution and the laws of the United States"- namely, due process of law.

The District Court held these counts of the indictment valid as to the sheriff, deputy sheriff and patrolman. But it dismissed them as against the nonofficial defendants because the counts do not charge that the latter were "officers in fact, or de facto in anything allegedly done by them 'under color of law.'"

We note that by sustaining these counts against the three officers, the court again necessarily concluded that an offense under §242 is properly stated by allegations of willful deprivation, under color of law, of life and liberty without due process of law. We agree. No other result would be permissible under the decisions of this Court. (Footnote omitted).

But we cannot agree that the Second, Third or Fourth Counts may be dismissed as against the nonofficial defendants. Section 242 applies only where a person indicted has acted "under color" of law. Private persons, jointly engaged with state officials in the prohibited action, are acting "under color" of law for purposes of the statute. To act "under color" of law does not require that the accused be an officer of the State. It is enough that he is a willful participant in joint activity with the State or its agents. (Footnote omitted).

In the present case, according to the indictment, the brutal joint adventure was made possible by state detention and calculated release of the prisoners by an officer of the State. This action, clearly attributable to the State, was part of the monstrous design described by the indictment. State officers participated in every phase of the alleged venture: the release from jail, the interception, assault and murder. It was a joint activity, from start to finish... In effect, if the allegations are true, they were participants in official lawlessness, acting in willful concert with state officers and hence under color of law...

II. No. 59.

No. 59 charges each of the 18 defendants with a felony—a violation of §241. This indictment is in one count. It charges that the defendants "conspired together...to injure, oppress, threaten and intimidate "Schwerner, Chaney and Goodman "in the free exercise and enjoyment of the right and privilege secured to them by the Fourteenth Amendment to the Constitution of the United States not to be deprived of life or liberty without due process of law by persons acting under color of the laws of Mississippi." The indictment alleges that it was the purpose of the conspiracy that Deputy Sheriff Price would release Schwerner, Chaney and Goodman from custody in the Neshoba County jail at such time that Price and the other 17 defendants "could and would intercept" them "and threaten, assault, shoot and kill them." The penalty under §241 is a fine of not more than $5,000, or imprisonment for not more than 10 years, or both...

The District Court dismissed the indictment as to all defendants. In effect, although §241 includes rights or privileges secured by the Constitution or laws of the United States without qualification or limitation, the court held that it does not include rights protected by the Fourteenth Amendment...

The indictment specifically alleges that the sheriff, deputy sheriff and a patrolman participated in the conspiracy; that it was a part of the "plan and purpose of the conspiracy" that Deputy

Sheriff Price, "while having [the three victims]... in his custody in the Neshoba County Jail... would release them from custody at such time that he [and others of the defendants] could and would intercept [the three victims] threaten, assault, shoot and kill them."

This is an allegation of state action which, beyond dispute, brings the conspiracy within the ambit of the Fourteenth Amendment. It is an allegation of official, state participation in murder, accomplished by and through its officers with the participation of others. It is an allegation that the State, without the semblance of due process of law as required of it by the Fourteenth Amendment, used its sovereign power and office to release the victims from jail so that they were not charged and tried as required by law, but instead could be intercepted and killed. If the Fourteenth Amendment forbids denial of counsel, it clearly denounces denial of any trial at all...

We conclude, therefore, that it is incumbent upon us to read §241 with full credit to its language. Nothing in the prior decisions of this Court or of other courts which have considered the matter stands in the way of that conclusion. (Footnote omitted)...

Reversed and remanded.

D.

Murders of Addie Mae Collins, Denise McNair, Cynthia Wesley and Carole Robertson

On September 15, 1964, the 16th Street Baptist Church was bombed in Birmingham, Alabama, killing four young girls as they attended Sunday school. It was not until the early 70's that the Federal Bureau of Investigation (F.B.I.) gave to Alabama authorities secretly recorded tapes that would play a key role in the trials of the men arrested for the bombing. But why did the F.B.I. wait over eight years before turning over the evidence to Alabama authorities? Why did F.B.I. Director J. Edgar Hoover refuse to prosecute individuals when he had evidence of their Klan involvement in the bombings? And why did the Alabama authorities wait so long to bring the men who murdered the young black girls to justice?

Both governmental bodies blamed each other for the thirty-eight year delay in the prosecutions. William Baxley, the Alabama Attorney General in the 1970's, stated, in a New York Times Op-Ed article, that the F.B.I. deliberately thwarted the state's attempts to bring the killers to justice. Baxley "...said he had lobbied for years to gain access to the F.B.I. files and had succeeded only after Jack Nelson, a reporter for the Los Angeles Times, threatened to write that the bureau was stonewalling.[9] Baxley stated that the F.B.I. had in its possession secretly taped conversations of Blanton in his kitchen, where he implicated himself in making the bombs. Craig D. Dahle, a spokesperson for the F.B.I. laid the blame on the agency's unwillingness to expose confidential informers and on the distrust that existed between federal and Alabama agencies.[10]

The final defendant in the case, Bobby Frank Cherry, went to trial on May 6, 2002. Cherry, a former member of the Ku Klux Klan and age 71, had been free since the bombing of the church. He was scheduled to be tried with Blanton in 2001, but he faked mental incompetency which allowed him to delay his trial until January, 2002, when he was declared by a state judge to be competent.
On May 22, 2002, Cherry was convicted of the murders by a Jefferson County, Alabama jury made up of nine whites and three blacks, after deliberating for six hours.[11]

---

9   Kevin Sack, F.B.I. Denies It Hid Evidence in Church Blast, The New York Times, May 4, 2001.

10   Kevin Sack, F.B.I. Denies It Hid Evidence in Church Blast, The New York Times, May 4, 2001.

11   Rick Bragg, Ex-Klansman Gets Life Sentence for Killing 4 Alabama Girls, The New York Times, May 23, 2002.

These cases brought to a close racist terrorists who destroyed black lives yet went largely unpunished. Robert Chambliss ("Dynamite Bob") was reported to have been involved in over 40 bombings of black homes and institutions. He was convicted of the murders in 1977. Herman Frank Cash, another culprit in the bombing, died before he was tried. Thomas E. Blanton, Jr. was convicted and sentenced to life in 2001. Finally, Cherry faced the same fate in May, 2002 after 38 years of leave from punishment.

► Notes & Questions

1. On June 11, 2005 the United States Senate issued its first apology over its failure to ever pass anti-lynching laws. At a luncheon held for descendants of survivors, James Cameron, age 91, spoke of how he survived a lynching as a 16 year old boy in Marion, Indiana. He and two friends were accused of murdering a white man and raping a white woman. The two men were killed by a mob and Mr. Cameron narrowly escaped hanging. The rope had been placed around his neck when a white man came forward and said Mr. Cameron had nothing to do with the killing.

   The Senate resolution was supported by only 80 senators and was merely a voice vote.

   At the luncheon relatives of Anthony Crawford spoke of the lynching of their relative in 1916. Mr. Crawford, a wealthy cotton farmer in Abbeville, South Carolina was hanged after a dispute over the price of cotton seed. He was shot more than 200 times. One relative said of the senate apology: "I have to let God be the judge because I don't know if they meant it out of their heart or they're just saying it out of their mouth." (Sheryl Gay Stolberg, "Senate Issues Apology Over Failure on Lynching Law,"*The New York Times*, June 14, 2005.

2. Another racist who spent most of his adult lilfe free before finally being convicted of murdering Vernon Dahmer was Samuel Bowers. As the head of the Ku Klux Klan in Mississippi he ordered the firebombing of the home of Vernon Dahmer on January 10, 1966 because Mr. Dahmer was helping blacks to register to vote in his grocery store. On the night of his murder two carloads of Klansmen came to the Dahmer home and set it on fire. Mr. Dahmer tried to fight them off with his shotgun, but

▶ Notes & Questions

---

he died from smoke inhalation. His family did escape the house while he fought the racists with firepower. Bowers was convicted of killing Dahmer in 1998 and died in prison in 2006.

Before the Dahmer murder, Samuel Bowers had spent six years in federal prison for violating the civil rights of James Chaney, Andrew Goodman and Michael Schwerner. ("Samuel Bowers; convicted in bombing of activist,"*The Boston Globe*, November 6, 2006.)

E.

The Killing of Rev. Accelyn Williams (Boston)

On March 25, 1994, Boston police broke into the house of Rev. Accelyn Williams, a seventy-five year old black minister. The police raid occurred at 3 a.m. in the morning and was in search of drugs. The Police however, relying upon confidential information from an informant, entered the wrong house. Rev. Williams was chased, thrown to the floor and handcuffed by the police. He suffered a fatal heart attack as a result of these police actions. The next day Police Commissioner Paul F. Evans acknowledged that the police had made a mistake and apologized to the Williams family.

In April, 1996, the widow of Rev. Williams accepted a settlement of $1,000,000.00 from the City of Boston. One of the family's attorneys stated that if the victim had been white, the city would have paid more. Attorney Henry Owens opposed the settlement and argued that the raid represented a pattern of police violence against the black community.

Was the raid a mistake or the result of indifference to the rights of black individuals? Should the award have been larger? Is the public served by the $1,000,000.00 award? Shouldn't the police officers repay the public for the cost of their mistakes?

► Notes & Questions

1. Why didn't the Federal Government, in the *Price* case, bring the charges in state court?

2. Shouldn't the penalties under state law have been stronger, especially when the deprivation in this case was murder?

3. Two of the victims were white and one black. What does this fact illustrate about racism in the South? What does it reveal about the civil rights movement and the role of white supporters?

4. Do you agree with the Court's interpretation that private individuals can be indicted under the statute? Why is this interpretation important in terms of its ability to reach private individuals?

5. In 1996, a jury ordered Bernhard Goetz to pay Darrell Cabey $43 million in damages for shooting Cabey in a New York City subway in 1984. Goetz testified that he shot four black youth on the subway when they asked him for $5.00. Cabey, one of his victims is paralyzed with a mental capacity of an eight year old. Mr. Goetz has filed bankruptcy and is not expected to pay the judgment. Has Mr. Cabey received justice? Should Goetz have been convicted of the shootings in the earlier criminal trial? Was he justified in pulling the gun and firing at five youth in a crowded train? Did he have a legitimate right to protect himself? Under what circumstances should a citizen be allowed to shoot a gun in a train or other congested public place?

6. In December, 1996, Benjamin and Betty Mims of South Carolina received a two year jail sentence for brutalizing a 9 year old black boy. The youngster had come to the Mims'

▶ **Notes & Questions**

house to play with their children. The couple accused the young boy of trying to steal from them. They then took him into the woods, tied him to a tree, beat and punched him. Benjamin fired his shotgun in the direction of the youngster and Betty choked him mercilessly. The youngster passed out from these actions. The two convicted felons will be eligible for parole in a little over six months. Shouldn't the defendants have been punished more severely? What effect did these lenient sentences have upon the black community? Do they inspire confidence in the judicial system?

7. In the second (Federal) Rodney King trial, officers Stacey Koon and Lawrence Powell were sentenced to 2 1/2 years for beating King and fracturing his skull and eye socket. Given the rebellions in Los Angeles following the first (state) trial, shouldn't the judge have taken into consideration the outrage of the community and imposed a stiffer sentence? Should a judge be able to take into consideration a defendant's social status in the community before imposing a sentence? Isn't the loss of that status, as a result of a conviction, enough punishment?

8. Has the governmental response to white racist violence been sufficient? The end of the Civil War in 1865 did not halt the violent assaults against black people. In 1868 some whites engaged in a "niggerhunt" in Louisiana's Bossier County, which resulted in 120 blacks being killed. See *United States v. Guest*, 383 U.S. 745 (1966) for a glimpse of how the Federal Government responded to violence against blacks.

9. In July, 1917 white riots broke out in East St. Louis that resulted in 39 blacks being killed and 9 whites. Several months later

▶ Notes & Questions

in Houston, Texas, 2 black soldiers were killed and 17 white men.

10. On September 13, 1971, prisoners at New York's Attica Correctional Facility staged an uprising against oppressive prison conditions. Rather than listen to the grievances, Governor Nelson Rockefeller authorized state police shootings which resulted in the killing of 43 people, 10 of whom were guards. In January, 2000, the State of New York indicated that it would settle the civil law suit by paying $12,000,000.00 to former inmates and their families.[12] Once an individual becomes a prisoner, does he/she lose fundamental civil rights? Should society be so generous to former felons? Should the state have used less deadly force to re-take the prison?

11. Elmer "Geronimo" Pratt, a former Black Panther Party member, who had spent 25 years in prison for a crime he did not commit, settled his civil law suit against the City of Los Angeles for an estimated $4.5 million.[13] What steps must the public take to insure that no more innocent individuals are incarcerated?

---

12   Tom Wicker, Attica: Settled But Not Healed,
The New York Times, January 7, 2000.

13   The Boston Globe, April 24, 2000.

F.

Federal Assault upon Blacks: The Tuskegee Syphilis Experiments

The Tuskegee Syphilis Experiments, carried out by the United States Public Health Service over a forty year period, is an example of the potential abuses of the human experimentation process. The experiments, carried out in Alabama on black men by the United States Government, violated both Alabama and Federal law as well as ethical standards promulgated by the Federal Government and various medical associations. The Tuskegee Experiment, as it is sometimes called, was a long-term syphilis experiment initiated by the United States Public Health Service in 1932. The experiments, conducted in Macon County, Alabama, were secretly carried out for forty years until a former employee of the Department of Health, Education and Welfare leaked the facts of the experiments to the Associated Press in 1972.[14] During the period of the study approximately five hundred men used in the experiments died from untreated syphilis.

Due to public outcry from communities and responsible members of the medical profession several studies were initiated to determine what actually occurred in Alabama. A year after the Associated Press story, the Alabama Advisory Committee to the United States Commission on Civil Rights made a cursory review of the Tuskegee Experiments. The United States Commission on Civil Rights is a bipartisan group established by the Civil Rights Act of 1957 and charged with the responsibility of investigating "denials of the equal protection of the laws based on race, sex, religion, or national origin." In each of the fifty states of the union there is an advisory committee established pursuant to section 105(c) of the Civil Rights Act of 1955 as amended.[15]

---

14   The Tuskegee Study, "A Report of the Alabama Committee to the United States Commission on Civil Rights," March, 1973, page 1.

15   The Tuskegee Study, page 1.

This sixteen page report became the official investigative source on the experiment. Needless to say, it was wholly inadequate. Rather than call on friends and relatives of the victims who could testify to the nature of the experiments and of the human suffering that resulted, it merely documented accounts of individuals who worked in the study.

A more objective and thorough account of the experiments was carried out by an Ad Hoc Advisory Panel organized by the Department of Health, Education and Welfare. The authority for setting up the committee was derived from Section 222 of the Public Health Service Act as amended, 42 U.S.C. 217a and Executive Order 11671.[16] In contrast to the Alabama Advisory Committee, this committee consisted of non-Alabama citizens drawn from numerous professions. Their task was to advise the Assistant Secretary of the Department of Health, Education and Welfare on the following issues:

1. "Determine whether the study was justified in 1932 and whether it should have been continued when penicillin became generally available.

2. Recommend whether the study should be continued at this point in time, and if not, how it should be terminated in a way consistent with the rights and health needs of its remaining participants.

3. Determine whether existing policies to protect the rights of patients participating in health research conducted or supported by the Department of Health, Education and Welfare are adequate and effective and to recommend improvements in these policies, if needed."[17]

---

16   Ad Hoc Advisory Panel, page 1.

17   Ad Hoc Advisory Panel, page 1.

The report, which became available in April of 1973, demonstrated that the Tuskegee Experiment was an outgrowth of research efforts on syphilis that were being carried on in Sweden and in the United States. In 1929 the United States Public Health Service in conjunction with the Julius Rosenwald Fund conducted syphilis control tests in six southern states: Tennessee (Tipton County), Mississippi (Bolivar County), Georgia, (Glynn County), Alabama (Macon County), Virginia (Albermarlea County), and North Carolina (Pitt County). From these studies it was found that Macon County, Alabama had a positive syphilis ratio of 35%.[18]

In Oslo, Sweden a Doctor Bruusgaard released some interesting data in 1929 on the affects of untreated syphilis on males. The study observed the effects of the disease on four hundred and seventy-three (473) patients over a period of from three to forty years. Some of the research of Doctor Bruusgaard suggested that in the latter stages of syphilis a phenomenon he referred to as "spontaneous cure" occurred. In 1929 he reported that 42.5% of his patients recovered from the disease as a natural course.[19] The Tuskegee Experiments in Macon County, therefore, were designed to accomplish the following:

1. "Study the natural history of the disease.

2. Study the course of treated and untreated syphilis.

3. Study the difference in histological and clinical course of the disease in black versus white subjects.

4. Study with an 'acceptance' of the postulate that there was a benign course of the disease in later stages vis-à-vis the dangers of available therapy.

---

18   Ad Hoc Advisory Panel, page 6.

19   Ad Hoc Advisory Panel, page 6.

5. Short term study (6 months or longer) of the incidence and clinical course of late latent syphilis in the Negro people.

6. Provide valuable data for a syphilis control program for a rural impoverished community."[20]

To be sure, the Tuskegee Experiments promised different individuals and institutions different results. Some of the data submitted to the Alabama Advisory Committee justified the study on the basis that it was designed to find the means to curtail the spread of it in the County. *The Milbank Memorial Fund Quarterly,* a publication of the chief private supporter of the syphilis experiments estimated that more potential service men in World War One were rejected for military service because of syphilis than for any other disease.[21] Therefore, according to the Milbank Fund, the purpose of the syphilis experiments was to determine the effectiveness of treatment in preventing the spread of the disease.

Austin Deibert and Martha Bruyere, two doctors associated with the study, had a slightly different view of the purpose. According to them the purpose was to follow the course of the disease in an untreated state to determine its effects upon the subject's cardiovascular system.[22]

Although the experimenters differed in their rationales for the experiments, the ultimate results in terms of human life and suffering was clear. Although it is hard to determine the exact number of men utilized in the study, it has been estimated that as many as 625 men were actually involved; of this number 127

---

20   Ad Hoc Advisory Panel, page 6. A considerable amount of this information was gathered from an October 29, 1932 correspondence between T. Clark, Assistant Surgeon General, and M.M. Davis of the Rosenwald Fund.

21   The Tuskegee Study, page 3.

22   Deibert, Austin, Bruyere, Martha, "Untreated Syphilis in the Male Negro," The Journal of Venereal Disease Information, Public Health Service, Vol. 27, December, 1946.

survived, 430 died and 68 either left Macon County or died.[23] All of them were black, uneducated and for the most part married. All were over the age of forty and thirty percent over the age of fifty. The majority only had a sixth grade education. Macon County, where most of the subjects came from, had in 1930 a population of 27,102 of which 22,376 were black, representing 82.3 percent of the total.[24]

The fact that the experiments were carried out in impoverished Macon County among black people was no coincidence. Rather, the area was chosen because of the people's relatively low level of educational attainment and therefore their greater gullibility. Consequently, many of the people volunteered to be in the study after being offered free medical care for their families as an inducement. Some were promised that if they allowed the experimenters to conduct autopsies on their bodies, that the other members of the family would be given free burial insurance. However, the height of deception was that approximately four hundred of the men and their families were never even told that they had syphilis, but that they suffered from "bad blood" or anemia.[25] These men died in the back country of Alabama, never realizing that they had been utilized in an experiment funded by the United States Government.

However, the United States Government cannot take the sole blame for the tragedy that occurred in Macon County because several other institutions were so intimately involved; chief among them being the Milbank Memorial Fund (a private foundation) and Tuskegee Institute (a private Negro college).[26] The Milbank Memorial Fund located in New York City donated funds for burial expenses and autopsies.[27] The John A. Andrew Memorial Hospital at Tuskegee Institute was used to channel funds from the Milbank

23   The Tuskegee Study, page 11.

24   The Tuskegee Study, page 12.

25   The Tuskegee Study, page 9.

26   Ad Hoc Advisory Panel, page 10.

27   The Tuskegee Study, page 5.

Memorial Fund to the doctors who performed autopsies and paid burial expenses. All of the major public health organizations in Macon County and the State of Alabama were involved in the study. The Macon County Health Department served as the initial liaison to the Public Health Service and continued to coordinate the inflow of funds from Washington, D.C. In addition, the Alabama Department of Health reviewed the experiments periodically and the Macon County Medical Society was consulted by the doctors directly involved.[28] Black morticians in Macon County experienced periodic upsurges in their business as a result of the funds they received for laying their "brothers" to rest.[29]

Finally, the Tuskegee syphilis experiments represented a grand example of institutional and governmental deception. Such deception caused untold misery in the lives of both the victims and their families. Jay Katz, a member of the Ad Hoc Advisory Panel echoed the sentiments of an outraged public:

> There is ample evidence in the records available to us that the consent to participation was not obtained from the Tuskegee Syphilis Study Subjects, but that instead they were exploited, manipulated, and deceived. They were treated not as human beings, but as objects of research.[30]

Finally, society has a particular responsibility to protect the powerless and oppressed in American society from the excesses of governmental overzealousness. In Tuskegee this protection was nonexistent as doctors deliberately allowed over five hundred men to infect their wives and children with a disease that was in the power of medical science to control.

---

28   The Tuskegee Study, page 7.

29   The Tuskegee Study, page 6.

30   Ad Hoc Advisory Panel, page 14.

As a result of the experiment, countless numbers of children in Macon County suffered and their offspring continue to suffer from blindness, distorted bone structure, brain disease and other abnormalities associated with the disease.

In the final analysis only an aware black community can guard against these kinds of violations of law and ethics. black people in this country have a particular responsibility to make sure that medical researchers obtain consent from potential subjects before any form of experimentation is allowed to take place within their communities.

▶ Notes & Questions

A good book that chronicles the medical exploitation of blacks from colonial times to the president is *Medical Apartheid: The Dark History of Medical Experimentation on Black Americans From Colonial Times to the Present* by Harriet A. Washington (Doubleday Press).

G.
Police Assaults Upon Diallo and Louima

The police assaults upon Amadou Diallo and Abner Louima exposes the extent of racist intimidation and brutalization of African people. Not only are African-Americans subjected to blatant forms of discriminatory treatment, assault and death at the hands of the police, but so have other descendants of Africa, such as the Guinean immigrant, Amadou Diallo and the Haitian-American, Abner Louima.

Amadou Diallo-(Guinean-Immigrant)

The twentieth century ended as it began with people of African descent oppressed by white supremacist political and economic systems. The case of the 22 year old immigrant from Guinea illustrates this point well. On February 4, 1999, when Amadou Diallo, an unarmed African, was fired at 41 times and hit 19 times in the vestibule of his home by New York City police bullets, the world community became outraged at such a blatant act of official misconduct.

When the officers implicated in the shooting came to trial, the case was moved to Albany, New York. The lawyers for the officers successfully argued that the move was necessary in order to insure a fair trial. People of color and their supporters, however, viewed the move as an attempt to obtain a white jury that would be sympathetic to the white police officers. Bob Herbert in *The New York Times* wrote: "...the reality is this: An all-white panel of five judges, one of whom is a crony of the lawyer for one of the accused cops, took the case out of the Bronx (and out of the hands of a black judge) and sent it to a place where *all* the judges and nearly all of the potential jurors are white..."[31]

---

31   Bob Herbert, A Whitewash in Albany, The New York Times, December 27, 1999.

Should the trial have been transferred? Shouldn't the people in New York City have had an opportunity to be heard in such a controversial case that involved volatile issues of race and police violence? Police said they thought the wallet was a gun. If a white man had been stopped in a similar neighborhood and reached for his wallet, would he have been shot at 41 times? A public policy that equates a wallet with a gun in the black community and no where else is racist and should be subjected to international scrutiny and prosecution.

It is clear that the city policy has not done much to get guns off the streets. It has, however, deprived inner city men of their right to travel freely within the city without police harassment. "The unit's officers frisked 27,061 people in 1998, but arrested only 4,647; more than 22,000 were not even accused of wrongdoing, just stopped and searched."[32] Furthermore, the Street Crime Unit had been encouraged to be aggressive in their stopping of black males, a unit that was 80% white, 16% Hispanic and a mere 3% black.[33]

What about the very public policy that led to Mr. Diallo being killed? Shouldn't there have been scrutiny of that policy which resulted in countless numbers of innocent black men being stopped and Diallo killed? Shouldn't it have been examined under the strict scrutiny of the judicial process? Officer Carroll testified that he stopped Mr. Diallo to question him, and that Mr. Diallo reached into his pocket for his wallet, which was greeted by 41 police bullets.

As was expected by many, after the move to Albany, the four officers (Sean Carroll, Edward McMellon, Kenneth Boss, and Richard Murphy) were acquitted on February 25, 2000. How could the officers be acquitted when 41 shots were fired at an unarmed man? Two of the officers emptied their 9mm pistols that carried 16 bullets each. The other two officers fired a total of 9 bullets.

32   Joyce Purnick, Big Issues are Left Unsaid in Trial on Diallo Slaying, The New York Times, February 21, 2000.

33   Fred Kaplan, After verdicts, seeking answers in NYPD, The Boston Globe, February 27, 2000.

Isn't this clear evidence of unreasonable use of police power or of reckless use of deadly force? Why couldn't the jury recognize that to shoot an unarmed man 19 times was clear evidence of reckless endangerment or of deliberate intent to kill Diallo?

The conscience of Americans was aroused as many resorted to protests over the verdict. Many marched from Central Park to city hall chanting "No Justice, No Peace" and "Don't shoot. It's a wallet" as they held up their wallets. They listened to Mayor Rudolph W. Giuliani applaud the peaceful protests yet acknowledge that the verdict proved that the officers committed no crime. Rev. Al Sharpton countered the mayor's remarks with his own question: "How are you going to call beating Rodney King excessive, but now in the Bronx, you replace fists with bullets, and it's not excessive enough? This was Rodney King multiplied by lead."[34] Many blacks were troubled by the fact that four black women were on the jury that rendered the verdict. The forewoman of the jury, Arlene Taylor, a black woman, stated to the press that race was not an issue. In addition, some people have criticized Robert T. Johnson, the Bronx district attorney, who was also black, for not being up to the case, or being less than aggressive. For example, many have stated that the prosecutors should have cross-examined the defense expert witness on police procedures, James J. Fyfe, and the last defense witness.

The outrage was overwhelming throughout New York City. Otherwise moderate community leaders spoke out against the verdict. Norman Siegel, Executive Director of New York Civil Liberties Union called for a special prosecutor of police brutality cases. Rev. Calvin O. Butts III of Abyssinian Baptist Church told his congregation on February 27, 2000 "I feel a little like my Lord, I want to kick over some tables."[35] He was more direct in his criticism of Mayor Giuliani: "...I can say he has created in this city a divisiveness, a climate that gives a chance for people who

34   Francie Latour, Protests rise over Diallo verdict,
The Boston Globe, February 27, 2000.

35   Eric Lipton, From Pulpits to Politics, Angry Voices on
Diallo, The New York Times, February 28, 2000.

are filled with rage, people who are racist, to strike out against the poor or downtrodden."[36]

After the state trials, activists hoped that justice would be obtained through the federal judicial system. The key question that confronted everyone was: Would the federal government take up the case? In order for the federal courts to get involved there had to be evidence of the following factors: 1. substantial federal interest; 2. the interest had to be un-vindicated by the state proceedings. In determining whether the second factor was satisfied, the federal government would have to conclude that either the state prosecution was incompetent or that jury nullification occurred, i.e. the jury ignored evidence before it.

Concerned citizens around the country wrote the federal government to insist that it take action against the four police officers. On March 3, 2000, the Boston Pan-African Forum, a scholarly/activist organization in New England wrote Attorney General Janet Reno and urged her department to investigate the killing. The organization wrote in part: "...we refuse to believe that the shooting of Mr. Diallo, an unarmed civilian, was justifiable under any reasonable notions of justice and human rights... It appears to us that Mr. Diallo was singled out for surveillance, stopping and shooting because he was a person of African descent. For example, it has been reported that between 1997 and 1998, the Street Crime Unit stopped and frisked 45,000 people of African descent. Eighty percent of those stopped had no guns on their persons, or had been engaged in criminal activity. This unacceptable practice of racial profiling has its roots in immoral racial subjugation policies of the past that continue to manifest itself with deadly consequences..."[37]

On January 31, 2001, the United States decided against prosecuting the officers. The United States Attorney in Manhattan concluded "the officers did not fire at Mr. Diallo with specific intent to use unreasonable force." In short, the government believed that there was no evidence of intent or wilfulness. Acting

---

36   Ibid.

37   The author was President of Boston Pan-African Forum at the time.
The letter to Attorney General Reno is in the files of the organization.

Attorney General Eric H. Holder, Jr., a black man in the new Clinton administration, issued a statement from Washington, D.C. in support of this decision.[38] Amadou's mother, Kadiatou Diallo responded to the government's decision by stating: "I have been betrayed by the criminal justice system because I believe for me, as a mother, a child is a child. If someone has been executed like Amadou was, there should be accountability."[39]

The other avenue of redress for those who felt outraged by the killing was an internal investigation. Would New York Police Commissioner Howard Safir discipline the officers for violating police procedures and protocols? This question was quickly answered. The police commissioner decided against disciplining the officers on April 27, 2001. He believed the officer's contention that they believed Mr. Diallo had a gun and that their lives were threatened. He did order that they undergo retraining.

---

38 Susan Sachs, U.S. Decides Against Prosecuting 4 Officers who Killed Immigrant, The New York Times, February 1, 2001.

39 Ibid.

► Notes & Questions

1. On March 1, 2000, a young black man, Malcolm Ferguson, was killed by plain clothes police in the Bronx, a few blocks from where Diallo was killed. Ferguson was unarmed and shot in the head. He was one of two protestors arrested earlier in the week at a Diallo protest rally. The officer who shot Mr. Ferguson was Louis Rivera, a Latino officer. Is it more likely that black or Latino police officers will be less likely to use deadly force in communities of color? Mayor Giuliani quickly pointed out that Mr. Ferguson had a history of drug crimes. Is this statement relevant to the question of whether Officer Rivera used excessive force? Juanita Young, Mr. Rivera's mother argued forcefully that her son was still a human being with rights: "... They murdered my son. The mayor is going to judge a person just by what's on a piece of paper? What they're saying about him is a stonefaced lie. That boy was human, like you and me. They didn't have to kill him."[40] Should these killings of black males by the New York Police Department be brought before the United Nations as a violation of human rights?

2. On October 10, 2005 three white New Orleans police officers were arrested and charged with battering Robert Davis. Mr. Davis' assault was caught on videotape by a news crew, which showed the police officers punching the 64 year old black man.

---

40   Robert D. McFadden, Juan Forero, Giuliani Says Latest Bronx Shooting by Police Isn't Another Diallo Case, The New York Times, March 3, 2000.

Abner Louima-Haitian-American

UNITED STATES OF AMERICA v.
CHARLES SCHWARTZ, THOMAS WIESE, and
THOMAS BRUDER, Defendants-Appelllants,
JUSTIN A. VOLPE and MICHAEL BELLOMO, Defendants.
United States Court of Appeals for the Second Circuit
283 F.3d 76 (2002)

OPINION BY: JOHN M. WALKER, JR., Chief Judge:

Defendants-Appellants Charles Schwarz, Thomas Bruder, and Thomas Wiese appeal from their convictions, after two jury trials, on charges brought related to the events surrounding the brutal assault on Abner Louima in the early hours of August 9, 1997, while he was in custody at the 70th Police Precinct in Brooklyn, New York, and its aftermath.

The three appellants and defendant Justin Volpe were ultimately charged, in a twelve-count superseding indictment handed down on March 3, 1999, with conspiracy to deprive and with depriving Louima of his civil rights, in violation of 18 U.S.C. §§ 241 and 242, by assaulting him in a police car ("the car assaults"); Schwarz and Volpe were charged with conspiracy to deprive and with depriving Louima of his civil rights by sexually assaulting him in the bathroom of the 70th Precinct; and Schwarz, Bruder, and Wiese were charged with conspiracy to obstruct justice, in violation of 18 U.S.C. §§ 371 and 1503, by lying to state and federal prosecutors in an effort to exculpate Schwarz with respect to the bathroom assault. See *United States v. Volpe*, 42 F. Supp. 2d 204, 208 (E.D.N.Y. 1999). In addition, Volpe and defendant Michael Bellomo were charged with various offenses in connection with an arrest unrelated to the assaults on Louima. Id. Neither Volpe nor Bellomo are appellants in this appeal. The district court severed the charge of conspiracy to obstruct justice (Count Twelve) from the remaining counts, which were tried first.

Prior to the close of the first trial, before the government rested and out of the jury's presence, Volpe entered a guilty plea to six of the seven counts with which he was charged, including assaulting Louima in the patrol car and in the bathroom. See *United States v. Volpe*, 78 F. Supp. 2d 76, 81 (E.D.N.Y. 1999). At the end of that trial, the jury found Schwarz guilty of both conspiring to violate and violating Louima's civil rights based on the bathroom assault, but acquitted Schwarz, Wiese, and Bruder of all charges related to the car assaults.

At the second trial, the jury found Wiese, Bruder, and Schwarz guilty on the single charge at issue: conspiracy to obstruct a federal grand jury proceeding based on their statements to various investigators to the effect that Schwarz did not participate in the bathroom assault.

On June 27, 2000, the United States District Court for the Eastern District of New York (Eugene H. Nickerson, District Judge) sentenced Schwarz to 188 months of imprisonment, five years of supervised release with a special prohibition on possession of a firearm, and a special assessment of $300, and ordered restitution to Louima in the amount of $277,495. See *United States v. Bruder,* 103 F. Supp. 2d 155, 185 (E.D.N.Y. 2000). Bruder and Wiese were each sentenced to 60-month prison terms, three years of supervised release with a special prohibition on possession of a firearm, and a $100 special assessment. See id. at 190.

Appellants raise a host of challenges to their convictions. We discuss only those claims that are dispositive of this case and intimate no view on other issues on appeal that we have found unnecessary to address. The first part of our discussion will review the facts and proceedings relevant to the first trial, and will then consider Schwarz's challenges to that trial, specifically addressing: (A) whether Schwarz's attorney labored under an unwaivable conflict of interest that required his disqualification; and (B) whether the district court erred in denying without a hearing Schwarz's motion for a new trial based on the jury's exposure during jury deliberations to extrinsic information that Volpe's guilty plea referred to another police officer in the bathroom. The second part of our discussion will review the facts and proceedings relevant to the second trial and will consider the challenge made by all three appellants with respect to their convictions at the second trial: that there was insufficient evidence that appellants conspired to obstruct a federal grand jury investigation, as required by 18 U.S.C. § 1503.

For the reasons that follow, we hold that Schwarz's convictions for the civil rights violations must be vacated and remanded for a new trial because his attorney's unwaivable conflict of interest denied him effective assistance of counsel and because the jury was improperly exposed to prejudicial extrinsic information during jury deliberations. We also hold that all three appellants' convictions at the second trial for conspiracy to obstruct justice must be reversed for insufficient evidence.

THE FIRST TRIAL

I. Factual Background (Note omitted)

A. Pre-trial Proceedings

Shortly after the assault on Louima in August 1997, the law firm that represented the Policeman's Benevolent Association ("PBA"), the police officers' union, hired Stephen Worth and Stuart London as trial counsel to represent Schwarz and Bruder respectively. Both attorneys were hired as outside conflict counsel to avoid any conflicts of interest that might arise if the PBA's regular retained law firm were to represent multiple defendants. Worth's and London's fees were to be paid by the PBA.

In February 1998, after Schwarz had been indicted by the federal grand jury, Worth, London, and some other attorneys formed a law firm, Worth, Longworth & Bamundo, LLP (the "Worth firm"). In May 1998, the Worth firm entered into a two-year $10 million retainer agreement with the PBA (the "PBA retainer") to represent all police officers in administrative, disciplinary, and criminal matters as well as to provide them with civil legal representation. After entering into the PBA retainer, Worth and London agreed to continue their representation of Schwarz and Bruder without charging further fees beyond the PBA retainer.

Shortly after learning of the formation of the Worth firm and its agreement with the PBA, the government wrote a letter to the district court dated May 28, 1998, to advise it of potential conflicts of interest arising from the joint representation of Schwarz and Bruder by partners in the same law firm and from the Worth firm's PBA retainer. The government urged the district court to conduct a hearing pursuant to *United States v. Curcio*, 680 F.2d 881 (2d Cir. 1982)....

On September 11, 1998, with the first trial still several months away, the district judge held a hearing in which he advised Schwarz and Bruder regarding the risks presented by the potential conflicts...

At the Curcio hearing, the government once again took the position that the conflict resulting from the PBA retainer was so serious that it could not be waived... (Citation omitted)...

B. Trial Proceedings

The first trial began on May 4, 1999. (Citation omitted). It concerned all of the charges against the defendants except for the single charge of conspiracy to obstruct justice, which had been severed by the district court, on consent of the government and without objection by the defendants, and would be the subject of the second trial...

In the early morning hours of Saturday, August 9, 1997, several New York City police officers were summoned from the 70th Precinct to the Club Rendez-Vous in Brooklyn, New York to disperse a crowd gathered around a street fight between two of the club's patrons. (Citation omitted). Appellants Schwarz, Bruder, and Wiese and defendant Volpe were among the officers who arrived at the scene at approximately 4:00 a.m. (Citation omitted). The crowd, which had spilled out into the street to watch the fight, was noisy and boisterous. (Citation omitted). At one point, Louima had a verbal altercation with Volpe and, while this was going on, another individual struck Volpe and knocked him to the ground. (Citation omitted).Volpe thought--mistakenly, as it turned out--that Louima was the person who struck him. (Citation omitted). Louima was then arrested and handcuffed by Schwarz and other officers, including Wiese, who was Schwarz's regular patrol partner, and Officer Eric Turetzky. (Citation omitted). Schwarz and Wiese put Louima in the back of their patrol car to be transported to the 70th Precinct. (Citation omitted). It was undisputed that Schwarz drove the patrol car, Wiese sat in the passenger seat, and Louima sat alone in the back seat. (Citation omitted).

Louima testified that the patrol car made three stops en route to the station house and that during two of these stops he was assaulted by Volpe, Schwarz, Wiese, and Bruder. (Citation omitted). Because Volpe pled guilty and the other defendants were acquitted on these charges, none of these alleged assaults are at issue in this appeal.

When the patrol car arrived at the stationhouse, Louima was taken to the front desk. (Citation omitted). Schwarz searched him and removed his wallet and cash from his pockets. (Citation omitted). Turetzky testified that when Schwarz searched Louima, Louima's pants fell down, and that Schwarz "left the pants down by Mr. Louima's knees." (Citation omitted). Similarly, Louima testified that "the driver"pulled his pants and underwear down to his knees. (Citation omitted). Schwarz and Sergeant Jeffrey Fallon, the desk officer on duty, counted Louima's money, and Schwarz filled out a "pedigree card"c ontaining basic information about Louima. (Citation omitted).

Officer Mark Schofield testified that when he returned to the precinct following the events at the Club Rendez-Vous, he saw Volpe standing at the rear of the station house holding a stick-like object two to three feet in length. (Citation omitted). Volpe later approached Schofield when he was standing near the front desk and borrowed a pair of leather gloves from him. (Citation omitted).

The events that followed the processing of Louima at the front desk were central to the government's case and were hotly contested at both trials; however, evidence and testimony that strongly contradicted the government's version of events was not introduced until the second trial. At the first trial, two government witnesses, Officers Turetzky and Schofield, testified that they saw Schwarz lead Louima away from the front desk and toward the back area of the station house. (Citation omitted). The back area contained a room of holding cells and, after a right-hand turn, a bathroom. Turetzky stated that he saw Schwarz walk Louima to within a few feet of the bathroom. (Citation omitted). Both witnesses stated that Louima's pants were down around his ankles, although Schofield testified that he did not see Louima's bare buttocks. (Citation omitted).

Sergeant Fallon testified that Louima was not led away from the front desk until after the pedigree card was filled out and the cash was counted and returned to Louima. (Citation omitted). Similarly, Turetzky told state investigators that he saw Schwarz "put the [pedigree] card on the top of the [front] desk"before Louima was led away. (Citation omitted). Fallon testified that, after receiving the completed pedigree card, he ordered that Louima be taken to a cell in the back of the station house and that when he gave that order, Schwarz was "right up next to [Louima] "and "just pretty much [had] control of [him]." (Citation omitted).

Schofield stated that a few minutes after he saw Schwarz leading Louima to the back of the precinct, he, Wiese, and other officers, but not Schwarz, waited together by the front desk to go to the hospital, and that a few minutes later, Volpe "walked out from the back area"and "gave back the gloves that he borrowed"from Schofield. (Citation omitted).

Louima consistently testified that two officers led him toward and into the bathroom and that both took part in the assault that took place there. (Citation omitted). However, he could identify only one of them. Louima was able to identify Volpe, both in court and previously from a photo array, as one of the men who led him to the bathroom and attacked him there. (Citation omitted). The most he could offer about the second officer was that he was "the driver." (Citation omitted). However, Louima was unable to identify Charles Schwarz, either from a photo array or in court, as the driver. (Citation omitted). Louima was never shown a photo array containing Wiese's photo. (Citation omitted). Louima testified that the "face . . . and hair style" of the driver and passenger were similar. (Citation omitted).

The government offered evidence to support a finding that Louima's testimony about "the driver" referred to Schwarz. (Citation omitted). In addition to the undisputed fact that Schwarz was the driver of the patrol car and Wiese was the passenger, (Citation omitted). Louima's statement that "the driver" handcuffed him was consistent with Turetzky's testimony that Schwarz was one of the officers that arrested Louima and put handcuffs on him, (Citation omitted), although according to Turetzky, he and Wiese also participated in handcuffing Louima.(Citation omitted). Louima also stated that it was "the driver" who searched him at the front desk. (Citation omitted). Fallon and Turetzky both testified that Schwarz searched Louima. (Citation omitted). And, as we have described, Turetzky and Schofield corroborated Louima's testimony that it was the driver who led him away from the front desk toward the bathroom. (Citation omitted).

Once in the bathroom, according to Louima, the driver participated in the assault with Volpe by hitting him, putting his foot on Louima's mouth when he cried out, and pulling him up by the handcuffs while Volpe brutally forced a broken broomstick into Louima's rectum. (Citation omitted).

Turetzky testified that sometime after seeing Schwarz lead Louima toward the bathroom, he saw Volpe walking from the bathroom carrying a stick and leading Louima toward the arrest room and holding cells...

After he was placed in the holding cell, Louima asked for and received assistance from a police officer whom he could not identify. (Citation omitted). Other evidence indicated that it was Bruder. Later, Louima was taken to Coney Island Hospital, where he was treated for head injuries and underwent surgery for internal injuries to his bladder and rectum. (Citation omitted).

Meanwhile, several officers involved in the events outside the nightclub, including Volpe, Schwarz, Wiese, and Schofield, drove to New York Community Hospital to be treated for minor injuries.

(Citation omitted). Volpe shared a patrol car with Schofield and Police Officer Christopher Barr. (Citation omitted). Wiese and Schwarz were in a separate car. (Citation omitted). Schofield testified that when he, Barr, and Volpe arrived at the hospital, Volpe remained outside for a few moments, and then came in with Wiese and Schwarz. See id. Schofield testified that as he entered the hospital's waiting room, he overheard Volpe say, "I broke a man down." (Citation omitted). As Volpe said this, he was sitting across from Wiese and about six feet away from where Schwarz was standing. (Citation omitted).

On May 25, 1999, shortly before the scheduled close of the government's case-in-chief, the first trial was interrupted so that Volpe could plead guilty, out of the jury's presence, to six counts of the superseding indictment. During the plea allocution, Volpe stated under oath,

> While I was in the bathroom, there was another police officer in the bathroom with me. That police officer saw what was going on, did nothing to stop it. It was understood from the circumstances that the police officer would do nothing to stop me or to report it to anyone. (Citation omitted).

The jury, which would continue to hear evidence on all assault charges against Schwarz, Bruder, and Wiese, was informed by the district court that Volpe had pleaded guilty...

Schwarz's principal defense at the first trial was that Volpe acted alone. In opening and closing arguments, Schwarz's attorney, Stephen Worth, argued that Louima had fabricated the presence of a second officer in the bathroom to support his claim that the bathroom assault was the result of "systemic" police brutality and not the actions of one aberrant cop. (Citation omitted). During closing arguments, Schwarz's attorney also suggested that an additional motive for Louima to fabricate the presence of a second officer in the bathroom was to preserve his "manhood" or "dignity."

On June 2, 1999, the jury found Schwarz guilty of participating in and conspiring with Volpe to participate in the sexual assault of Louima in the bathroom, and acquitted Schwarz, Wiese, and Bruder of the patrol car assaults. (Citation omitted).

C. Post-trial Proceedings

Following his conviction, Schwarz moved for a new trial on the ground, among others, that the jury's verdict was tainted because the jury was exposed to facts that were not in evidence. In support of his motion, Schwarz submitted three nearly identical affidavits from members of the anonymous jury that had convicted him. (Citation omitted). Two of them, executed the same day Schwarz filed his motion, were signed "Juror # 2" and "Juror # 6." The third affidavit was unsigned, but appeared to have been prepared for "Juror No. 3." Each affidavit stated that the juror contacted Schwarz's attorney after the verdict and "discussed certain aspects of the jury's deliberations with him." (Citation omitted). The jurors asserted that despite their "best efforts to avoid publicity," they had learned from one juror during jury deliberations that Volpe had pleaded guilty to assaulting Louima in the bathroom and "had indicated that he had done this assault 'with' another police officer." (Citation omitted). The affidavits also stated that, after the verdict was returned and their service was completed, the jurors learned through press accounts that "Volpe's attorney had told the prosecutors that a second police officer was in the bathroom, but that the second officer was not Mr. Schwarz." (Citation omitted). The jurors asserted that had they known about the attorney's statements before reaching a verdict, they would have had reasonable doubt as to Schwarz's guilt. (Citation omitted).

The district judge refused to hold an evidentiary hearing and denied the motion for a new trial. He reasoned that (1) none of the jurors indicated in their affidavits that the first statement--the assertion that Volpe had admitted the presence of another officer--affected their deliberations; (2) there was ample evidence at trial that another officer had been present, thus it "could hardly have been news to the jury"--notwithstanding Schwarz's "fanciful" assertion that Volpe acted alone; (3) jurors are presumed to follow instructions and the jury had been repeatedly admonished by the district court to ignore extrinsic information and, in particular, had been told that Volpe's guilty plea had no bearing on the trial; and (4) there are strong policy reasons for not engaging in a post-verdict inquiry of the jury, including the presumption that jury deliberations were proper and the impropriety in defense counsel's communicating with the jurors without the district court's permission or supervision. (Citation omitted)...

II. Schwarz's Challenges to the First Trial

A. The Conflict of Interest Issue

On appeal, Schwarz, represented by new counsel, argues that the loyalties owed by his trial attorney, Worth, to the PBA and Worth's pecuniary interest in the PBA retainer created an actual conflict of interest that adversely affected Worth's representation of him and deprived him of his Sixth Amendment right to effective assistance of counsel. Schwarz further contends (1) that Worth's conflict was so serious as to be unwaivable and (2) that, in any event, the waiver he made during the district court's Curcio hearing was ineffective because he was not specifically apprised and had no reason to believe that Worth's interests in the PBA retainer would conflict with his defenses in the particular way that they did.

1. The Conflict of Interest

"A defendant's Sixth Amendment right to effective assistance of counsel includes the right to representation by conflict-free counsel." (Citation omitted). Whether a defendant's representation violates the Sixth Amendment right to effective assistance of counsel is a mixed question of law and fact that is reviewed de novo....

Because Louima had consistently maintained that he was assaulted in the bathroom by at least two officers, Schwarz had an obvious strategic interest in implicating another officer in the bathroom assault from the moment he was charged with that crime. As further discussed below, that interest became stronger during the course of his trial. Such a defense, however, could have hampered the PBA in its defense of the Louima civil suit. As a result, Worth faced an actual conflict between his representation of Schwarz, on the one hand, and both his professional obligation to the PBA and his self interest, on the other....

In short, we conclude that Worth's actual conflict adversely affected his performance in representing Schwarz. (Citation omitted). Accordingly, we find that Schwarz has established a violation of his Sixth Amendment right to effective assistance of counsel due to Worth's conflict unless, as the government maintains, Schwarz effectively waived the conflict at the Curcio hearing. We now turn to that question.

2. The Waiver...

In sum, we hold that Schwarz's counsel suffered an actual conflict, that the conflict adversely affected his counsel's representation, and that the conflict was unwaivable. Accordingly, we are required to vacate Schwarz's conviction in the first trial and remand for a new trial.

B. The Jury Contamination Issue

On appeal, Schwarz argues that the district court erred in denying him a new trial without holding a hearing on whether the exposure to extrinsic information affected the jury's deliberations....

In light of our conclusion that a new trial must be held because of the conflict of interest of Schwarz's attorney, however, there is no need for us to decide the issue.

THE SECOND TRIAL

I. Factual Background

On February 7, 2000, the second trial of Schwarz, Bruder, and Wiese began. (Citation omitted). The only count at issue, Count Twelve of the superseding indictment, alleged that beginning in the days immediately following the assault and continuing until December of 1997, Wiese, Bruder, Schwarz, and others conspired to obstruct the federal grand jury investigation into the sexual assault of Louima. The indictment alleged, in pertinent part, that "it was part of the conspiracy that [Bruder and Wiese] would provide false and misleading information to federal and local law enforcement [officials] in an effort to exculpate [Schwarz] with respect to the sexual assault"of Abner Louima. (Citation omitted). The sole object of the conspiracy as charged was to engage in conduct that would obstruct or impede a federal judicial proceeding, such as a grand jury proceeding, in violation of 18 U.S.C. § 1503. The government's proof at the second trial concerning the conspiracy fell generally into three categories. The first category consisted of substantially the same evidence that had been introduced at the first trial pertaining to the events of the early morning hours of Saturday, August 9, 1997. (Citation omitted)....

The third category of evidence the government presented to the jury consisted of various statements made by the appellants or by lawyers on their behalf to law enforcement officials and others during the state and federal investigations. (Citation omitted)....

On March 6, 2000, the jury found Bruder, Schwarz, and Wiese guilty of conspiracy to obstruct justice. (Citation omitted).

II. The Challenge to the Sufficiency of the Evidence in the Second Trial

Appellants' primary contention with respect to the second trial is that their convictions for conspiracy to obstruct justice in violation of 18 U.S.C. §§ 371 (the conspiracy statute) and 1503 (the obstruction of justice statute) must be reversed for insufficiency of the evidence under the Supreme Court's holding in United States v. Aguilar, 515 U.S. 593, 132 L. Ed. 2d 520, 115 S. Ct. 2357 (1995)...

Appellants carry a heavy burden in challenging the sufficiency of the evidence. They must establish that, viewing the evidence in the light most favorable to the government, no rational trier of fact could have found all of the elements of the crime beyond a reasonable doubt. (Citation omitted). Nevertheless, we agree that, under the teaching of *Aguilar*, the evidence was insufficient to convict the appellants and that their convictions must be reversed....

CONCLUSION

For the foregoing reasons, we hold that appellants' convictions on Count Twelve for conspiracy to obstruct justice under §§ 371 and 1503 must be REVERSED because there was insufficient evidence to support them, and we direct entry of a judgment of acquittal as to all defendants on that count (Docket Nos. 00-1479, 00-1483, and 00-1515). In addition, we hold that Schwarz's conviction on Counts One and Four for civil rights violations and conspiracy must be VACATED AND REMANDED FOR A NEW TRIAL because (1) an unwaivable actual conflict of interest adversely affected his attorney's performance and (2) the jury's exposure to extrinsic information during jury deliberations, when considered with other circumstances in this case, gives rise to a reasonable probability that the outcome of the jury's verdict would have been different (Docket No. 00-1479). The mandate shall issue forthwith.

▶ Notes & Questions

1. On March 16, 2000, Patrick M. Dorismond, age 26, was killed by New York City police who they wrongly thought was a drug dealer. In fact, Patrick was a security guard and the brother of Charles Dorismond, otherwise known as Bigga Haitian, a prominent New York entertainer, and the son of Andre Dorismond, one of Haiti's most celebrated vocalists.[41] Unarmed Dorismond was killed by undercover police. In July of the same year a grand jury refused to bring charges against the officer, Anthony Vasquez. In a press conference following the grand jury decision, Marie Dorismond cried out: "Help me God! Why did you create me black? Look at me. I'm suffering now."[42] What steps should be taken, particularly in New York City, to curtail these unjustifiable killings of Haitian and other people of color?

2. New York City, under Mayor Rudolph W. Giuliani, witnessed another killing of an unarmed black man by the police. This time Malcolm Ferguson was killed two blocks from where Amadou Diallo was killed. There was no evidence that Mr. Ferguson was armed or had drugs on his person. Would police be willing to use deadly force as freely in white neighborhoods? Are these killings a violation of the human rights of the victims?

---

41   David Barstow, Police Shooting Echoes Among Haitians, The New York Times, March 22, 2000.

42   C.J. Chivers, Grand Jury Clears Drug Detective Who Killed Unarmed Man, The New York Times, July 28, 2000.

▶ Notes & Questions

At a ceremony for police recruits, Mayor Giuliani stated that New York police were a "model" for other police forces throughout the country.[43]

3. In New Jersey police violence against Blacks is not limited to the poor. Attorney Felix Morka, in testifying before the New Jersey Legislative Black and Latino Caucus, described how he was choked by state troopers in January, 1997. This and other incidents led the state of New Jersey to admit that some state police officers racially profiled motorists. A report by New Jersey Attorney General's Office indicated that 77.2 percent of vehicles searched belonged to blacks or "Hispanics," compared to 21.4 percent for whites.[44] Given that, at least in New Jersey, racial profiling is not class based, should all black men fear for their safety? If more middle-class black men were subjected to police harassment would this lead to policy changes regarding police conduct toward black men?

4. In February, 2001, New Jersey settled a civil law suit brought by four young men shot on the New Jersey Turnpike in April, 1998. The settlement was for $13 million. Jermaine Grant, one of the victims, drew a parallel between what happened to him and what happened in the civil rights era: "It seems like we're still in the struggle, you know? Like Dr. King, Malcolm X, Rosa Parks, they took the back door so we could take the front door.

---

43   Elizabeth Bumiller, Giuliani Backs Police in Latest Bronx Killing, The New York Times, March 3, 2000.

44   Thomas Martello, New Jersey acknowledges racial profiling by police, The Boston Globe, April 21, 1999.

▶ **Notes & Questions**

But it seems to me now like we're still taking the back door."[45]
It is clear that racial profiling causes black males to perceive the
police as an oppressive force. Does the public have an interest
in creating and maintaining a wholesome image of the police in
the black community?

5. Dennis W. Archer, a black man and the son of the Mayor of
   Detroit, was stopped by the police in Detroit in July, 1999. His
   car was surrounded by six police cars and he was ordered out.
   Mr. Archer had a shotgun placed at his head. He was shoved
   into the back seat of a cruiser and handcuffed. He was released
   after police verified that he was not a suspect for a crime.
   Mayor Archer had experienced similar insults 15 years earlier.[46]
   Middle class status does not insulate you from harassment. The
   unwritten crime of Driving While Black applies to all black
   males.

6. Harold Dusenbury of Willingboro, New Jersey received a
   settlement of his civil law suit against New York City for $2.75
   million. Mr. Dusenbury was beaten by five New York police
   officers on July 25, 1996. An electrician, he was beaten on 8th
   Avenue and called racial slurs, after having his head slammed
   against a metal gate.

---

45   Iver Peterson, David M. Halbfinger, New Jersey Agrees to Settle Suit
from Turnpike Shooting, February 3, 2001.

46   Robyn Meredith, Near Detroit, a Familiar Sting in Being a Black Driver,
The New York Times, July 16, 1999.

▶ **Notes & Questions**

The District Attorney closed its investigation after concluding that there was a mistake.[47]

7. In Riverside, California 19 year old Tyisha Miller was shot and killed by police as she awakened from sleep in her car. She was struck twelve times. Police said when they approached the car, Ms. Miller was sleep with a gun in her lap, and when they broke the driver's window, she sat up whereupon she was shot. While the officers were not charged, community residents spoke out against the killing. Rev. Bernell Butler said: "Their plan was: 'We'll break the window and if she moves, we'll kill her,' It was an idiotic, doomed plan... They were racist. They murdered that girl."[48] Did the police murder her?

8. In the dragging death of James Bird, three white defendants (Shawn Allen Berry, John William King and Lawrence Russell Brewer) were found guilty of murder. The latter two (avowed white supremacists) were sentenced to death, while the former was given a sentence of life imprisonment. Mr. Bird, an African-American, was killed on June 7, 1998 when he was chained to Mr. Berry's pick-up truck and dragged in the town of Jasper, Texas. In Mr. Berry's case the all white jury found Berry guilty of murder, but failed to sentence him to death. In forty years he will be eligible for parole. At the time of his sentencing Berry was 24 years of age. Do you support the death penalty for the two white supremacists? Why were there convictions in the

---

47   Benjamin Weiser, New York to Pay $2.75 million to a Man Who Said the Police Beat Him, The New York Times, April 27, 1999.

48   Tom Gorman, Police not charged in Calif. shooting, The Boston Globe, May 7, 1999.

▶ Notes & Questions

Bird case, but such difficulty in obtaining convictions in the Louima case?

9. Why do some Whites become violent racists? A useful exercise would be to examine at least four of the following stories and gather as much information as possible on the lives of these violent white men. The following articles would serve as useful starting points: *Miss. shooting laid to racism, The Boston Globe*, April 14, 1996; P. Solomom Banda, *Racist pleads guilty in slaying, The Boston Globe*, December 21, 1999; Emery P. Dalesio, *Ex-paratrooper convicted in 2 N.C. racial killings, The Boston Globe*, March 7, 1997; *Ex-G.I. Draws Life Sentence for Racially Motivated Killings, The New York Times,* March 7, 1997; *Another Soldier Convicted in Race-Based Killings, The Boston Globe*, May 3, 1997; James Barron, *New York Officer Held in Beating in Racial Incident at a Bar on L.I., The New York Times*, May 30, 1996; Sam Howe Verhovek, *Leaders of Aryan Nation Found Negligent in Attack, The New York Times*, September 8, 2000; *FBI joins inquiry on slaying of black teen, The Boston Globe*, November 26, 1999; Cindy Rodriguez, *Three men charged in racial assault, Boston Globe*, Nov. 7, 1999.

10. One of the most important statements made by public officials on the *Diallo* case was made by Senator Bill Bradley: "When racial profiling seeps so deeply into somebody's mind, a wallet in the hands of a white man looks like a wallet, but a wallet in the hands of a blackman looks like a gun."

Chapter Nine

LEGAL RESPONSE TO
BLACK LIBERATION EFFORTS

A great deal has been written about the legal response to the Black Panther Party, Angela Davis and militant prison uprisings. The public has never been given the opportunity to compare and contrast the court proceedings of two of the leading black leaders of the twentieth century, Marcus Garvey and W.E.B. Du Bois. Although the two men were quite different in temperament and background, both had profound impacts upon the thinking of African Americans. Garvey was born in St. Anns Bay, Jamaica and came to the United States in 1916, bringing his organization for social uplift: The Universal Negro Improvement Association. (UNIA). Through his teachings of self-help and racial pride, he was able to organize the largest mass movement of blacks ever. In August of 1920, Garvey organized the International Convention of the Negro Peoples of the World in New York City. At the end of the thirty day convention, they issued a statement entitled "A Declaration of Rights of the Negro Peoples of the World," in which he condemned the enslavement and colonization of the black world, especially Africa. The American State Department quickly declared Garvey "an undesirable and indeed a very dangerous alien..." He was soon thereafter indicted by the United States Government.

Du Bois, on the other hand, was born in Great Barrington, Massachusetts to a middle class family. He attended Fisk University, Harvard College, University of Berlin and Harvard University, where he received a Ph.D. degree. He was born in 1868 and died in 1963. During this life time, he was one of the leading thinkers in the country and advocated for the unity of black people the world over. He was also a socialist, which led to the revocation of his passport by the State Department in 1951.

The passport of Paul Robeson had been revoked as well. Robeson, like Du Bois, was a part of a small elite of highly educated, but militant intellectuals who openly opposed the excesses of American capitalism. Robeson, though trained as a lawyer, became an actor and singer of international fame. While in self-imposed exile in Europe, he learned ten African languages and lectured about African culture and folklore. When he returned to the United States in 1939, he joined the growing left movement in Harlem.

In February, 1951 Du Bois was indicted and charged with being an agent for a foreign government. The indictment was brought against the Peace Information Center, Du Bois and several other officers. It is note worthy that these indictments against Garvey and Du Bois were brought by the United States Government against two black leaders whose Pan-African perspectives sought the unification of the black world and the end of European imperialism.

A.

Destruction of Reputation by False Charges: W. E. B Du Bois

W.E.B. Du Bois, a native of Great Barrington, Massachusetts, was a founder of the National Association for the Advancement of Colored People, and an outstanding scholar, educator and black activist. Although he was born to a middle-class background on February 23, 1868, he centered his life work around black people and their precarious position in the world. It was at Fisk University, Nashville, Tennessee where he had his first meaningful contact with black people. He was moved by the pervasive lynching of blacks during his early years. Between 1885-1894, seventeen (1700) hundred blacks were lynched. After graduating from Fisk in 1888, he studied at Harvard College and received a Bachelors

Degree cum laude in 1890. After graduation, he continued for another year at Harvard Graduate School to further his study in History and Political Science. In 1892 he was awarded the Slater Fund Fellowship for graduate study at the University of Berlin.

At the age of twenty-six he returned to the United States to teach at Wilberforce University and to receive his Ph.D. from Harvard University in 1896. For the next sixteen years of his life, Du Bois taught at three universities: Wilberforce for two years, University of Pennsylvania for one year and at Atlanta University for thirteen years.

From July 9, 1905 until his death in 1963, Du Bois became intimately involved with the black liberation struggle. In 1905 he and fifty-nine other individuals, representing seventeen states, gathered in Buffalo, New York to start the "Niagara Movement." In February, 1919, he organized black activists and intellectuals from around the world for the first Pan-African Congress, which was held in Paris, France. He organized several other congresses throughout the world in the years 1921, 1923, 1927 and 1945. These congresses attempted to unite the African race in a common assault against colonialism in Africa and racism in Europe and America. Increasingly, Du Bois began to gravitate toward socialism, which brought him and his organizational affiliations under the scrutiny of the United States Government.

Indictment- On February 10, 1951, Du Bois and four officers of the Peace Information Center were indicted by a Federal Grand Jury for allegedly failing to register under the Foreign Agents Registration Act. Du Bois' organization supported the Stockholm Peace Appeal, which had been signed by 11,350,000 Americans, and called for outlawing the atomic bomb. The government charged that Du Bois and the others had failed to register as an agent for a foreign principal. If convicted, they could face a fine of $10,000.00 and five years imprisonment. During this period of American history a number of Americans were called before Congress to explain their loyalty to the United States. The leader of this movement which intimidated many loyal Americans was

Senator Joseph McCarthy. Du Bois received the attention of the United States Government because of his favorable views on socialism, but also because of his status as an international leader of African people. He had successfully organized and held several Pan-African Congresses around the world, the last one being held in Manchester, England in 1945.

Du Bois was shocked by the indictment. He issued a statement denouncing it, which read in part: "...There is no basis, in fact or fancy, for the charge that the Peace Information Center was in any way a representative of a foreign principal... As chairman of the Peace Information Center during its existence, I can state categorically that we were an entirely American organization whose sole objective was to secure peace and prevent a third world war..." In fact, Du Bois stated that the organization had disbanded in October, 1950.

The defendants challenged the constitutionality of the Foreign Agents Registration Act in the United States District Court on April 27, 1951. On May 9, 1951 Judge Alexander Holtzoff upheld the Act and refused to dismiss the indictments. However, on November 20, 1951, after the trial had begun, the indictments were dismissed by Judge Matthew F. McGuire. He ruled that the government had failed to prove a link to a foreign principal.

Even though he was acquitted, Du Bois lost his leadership role among black people. He wrote: "...I lost my leadership of my race. It was a dilemma for the mass of Negroes; either they joined the current beliefs and actions of most whites or they could not make a living or hope for preferment. Preferment was possible. The color line was beginning to break. Negroes were getting recognition as never before. Was not the sacrifice of one man, small payment for this? Even those who disagreed with this judgment at least kept quiet. The colored children ceased to hear my name."[1]

---

1   W.E.B. Du Bois, The Autobiography of W. E. B. Du Bois (New York: International Press).

UNITED STATES v. PEACE INFORMATION CENTER
United States District Court
District of Columbia
97 F.Supp. 255 (1951)

HOLTZOFF, District Judge.

The defendant Peace Information Center has been indicted on a charge of violating the Foreign Agents Registration Act, (Footnote omitted) in failing to register as an agent of a foreign principal. The individual defendants are charged in their capacity as officers and directors of Peace Information Center with failure to cause the latter to register. The defendants move to dismiss the indictment on the ground that the statute is unconstitutional, and on the further ground that the indictment is defective.

The Foreign Agents Registration Act requires every agent of a foreign principal to file a registration statement with the Attorney General setting forth certain information specified in the statute. In brief, a foreign principal is defined as a government of a foreign country, a foreign political party, or an individual affiliated or associated with either of them; a person outside of the United States; an organization having its principal place of business in a foreign country; or a domestic concern subsidized by any one of the former. The Act further defines the term "agent of a foreign principal". In effect, the definition includes any person who acts as a publicity agent or public-relations counsel for a foreign principal; any person who collects information, or reports information to a foreign principal; and any person who engages in other similar activities that are described in the Act in considerable detail. Diplomatic and consular representatives, persons engaged in trade or commerce and press associations are expressly exempted. The Act provides that no person shall act as an agent of a foreign principal unless he has filed a registration statement with the Attorney General. The Act further requires every person who is an agent of a foreign principal to file a registration statement with the Attorney General. The contents of the statement are prescribed. A willful violation of the Act is made a criminal offense.

The intent and purpose of the Congress in enacting this measure appear from the following statement found in the report of the Committee on the Judiciary of the House of Representatives, recommending passage of the legislation (H.Rept.No.1381, 75th Cong. 1st Sess., July 28, 1937):

"Incontrovertible evidence has been submitted to prove that there are many persons in the United States representing foreign governments or foreign political groups, who are supplied by such foreign agencies with funds and other materials to foster un-American activities, and to influence the external and internal policies of this country, thereby violating both the letter and the spirit of international law, as well as the democratic basis of our own American institutions of government.

"Evidence before the Special Committee on Un-American Activities disclosed that many of the payments for this propaganda service were made in cash by the consul of a foreign nation, clearly giving an unmistakable inference that the work done was of such a nature as not to stand careful scrutiny.

"As a result of such evidence, this bill was introduced, the purpose of which is to require all persons who are in the United States for political propaganda purposes-propaganda aimed toward establishing in the United States a foreign system of government, or group action of a nature foreign to our institutions of government, or for any other purpose of a political propaganda nature—to register* * * and to supply information about their political propaganda activities, their employers, and the terms of their contracts.

"This required registration will publicize the nature of subversive or other similar activities of such foreign propagandists, so that the American people may know those who are engaged in this country by foreign agencies to spread doctrines alien to our democratic form of government, or propaganda for the purpose of influencing American public opinion on a political question."

In *Viereck v. United States*, 318 U.S. 236, 241, 63 S.Ct. 561, 563, 87 L.Ed. 734, which involved a conviction under this statute, Chief Justice Stone gave the following explanation of the objectives of the Act: "The Act of 1938 requiring registration of agents for foreign principals was a new type of legislation adopted in the critical period before the outbreak of the war. The general purpose of the legislation was to identify agents of foreign principals who might engage in subversive acts or in spreading foreign propaganda, and to require them to make public record of the nature of their employment. But the means adopted to accomplish that end are defined by the statute itself, which, as will presently appear more in detail, followed the recommendations of a House Committee which had investigated foreign propaganda. These means included the requirement of registration of agents for foreign principals-with which it appears that petitioner complied-and the requirement that the registrant gave certain information concerning his activities as such agent." The constitutionality of the statute was evidently assumed in that case, for it was not discussed...

The second foundation for the statute here under consideration is found in the powers conferred on the Congress by the Constitution to legislate concerning national defense. As indicated in *United States v. Curtiss-Wright Export Corp.*, 299 U.S. 304, 315, 57 S.Ct. 216, 81 L.Ed. 255, the powers of the Federal government in respect to internal affairs are those that are specifically enumerated in the Constitution as well as such implied powers as are necessary and proper to carry into effect the enumerated powers. The enumerated powers are to be broadly construed. (Footnote omitted). Support for legislation need not necessarily be found in a single power, but may be derived from a composite of several powers.

The government has the power of self preservation. It must have the capacity to protect itself from attempts to destroy it. It must assure its own survival. Americans are a freedom-loving people. They want their liberty to endure permanently. They have a right to defend it against all efforts, be they open or insidious, to subvert or destroy it...

This brings us to a consideration of the second phase of the issue of constitutionality, namely, whether the statute transcends any limitations on the powers of the Congress. The defendants advance three contentions in respect to this matter: first that the statute is repugnant to the guarantee of freedom of speech contained in the First Amendment; second, that the statute violates the privilege against self incrimination found in the Fifth Amendment; and third, that the statute is violative of the due process clause of the Fifth Amendment, in that it is too indefinite and does not formulate an ascertainable standard of guilt. The greatest emphasis is laid by the defendants on the first of these objections, namely, the alleged interference with the right of freedom of speech guaranteed by the First Amendment.

Freedom of speech is one of the basic rights safeguarded by the Constitution. It is perhaps one of the greatest of these privileges, second only to the right to a fair trial. It is an elementary principle, however, that freedom of speech is not absolute and unlimited, but is bounded by the rights of others than the speaker. For example, no one may disseminate obscene matter in the name of freedom of speech. No one is permitted to make a statement that may incite a riot or create a panic. No one may urge or advise the commission of a crime. No one may advocate the overthrow of the government by force or violence. No one may justify fraudulent or deceptive advertising by recourse to the right of freedom of speech. Many a crime is committed purely by word of mouth, such as obtaining money by false pretenses, extortion, broadcasting treasonable utterances, and many others. This list may be multiplied *ad infinitum*. The right of freedom of speech is no defense to a prosecution for any of these offenses.

The statute under consideration neither limits nor interferes with freedom of speech. It does not regulate expression of ideas. Nor does it preclude the making of any utterances. It merely requires persons carrying on certain activities to identify themselves by filing a registration statement...

Motion to dismiss the indictment is denied.

▶ Notes & Questions

1. By the time of his indictment, Du Bois had publicly announced his conversion to socialism. Given that the nation was suffering from the "red scare," which caused many innocent Americans to be subjected to governmental scrutiny, was Du Bois indicted primarily because of his political beliefs or because of his color?

2. Why didn't the Court dismiss the indictments? The fact that the indictments survived legal challenge meant that Du Bois had to go to trial. He was ultimately cleared of the charges after considerable damage to his reputation, particularly in the United States.

3. In 2007 the Internal Revenue Service raided the offices of Rev. Al Sharpton and seized certain documents related to his business activities. These moves by the federal government came after Rev. Sharpton led a large march protesting the failure of the FBI to investigate the Jenna Six cases in Louisiana. The Jenna Six cases grew out of the arrest and prosecution of black high school students for alleged assaults upon a white student. The government failed to investigate the racist statements and actions by white students directed at black students, including the hanging of a noose from a tree on campus. Is the investigation of Rev. Sharpton another example of governmental attempts to intimidate civil rights activities?

B.

Destruction of Reputation and Livelihood Through Political Intimidation: Leonard Jeffries

Professor Jeffries is one of a core of black academics who have challenged the Eurocentric view of history. As Chairperson of the Black Studies Department at City University of New York, he directed the program into an area of scholarship that was not readily accepted by the traditional departments. In addition, Professor Jeffries became a public speaker who was widely sought after on the national lecture circuit. As a result of certain statements he made concerning Jews and their involvement in the African slave trade, he became the subject of protracted criticism and assault. Are black intellectuals fair targets for governmental officials who may disagree with the content of their speech? Should the powers of government be used to silence such controversial speech? Should a radical intellectual perspective be tolerated even though it may offend some segments of the public?

In 1994 this same court rendered a decision in favor of Professor Jeffries, which was appealed to the United States Supreme Court. On November 14, 1994 the Court vacated the decision of the United States Court of Appeals for the Second Circuit and remanded it for further consideration in light of *Waters v. Churchill,* 511 U.S. 661 (1994). The following decision resulted upon remand.

JEFFRIES v. HARLESTON
United States Court of Appeals for the Second Circuit
21 F.3d 1238 (1995)

OPINION: McLAUGHLIN, Circuit Judge:

In *Jeffries v. Harleston,* 21 F.3d 1238 (2d Cir. 1994), we affirmed the district court's judgment that 15 university officials violated the First Amendment rights of a professor, Leonard Jeffries, by reducing his term as a department chairman because of a controversial speech (the "Albany speech") he had given off campus. Our decision rested on what we understood to be the applicable rule that the government cannot take action against an employee for speaking on public issues, unless it first shows that the speech actually "impaired the efficiency of government operations." (Citation omitted). We also vacated the part of the judgment that found six of the defendants liable for punitive damages, as the jury's special verdict responses were "hopelessly irreconcilable" on whether these defendants harbored the necessary evil motives. (Citation omitted).

A month after our decision in *Jeffries*, the United States Supreme Court decided *Waters v. Churchill*, 511 U.S. 661, 114 S. Ct. 1878 (1994) (plurality opinion). A four-justice plurality in *Waters* held that the government could fire an employee for disruptive speech based on its reasonable belief of what the employee said, regardless of what was actually said. (Citation omitted). In addition, when weighing the value of the employee's speech against the interference with government operations, the *Waters* plurality also indicated that a government employer need only show that the speech is likely to be disruptive before the speaker may be punished. (Citation omitted).

The Jeffries defendants, relying on *Waters*, petitioned the Supreme Court for a writ of certiorari. The Supreme Court granted certiorari, and, without comment, vacated *Jeffries* and remanded to us for reconsideration in light of *Waters*. (Citation omitted).

On remand from the Supreme Court, we reverse the district court's judgment because defendants made a substantial showing at trial that their decision to limit Jeffries' term was based upon a reasonable prediction that the Albany speech would disrupt university operations.

BACKGROUND

We summarize the facts briefly; a more detailed account appears in our initial opinion. (Citation omitted).

Leonard Jeffries was the chairman of the Black Studies department at City College of New York ("City College"), which is part of the City University of New York ("CUNY") system.

In delivering the Albany speech, which addressed the bias of New York State's public school curriculum and the history of black oppression, Jeffries made several derogatory statements, particularly about Jews. After the speech, City College President Bernard Harleston and CUNY Chancellor Ann Reynolds arranged for the CUNY Board of Trustees to vote as to whether to limit Jeffries' term as department chair to one year, even though such terms normally last three years. A majority of the 14 members of the CUNY Board of Trustees voted to limit Jeffries' term. The votes were cast as follows: Nine of the Trustees voted to limit Jeffries' term to a year; four voted to remove him immediately; one abstained because she had made critical comments about Jeffries in the past. Harleston and Reynolds did not vote because they were not Trustees.

Jeffries sued Harleston, Reynolds, and all 14 of the individual CUNY trustees under 42 U.S.C. ' 1983 in the United States District Court for the Southern District of New York (Kenneth Conboy, Judge), alleging that they removed him in violation of the First Amendment. (One of the 16 original defendants, Trustee Blanche Bernstein, died during the trial, and Jeffries discontinued his claims against her.) Jeffries sought reinstatement and punitive damages.

The jury was given several sets of interrogatories to answer. In response to the first wave, the jury found that the defendants demoted Jeffries because of the Albany speech. The jury's answers also indicated that the Albany speech did not disrupt "the effective and efficient operation of the Black Studies Department, the College, or the University," but that the defendants "were motivated in their actions by a reasonable expectation" that the speech would cause such a disruption. The judge concluded from these responses that all 15 remaining defendants had violated Jeffries' First Amendment rights because the speech was substantially on matters of public concern, and did not cause actual harm to CUNY.

The judge then submitted another wave of questions to the jury to discern the individual liability of each of the 15 defendants. In response, the jury found that only six defendants -- Harleston, Reynolds, and Trustees Edith Everett, Herman Badillo, Sylvia

Bloom, and Harold Jacobs (together, the "Harleston defendants") -- took action against Jeffries because of the Albany speech, and would not have done so had Jeffries not given the speech. Of the four Trustees who are Harleston defendants, three had voted to remove Jeffries from his post immediately, and one had abstained because of the negative statements she had made about Jeffries in the past. (The fourth vote to remove Jeffries immediately came from Trustee Bernstein, who died during the trial, and is not part of this appeal.) The jury found that the other nine defendants, all of whom had voted to limit Jeffries' term to one year, did not act with the same retaliatory animus.

On the third and final wave of interrogatories, the jury found that all six of the Harleston defendants had "acted with malicious intent to violate the plaintiff's rights under the First Amendment... or with malicious intent to unlawfully injure him, or... with a callous or reckless disregard of the plaintiff's First Amendment rights." Based on these findings, the jury awarded punitive damages against the Harleston defendants.

After finding that the defendants were not shielded from liability by qualified immunity, the district judge entered judgment consistent with the jury responses (although he reduced the punitive damage amounts). In addition, the judge ordered the defendants to reinstate Jeffries as chairman of the department for two years. The defendants appealed.

We affirmed the reinstatement order, agreeing with the district court that the defendants had violated Jeffries' right to free speech, and that the Harleston defendants were not shielded by qualified immunity. (Citation omitted)...

Upon the defendants' petition, the Supreme Court granted certiorari, vacated our judgment, and remanded with instructions to reconsider our opinion in light of Waters.

DISCUSSION

One of the principles driving our earlier Jeffries decision was that the First Amendment protects a government employee who speaks out on issues of public interest from censure by his employer unless the speech actually disrupted the employer's operations. (Citation omitted). We expressly held that a mere reasonable belief that the speech would interfere with the employer's operations is not enough to discipline an employee, unless the employee holds a high-level, policymaking position. (Citation omitted).

Applying that standard, we studied the Albany speech, and found that it squarely involved issues of public concern -namely, the New York state public school curriculum, and black oppression throughout history. (Citation omitted). Then, after examining CUNY's bylaws, and the testimony of CUNY officials, we agreed with the district court that the position of Black Studies Chairman was a ministerial position at CUNY, and carried no policymaking authority. (Citation omitted). Thus, we held that the defendants bore the burden at trial to show that the speech actually interfered with CUNY operations. (Citation omitted).

Given the jury's finding that the defendants had failed to make this showing, we held that the defendants had violated Jeffries' free speech rights. (Citation omitted)...

I.

In *Waters*, a four-justice plurality held that the government could fire an employee for disruptive speech based on the government's reasonable belief of what the employee said, regardless of what was actually said. (Citation omitted). Here, however, there is no dispute as to what Jeffries actually said in the Albany speech. Accordingly, we need pursue only that part of *Waters* dealing with the disruptiveness of the speech.

The *Waters* plurality reiterated the test of *Connick v. Myers*, 461 U.S. 138, 75 L. Ed. 2d 708, 103 S. Ct. 1684 (1983), to determine when the First Amendment protects speech by a government employee:

"To be protected, the speech must be on a matter of public concern, and the employee's interest in expressing herself on this matter must not be outweighed by any injury the speech could cause to the 'interest of the State, as an employer, in promoting the efficiency of the public services it performs through its employees.'"

114 S. Ct. at 1884 (quoting *Connick*, 461 U.S. at 142 (quoting *Pickering v. Board of Ed. of Township High School Dist.,* 391 U.S. 563, 568, 20 L. Ed. 2d 811, 88 S. Ct. 1731 (1968))).

The plurality then explained that, in applying this test, the extent of the injury caused by the employee's speech need not be actual; rather, the government's burden is just to show that the speech threatened to interfere with government operations. (Citation omitted)...

[A] government employee, like any citizen, may have a strong, legitimate interest in speaking out on public matters. In many such situations the government may have to make a substantial showing that the speech is, in fact, likely to be disruptive before it may be punished. (Citation omitted).

We read the *Waters* plurality opinion to hold that the closer the employee's speech reflects on matters of public concern, the greater must be the employer's showing that the speech is likely to be disruptive before it may be punished. (Citation omitted). There is, thus, a proportion between the nature of the speech and the nature of the sanction that may ensue. Nevertheless, even when the speech is squarely on public issues, -- and thus earns the greatest constitutional protection -- *Waters* indicates that the government's burden is to make a substantial showing of likely interference and not an actual disruption. (Citation omitted).

II.

Whittled to its core, Waters permits a government employer to fire an employee for speaking on a matter of public concern if:
(1) the employer's prediction of disruption is reasonable; (2) the potential disruptiveness is enough to outweigh the value of the speech;

and (3) the employer took action against the employee based on this disruption and not in retaliation for the speech. (Citation omitted). By stressing that actual disruption is not required, *Waters* pulls a crucial support column out from under our earlier *Jeffries* opinion. We are now constrained to hold under Waters that the defendants did not violate Jeffries' free speech rights if: (1) it was reasonable for them to believe that the Albany speech would disrupt CUNY operations; (2) the potential interference with CUNY operations outweighed the First Amendment value of the Albany speech; and (3) they demoted Jeffries because they feared the ramifications for CUNY, or, at least, for reasons wholly unrelated to the Albany speech.

In the district court, the jury's central finding was that all 15 defendants were "motivated" to demote Jeffries by a "reasonable expectation" that the Albany speech would harm CUNY. This jury finding establishes that because the defendants were motivated by a reasonable prediction of disruption, they did not demote him for an improper retaliatory motive. Moreover, we hold that, as a matter of law, this potential disruptiveness was enough to outweigh whatever First Amendment value the Albany speech might have had. Under *Waters*, then, the jury's finding, if it stood alone, would suffice to show that none of the defendants violated Jeffries' free speech rights...

Finally, we note that an amicus curiae argues that we should not apply *Waters* at all because Jeffries, as a faculty member in a public university, deserves greater protection from state interference with his speech than did the nurse in Waters who complained about the obstetrics division of the hospital. We recognize that academic freedom is an important First Amendment concern. (Citation omitted). Jeffries' academic freedom, however, has not been infringed here. As we held in the earlier *Jeffries*, and as Jeffries himself has argued, the position of department chair at CUNY is ministerial, and provides no greater public contact than an ordinary professorship. (Citation omitted). Jeffries is still a tenured professor at CUNY, and the defendants have not sought to silence him, or otherwise limit his access to the "marketplace of ideas" in the classroom. (Citation omitted).

CONCLUSION

Because the only defendants who voted in favor of limiting Jeffries' term did so constitutionally, and because the Harleston defendants did not contribute to the decision to limit Jeffries' term, we conclude that Jeffries has not suffered a deprivation of his constitutional rights.

We reverse the judgment of the district court, and remand with instructions to enter judgment for the defendants.

REVERSED and REMANDED with instructions to enter judgment for the defendants.

► **Notes & Questions**

1. Professor Jeffries, according to the first decision of the Court, possessed a First Amendment right to speak on issues of public concern. What was the competing interest that the government possessed with respect to the running of its educational institutions?

2. The above decision was ultimately appealed back to the United States Supreme Court which refused to hear it on October 2, 1995.

C.

Destruction of Popular Leadership in the Black Community

1. <u>**The Case of Marcus Mosiah Garvey**</u>

When Marcus Garvey arrived in the United States on March 23, 1916, he had already established his Universal Negro Improvement Association in his native Jamaica. Born on August 17, 1887, he had already set as a goal of his new organization "...The establishment of a central nation for black people..."[2] Shortly after the incorporation of his organization on July 2, 1918, he began to organize the poor and dispossessed blacks of New York City and throughout the United States. By 1919, the Universal Negro Improvement Association had an estimated thirty branches and two million members.[3] Garvey launched a newspaper, *The Negro World* and a steamship company, Black Star Line. In 1920, he successfully organized and held the First International Convention of the Negro Peoples of the World. At this meeting the organization issued the Declaration of Rights of the Negro Peoples of the World and elected Garvey president of the organization.

Although Garvey appealed to the black masses, who were experiencing difficult economic times and lynchings, he was not generally accepted by the "Negro Intelligentsia." Because of his stand on communism, he was not supported by the white left and the white capitalist class saw him as a potential threat to their imperialist holdings in Africa.

On January 12, 1922, Garvey was arrested and charged with using the United States mails to defraud investors in the Black Star Line. In 1923, he was convicted, sentenced to five years, fined $1,000.00 and ordered to pay court costs for the trial. In 1925, after his appeal failed, he entered federal prison in Atlanta. By the time he entered prison, his organization had approximately 996 branches

---

2   Tony Martin, Race First (Dover: The Majority Press, 1976), p. 6.

3   Martin, p. 11.

in the United States and around the world.[4] In December, 1927, his sentence was commuted and he was deported to Jamaica. After continuing to work in his organization in Jamaica and England, he died in June, 1940.

The legal process had been used successfully to curb the impetus of his organization in the United States. The prosecution was deliberate and politically inspired. Before the legal proceedings were convened, Garvey's movement was closely monitored by the government, in particular by J. Edgar Hoover of the Bureau of Investigations. Informants were also planted within Garvey's movement.

At trial, Garvey dismissed his attorney, Cornelius W. McDougald, and defended himself. The key evidence of the government was an empty envelope addressed to Benny Dancy. It was the government's contention that Garvey had mailed solicitation materials to Dancy. Dancy testified that he could not remember the contents of the envelope, and whether it contained Black Star Line materials. Furthermore, Garvey was convicted on the third count of the second indictment. However, no evidence was presented on that count. The other three co-defendants were found not-guilty.

The Judge imposed the most severe penalty allowable under the law for the conviction. On August 4, 1924, the government brought an income tax fraud indictment against Garvey. Garvey, however, appealed the mail fraud conviction and based his argument primarily upon the insufficiency of the evidence regarding the Dancy letter. After he was deported, the income tax case was dismissed.

GARVEY v. UNITED STATES
Circuit Court of Appeals. Second Circuit.
4 F2 974 (1926)

Before ROGERS, HOUGH, and LEARNED HAND, Circuit Judges.

---

4   Martin, p. 15.

HOUGH, Circuit Judge (after stating the facts as above), Justice to the community and rules of law combine to prevent courts or juries from looking upon the testimony in this case in the spirit sought to be aroused by the brief for plaintiff in error.

It may be true that Garvey fancied himself a Moses, if not a Messiah; that he deemed himself a man with a message to deliver, and believed that he needed ships for the deliverance of his people; but with this assumed, it remains true that if his gospel consisted in part of exhortations to buy worthless stock, accompanied by deceivingly false statements as to the worth thereof, he was guilty of a scheme or artifice to defraud, if the jury found the necessary intent about his stock scheme, no matter how uplifting, philanthropic, or altruistic his larger outlook may have been. And if such scheme to defraud was accompanied by the use of the mails defined by the statute, he was guilty of an offense under Criminal Code, s. 215.

We need not delay to examine in detail the fraud scheme exhibited by practically uncontradicted evidence. Stripped of its appeal to the ambitions, emotions, or race consciousness of men of color, it was a simple and familiar device of which the object (as of so many others) was to ascertain how "it could best unload upon the public its capital stock at the largest possible price."*Horn v. United States*, 182 F. 721, at 731, 105 C. C. A. 163, 173. At this bar there is no attempt to justify the selling scheme practiced and proven; it was wholly without morality or legality.

This writ rests solely on an asserted failure to prove the "indictment letter" in the single count on which Garvey was convicted.

We pointed out in *Hart v. United States*, 240 F. 911, at 917, 153 C. C. A. 597, that Congress, by section 215, has made any fraudulent scheme a crime, if for the purpose of executing the same any letter, etc., be sent or received by post. The corollary is that in this case it was necessary for the prosecution to prove not only that there was a scheme to defraud, but to show that there was a communication sent through the mail to Dancy within the jurisdiction of the court for the purpose of executing or attempting to execute the same.

As was said in *Lefkowitz v. United States* (C. C. A.) 273 F. 664, certiorari denied 257 U. S. 637, 42 S. Ct. 49, 66 L. Ed. 409, in such a prosecution as this it is competent to show every part of the method of conducting the scheme that is calculated to shed light on the intent and purpose of its deviser. Some schemes have a relation to the use of the mails so plain that any court or juryman can take notice thereof; and so the general use of the mails may be established by showing that the success of the scheme depended on a wholesale utilization of the post. This is fully set forth in *Kellogg v. United States*, 126 F. 323, 61 C. C. A. 229. And in this case there was proven a widespread and wholesale use of the mails for the purpose of soliciting subscriptions to the worthless stock offered by Garvey to the public. The connection between his scheme and the use of postal facilities was manifest, and this circumstance was proper for the consideration of the jury.

Starting with this, there was abundant proof of the style of "literature" used in falsely puffing the Black Star Line stock. It was directly proven that Dancy received through the mail an envelope addressed as in the indictment averred, that such envelope was like many similarly proven to have been mailed by Garvey's mailing agent, and bearing upon them the legend "Black Star Line, New York City."

It was also directly proven that Dancy received many communications not only from the Black Star Line but from other organizations with which Garvey was concerned, and that some of the letters thus received advised him to "invest more money in the Black Star Line"; and he did purchase some 50 shares. But there was no direct evidence as to what particular circular, letter, or the like came in the envelope identified by Dancy as having been sent to and received by him through the post, and mentioned in the indictment. It was further directly proven that Dancy had received through the post communications distinctly calculated to aid in executing the scheme to defraud; so that the point raised by this writ is that this evidence is insufficient to justify a conviction upon the single count before us, because there was no direct proof of what the envelope had contained.

To this we cannot agree; the circumstantial evidence is sufficient. The rule is elementary that any fact which becomes material in a criminal prosecution may as a rule be established by circumstantial as well as by direct evidence. 16 C. J. 762. So also is the rule fundamental that in arriving at their verdict a jury is not confined to considering the palpable facts in evidence, but it may draw reasonable inferences and make reasonable deductions therefrom. 16 C. J. 760. Consequently a conviction may well be had upon circumstantial evidence, although to warrant such conviction the proven facts must clearly and satisfactorily exclude every other reasonable hypothesis save that of guilt. *United States v. Greene* (D. C.) 146 F. 803, affirmed 154 F. 401, certiorari denied 207 U.S. 596, 28 S.Ct. 261, 52 L.Ed. 357.

The only matter here not proven by direct evidence is that some particular circular or letter was enclosed in the envelope produced by Dancy—a man evidently both emotional and ignorant, whose caliber may be judged by the following excerpts from a cross-examination conducted by Garvey pro se:

"Q. You don't know whether they (letters or circulars) reached you through the mail or not; you just saw things about Black Star Line."

"A. I saw things about it."

"Q. Yes."

"A. I didn't saw things, I saw it in the letters."

"Q. Can you remember what you saw in the letter positively?"

"A. I just told you I couldn't remember all; do you understand its?..."

"Q. The letters that the district attorney showed you, they weren't the letters?"

"A. They weren't the letters?"

"Q. Yes."

"A. Yes, they were the letters."

"Q. And you don't remember what was in them?"

"A. I can't remember all of them; I got so many letters I couldn't remember all the letters."

It is a reasonable inference that men regularly sending out circulars in envelopes do not send out empty envelopes; also, that one who received an empty envelope would remember the emptiness; and further and finally, that when Dancy identified the envelope and testified to letters and circulars so numerous that he could not remember all of them, the inference was justifiable that some or one of those documents came in the envelope. Which one was of no importance? The nature of the matter sent by mail is immaterial; it is the purpose inspiring the sending that brings the scheme deviser under national law, not the language of his communication.

Thus the circumstantial evidence justified the jury in finding that the envelope did not come empty to Dancy. We note that it is the language of the count that requires the envelope to have contained a letter or the like; so far as the statute goes, it would be quite possible so to use an empty envelope or a postal card blank except for address, as to satisfy the statute.

Judgment affirmed.

▶ Notes & Questions

1. Given that Garvey's conviction was based upon the sole letter to Dancy, should this conviction have been overturned? Was the evidence of Garvey mailing the letter sufficient to warrant his conviction under a standard of "beyond a reasonable doubt"?

2. Upon conviction, Garvey was sentenced to five years in federal prison. Was this sentence severe given the weight of the evidence?

3. Colonel Muammar el-Khadafy of Libya promised the Nation of Islam a gift of $1 billion dollars. The Clinton Administration blocked the gift on the grounds that Libya was a terrorist nation. The government also barred Minister Farrakhan from receiving a $250,000.00 humanitarian award from Libya. Minister Louis Farrakhan stated that the money would be used to benefit American people and should be allowed into the country. He further stated that the money would be used for voter registration drives and for religious and humanitarian purposes. Because the Nation of Islam had to get permission to receive the money from the Office of Foreign Assets Control of the Treasury Department, Representative King asked the State Department to revoke the passport of Minister Farrakhan so he could not make another trip to Libya. Shouldn't the Nation of Islam be allowed to accept the money from Libya given the new United States welfare bill that effectively left many poor people without financial support? If the funds would be used to bring about economic development in the inner cities, wouldn't this be in the public interest?

2. The Case of Malcolm X

After Malcolm X broke with the Honorable Elijah Muhammad on March 8, 1964, he had less than a year to live. Within this period Malcolm increasingly became the target of FBI surveillance and Black Muslim terror. These two forces, the FBI and the Black Muslims, contributed to the death of Malcolm. It is quite clear that neither of the groups wanted to see Malcolm maintain his leadership of the Black liberation movement.

Through FBI wiretaps of the home of Elijah Muhammad, we learn that the leader of the Nation of Islam wanted Malcolm X killed. In FBI memoranda, one can read Elijah stating that Malcolm's eyes should be closed, his head cut off and that he deserved to die.[5] It would appear that the Muslims successfully carried out their motives because the three men arrested and convicted for Malcolm's death were all muslims: Talmadge Hayer, Norman 3X Butler and Thomas 15X Johnson.

Malcolm had attracted the attention of the FBI before his break with Elijah Muhammad on March 8, 1964. The Bureau had become concerned about the widening appeal of the Muslim sect. By the end of December, 1956, J. Edgar Hoover requested permission to wire tap offices and meeting places of the Nation of Islam around the country.[6] One of the primary goals of the Bureau was to discredit the Nation of Islam around the world. The Bureau was particularly alarmed by the favorable accolades that President Kwame Nkrumah of Ghana directed toward both Rev. Martin Luther King, Jr. and Malcolm X.

---

5   Evanzz, Karl, The Judas Factor "The Plot to Kill Malcolm X" (New York, Thunder's Mouth Press, 1992), p. xviii.

6   Evanzz. pp. 66-67.

After Malcolm X met with Kwame Nkrumah for a second time on August 17, 1958, the Central Intelligence Agency (CIA) asked the FBI for its file on the Nation of Islam.[7] The FBI provided a list of members in all chapters of the United States, including those in prison. They were able to get these internal records from informants who had been planted in high ranking positions within the organization. Ultimately the FBI hoped to "neutralize" Rev. King, Malcolm x and Elijah Muhammad. Agent William Sullivan explained:

> "...When this is done, and it can and will be done, obviously much confusion will reign, particularly among the Negro people... The Negroes will be left without a national leader of sufficiently compelling personality to steer them in the proper direction."[8]

In February of 1965, the Bureau had even more reasons to get rid of Malcolm. Despite the Nation of Islam applying more pressure upon Malcolm and his family to leave their home in Queens, Malcolm continued to seek audiences beyond the shores of the United States. As he traveled to more developing, non-white countries and consulted with progressive leaders around the world, he developed an internationalist perspective that de-emphasized race. On February 8, he spoke before the First Congress of the Council of African Organizations in London. He also spoke with London branch members of the Organization of Afro-American Unity (OAAU). He had been invited to the February 27th Afro-Asian Conference in Algiers along with Che Guevara and other revolutionaries from organizations such as Southwest African

---

7 Evanzz, p. 75. The FBI and the CIA was particularly concerned about the alliance between Malcolm X and Kwame Nkrumah because they represented two aspects of the developing Black liberation movement. Nkrumah as the President of newly independent Ghana (1957) was a leader of the African independence movement. He also embraced a non western view of development and espoused African unity as key to development of the entire continent.

8 Evanzz, p. 172.

People's Organization (SWAPO), and the Palestine Liberation Organization (PLO).[9]

At this point in Malcolm's career he was a man of international stature. Between February 6-13, 1965 he was in Britain and France. He gave speeches and interviews in London. But on February 9, he was refused entrance into France. He believed that the decision to exclude him was made at the request of the American government.[10] The FBI was not happy about the anti-imperialist content of Malcolm's speeches. For example, on February 11, 1965 at the London School of Economics he spoke of "The Oppressed Masses of the World Cry Out for Action Against the Common Oppressor." In this speech Malcolm rejected the notion that black people are a minority, rather he argued that blacks are a part of a black oppressed majority who struggled against a common oppressor.

He continued his focus upon the international dimension of oppression when he returned to the United States. At a speech in Rochester, New York on February 16, 1965, he stressed the need to downplay "civil rights." Human rights violations, he argued, could be brought before the world and the United Nations. Malcolm had begun to de-emphasize the racial nature of the black struggle and to accept the need for coalitions between whites and blacks within the United States. He stated a few days before he was assassinated: "There is a conspiracy to kill me because the racists know that I now believe the only way to help the black man in this country is unity among black people and white people."[11] Consequently Malcolm had come to the point in his life where he realized that world unity against imperialism and racism, both inside and outside the United States, was necessary in order to fundamentally change political and economic power.

On February 21, 1965, at about 2:30 p.m., Malcolm was shot while he was beginning a speech at the Audubon Ballroom in

---

9   Evanzz, pp. 288-289.

10   Carter, Steve, Editor, Malcolm X: The Final Speeches (New York, Pathfinder, 1992), p. 35.

11   Clark, p. 181.

Harlem, New York. The first person to Malcolm's side as he lay on the floor, bleeding from his several wounds to the chest, was Gene X Roberts, an undercover officer, a member of New York Police Department's Bureau of Special Services (BOSS). These undercover officers were organized and trained by the Federal Bureau of Investigation (FBI).

3. <u>The Case of the Black Panther Party: Cointelpro</u>

At the dawn of the twentieth century blacks increasingly moved from the rural sectors of America to the urban metropolis. It was here that they began to take control of their destinies. In the South they had to fight, usually unsuccessfully against both private and state sanctioned violence. The beginnings of the twentieth century, however, ushered in an era of political activism, beginning with the massive Marcus Garvey movement and continuing to the present era. Concomitant with this rise of black activism was the development of FBI oversight, infiltration and destruction of these movements and their leaders. The Federal government could not allow the rise of independent and militant political leadership in the black community.

<u>The Marcus Garvey Precedent</u>
The Federal government assault against black leadership did not begin in the 1960's and 1970's. Rather, as early as October 11, 1919, J. Edgar Hoover had targeted the most militant black leader of the period, Marcus Garvey, for surveillance and eventual deportation to Jamaica. On that day Hoover wrote a letter to the Attorney General indicating that Garvey was a popular leader who had not violated any laws yet.[12] As with the Panthers, Hoover was able to enlist the services of key informers to infiltrate Garvey's Universal Negro

---

12   Churchill, Ward and Vanderwall, Jim, The Cointelpro Papers
"Documents from the FBI's Secret Wars Against Dissent in the United States"
(Boston, South End Press, 1990), p. 12.

Improvement Association. James Wormley Jones received that key role of spy on the Black popular movement.[13]

On October 11, 1919, Hoover wrote the following letter to Attorney General Ridgely:

"...I am transmitting herewith a communication which has come to my attention from the Panama Canal, Washington office, relative to the activities of MARCUS GARVEY. Garvey is a West-Indian negro and in addition to his activities in endeavoring to establish the Black Star Line Steamship Corporation he has also been particularly active among the radical elements in New York City in agitating the negro movement. Unfortunately, however, he has not as yet violated any federal law whereby he could be proceeded against on the grounds of being an undesirable alien, from the point of view of deportation. It occurs to me, however, from the attached clipping that there might be some proceeding against him for fraud in connection with his Black Star Line propaganda and for this reason I am transmitting a communication to you for your appropriate attention."

"The following is a brief statement of Marcus Garvey and his activities: Subject a native of West Indies and one of the most prominent negro agitators in New York; He is a founder of the Universal Negro Improvement Association and African Communities League; He is the promulgator of the Black Star Line and is the managing editor of the Negro World; He is an exceptionally fine orator, creating much excitement among the negroes through his steamship proposition; In his paper the "Negro World" the Soviet Russian Rule is upheld and there is open advocation of Bolshevism"[14]

---

13   Churchill, p. 12.

14   Churchill, p. 12.

It was during the liberal Democratic administrations that the infiltration of black liberation movements reached its peak. On August 25, 1967, the Federal Bureau of Investigations (FBI) launched a full scale infiltration of the Southern Christian Leadership Conference, the Black Panther Party and other organizations. Since Malcolm X had been assassinated on February 21, 1965, he and his movement were not subject to this policy.

In a memorandum to twenty-two (22) local FBI offices, J. Edgar Hoover launched a political onslaught entitled: Counterintelligence Program-Black Nationalist-Hate Groups, Internal Security. The memorandum set forth the purposes of the program in clear terms:

"...The purpose of this new counterintelligence endeavor is to expose, disrupt, misdirect, discredit, or otherwise neutralize the activities of Black nationalist, hate type organizations and groupings, their leadership, spokesmen, membership, and supporters, and to counter their propensity for violence and civil disorder. The activities of all such groups of intelligence interest to this Bureau must be followed on a continuous basis so we will be in a position to promptly take advantage of all opportunities for counterintelligence and to inspire action in instances where circumstances warrant. The pernicious background of such groups, their duplicity, and devious maneuvers must be exposed to public scrutiny where such publicity will have a neutralizing effect. Efforts of the various groups to consolidate their forces or to recruit new or youthful adherents must be frustrated. No opportunity should be missed to exploit through counterintelligence techniques the organizational and personal conflicts of the leadership of the groups and where possible an effort should be made to capitalize upon existing conflicts between competing black nationalist organizations. When an opportunity is apparent to disrupt or neutralize black nationalist, hate-type organizations through the cooperation of established local news media contacts or through such contact with sources available to the seat of Government, in every instance careful attention must be given to the proposal to insure the targeted group is disrupted, ridiculed, or discredited through the publicity and not merely publicized. Consideration should be given to techniques to preclude violence-proved or rabble-rouser leaders of hate groups from spreading their philosophy publicly or through various mass communication media."

"Many individuals currently active in black nationalist organizations have backgrounds of immorality, subversive activity, and criminal records. Through your investigation of key agitators, you should endeavor to establish their unsavory backgrounds. Be alert to determine evidence of misappropriation of funds or other types of personal misconduct on the part of militant nationalist leaders so any practical or warranted counterintelligence may be instituted..."[15]

By March 4, 1968, the Counterintelligence Program had been expanded by the FBI to include forty-one (41) local offices. In new directives to these offices, Hoover instructed his staff to accomplish the following goals:

"1. Prevent the coalition of militant black nationalist groups. In unity there is strength; a truism that is no less valid for all its triteness. An effective coalition of black nationalist groups might be the first step toward a real "Mau Mau" in America, the beginning of a true black revolution.

"2. Prevent the rise of a "messiah" who could unify, and electrify, the militant black nationalist movement. Malcolm X might have been such a "messiah;" he is the martyr of the movement today. Martin Luther King, Stokely Carmichael and Elijah Muhammed all aspire to this position. Elijah Muhammed is less of a threat because of his age. King could be a very real contender for this position should he abandon his supposed "obedience" to "white, liberal doctrines" (nonviolence) and embrace black nationalism. Carmichael has the necessary charisma to be a real threat in this way.

"3. Prevent violence on the part of black nationalist groups. This is of primary importance, and is, of course, a goal of our investigative activity; it should also be a goal of the Counterintelligence Program.

---

15   Churchill, pp. 92-93.

Through counterintelligence it should be possible to pinpoint potential troublemakers and neutralize them before they exercise their potential for violence.

"4. Prevent militant black nationalist groups and leaders from gaining respectability, by discrediting them to three separate segments of the community. The goal of discrediting black nationalists must be handled tactically in three ways. You must discredit these groups and individuals to, first, the responsible Negro community. Second, they must be discredited to the white community, both the responsible community and to "liberals" who have vestiges of sympathy for militant black nationalist simply because they are Negroes. Third, these groups must be discredited in the eyes of Negro radicals, the followers of the movement. This last area requires entirely different tactics from the first two. Publicity about violent tendencies and radical statements merely enhances black nationalists to the last group; it adds "respectability" in a different way.

"5. A final goal should be to prevent the long- range growth of militant black nationalist organizations, especially among youth. Specific tactics to prevent these groups from converting young people must be developed..."[16]

Neutralizing (Killing) of Blacks by Government

This policy of the government was quickly implemented. More than 4000 agents and informants infiltrated the Black liberation movements at their highest levels. In 1968, the FBI disseminated false information about Imari Abubakari Obadele (Richard Henry), who was the President of the Republic of New Afrika (RNA). Several years later the FBI, through its agents, disrupted a meeting of RNA in Jackson, Mississippi. The organization had plans to establish a black nation in five southern states. On October 10, 1970, agents spoke to an elderly black man in Mississippi who had agreed to sell to RNA 560 acres of land. After the agents provided false information about the organization, the man refused to sell the land to the RNA.

---

16   Churchill, pp. 110-111.

The most extensive assault by the FBI was directed toward the Black Panther Party. The party was formed by Huey P. Newton and Bobby Seale in the San Francisco Bay area in October, 1966. By September 8, 1968, J. Edgar Hoover stated that the Party was "...the greatest (single) threat to the internal security of the country."[17]

The FBI, therefore, accelerated its efforts to accomplish the goals set forth in the initial policy statements. The Bureau soon thereafter engaged in a protracted program to disrupt the merger between the Party and the Student Nonviolent Coordinating Committee (SNCC). This goal was achieved by "neutralizing" the leadership of these organizations. H. Rap Brown, was "charged with inciting a race riot in Maryland." Stokely Carmichael was accused of being a CIA informant, which required him to leave the country for Africa to avoid being killed by misguided Party members. On or about November 27, 1968, Eldridge Cleaver fled the country to Cuba, Algeria and France to avoid being apprehended for his alleged involvement in a shootout on April 6, 1968 when Bobby Hutton was killed by Oakland police.[18]

There is also evidence that the FBI distributed false information to the Panthers and United Slaves (US) led by cultural nationalist Ron Karenga. The false information distributed by the FBI ultimately led to a shootout between the two organizations on January 17, 1969 where members of the Panthers were shot to death by US members in a UCLA classroom.[19]

One of the most brutal attacks by the FBI against the Panthers occurred in Chicago. The target was Fred Hampton, a very charismatic leader of the Party who had received considerable support from the black community as a result of his free breakfast and other programs. In addition, he had formed an alliance with street gangs, such as the Black Stone Rangers. He was clearly a threat, according to the FBI, and had to be neutralized. The Bureau attempted to divide and get the two organizations to fight each other by sending a false letter to

---

17　Churchill, pp. 110-111.

18　Churchill, pp. 128-129.

19　Churchill, p. 133.

Jeff Fort, the leader of the Rangers, indicating that Fred Hampton had a hit out on him.[20]

The final plan was to neutralize Hampton. In November, 1969, FBI informant, William O'Neal, who had become Hampton's personal body guard and chief of security, began to play a key role in the FBI's plan to get rid of Fred Hampton. Agent Roy Mitchell obtained a floor plan of the apartment where Hampton slept from O'Neal. On December 3, 1969 O'Neal slipped some secobarbital into a glass of kool aid that he gave Hampton. At about 4 a.m., on December 4, 1969, Hampton's apartment was raided by fourteen policemen. Hampton was shot once in the chest and twice in the head.[21] The police fired a total of 98 rounds into the apartment. William O'Neal was paid a bonus of $300.00 for his work in helping the police to neutralize Hampton. The families of Hampton and Mark Clark (also killed) filed a $47 million civil wrongful death suit against state defendants and the FBI. In November 1982, the plaintiffs received a judgment of $1.85 million for the wrongful deaths.[22]

---

20   Churchill, p. 135.

21   Churchill, p. 140.

22   Churchill, p. 141.

► Notes & Questions

1. Should the FBI be allowed to infiltrate domestic organizations, plant false information, and "neutralize" dissident groups?

2. Are there ever sufficient circumstances that would justify such involvement?

3. Why do blacks join organizations such as the FBI or become informants for such agencies, when they know that they will be used to disrupt or destroy black organizations?

4. **The Case of Rev. Martin Luther King, Jr.** When James Earl Ray pled guilty to the murder of Rev. Martin Luther King, Jr. on March 10, 1969, the question of whether a conspiracy existed to kill Rev. King became moot. At least the FBI had hoped. Ray was sentenced to 99 years in the penitentiary, but later recanted his confession that he had acted alone in the assassination. Many observers were upset that a public trial was never conducted. The examination and cross examination of witnesses would have revealed the weight of the overall evidence. More importantly, evidence of the extent to which the FBI had hoped that Dr. King would be killed, would have been made public.

Dick Gregory, the black social activist and comedian, has written: "...The FBI hated King with a passion..."[23] The Church Committee, established by the United States Congress to investigate domestic intelligence activities, wrote: "...The Committee finds that covert action programs have been used to disrupt the lawful political activities of individual Americans and groups and to

---

23 Mark Lane and Dick Gregory, Murder in Memphis" The FBI and the Assassination of Martin Luther King" (New York, Thunder's Mouth Press, 1993), p. 6.

► **Notes & Questions**

discredit them, using dangerous and degrading tactics which are abhorrent in a free and decent society... The sustained use of such tactics by the FBI in an attempt to destroy Dr. Martin Luther King, Jr., violated the law and fundamental human decency..."[24] The FBI was obsessed with Rev. King and engaged in extensive wiretapping of his home, offices and hotel rooms. The FBI fabricated letters and mailed them to his wife, Coretta Scott King, the media and others in an attempt to discredit Rev. King. It was hoped that the communications to Mrs. King would cause marital discord. The FBI hoped that the marital discord would cause Rev. King to abandon his campaign for human rights and civil rights. When J. Edgar Hoover learned that Rev. King would receive the Nobel Peace Prize, he authorized the mailing of a threatening letter to Rev. King. In the letter the FBI warned that it would release to the press alleged immoral information that it had received from wiretaps of Rev. King if he did not commit suicide. [25]

Rather than viewing Rev. King as a religious man who was seeking justice for African Americans, Hoover considered him a hypocrite and a potential criminal. In fact, Rev. King was classified by the FBI in May, 1962 as a person who the government would detain and imprison during national emergencies.[26] In that same year the Bureau investigated the Southern Christian Leadership Conference (SCLC). The justification raised by the agency was a suspicion that certain communists had infiltrated the organization.

Hoover did not invade the privacy of Rev. King and other Americans without the approval of higher governmental officials.

---

24   Lane, p. 77.

25   Lane, p. 78.

26   Lane, p. 80.

▶ Notes & Questions

Attorney General Robert Kennedy had been made aware of the surveillance of Rev. King and on October 7, 1963, he gave Hoover permission to wiretap Rev. King's home and the offices of SCLC.[27] The Attorney General gave Hoover the authorization to wiretap Rev. King's current address or "...any future address." Hoover interpreted this authorization to mean hotels and motels and homes of friends who may have provided lodging for Rev. King.

If the attempts to discredit Rev. King failed, the FBI was prepared to take even more draconian steps. Hoover had developed a plan whereby he would attempt to recruit a substitute leader who would exert leadership over the black movement and be controlled by the FBI. This plan never came to fruition.[28]

In 1968, the FBI became even more desperate in their efforts to control King. Not only was Rev. King continuing his efforts to bring dignity to blacks, but he also was beginning to develop a much broader strategy. His new strategy would be much broader and include all poor people. His Poor People's March would unite black, White and other poor people in a united movement for human dignity. This unity among the oppressed majority, the FBI believed, would make Rev. King even more powerful and thus pose a threat to the United States. This shift from civil rights to economic rights was clearly manifested in the garbage workers strike in Memphis, Tennessee where Rev. King went on March 29, 1968 to join their protests.

The FBI followed the activities of Rev. King very closely. They wrote a letter entitled "Do As I Say, Not As I Do," which they intended to distribute to the local news outlets. The letter criticized

---

27   Lane, p. 84.

28   Lane, p. 91.

▶ Notes & Questions

Rev. King for staying in a downtown Holiday Inn, rather than in the black owned Lorraine Motel. The FBI wrote that it was hypocritical for him to urge blacks to boycott downtown businesses, when he stayed in white downtown motels.

On April 3, 1968, when Rev. King returned to Memphis for a rally, he stayed in the Lorraine Motel as the FBI had wanted. That night he gave his last speech, "I've Been to the Mountaintop," at the Mason Temple. His speech was prophetic:

"...Well, I don't know what will happen now. We've got some difficult days ahead. But it doesn't matter with me now. Because I've been to the mountaintop. And I don't mind. Like anybody, I would like to live a long life. Longevity has its place. But I'm not concerned about that now. I just want to do God's will. And he's allowed me to go to the mountain. And I've looked over. And I've seen the promised land. I may not get there with you. But I want you to know tonight, that we, as a people will get to the promised land. And I'm happy, tonight. I'm not worried about anything. I'm not fearing any man. Mine eyes have seen the glory of the coming of the Lord."[29]

On April 4, 1968, at about 6:15 p.m., Rev. King was shot and killed by a gunman, as he stood outside on the balcony of the Lorraine Motel.

---

29   Lane, p. 117.

D.

Native American Land and Its Theft and Control

Under what circumstances should the government take the land of individuals who owned and enjoyed it prior to the arrival of Europeans? Is the rationale for extinguishing the rights of Native Americans convincing? Is it self-serving? Should the government compensate Native Americans for the loss of their land?

STATE OF VERMONT v. RALEIGH ELLIOTT, et al.
Vermont Supreme Court
616 A.2d 210 (1992)

Morse, J. Defendants are individuals in a group of thirty-six people who were charged with fishing without a license under 10 V.S.A. '' 4251(a), 4266. The cases arose primarily from an October 18, 1987 "fish-in" demonstration and were consolidated for trial. Before trial, defendants moved to dismiss based on the doctrine of "aboriginal rights." They claimed the doctrine prohibited the prosecution of Native Americans if they were members of a currently viable Indian tribe which had from "time immemorial" continuously occupied the land where the offenses occurred. According to defendants, because they held "aboriginal title" to the land, they were not subject to state regulation for fishing without a license.

The trial court agreed and dismissed the charges against most of the defendants because they were members of the Missisquoi Tribe, a subpart of the Western Abenaki Tribe whose aboriginal title had not been extinguished. The State took an interlocutory appeal, arguing that the Abenakis (as we shall refer to them for purposes of this opinion) are no longer a tribe, and, even if they are, any aboriginal title to the land was extinguished by governmental action long ago. We agree that aboriginal rights were extinguished and, accordingly, reverse.

I.

"Aboriginal title" gives members of a viable Native American tribe a right of occupancy to lands that is protected against claims by anyone else unless the tribe abandons the lands or the sovereign extinguishes the right. *United States v. Santa Fe Pacific R.R.,* 314 U.S. 339, 345-47 (1941). The right arises from a tribe's occupation of a definable, ancestral homeland before the onset of European colonization. The occupation must have been exclusive of the occupation by other tribes. *Id.* at 345. The validity of aboriginal title is not dependent on treaty, statute, or other formal governmental recognition, (Citation omitted), but a group making a claim under the doctrine must present sufficient proof that they have constituted a tribe throughout relevant history and have never voluntarily abandoned their tribal status. (Citation omitted).

This property concept flowed from the "doctrine of discovery," which in turn, derived from natural law. See F. Cohen, *Handbook of Federal Indian Law* 486 n.128 (1982). The discovery doctrine was recognized by European countries during the colonization of North America. During the territorial expansion of the sixteenth, seventeenth, and eighteenth centuries, European governments reconciled their claims to newly acquired lands with claims of other European governments and the aboriginals who were already occupying the lands. (Citation omitted). As a result of these compromises, it was generally understood that a discovering nation-the European government whose arrival was first in time-held title to lands "subject to the Indians' right of occupancy and use." (Citation omitted). Hence, the phrase "aboriginal title" or "Indian title" describes the ownership interest retained by Native Americans in lands which European nations appropriated. (Citation omitted). The United States Supreme Court adopted the doctrine in *Johnson v. McIntosh,* 21 U.S. (8 Wheat.) 543, 592 (1823). In that case and later, the Court applied the doctrine by "assigning dual, or split, property rights to the discoverer nation on the one hand, and Indian nations on the other." Norgren, *supra,* at 85. As case law developed, it became clear that discovering nations did not hold fee simple absolute because their interest was encumbered by the occupancy rights held by Native Americans. (Citation omitted). The interest that the discovering nation did hold, however, significantly impaired the rights of the original inhabitants because the discoverer had the "'exclusive right... to appropriate the lands occupied by the Indians,'" (Citation omitted), and could terminate aboriginal rights at any time. *Santa Fe,* 314 U.S. at 347.

Although the doctrine of aboriginal rights is long standing, (Citation omitted), the nature of the various interests in aboriginal lands has not been easily defined or applied. A sovereign's transfer of such land is subject to continuing Indian rights of occupancy and use, until those underlying rights are extinguished. (Citation omitted). The interest transferred is termed the "naked fee." (Citation omitted). Absolute ownership does not vest until Indian title is extinguished, a phenomenon that cannot occur without the act or consent of the sovereign. (Citation omitted). Therefore, where the terms of a land grant do not rise to the level of extinguishment, or where there has been no action by the sovereign demonstrating an intent to extinguish, the grant of land conveys only an inchoate interest in the land. (Citation omitted).

II.

Indian title may be abolished, or "extinguished," causing the Native Americans to lose their right of occupancy and use, and vesting fee simple absolute in either the sovereign or a third party. (Citation omitted). Extinguishment differs from a transfer of the naked fee, because when the former occurs, no rights are left in the Indians. Extinguishment may be accomplished "by treaty, by the sword, by purchase, by the exercise of complete dominion adverse to the right of occupancy, or otherwise." (Citation omitted).

Even though aboriginal title has been deemed "as sacred as the fee simple of the whites," (Citation omitted), it may nevertheless be taken without compensation. *Tee-Hit-Ton Indians v. United States,* 348 U.S. 272, 279 (1955). The federal policy is that extinguishment occur through negotiation rather than by force, but an extinguishment by force is valid. (Citation omitted). (extinguishment need not be accomplished by treaty or voluntary cession because the "relevant question is whether the governmental action was intended to be a revocation of Indian occupancy rights, not whether the revocation was effected by permissible means"). The manner, time, and conditions of extinguishment are determined by the sovereign. *Buttz v. Northern Pacific R.R.,* 119 U.S. 55, 66 (1886). Extinguishment is irrevocable; once it takes place, Indian title cannot be revived.

Before the American Revolution, Great Britain held the power to extinguish aboriginal rights in the colonies. (Citation omitted). The right to extinguish may pass to succeeding sovereigns, and with the adoption of the federal constitution, the right to extinguish became the exclusive right of the federal government. (Citation omitted). Sovereign intent to extinguish need not be express, but there must be evidence that demonstrates a "plain and unambiguous" intent to extinguish exclusive aboriginal rights. (Citation omitted). Because of the federal policy to respect Indian rights of occupancy, the intent to extinguish Indian title will not be "lightly implied." (Citation omitted).

An historical event, although insufficient by itself to establish an extinguishment, may contribute to a finding of extinguishment when analyzed together with other events. *Gemmill,* 535 F.2d at 1148 (ambiguity in single act of federal government is not fatal to claim of extinguishment when series of subsequent acts resolves ambiguity to demonstrate extinguishment); (Citation omitted).

Moreover, a century-long course of conduct may demonstrate extinguishment, even though the exact date on which Indian title is extinguished is difficult to determine. (Citation omitted); see also *Ildefonso,* 513 F.2d at 1390 ("there are no fine spun or precise formulas for determining the end of aboriginal ownership").

As seen from our discussion so far, the doctrine of Indian title and its extinguishment lacks precision in delineating between competing interests...

III.

We do not decide whether the trial court ruled correctly on the issue of tribal status and assume for the purposes of this case that defendants are members of a bonafide tribe of Native Americans. We conclude, however, that a series of historical events, beginning with the Wentworth Grants of 1763, and ending with Vermont's admission to the Union in 1791, extinguished the aboriginal rights claimed here.

IV.

In deciding the issue of extinguishment, we first place the pertinent historical facts in context. Although historical scholarship may be based on conflicting interpretations of recorded history, we briefly recite the political backdrop against which European settlement was set, in order to put into perspective the events leading to the extinguishment of the Abenakis' aboriginal rights to the land at issue.

A.

The area covering what is now the states of New York, New Hampshire, and Vermont was colonized in the seventeenth century by European settlers. The English had full control of the New York area by 1669. New Hampshire was also colonized by the English, and was officially under British rule as a royal province by 1679. After the American Revolution, the New York and New Hampshire colonies (also known as provinces) were admitted as two of the thirteen original states in 1788.

The Abenaki occupied what is now northwestern Vermont long before white presence began in the area in 1609 with the arrival of Samuel de Champlain. (Citations omitted). In 1724, Dutch settlers established a community in southern Vermont. After the British won the French and Indian War (1754-63), the land was opened for further European settlement. When the American Revolution began in 1775, approximately 20,000 people lived in what is now the State of Vermont.

B.

As provinces, New York and New Hampshire were administered on behalf of the Crown by royal governors authorized to grant, "for and in the name of the King, any unchartered lands in (their) province." H. Hall, *Early History of Vermont* (1868). The Crown, however, retained full control over boundaries, and could enlarge or contract them at will. *Id.* The first significant historical event relevant to extinguishment of Abenaki aboriginal title was the royal grant of lands to European settlers in the area claimed by the Abenakis in this case...

Conflict between New Hampshire claimants and New York authorities persisted. In 1769, the royal government of New York initiated the first in a series of ejectment suits in an attempt to remove the New Hampshire grantees from the land granted by New York. V. Orton, *Personal Observations on the Republic of Vermont* 45 (1977). The New Hampshire grantees subsequently revolted against the New York authorities, and in the years between 1770 and 1775 settlers formed a militia called the "Green Mountain Boys." Led by Ethan Allen, this group of claimants repulsed the "Yorkers" who tried to attain lands in Vermont. The rebellion prompted the decision to establish an independent government for the New Hampshire grantees. C. Williamson, *Vermont in Quandary: 1768-1825* 7-23(1949); see also *Vermont v. New Hampshire,* 289 U.S. at 607 (finding of special master that attempts by New York authorities to interfere with holdings of New Hampshire grantees "led to protest and forcible resistance which assumed the proportions of a revolutionary movement"). Consequently, in January 1777, Vermont declared its independence as a "Republic." By this declaration, Vermont rejected all governing authority except its own. The preamble to the document in which Vermont announced its autonomy from New York and British rule, as well as that of the rest of the world, asserted Vermont's dominion over the lands granted by Governor Wentworth:

> And whereas, the territory which now comprehends the State of Vermont, did antecedently, of right, belong to the government of New Hampshire; and the former Governor thereof, viz. his excellency Benning Wentworth, Esq., granted many charters of lands and corporations, within his State, to the present inhabitants and others.
>
> Vt.Const., preamble (1777)...

Before Vermont's admission to the Union as the fourteenth state, statements made on behalf of the-self-proclaimed "Republic" and the federal Congress shed light on the understanding held by both Vermont and Congress as to who had rights to the territory of Vermont...

V.

The trial court examined the events leading to Vermont's statehood and concluded that no single event constituted express or implied termination of aboriginal rights... The court also stated that Vermont's 1777 Constitution and subsequent admission to the Union did not accomplish an extinguishment of aboriginal rights. As a result, according to the trial court, the State failed to satisfy its burden of showing, by a preponderance of the evidence, a "clear and unambiguous intent to extinguish" aboriginal rights. For the reasons that follow, we disagree.

We differ with the trial court principally in its application of the test for extinguishment to discrete events in Vermont's history, rather than to the cumulative effect of many historical events. The legal standard does not require that extinguishment spring full blown from a single telling event. Extinguishment may be established by the increasing weight of history.

Governor Wentworth's grants of the lands at issue may not have been authorized by the Crown, but any ultra vires exercise of power by him does not detract from the vast political changes it inspired. These grants triggered the emergence of Vermont for a short time in history as an entity separate from the authority of Great Britain and its provinces of New Hampshire and New York, or any other government. A drastic realignment of jurisdictional boundaries was induced by Wentworth's Grants. Appreciation of the various authorities' conduct toward the area that is now the State of Vermont is critical to our determination that intent to extinguish became unquestionable. The Crown's sanctioning of European dominion over the area, the zeal with which the founders of the "Republic" of Vermont protected the New Hampshire Grants, and the negotiations with Congress in anticipation of Vermont joining the Union remove any doubt that extinguishment of Abenaki aboriginal title was complete by 1791, when Vermont became the fourteenth state...

A.

We agree with defendants that non-Indian, or "white," encroachment causing Indian withdrawal is not, in itself, effective to extinguish aboriginal rights. (Citation omitted). We do, however, include the phenomenon of white settlement in our analysis as evidence of an intent to extinguish by the assertion of dominion over the area. This is because "[m]aking lands available for white settlement...in an appropriate factual context, constitute[s] termination of aboriginal ownership." *Id.;* see also *Gila River Pima Maricopa Indian Community v. United States,* 494 F.2d 1386, 1391 (Ct. Cl. 1974) (authorized white settlement is one factor in determining when Indian title ceased and "'in an appropriate factual context' the opening up of an area for settlement can be tantamount to the ending of aboriginal title over the whole region"). Here, there was much more than "expectation." There was actual settlement and appropriation to the exclusion of other competing claims, and ratification by Congress when it admitted Vermont to the Union. Defendants' claims that the Abenakis never voluntarily abandoned the area and that they were never completely removed have no effect on a finding of an intent to assert complete control over the area in a manner adverse to the Abenakis. (Note omitted).

B.

We concede that the period preceding Vermont's statehood was a confusing era, and that valid questions remain as to the legitimacy of the opposing governing entities. Nevertheless, the tumultuous political context does not preclude a finding of extinguishment. (Citation omitted). Vermont's admission to the Union provided closure to a long period of authority transferred from one body politic to another, giving final, official sanction to the previous events, and eliminating any remaining ambiguity about who had dominion over lands once controlled by the Abenakis. Short of an express statement declaring an intent to extinguish, it is difficult to imagine a demonstration of intent that could be more unequivocal than these cumulative events leading to statehood. We conclude that, by the year 1791, aboriginal rights to the area now known as St. Albans, Highgate and Swanton had been extinguished.

Reversed and remanded for further proceedings.

Native Americans and Economic Opportunity

Should the law stand in the way of Native Americans acquiring economic opportunity, given the history of genocide directed towards the native population? Approximately twenty four states have allowed some form of casino gambling to take place on Native American land. The casino business across the country is worth an estimated 4 billion dollars annually. When a state refuses to bargain with a tribal group in "good faith" should the Native Americans be allowed to bring suit in federal court to compel the state to abide by the law?

SEMINOLE TRIBE v. FLORIDA
Supreme Court of the United States
116 S.Ct. 1114 (1996)

Chief Justice REHNQUIST delivered the opinion of the Court.

The Indian Gaming Regulatory Act provides that an Indian tribe may conduct certain gaming activities only in conformance with a valid compact between the tribe and the State in which the gaming activities are located. (Citation omitted). The Act, passed by Congress under the Indian Commerce Clause, U.S. Const., Art. I, '8, cl. 3, imposes upon the States a duty to negotiate in good faith with an Indian tribe toward the formation of a compact, (Citation omitted), and authorizes a tribe to bring suit in federal court against a State in order to compel performance of that duty, (Citation omitted). We hold that notwithstanding Congress' clear intent to abrogate the States' sovereign immunity, the Indian Commerce Clause does not grant Congress that power, and therefore ' 2710(d)(7) cannot grant jurisdiction over a State that does not consent to be sued. We further hold that the doctrine of *Ex parte Young,* 209 U.S. 123, 28 S.Ct. 441, 52 L.Ed. 714 (1908), may not be used to enforce '2710(d)(3) against a state official.

I.

Congress passed the Indian Gaming Regulatory Act in 1988 in order to provide a statutory basis for the operation and regulation of gaming by Indian tribes. Citation omitted). The Act divides gaming on Indian lands into three classes-I, II, and III - and provides a different regulatory scheme for each class. Class III gaming- the type with which we are here concerned-is defined as "all forms of gaming that are not class I gaming or class II gaming," (Citation omitted), and includes such things as slot machines, casino games, banking card games, dog racing, and lotteries. (Note omitted). It is the most heavily regulated of the three classes. The Act provides that class III gaming is lawful only where it is: (1) authorized by an ordinance or resolution that (a) is adopted by the governing body of the Indian tribe, (b) satisfies certain statutorily prescribed requirements, and (c) is approved by the National Indian Gaming Commission; (2) located in a State that permits such gaming for any purpose by any person, organization, or entity; and (3) "conducted in conformance with a Tribal-state compact entered into by the Indian tribe and the State under paragraph (3) that is in effect." (Citation omitted).

The "paragraph (3)" to which the last prerequisite of '2710(d)(1) refers is '2710(d)(3), which describes the permissible scope of a Tribal-State compact, see '2710(d)(3)(C), and provides that the compact is effective "only when notice of approval by the Secretary [of the Interior] of such compact has been published by the Secretary in the Federal Register," (Citation omitted). More significant for our purposes, however, is that '2710(d)(3) describes the process by which a State and an Indian tribe begin negotiations toward a Tribal-State compact: " (A) Any Indian tribe having jurisdiction over the Indian lands upon which a class III gaming activity is being conducted, or is to be conducted, shall request the State in which such lands are located to enter into negotiations for the purpose of entering into a Tribal-State compact governing the conduct of gaming activities. Upon receiving such a request, the State shall negotiate with the Indian tribe in good faith to enter into such a compact."

The State's obligation to "negotiate with the Indian tribe in good faith," is made judicially enforceable by ''2710(d)(7)(A)(i) and(B)(i):

" (A) The United States district courts shall have jurisdiction over—

" (i) any cause of action initiated by an Indian tribe arising from the failure of a State to enter into negotiations with the Indian tribe for the purpose of entering into a Tribal-State compact under paragraph (3) or to conduct such negotiations in good faith...

" (B)(i) An Indian tribe may initiate a cause of action described in subparagraph (A)(i) only after the close of the 180-day period beginning on the date on which the Indian tribe requested the State to enter into negotiations under paragraph (3)(A)."

In September 1991, the Seminole Tribe of Indians, petitioner, sued the State of Florida and its Governor, Lawton Chiles, respondents. Invoking jurisdiction under 25 U.S.C. '2710(d)(7)(A), as well as 28 U.S.C. ' 1331 and 1362, petitioner alleged that respondents had "refused to enter into any negotiation for inclusion of [certain gaming activities] in a tribal-state compact," thereby violating the "requirement of good faith negotiation" contained in '2710(d)(3). (Citation omitted). Respondents moved to dismiss the complaint, arguing that the suit violated the State's sovereign immunity from suit in federal court. The District Court denied respondents' motion, (Citation omitted), and the respondents took an interlocutory appeal of that decision. (Citation omitted).

The Court of Appeals for the Eleventh Circuit reversed the decision of the District Court, holding that the Eleventh Amendment barred petitioner's suit against respondents. (Citation omitted)...

Petitioner sought our review of the Eleventh Circuit's decision, (Note omitted) and we granted certiorari, (Citation omitted), in order to consider two questions: (1) Does the Eleventh Amendment prevent Congress from authorizing suits by Indian tribes against States for prospective injunctive relief to enforce legislation enacted pursuant to the Indian Commerce Clause?; and (2) Does the doctrine of *Ex parte Young* permit suits against a State's governor for prospective injunctive relief to enforce the good faith bargaining requirement of the Act? We answer the first question in the affirmative, the second in the negative, and we therefore affirm the Eleventh Circuit's dismissal of petitioner's suit. (Note omitted).

The Eleventh Amendment provides:

"The Judicial power of the United States shall not be construed to extend to any suit in law or equity, commenced or prosecuted against one of the United States by Citizens of another State, or by Citizens or Subjects of any Foreign State."

Although the text of the Amendment would appear to restrict only the Article III diversity jurisdiction of the federal courts, "we have understood the Eleventh Amendment to stand not so much for what it says, but for the presupposition...which it confirms. (Citation omitted). That presupposition, first observed over a century ago in *Hans v. Louisiana,* 134 U.S. 1, 10 S.Ct. 504, 33 L.Ed. 842 (1890), has two parts: first, that each State is a sovereign entity in our federal system; and second, that "'[i]t is inherent in the nature of sovereignty not to be amenable to the suit of an individual without its consent.'" (Citation omitted). For over a century we have reaffirmed that federal jurisdiction over suits against unconsenting States "was not contemplated by the Constitution when establishing the judicial power of the United States." (Citation omitted).

Here, petitioner has sued the State of Florida and it is undisputed that Florida has not consented to the suit. See *Blatchford, supra,* at 782, 111 S.Ct., at 2582 (States by entering into the Constitution did not consent to suit by Indian tribes). Petitioner nevertheless contends that its suit is not barred by state sovereign immunity. First, it argues that Congress through the Act abrogated the States' sovereign immunity. Alternatively, petitioner maintains that its suit against the Governor may go forward under *Ex parte Young, supra.* We consider each of those arguments in turn.

II.

Petitioner argues that Congress through the Act abrogated the States' immunity from suit. In order to determine whether Congress has abrogated the States' sovereign immunity, we ask two questions: first, whether Congress has "unequivocally expresse[d] its intent to abrogate the immunity," *Green v. Mansour,* 474 U.S. 64, 68, 106 S.Ct. 423, 426, 88 L.Ed.2d 371 (1985); and second, whether Congress has acted "pursuant to a valid exercise of power." Ibid...

A.

In sum, we think that the numerous references to the "State" in the text of '2710(d)(7)(B) make it indubitable that Congress intended through the Act to abrogate the States' sovereign immunity from suit. (Note omitted).

B.

Having concluded that Congress clearly intended to abrogate the States' sovereign immunity through '2710(d)(7), we turn now to consider whether the Act was passed "pursuant to a valid exercise of power." *Green v. Mansour,* 474 U.S., at 68, 106 S.Ct., at 425-426...

The Eleventh Amendment prohibits Congress from making the State of Florida capable of being sued in federal court... The Eleventh Circuit's dismissal of petitioner's suit is hereby affirmed. (Note omitted).

It is so ordered.

Justice STEVENS, dissenting.

This case is about power, the power of the Congress of the United States to create a private federal cause of action against a State, or its Governor, for the violation of a federal right. In *Chisholm v. Georgia,* 2 Dall. 419, 1 L.Ed. 440 (1793), the entire Court, including Justice Iredell whose dissent provided the blueprint for the Eleventh Amendment, assumed that Congress had such power...

Justice SOUTER, with whom Justice GINSBURG and Justice BREYER join, dissenting.

In holding the State of Florida immune to suit under the Indian Gaming Regulatory Act, the Court today holds for the first time since the founding of the Republic that Congress has no authority to subject a State to the jurisdiction of a federal court at the behest of an individual asserting a federal right...

► Notes & Questions

1. Has there ever been an equal opportunity era for Native-Americans?

2. Given the unequal bargaining power of Europeans and Native-Americans, should an impartial third party decide these issues of land control? Should the United Nations intervene on behalf of native people around the world, who have been stripped of their land and culture, without any compensation or recognition?

3. Compare and contrast the political and socio-economic status of African-Americans and Native-Americans today. Why have there been such monumental changes in the law and socio-economic condition of the former, but little change in the law and socio-economic condition of the latter?

E.

Concentration Camps: A Precedent for People of Color

Should the government be allowed to place people of color in detention when there has been no evidence of a direct threat to national security? When is a detention center a concentration camp? What lessons can black people learn from the experience of the Japanese Americans?

TOYOSABURO KOREMATSU v. UNITED STATES
Supreme Court of the United States
324 U.S. 885 (1944)

Mr. Justice BLACK delivered the opinion of the Court.

The petitioner, an American citizen of Japanese descent, was convicted in a federal district court for remaining in San Leandro, California, a "Military Area", contrary to Civilian Exclusion Order No. 34 of the Commanding General of the Western Command, U.S. Army, which directed that after May 9, 1942, all persons of Japanese ancestry should be excluded from that area. No question was raised as to petitioner's loyalty to the United States. The Circuit Court of Appeals affirmed, (Citation omitted) and the importance of the constitutional question involved caused us to grant certiorari.

It should be noted, to begin with, that all legal restrictions which curtail the civil rights of a single racial group are immediately suspect. That is not to say that all such restrictions are unconstitutional...

In the instant case prosecution of the petitioner was begun by information charging violation of an Act of Congress, of March 21, 1942, 56 Stat. 1' 97a, which provides that"... whoever shall enter, remain in, leave, or commit any act in any military area or military zone prescribed, under the authority of an Executive order of the President, by the Secretary of War, or by any military commander designated by the Secretary of War, contrary to the restrictions applicable to any such area or zone or contrary to the order of the Secretary of War or any such military commander, shall, if it appears that he knew or should have known of the existence and extent of the restrictions or order and that his act was in violation thereof, be guilty of a misdemeanor and upon conviction shall be liable to a fine of not to exceed $5,000 or to imprisonment for not more than one year, or both, for each offense."

Exclusion Order No. 34, which the petitioner knowingly and admittedly violated, was one of a number of military orders and proclamations, all of which were substantially based upon Executive Order No. 9066, 7 Fed. Reg. 1407. That order, issued after we were at war with Japan, declared that "the successful prosecution of the war requires every possible protection against espionage and against sabotage to national defense material, national-defense premises, and national-defense utilities..."

One of the series of orders and proclamations, a curfew order, which like the exclusion order here was promulgated pursuant to Executive Order 9066, subjected all persons of Japanese ancestry in prescribed West Coast military areas to remain in their residences from 8 p. m. to 6 a. m. As is the case with the exclusion order here, that prior curfew order was designed as a "protection against espionage and against sabotage." In *Kiyoshi Hirabayashi v. United States*, 320 U.S. 81, 63 S.Ct. 1375, 87 L.Ed. 1774, we sustained a conviction obtained for violation of the curfew order. The Hirabayashi conviction and this one thus rest on the same 1942 Congressional Act and the same basic executive and military orders, all of which orders were aimed at the twin dangers of espionage and sabotage.

The 1942 Act was attacked in the Hirabayashi case as an unconstitutional delegation of power; it was contended that the curfew order and other orders on which it rested were beyond the war powers of the Congress, the military authorities and of the President, as Commander in Chief of the Army; and finally that to apply the curfew order against none but citizens of Japanese ancestry amounted to a constitutionally prohibited discrimination solely on account of race. To these questions, we gave the serious consideration which their importance justified. We upheld the curfew order as an exercise of the power of the government to take steps necessary to prevent espionage and sabotage in an area threatened by Japanese attack.

In the light of the principles we announced in the Hirabayashi case, we are unable to conclude that it was beyond the war power of Congress and the Executive to exclude those of Japanese ancestry from the West Coast war area at the time they did. True, exclusion from the area in which one's home is located is a far greater deprivation than constant confinement to the home from 8 p.m. to 6 a.m. Nothing short of apprehension by the proper military authorities of the gravest imminent danger to the public safety can constitutionally justify either. But exclusion from a threatened area, no less than curfew, has a definite and close relationship to the prevention of espionage and sabotage. The military authorities, charged with the primary responsibility of defending our shores, concluded that curfew provided inadequate protection and ordered exclusion. They did so, as pointed out in our Hirabayashi opinion, in accordance with Congressional authority to the military to say who should, and who should not, remain in the threatened areas.

In this case the petitioner challenges the assumptions upon which we rested our conclusions in the Hirabayashi case. He also urges that by May 1942, when Order No. 34 was promulgated, all danger of Japanese invasion of the West Coast had disappeared. After careful consideration of these contentions we are compelled to reject them.

Here, as in the Hirabayashi case, supra, 320 U.S. at page 99, 63 S.Ct. at page 1385, 87 L.Ed. 1774, "* * * we cannot reject as unfounded the judgment of the military authorities and of Congress that there were disloyal members of that population, whose number and strength could not be precisely and quickly ascertained. We cannot say that the war-making branches of the Government did not have ground for believing that in a critical hour such persons could not readily be isolated and separately dealt with, and constituted a menace to the national defense and safety, which demanded that prompt and adequate measures be taken to guard against it."

Like curfew, exclusion of those of Japanese origin was deemed necessary because of the presence of an unascertained number of disloyal members of the group, most of whom we have no doubt were loyal to this country. It was because we could not reject the finding of the military authorities that it was impossible to bring about an immediate segregation of the disloyal from the loyal that we sustained the validity of the curfew order as applying to the whole group. In the instant case, temporary exclusion of the entire group was rested by the military on the same ground. The judgment that exclusion of the whole group was for the same reason a military imperative answers the contention that the exclusion was in the nature of group punishment based on antagonism to those of Japanese origin. That there were members of the group who retained loyalties to Japan has been confirmed by investigations made subsequent to the exclusion. Approximately five thousand American citizens of Japanese ancestry refused to swear unqualified allegiance to the United States and to renounce allegiance to the Japanese Emperor, and several thousand evacuees requested repatriation to Japan". (Footnote omitted).

We uphold the exclusion order as of the time it was made and when the petitioner violated it. Cf. *Chastleton Corporation v. Sinclair*, 264 U.S. 543, 547, 44 S.Ct. 405, 406, 68 L.Ed. 841; *Block v. Hirsh*, 256 U.S. 135, 154, 155, 41 S.Ct. 458, 459, 65 L.Ed. 865, 16 A.L.R 165. In doing so, we are not unmindful of the hardships imposed by it upon a large group of American citizens. Cf. *Ex parte Kumezo Kawato*, 317 U.S. 69, 73, 63 S.Ct. 115, 117, 87 L.Ed. 58. But hardships are part of war, and war is an aggregation of hardships. All citizens alike, both in and out of uniform, feel the impact of war in greater or lesser measure. Citizenship has its responsibilities as well as its privileges, and in time of war the burden is always heavier. Compulsory exclusion of large groups of citizens from their homes, except under circumstances of direst emergency and peril, is inconsistent with our basic governmental institutions. But when under conditions of modern warfare our shores are threatened by hostile forces, the power to protect must be commensurate with the threatened danger...

We are thus being asked to pass at this time upon the whole subsequent detention program in both assembly and relocation centers, although the only issues framed at the trial related to petitioner's remaining in the prohibited area in violation of the exclusion order. Had petitioner here left the prohibited area and gone to an assembly center we cannot say either as a matter of fact or law, that his presence in that center would have resulted in his detention in a relocation center. Some who did report to the assembly center were not sent to relocation centers, but were released upon condition that they remain outside the prohibited zone until the military orders were modified or lifted. This illustrates that they pose different problems and may be governed by different principles. The lawfulness of one does not necessarily determine the lawfulness of the others. This is made clear when we analyze the requirements of the separate provisions of the separate orders. These separate requirements were that those of Japanese ancestry (1) depart from the area; (2) report to and temporarily remain in an assembly center; (3) go under military control to a relocation center there to remain for an indeterminate period until released conditionally or unconditionally by the military authorities. Each of these requirements, it will be noted, imposed distinct duties in connection with the separate steps in a complete evacuation program. Had Congress directly incorporated into one Act the language of these separate orders, and provided sanctions for their violations, disobedience of any one would have constituted a separate offense. Cf. *Blockburger v. United States*, 284 U.S. 299, 304, 32 S. ct. 180, 182, 76 L.Ed. 306. There is no reason why violations of these orders, insofar as they were promulgated pursuant to congressional enactment, should not be treated as separate offenses...

It is said that we are dealing here with the case of imprisonment of a citizen in a concentration camp solely because of his ancestry, without evidence or inquiry concerning his loyalty and good disposition towards the United States. Our task would be simple, our duty clear, were this a case involving the imprisonment of a loyal citizen in a concentration camp because of racial prejudice. Regardless of the true nature of the assembly and relocation centers, and we deem it unjustifiable to call them concentration camps with all the ugly connotations that term implies, we are dealing specifically with nothing but an exclusion order. To cast this case into outlines of racial prejudice, without reference to the real military dangers which were presented, merely confuses the issue. Korematsu was not excluded from the Military Area because of hostility to him or his race. He was excluded because we are at war with the Japanese Empire, because the properly constituted military authorities feared an invasion of our West Coast and felt constrained to take proper security measures, because they decided that the military urgency of the situation demanded that all citizens of Japanese ancestry be segregated from the West Coast temporarily, and finally, because Congress, reposing its confidence in this time of war in our military leaders, as inevitably it must, determined that they should have the power to do just this. There was evidence of disloyalty on the part of some, the military authorities considered that the need for action was great, and time was short. We cannot, by availing ourselves of the calm perspective of hindsight, now say that at that time these actions were unjustified.

Affirmed...

Mr. Justice MURPHY, dissenting.

This exclusion of "all persons of Japanese ancestry, both alien and non-alien," from the Pacific Coast area on a plea of military necessity in the absence of martial law ought not to be approved. Such exclusion goes over "the very brink of constitutional power" and falls into the ugly abyss of racism...

The judicial test of whether the Government, on a plea of military necessity, can validly deprive an individual of any of his constitutional rights is whether the deprivation is reasonably related to a public danger that is so "immediate, imminent, and impending" as not to admit of delay and not to permit the intervention of ordinary constitutional processes to alleviate the danger. *United States v. Russell*, 13 Wall. 623, 627, 628, 20 L.Ed. 474; *Mitchell v. Harmony*, 13 How. 115, 134, 135, 14 L.Ed. 75; *Raymond v.*

Thomas, 91 U.S. 712, 716, 23 L.Ed. 434. Civilian Exclusion Order No. 34, banishing from a prescribed area of the Pacific Coast "all persons of Japanese ancestry, both alien and non-alien," clearly does not meet that test. Being an obvious racial discrimination, the order deprives all those within its scope of the equal protection of the laws as guaranteed by the Fifth Amendment. It further deprives these individuals of their constitutional rights to live and work where they will, to establish a home where they choose and to move about freely. In excommunicating them without benefit of hearings this order also deprives them of all their constitutional rights to procedural due process. Yet no reasonable relation to an "immediate, imminent, and impending" public danger is evident to support this racial restriction which is one of the most sweeping and complete deprivations of constitutional rights in the history of this nation in the absence of martial law... Justification for the exclusion is sought, instead, mainly upon questionable racial and sociological grounds not ordinarily within the realm of expert military judgment, supplemented by certain semi-military conclusions drawn from an unwarranted use of circumstantial evidence. Individuals of Japanese ancestry are condemned because they are said to be "a large, unassimilated, tightly knit racial group, bound to an enemy nation by strong ties of race, culture, custom and religion." (Footnote omitted). They are claimed to be given to "emperor worshipping ceremonies" and to "dual citizenship." (Footnote omitted). Japanese language schools and allegedly pro-Japanese organizations are cited as evidence of possible group disloyalty, (Footnote omitted) together with facts as to certain persons being educated and residing at length in Japan...

I dissent, therefore, from this legalization of racism. Racial discrimination in any form and in any degree has no justifiable part whatever in our democratic way of life. It is unattractive in any setting but it is utterly revolting among a free people who have embraced the principles set forth in the Constitution of the United States. All residents of this nation are kin in some way by blood or culture to a foreign land. Yet they are primarily and necessarily a part of the new and distinct civilization of the United States.

They must accordingly be treated at all times as the heirs of the American experiment and as entitled to all the rights and freedoms guaranteed by the Constitution.

Mr. Justice JACKSON, dissenting.

Korematsu was born on our soil, of parents born in Japan. The Constitution makes him a citizen of the United States by nativity and a citizen of California by residence. No claim is made that he is not loyal to this country. There is no suggestion that apart from the matter involved here he is not law-abiding and well disposed. Korematsu, however, has been convicted of an act not commonly a crime. It consists merely of being present in the state whereof he is a citizen, near the place where he was born, and where all his life he has lived...

Now, if any fundamental assumption underlies our system, it is that guilt is personal and not inheritable. Even if all of one's antecedents had been convicted of treason, the Constitution forbids its penalties to be visited upon him, for it provides that "no Attainder of Treason shall work Corruption of Blood, or Forfeiture except during the Life of the Person attained." Article 3, '3, cl. 2. But here is an attempt to make an otherwise innocent act a crime merely because this prisoner is the son of parents as to whom he had no choice, and belongs to a race from which there is no way to resign...

I should hold that a civil court cannot be made to enforce an order which violates constitutional limitations even if it is a reasonable exercise of military authority. The courts can exercise only the judicial power, can apply only law, and must abide by the Constitution, or they cease to be civil courts and become instruments of military policy...

My duties as a justice as I see them do not require me to make a military judgment as to whether General DeWitt's evacuation and detention program was a reasonable military necessity. I do not suggest that the courts should have attempted to interfere with the Army in carrying out its task. But I do not think they may be asked to execute a military expedient that has no place in law under the Constitution. I would reverse the judgment and discharge the prisoner.

▶ **Notes & Questions**

1. Do you agree with the majority opinion that Korematsu's rights were not violated? Was "military necessity" a sufficient justification for the internment of Japanese-Americans?

2. Justice Murphy, in his dissent, states that the exclusion cannot be justified in the absence of a declaration of martial law. What is martial law? Do you agree with Justice Murphy's position?

3. Justice Jackson writes that guilt, under the American system of laws, is personal, and not inheritable. Given the Justice's position, should an American citizen ever be subjected to involuntary internment?

4. It is the year 2004. The United States has just bombed Khartoum, Sudan, East Africa on the grounds that it is a haven for Islamic terrorists. Two weeks after the bombing a major news agency revealed that at least 700 civilians were killed by the bombing, including at least 100 children. The news of the atrocities quickly spread throughout the United States, causing major popular eruptions throughout the country. Several cities, including New York, Chicago and Los Angeles are in flames and civil disobedience appears to be the rule, instead of law and order.

   In order to quell the violence that was spreading rapidly across the country, the President of the United States signed a curfew order for inner city communities in the three cities (New York, Chicago and Los Angeles) most affected by the violence. The order prohibited individuals from being on the public streets from 7 pm until 6 am each calendar day. In addition, since the violence was very rampant in the Harlem section of New York City, the order required all residents to report to an assembly

► Notes & Questions

center where they were to remain until further notice. Anyone failing to abide by the order would be arrested and held without bail until the emergency was declared over.

Furthermore, African students from Moslem countries have been required to leave the United States within 24 hours. Moslem-Americans have been ordered to report to their local police departments, register and receive an identification card.

Entire communities refused to report to the assembly centers and were arrested and held without bail. You have been hired as a legal advisor to the group and have been asked to research their legal rights. In a memorandum of at least ten pages outline and discuss the government's legal position and that of the defendants. What are the key legal issues that grow out of this case and controversy?

Chapter Ten

LAW AND
THE GLOBALIZATION OF RACISM

Racism, which was born of capitalism and its inhumane methods of accumulation, i.e. slavery, colonialism and neo-colonialism, manifests itself within all national boundaries touched by capitalism. Given that the United States formed the lynchpin in early capitalist development, racism would be particularly manifested there. Even in the 21st century, civil rights activists find themselves resisting racist symbols that should have died with the civil war, i.e. the noose. For example, in Jena, Louisiana the fact that a black student sat under a tree where traditionally white students sat prompted someone on August 31, 2006 to hang 3 nooses from the tree. Later six black students were arrested and charged with attempted murder of a white student who was believed involved in the hanging of the noose. Soon thereafter similar incidents of noose hangings appeared throughout the country. For example, in New York State, nine incidents occurred. See Mark Potok, Luke Visconti, Barbara Frankel and Nigel Holmes, "The Geography of Hate" *The New York Times*, *Op-Ed*, November 25, 2007.

Given that the Southern Poverty Law Center estimates that hate crimes have increased by 40% over the past few years, it is clear that the United States, particularly under the Bush administration has seen a sharp increase in public acts of racism.

Many believe that the Bush administration has demonstrated indifference to the suffering of those who have been victimized historically by capitalism.

Is the United States Indifferent to the Suffering of People in the Developing World?

At the September, 2001 World Conference Against Racism, Fidel Castro castigated the United States for boycotting the conference and not recognizing the precarious condition of the Palestinian people.

KEY ADDRESS BY DR. FIDEL CASTRO RUZ, PRESIDENT OF THE REPUBLIC OF CUBA, AT THE WORLD CONFERENCE AGAINST RACISM, RACIAL DISCRIMINATION, XENOPHOBIA AND RELATED INTOLERANCE
DURBAN, SOUTH AFRICA. SEPTEMBER 1, 2001

Excellencies:
Delegates and guests:

Racism, racial discrimination and xenophobia are not naturally instinctive reactions of the human beings but rather a social, cultural and political phenomenon born directly of wars, military conquests, slavery and the individual or collective exploitation of the weakest by the most powerful all along the history of human societies.

No one has the right to boycott this Conference which tries to bring some sort of relief to the overwhelming majority of mankind afflicted by unbearable suffering and enormous injustice. Neither has anyone the right to set preconditions to this conference or urge it to avoid the discussion of historical responsibility, fair compensation or the way we decide to rate the dreadful genocide perpetrated, at this very moment, against our Palestinian brothers by extreme right leaders who, in alliance with the hegemonic superpower, pretend to be acting on behalf of another people which throughout almost two thousand years was the victim of the most fierce persecution, discrimination and injustice that history has known.

Cuba speaks of reparations, and supports this idea as an unavoidable moral duty to the victims of racism, based on a major precedent, that is, the indemnification being paid to the descendants of the Hebrew people which in the very heart of Europe suffered the brutal and loathsome racist holocaust... The irrefutable truth is that tens of millions of Africans were captured, sold like a commodity and sent beyond the Atlantic to work in slavery while 70 million indigenous people in that hemisphere perished as a result of the European conquest and colonization.

The inhuman exploitation imposed on the peoples of three continents, including Asia, marked forever the destiny and lives of over 4.5 billion people living in the Third World today whose poverty, unemployment, illiteracy and health rates as well as their infant mortality, life expectancy and other calamities --too many, in fact, to enumerate here-- are certainly awesome and harrowing. They are the current victims of that atrocity which lasted centuries and the ones who clearly deserve compensation for the horrendous crimes perpetrated against their ancestors and peoples.

Actually, such a brutal exploitation did not end when many countries became independent, not even after the formal abolition of slavery. Right after independence, the main ideologists of the American Union that emerged when the 13 colonies got rid of the British domination at the end of the 18th century, advanced ideas and strategies unquestionably expansionist in nature.

It was based on such ideas that the ancient white settlers of European descent, in their march to the West, forcibly occupied the lands in which Native-Americans had lived for thousands of years thus exterminating millions of them in the process. But, they did not stop at the boundaries of the former Spanish possessions; consequently Mexico, a Latin American country that had attained its independence in 1821, was stripped of millions of square kilometers of territory and invaluable natural resources.

Meanwhile, in the increasingly powerful and expansionist nation born in North America, the obnoxious and inhumane slavery system stayed in place for almost a century after the famous Declaration of Independence of 1776 was issued, the same that proclaimed that all men were born free and equal.

After the purely formal slave emancipation, African-Americans were subjected during one hundred more years to the harshest racial discrimination, and many of its features and consequences still persist after almost four more decades of heroic struggles and the achievements of the 1960's, for which Martin Luther King, Jr., Malcolm X and other outstanding fighters gave their lives. Based on a purely racist rationale, the longest and most severe legal sentences are passed against African-Americans who in the wealthy American society are bound to live in dire poverty and with the lowest living standards.

Likewise, what is left of the Native-American peoples, which were the first to inhabit a large portion of the current territory of the United States of America, remain under even worse conditions of discrimination and neglect.

Needless to mention the data on the social and economic situation of Africa where entire countries and even whole regions of Sub-Saharan Africa are in risk of extinction the result of an extremely complex combination of economic backwardness, excruciating poverty and grave diseases, both old and new, that have become a true scourge. And the situation is no less dramatic in numerous Asian countries. On top of all this, there are the huge and unpayable debts, the disparate terms of trade, the ruinous prices of basic commodities, the demographic explosion, the neoliberal globalization and the climate changes that produce long droughts alternating with increasingly intensive rains and floods. It can be mathematically proven that such a predicament is unsustainable.

The developed countries and their consumer societies, presently responsible for the accelerated and almost unstoppable destruction of the environment, have been the main beneficiaries of the conquest and colonization, of slavery, of the ruthless exploitation and the extermination of hundreds of millions of people born in the countries that today constitute the Third World. They have also reaped the benefits of the economic order imposed on humanity after two atrocious and devastating wars for a new division of the world and its markets, of the privileges granted to the United States and its allies in Bretton-Woods, and of the IMF and the international financial institutions exclusively created by them and for them.

That rich and squandering world is in possession of the technical and financial resources necessary to pay what is due to mankind. The hegemonic superpower should also pay back its special debt to African-Americans, to Native-Americans living in reservations, and to the tens of millions of Latin American and Caribbean immigrants as well as others from poor nations, be they mulatto, yellow or black, but victims all of vicious discrimination and scorn.

It is high time to put an end to the dramatic situation of the indigenous communities in our hemisphere. Their own awakening and struggles, and the universal admission of the monstrosity of the crime committed against them make it imperative.

There are enough funds to save the world from the tragedy.

May the arms race and the weapon commerce that only bring devastation and death truly end.

Let it be used for development a good part of the one trillion US dollars annually spent on the commercial advertising that creates false illusions and inaccessible consumer habits while releasing the venom that destroys the national cultures and identities.

May the modest 0.7 percentage point of the Gross National Product promised as official development assistance be finally delivered.

May the tax suggested by Nobel Prize Laureate James Tobin be imposed in a reasonable and effective way on the current speculative operations accounting for trillions of US dollars every 24 hours, then the United Nations, which cannot go on depending on meager, inadequate, and belated donations and charities, will have one trillion US dollars annually to save and develop the world. Mark my words! One trillion US dollars every year! There are no few people in the world who can add, subtract, divide and multiply. This is not an overstatement! Given the seriousness and urgency of the existing problems, which have become a real hazard for the very survival of our specie on the planet, that is what would actually be needed before it is too late.

Put an end to the ongoing genocide against the Palestinian people that is taking place while the world stares in amazement. May the basic right to life of that people, children and youth, be protected. May their right to peace and independence be respected; then, there will be nothing to fear from UN documents.

I am aware that the need for some relief from the awful situation their countries are facing has led many friends from Africa and other regions to suggest the need for such prudence as would allow something to come out of this conference. I sympathize with them but I cannot renounce my convictions, as I feel that the more candid we are in telling the truth the more possibilities there will be to be heeded and respected. There have been enough centuries of deception.

I have only three other short questions based on realities that cannot be ignored.

The capitalist, developed and wealthy countries today participate of the imperialist system born of capitalism itself and the economic order imposed to the world based on the philosophy of selfishness and the brutal competition between men, nations and groups of nations which is completely indifferent to any feelings of solidarity and honest international cooperation. They live under the misleading, irresponsible and hallucinating atmosphere of consumer societies. Thus, regardless the sincerity of their blind faith in such a system and the convictions of their most serious statesmen, I wonder: Will they be able to understand the grave problems of today's world which in its incoherent and uneven development is ruled by blind laws, by the huge power and the interests of the ever growing and increasingly uncontrollable and independent transnational corporations?

Will they come to understand the impending universal chaos and rebellion? And, even if they wanted to, could they put an end to racism, racial discrimination, xenophobia and other related issues, which are precisely the rest of them all?

From my viewpoint we are on the verge of a huge economic, social and political global crisis. Let's try to build an awareness about these realities and the alternatives will come up. History has shown that it is only from deep crisis that great solutions have emerged. The peoples' right to life and justice will definitely impose itself under a thousand different shapes.

I believe in the mobilization and the struggle of the peoples! I believe in the idea of justice! I believe in truth! I believe in man!

Thank you.

The above speech was taken from http://afrocubaweb.com/wcr. htm.

Attempts at Preservation of Cultural Heritage: The Case of Hawaii

When individuals and governmental bodies move to redress past discrimination, some whites institute legal challenges to initiatives that are important to blacks and other people of color. An example can be found in *Rice v. Cayetano* decided by the Supreme Court in February, 2000. Hawaii enacted a law that only allowed Native-Hawaiians to vote for trustees of a benevolent organization that benefited Native-Hawaiians. This law was challenged by whites.

RICE *v.* CAYETANO, GOVERNOR OF HAWAII
Supreme Court of the United States
528 U.S. 495 (2000)

The Hawaiian Constitution limits the right to vote for nine trustees chosen in a statewide election. The trustees compose the governing authority of a state agency known as the Office of Hawaiian Affairs, or OHA. The agency administers programs designed for the benefit of two subclasses of Hawaiian citizenry, "Hawaiians" and "native Hawaiians." State law defines "native Hawaiians" as descendants of not less than one-half part of the races inhabiting the Islands before 1778, and "Hawaiians"- a larger class that includes "native Hawaiians"- as descendants of the peoples inhabiting the Hawaiian Islands in 1778. The trustees are chosen in a statewide election in which only "Hawaiians" may vote. Petitioner Rice, a Hawaiian citizen without the requisite ancestry to be a "Hawaiian"under state law, applied to vote in OHA trustee elections. When his application was denied, he sued respondent Governor (hereinafter State), claiming, *inter alia,* that the voting exclusion was invalid under the Fourteenth and Fifteenth Amendments. The Federal District Court granted the State summary judgment. Surveying the history of the Islands and their people, it determined that Congress and Hawaii have recognized a guardian-ward relationship with the native Hawaiians, which is analogous to the relationship between the United States and Indian tribes. It examined the voting qualifications with the latitude applied to legislation passed pursuant to Congress' power over Indian affairs, see *Morton* v. *Mancari,* 417 U.S. 535, and found that the electoral scheme was rationally related to the State's responsibility under its Admission Act to utilize a part of the proceeds from certain public lands for the native Hawaiians' benefit. The Ninth Circuit affirmed, finding that Hawaii "may rationally conclude that Hawaiians, being the group to whom trust obligations run and to whom OHA trustees owe a duty of loyalty, should be the group to decide who the trustees ought to be."146 F.3d 1075, 1079.

Held: Hawaii's denial of Rice's right to vote in OHA trustee elections violates the Fifteenth Amendment. Pp. 15-28.

(a) The Amendment's purpose and command are set forth in explicit and comprehensive language. The National Government and the States may not deny or abridge the right to vote on account of race. The Amendment reaffirms the equality of races at the most basic level of the democratic process, the exercise of the voting franchise. It protects all persons, not just members of a particular race. Important precedents give instruction in the instant case. The Amendment was quite sufficient to invalidate a grandfather clause that did not mention race but instead used ancestry in an attempt to confine and restrict the voting franchise, *Guinn* v. *United States,* 238 U.S. 347, 364-365; and it sufficed to strike down the white primary systems designed to exclude one racial class (at least) from voting, see, *e.g., Terry* v. *Adams,* 345 U.S. 461, 469-470. The voting structure in this case is neither subtle nor indirect; it specifically grants the vote to persons of the defined ancestry and to no others. Ancestry can be a proxy for race. It is that proxy here. For centuries Hawaii was isolated from migration. The inhabitants shared common physical characteristics, and by 1778 they had a common culture. The provisions at issue reflect the State's effort to preserve that commonality to the present day. In interpreting the Reconstruction Era civil rights laws this Court has observed that racial discrimination is that which singles out "identifiable classes of persons... solely because of their ancestry or ethnic characteristics." *Saint Francis College* v. *Al&nbhyph; Khazraji,*

481 U.S. 604, 613. The very object of the statutory definition here is
to treat the early Hawaiians as a distinct people, commanding their
own recognition and respect. The history of the State's definition
also demonstrates that the State has used ancestry as a racial
definition and for a racial purpose. The drafters of the definitions
of "Hawaiian" and "native Hawaiian" emphasized the explicit
tie to race. The State's additional argument that the restriction
is race neutral because it differentiates even among Polynesian
people based on the date of an ancestor's residence in Hawaii is
undermined by the classification's express racial purpose and its
actual effects. The ancestral inquiry in this case implicates the same
grave concerns as a classification specifying a particular race by
name, for it demeans a person's dignity and worth to be judged by
ancestry instead of by his or her own merit and essential qualities...
The law itself may not become the instrument for generating the
prejudice and hostility all too often directed against persons whose
particular ancestry is disclosed by their ethnic characteristics and
cultural traditions. The State's electoral restriction enacts a race-
based voting qualification. Pp. 15-21.

(b) The State's three principal defenses of its voting law
are rejected. It argues first that the exclusion of non-Hawaiians
from voting is permitted under this Court's cases allowing the
differential treatment of Indian tribes. However, even if Congress
had the authority, delegated to the State, to treat Hawaiians or native
Hawaiians as tribes, Congress may not authorize a State to create a
voting scheme of the sort created here. Congress may not authorize
a State to establish a voting scheme that limits the electorate for
its public officials to a class of tribal Indians to the exclusion of all
non-Indian citizens. The elections for OHA trustee are elections of
the State, not of a separate quasi-sovereign, and they are elections
to which the Fifteenth Amendment applies. *Morton* v. *Mancari,*
417 U.S. 535, distinguished. The State's further contention that
the limited voting franchise is sustainable under this Court's cases
holding that the one-person, one-vote rule does not pertain to
certain special purpose districts such as water or irrigation districts
also fails, for compliance with the one-person, one-vote rule of

the Fourteenth Amendment does not excuse compliance with the Fifteenth Amendment. Hawaii's final argument that the voting restriction does no more than ensure an alignment of interests between the fiduciaries and the beneficiaries of a trust founders on its own terms, for it is not clear that the voting classification is symmetric with the beneficiaries of the programs OHA administers. While the bulk of the funds appears to be earmarked for the benefit of "native Hawaiians," the State permits both "native Hawaiians" and "Hawaiians" to vote for trustees. The argument fails on more essential grounds; it rests on the demeaning premise that citizens of a particular race are somehow more qualified than others to vote on certain matters. There is no room under the Amendment for the concept that the right to vote in a particular election can be allocated based on race. Pp. 21-27.

Kennedy, J., delivered the opinion of the Court, in which Rehnquist, C. J., and O'Connor, Scalia, and Thomas, JJ., joined. Breyer, J., filed an opinion concurring in the result, in which Souter, J., joined. Stevens, J., filed a dissenting opinion, in which Ginsburg, J., joined as to Part II. Ginsburg, J., filed a dissenting opinion.

Brazil: Is There a Need for Affirmative Action?

More slaves were brought to Brazil than to any other western country and it was not eliminated until 1888. After the end of slavery, conditions did not improve much for Africans under Portugeuse colonialism. With the end of colonialism in 1822, Africans were prohibited from attending schools and generally discriminated against in all aspects of public life.[1]

Consequently, today more Afro-Brazilians exist in the western hemisphere than in the United States. Yet, due to racism many of these former slaves are found at the bottom of the socio-economic strata. The proposed Racial Equality Act would begin to change this state of affairs by developing a comprehensive affirmative action program for the nation of 170 million. If the act is passed, it would

---

1   Larry Rohter, "Multiracial Brazil Planning Quotas for Blacks" The New York Times, October 2, 2001..

set quotas for hiring throughout the economy and government such as 25% in theatre arts, 40% in television commercials, 20% in university admissions and 20% in civil service jobs.

Racism in France and Europe?

Throughout Europe where a substantial percentage of the population is composed of people of African descent, racism has become increasing evident in public life. In 1996 a report to the UN Human Rights Commission concluded that racist incidents increased after France passed anti-immigration laws in 1993. The report examined attacks on immigrants particularly from former North African colonies. Of France's population of 58 million, approximately 5 million are immigrants.[2]

Nine years after the passage of France's anti-immigration statute, racism was directly confronted by Christiane Taubira, an economist from French Guiana who ran unsuccessfully for the presidency of France. She was elected to the French Parliament as a representative from French Guiana in 1993, the same year that the anti-immigration statute was passed. Though unsuccessful in her bid for the presidency, she brought to the attention of the public the blatant and rampant discrimination that Africans, women, gays and other immigrants of color experienced in France.

Furthermore, in 2001, Ms. Taubira successfully authored a bill that designated the slave trade and slavery of any form as crimes against humanity. (See Marlise Simons, "Pushing Equality from Outside the Fraternity" *The New York Times,* April 18, 2002.) She spoke for all people who believed that Europe in general had taken a hands-off approach to immigrants of color who have been housed in urban ghettoes. She spoke out on behalf of these forgotten people: "We have to stop declaring war on the poor young people." (See Marlise).

---

2   "UN Report Blasts Racism in France," The Boston Globe, April 12, 1996.

Black Aboriginals in Australia

In 1967 a referendum was passed in Australia codifying the rights of Aboriginals who constituted 300,000 of the 19 million population. (See James Regan, "Aboriginals boo Australia's Premier" *The Boston Globe*, May 28, 2000). There has been a movement on the island to have the Australian government apologize for how it has treated the Aboriginals in the past, particularly the forceful removal of 100,000 children from their homes between 1910 and 1970. Furthermore, the Aboriginals have been discriminated against and as a result of hopelessness, many have become alcoholics. It would appear that not only would a public apology be in order, but that some form of reparations should be instituted for the centuries of neglect and out right denial of human rights.

Affirmative Action, AIDS and South Africa

When Nelson Mandela emerged from prison in 1990 after over 26 years behind bars because he fought for South Africa's freedom, black South Africans believed that prosperity would finally come to them. Such was not the case. Although the African majority experienced political independence, they did not escape the wrenching poverty of their existence and the West continued to reap the financial benefits of centuries of economic exploitation.

One approach that has been debated and adopted to some degree in South Africa is a policy of affirmative action that would give preferences to the 88% majority. The new policies would require all companies doing business with the government to establish hiring targets. The purpose of these laws has been to reach the 70 percent of the South African population who live below the poverty line and the 50 percent who are illiterate. (See Suzanne Daley, "Reversing Roles in a South African Dilemma" *The New York Times*, October 26, 1997).

Another struggle initiated by the government is an effort to get drug companies doing business in South Africa to allow the government to purchase cheaper anti-AIDS drugs on the world market. When the government went abroad to find cheaper generic drugs, 39 pharmaceutical companies sued the government in 1998, seeking to block the cheaper sales. On April 20, 2001 the companies ended their lawsuits after mounting pressure from the international community, in particular, the European Union and the World Health Organization. For example, the United Nations estimated that 25.3 million people in sub-Saharan Africa had contracted AIDS or HIV. (See Rachel L. Swarno, "Drug Makers Drop South African Suit over AIDS Medicine,"*The New York Times*, April 20, 2001).

Africa and China

The late esteemed Sociologist W.E.B. Du Bois wrote in 1962 that Africa must establish a closer economic relationship with China. Certainly he would have been pleased to witness the $1.9 billion trade deal between Africa and China signed on November 5, 2006. Forty heads of African states met in Beijing for a summit on building economic relationships with Africa. Delegates (1700) came from forty-eight countries. China promised that it would double its investments in Africa and make $5 billion available in loans and credits. (See Tim Johnson, "China, African nations sign $1.96 billion in new trade deals,"*The Boston Globe*, November 6, 2006). China agreed to increase its deployment of advisors to the continent and stated that its initiative in Africa was its most significant diplomatic initiative with any region since its independence in 1949.

Chapter Eleven

INTERNATIONAL TERRORISM AND CIVIL LIBERTIES

Many Americans believe that George Bush has engaged in a war against terrorism at the expense of Americans' civil liberties. In addition, many argue that America's status in the world has been adversely affected by international policies that involve torture and possible crimes against humanity, particularly in the treatment of detainees in Guantanomo Bay, Cuba. The administration has justified its actions under the rubric of fighting international terrorism.

What is International Terrorism?

United States Code, 18 U.S.C. 2332b(a)(2000) defines terrorism as the killing or injury to people in the United States involving special circumstances and "involving conduct transcending national boundaries."

In the September 11th assault special circumstances were met for the following reasons:

1. Commercial airlines were used, each, thus constituting a "...facility of interstate commerce...";
2. The attack "...obstructed, affected, or delayed interstate or foreign commerce...";
3. Victims included United States Government officials;
4. Pentagon was damaged.

The last factor "...conduct transcending national boundaries..." which is defined as "...conduct occurring outside of the United States in addition to the conduct occurring in the United States..." has been satisfied due to foreign al-Qaeda involvement.[1] At least, this is the contention of the United States Government. It is hoped that actual proof of this connection will be provided to the American public in detail at some point in the future. Following the attack, George Bush quickly obtained authorization from Congress to wage the war against terrorism.[2]

Later it became clear that the administration did not provide truthful information on the key issue of whether Iraq possessed weapons of mass destruction (WMD), as alleged by the Bush Administration. Once it was clear that no WMD's existed, many members of Congress felt that they had been purposefully misled by the administration. Some even suggested that George Bush be impeached because of his lying to Congress and the American people.

While there have been several terrorist attacks upon United States interests abroad, September 11th was the first major attack against the country since Pearl Harbor. Given that the attack occurred at both the centers of capitalist activity (Wall Street) and of military operations (The Pentagon), the United States believed it had to respond forcefully. In addition and most importantly, thousands of "innocent" Americans and foreigners died. As a result, the American people demanded a military response.

Prior Acts of Terrorism

The United States Government certainly had prior evidence of hostile intentions toward its foreign establishments and personnel. On December 21, 1988, 259 people, including 188 Americans were killed in Pan-American Flight 103 over Lockerbie, Scotland.

1　Note: Responding to Terrorism: Crime, Punishment, and War, 115 Harvard L Rev. 1217, N. 60.

2　Authorization for Use of Military Force, Pub. L. No. 107-40, 115 Stat. 224 (2001).

One Libyan man was convicted and another acquitted in a Scottish court established in The Netherlands.[3]

On February 26, 1993, a car bomb went off in the basement of the World Trade Center, killing six people and injuring many others. Islamic fundamentalists were arrested and convicted for the bombing. The rationale for the attacks, which became clear in the legal proceedings revolved around United States support for Israel and its refusal to recognize the right of the Palestinian people to exist as a sovereign.[4] Other Islamic leaders, not directly implicated in the bombing, such as Egyptian cleric Sheik Omar Abdel Rahman, were convicted of conspiracy and sentenced to long prison terms.[5]

The last terrorist attack before September 11th occurred on August 7, 1998 in Nairobi, Kenya and Dar es Salaam, Tanzania when twelve Americans and over two hundred Africans were killed as a result of explosions at the American embassies. While it did not have proof, the United States Government believed that the African strikes were engineered by Osama Bin Laden. President Clinton, therefore, ordered two military strikes, one in Afghanistan (training camp) and the other in Sudan (chemical plant). Both of the strikes were ineffective and there was mounting evidence that the target in the Sudan had no terrorist connections at all. Four individuals, however, believed responsible for the bombings were arrested due to international cooperation and subsequently convicted.[6]

---

3   Her Majesty's Advocate v. Al Megrahi, Case No. 1475/99, at 79, 82 (H.C.J. 2001) (Scot) at http://www.scotscourts.gov.uk/download/lockerbiejudgement. pdf.

4   United States v. Salameh, 152 F. 3d 88, 108 (2d Cir. 1998) and Note: Responding to Terrorism: Crime, Punishment, and War, 115 Harv. L. Rev. 1217 (Feb. 2002).

5   United States v. Rahman, 189 F. 3d 88, 103-11 (2d Cir. 1999).

6   United States v. Bin Laden, 92 F. Supp. 2d 225 (S.D.N.Y. 2000); United States v. Bin Laden, 156 F. Supp. 2d 359 (S.D.N.Y. 2000).

One can conclude from a review of these earlier terrorist attacks that all were orchestrated by Islamic fundamentalists who objected to United States policies toward the Middle East, particularly towards Israel. Two key issues formed the basis for their assaults against the United States: United States military presence in Saudi Arabia (the birthplace of Muhammed) and the Palestinian condition (land occupation). When the Bush administration came into power shouldn't these issues have been at the top of his agenda? Shouldn't he have used the prestige and resources of the United States to attack and resolve the Palestinian question through diplomatic channels? Instead of being a leader, Bush boycotted the September 1, 2001 Durban conference and assumed an isolationist posture concerning many pressing international issues, such as global warming and pollution, forgiveness of debt and reparations. Instead he pursued a military strategy that has cost American taxpayers billions of dollars, four thousand young American lives, hundreds of thousands of Iraqi lives and plummeted the nation's reputation abroad.

It is ironic that in George Bush's misguided policies, an assault upon terrorism had to be made at the expenses of Americans' civil liberties. It was in the so-called Patriot Act that the administration orchestrated a sweeping review of all federal laws for the purpose of strengthening American domestic security.

The United States Legal Response to September 11

Civil Liberties Assaulted
The Bush Administration has authorized secret monitoring of conversations between lawyers and individuals held on suspicion of being terrorists. Senate Judiciary Committee chairman Patrick Leahy of Vermont warned that this is an attempt by the executive branch to exercise extraordinary powers without judicial scrutiny or legislative authorization. Senator Leahy has stated the following about the governmental assaults upon civil liberties: "I want to see us protected from terrorism. But I want it done in a way that does

not diminish the basic protections of the Constitution."[7] Senator Edward Kennedy has lashed out at Bush's attempt to deprive defendants of the right to confidential conversation with their attorneys as well. Should government be allowed to circumvent an important right such as this?

Another civil liberties issue that is causing great concern is the government's increased monitoring of American citizens. Are activities such as the government surfing the web or attending public meetings to spy on Americans violations of the 4th Amendment? Professor David Cole at Georgetown University believes the government actions may infringe First Amendment rights. "There is a real cost to the openness of a free political society if every discussion group needs to be concerned that the F.B.I. is listening in on its public discussions or attending its public meetings."[8] Nevertheless, since F.B.I. authorization extends to churches and mosques, it is likely that the government will be intimately involved in what has been considered outside of governmental interference, i.e. religious activities and freedoms. Has the government gone too far in spying on Americans during their worship services?

USA Patriots Act (Uniting and Strengthening America by Providing Appropriate Tools Required to Intercept and Obstruct Terrorism). George Bush signed the USA Patriots Act on October 26, 2001. (Act of 2001, Pub. L. No. 107-56, 115 Stat. 272 (Oct. 26, 2001). The document is 342 pages long and amends fifteen (15) statutes. This statute has been used extensively by the Bush Administration to curtail civil liberties.

<u>Secret Detentions in the United States</u>

More than 800 people have been detained in the United States since September 11, 2002 without being charged. In many cases these are illegal aliens who have been sent to maximum security

---

7   Robin Toner, Ashcroft and Leahy Battling Over Greater Police Powers, The New York Times, December 2, 2001.

8   Adam Liptak, Changing the Standard, The New York Times, May 31, 2002.

prisons where they wait for a hearing before an Immigration Naturalization Service judge. Some are being held indefinitely as a "material witness." On April 30, 2002, Federal District Judge Shira A. Scheindlin dismissed charges against a Jordanian student studying in San Diego, Osama Awadallah who was held as a material witness in the government's terror investigation. He was detained on September 21, 2001 and held in solitary confinement without charges. The judge wrote in her opinion: "Relying on the material witness statute to detain people who are presumed innocent under our Constitution in order to prevent potential crimes is an illegitimate use of the statute."[9]

This decision was one of the first blows to the Bush administration's sweeping edicts that compromised Constitutional rights. The ultimate test of these type of public policies during the war on terrorism will have to be decided by the Supreme Court of the United States. Given its poor record on civil liberties issues and its conservative ideological bent, there is little reason to be optimistic. However, in June, 2001, the Court in a 5-4 decision did rule that the government cannot detain indefinitely illegal immigrants it considers dangerous. (*Zadvydas v. Davis*).

Should the government be allowed to use racial profiling in its terrorist investigations? Is it just to hold foreigners without charges indefinitely?

Secret Detentions in Guantanamo

At the heart of the Bush Administration's scheme to fight terrorism was its plan to try foreign detainees in military tribunals in Guantanamo, Cuba. Some legislators questioned whether the president had the authority to set up such tribunals in the absence of Congressional authorization. Some 300 law professors questioned whether the tribunals violated the separation of powers doctrine and whether the detainees would receive due process of law. The essential question was whether the detainees should be tried in civilian courts?

9   Benjamin Weiser, Judge Rules Against U.S. on Material-Witness Law, The New York Times, May 1, 2002.

Recently, families of Kuwaitis held in Guantanamo Bay filed suit in United States District Court in Washington, D.C. They wanted to visit their loved ones, have them seen by attorneys and ultimately have the legality of their detentions determined by a court of law.

The suit has been paid for by the Kuwaiti government and handled by the firm of Shearman & Sterling. The plaintiffs argued that the base at Guantanamo Bay was a United States territory since it has been under United States control since 1903 and that therefore, the detainees are entitled to the protections of United States and international law.[10] Some of the relatives of the detainees believed that racial profiling played a role in the detention. In an interview with an American newspaper, one relative said: "If you are an Arab you are accused- not just accused, guilty."[11]

Race and Terrorism: Unequal Prosecutions

With many people of color being held in detention or undergoing prosecution, race and ethnicity have become a question of academic and legal discourse. Furthermore, race has become an issue particularly among Arab-Americans who have found themselves subjected to extensive public scrutiny and discrimination. This hostility against Muslims will have a direct impact upon African-Americans, who make up 25 to 40 percent of Muslims in the United States.[12] Some observers have suggested that African-American Muslims will now be subjected to two forms of profiling: racial and religious.

In addition, with three Americans being implicated in allegations of support for Al-Qaeda, John Walker Lindh (white), Jose Padilla (Latino) and Yasser Esam Hamdi (Saudi-American), will the government apply similar standards of prosecution toward each man?

---

10 Neil MacFarquhar, Kuwaitis Press U.S. Over 12 Held at Guantanamo, The New York Times, June 26, 2002.

11 Ibid.

12 John E. Fountain, Sadness and Fear as a Group Feels Doubly at Risk, The New York Times, October 6, 2001.

Yasser Esam Hamdi

YASER ESAM HAMDI and ESAM FOUAD HAMDI, as next friend of YASER ESAM HAMDI, PETITIONERS v. DONALD H. RUMSFELD, SECRETARY OF DEFENSE, et al.
Supreme Court of the United States
542 U.S. 507 (2007)

Justice O'Connor announced the judgment of the Court and delivered an opinion, in which The Chief Justice, Justice Kennedy, and Justice Breyer join.

At this difficult time in our Nation's history, we are called upon to consider the legality of the Government's detention of a United States citizen on United States soil as an "enemy combatant" and to address the process that is constitutionally owed to one who seeks to challenge his classification as such. The United States Court of Appeals for the Fourth Circuit held that petitioner's detention was legally authorized and that he was entitled to no further opportunity to challenge his enemy-combatant label. We now vacate and remand. We hold that although Congress authorized the detention of combatants in the narrow circumstances alleged here, due process demands that a citizen held in the United States as an enemy combatant be given a meaningful opportunity to contest the factual basis for that detention before a neutral decisionmaker.

I.

On September 11, 2001, the al Qaeda terrorist network used hijacked commercial airliners to attack prominent targets in the United States. Approximately 3,000 people were killed in those attacks. One week later, in response to these "acts of treacherous violence," Congress passed a resolution authorizing the President to "use all necessary and appropriate force against those nations, organizations, or persons he determines planned, authorized, committed, or aided the terrorist attacks" or "harbored such organizations or persons, in order to prevent any future acts of international terrorism against the United States by such nations, organizations or persons." Authorization for Use of Military Force ("the AUMF"), 115 Stat. 224. Soon thereafter, the President ordered United States Armed Forces to Afghanistan, with a mission to subdue al Qaeda and quell the Taliban regime that was known to support it.

This case arises out of the detention of a man whom the Government alleges took up arms with the Taliban during this conflict. His name is Yaser Esam Hamdi. Born an American citizen in Louisiana in 1980, Hamdi moved with his family to Saudi Arabia as a child. By 2001, the parties agree, he resided in Afghanistan. At some point that year, he was seized by members of the Northern Alliance, a coalition of military groups opposed to the Taliban government, and eventually was turned over to the United States military. The Government asserts that it initially detained and interrogated Hamdi in Afghanistan before transferring him to the United States Naval Base in Guantanamo Bay in January 2002. In April 2002, upon learning that Hamdi is an American citizen, authorities transferred him to a naval brig in Norfolk, Virginia, where he remained until a recent transfer to a brig in Charleston, South Carolina. The Government contends that Hamdi is an "enemy combatant," and that this status justifies holding him in the United States indefinitely-without formal charges or proceedings-unless and until it makes the determination that access to counsel or further process is warranted.

In June 2002, Hamdi's father, Esam Fouad Hamdi, filed the present petition for a writ of habeas corpus under 28 U.S.C. § 2241 in the Eastern District of Virginia, naming as petitioners his son and himself as next friend. The elder Hamdi alleges in the petition that he has had no contact with his son since the Government took custody of him in 2001, and that the Government has held his son "without access to legal counsel or notice of any charges pending against him." (Citation omitted). The petition contends that Hamdi's detention was not legally authorized. (Citation omitted). It argues that, "[a]s an American citizen,... Hamdi enjoys the full protections of the Constitution," and that Hamdi's detention in the United States without charges, access to an impartial tribunal, or assistance of counsel "violated and continue[s] to violate the Fifth and Fourteenth Amendments to the United States Constitution." (Citation omitted). The habeas petition asks that the court, among other things, (1) appoint counsel for Hamdi; (2) order respondents to cease interrogating him; (3) declare that he is being held in violation of the Fifth and Fourteenth Amendments; (4) "[t]o the extent Respondents contest any material factual allegations in this Petition, schedule an evidentiary hearing, at which Petitioners may adduce proof in support of their allegations"; and (5) order that Hamdi be released from his "unlawful custody." (Citation omitted). Although his habeas petition provides no details with regard to the factual circumstances surrounding his son's capture and detention, Hamdi's father has asserted in documents found elsewhere in the record that his son went to Afghanistan to do "relief work," and that he had been in that country less than two months before September 11, 2001, and could not have received military training. (Citation omitted). The 20-year-old was traveling on his own for the first time, his father says, and "[b]ecause of his lack of experience, he was trapped in Afghanistan once that military campaign began." (Citation omitted).

The District Court found that Hamdi's father was a proper next friend, appointed the federal public defender as counsel for the petitioners, and ordered that counsel be given access to Hamdi. (Citation omitted). The United States Court of Appeals for the Fourth Circuit reversed that order, holding that the District Court had failed to extend appropriate deference to the Government's security and intelligence interests. (Citation omitted). It directed the District Court to consider "the most cautious procedures first," (Citation omitted), and to conduct a deferential inquiry into Hamdi's status, (Citation omitted). It opined that "if Hamdi is indeed an 'enemy combatant' who was captured during hostilities in Afghanistan, the government's present detention of him is a lawful one." (Citation omitted).

On remand, the Government filed a response and a motion to dismiss the petition. It attached to its response a declaration from one Michael Mobbs (hereinafter "Mobbs Declaration"), who identified himself as Special Advisor to the Under Secretary of

Defense for Policy. Mobbs indicated that in this position, he has been "substantially involved with matters related to the detention of enemy combatants in the current war against the al Qaeda terrorists and those who support and harbor them (including the Taliban)." (Citation omitted). He expressed his "familiar[ity]" with Department of Defense and United States military policies and procedures applicable to the detention, control, and transfer of al Qaeda and Taliban personnel, and declared that "[b]ased upon my review of relevant records and reports, I am also familiar with the facts and circumstances related to the capture of…Hamdi and his detention by U.S. military forces." (Citation omitted).

Mobbs then set forth what remains the sole evidentiary support that the Government has provided to the courts for Hamdi's detention. The declaration states that Hamdi "traveled to Afghanistan" in July or August 2001, and that he thereafter "affiliated with a Taliban military unit and received weapons training." (Citation omitted). It asserts that Hamdi "remained with his Taliban unit following the attacks of September 11"and that, during the time when Northern Alliance forces were "engaged in battle with the Taliban," "Hamdi's Taliban unit surrendered" to those forces, after which he "surrender[ed] his Kalishnikov assault rifle"to them. (Citation omitted). The Mobbs Declaration also states that, because al Qaeda and the Taliban "were and are hostile forces engaged in armed conflict with the armed forces of the United States," "individuals associated with" those groups "were and continue to be enemy combatants." (Citation omitted). Mobbs states that Hamdi was labeled an enemy combatant "[b]ased upon his interviews and in light of his association with the Taliban." (Citation omitted). According to the declaration, a series of "U.S. military screening team[s]" determined that Hamdi met "the criteria for enemy combatants," and "a subsequent interview of Hamdi has confirmed that he surrendered and gave his firearm to Northern Alliance forces, which supports his classification as an enemy combatant." (Citation omitted).

After the Government submitted this declaration, the Fourth Circuit directed the District Court to proceed in accordance with its earlier ruling and, specifically, to "'consider the sufficiency

of the Mobbs Declaration as an independent matter before
proceeding further.'" (Citation omitted). The District Court found
that the Mobbs Declaration fell "far short" of supporting Hamdi's
detention. (Citation omitted). It criticized the generic and hearsay
nature of the affidavit, calling it "little more than the government's
'say-so.' " (Citation omitted). It ordered the Government to turn
over numerous materials for *in camera* review, including copies
of all of Hamdi's statements and the notes taken from interviews
with him that related to his reasons for going to Afghanistan and
his activities therein; a list of all interrogators who had questioned
Hamdi and their names and addresses; statements by members of the
Northern Alliance regarding Hamdi's surrender and capture; a list
of the dates and locations of his capture and subsequent detentions;
and the names and titles of the United States Government officials
who made the determinations that Hamdi was an enemy combatant
and that he should be moved to a naval brig. (Citation omitted).
The court indicated that all of these materials were necessary for
"meaningful judicial review" of whether Hamdi's detention was
legally authorized and whether Hamdi had received sufficient
process to satisfy the Due Process Clause of the Constitution and
relevant treaties or military regulations. (Citation omitted).

The Government sought to appeal the production order, and
the District Court certified the question of whether the Mobbs
Declaration, "'standing alone, is sufficient as a matter of law to
allow meaningful judicial review of [Hamdi's] classification as
an enemy combatant.'" (Citation omitted). The Fourth Circuit
reversed, but did not squarely answer the certified question. It
instead stressed that, because it was "undisputed that Hamdi was
captured in a zone of active combat in a foreign theater of conflict,"
no factual inquiry or evidentiary hearing allowing Hamdi to be
heard or to rebut the Government's assertions was necessary or
proper. (Citation omitted). Concluding that the factual averments
in the Mobbs Declaration, "if accurate," provided a sufficient basis
upon which to conclude that the President had constitutionally
detained Hamdi pursuant to the President's war powers, it ordered
the habeas petition dismissed. (Citation omitted). The Fourth
Circuit emphasized that the "vital purposes"of the detention of

uncharged enemy combatants–preventing those combatants from rejoining the enemy while relieving the military of the burden of litigating the circumstances of wartime captures halfway around the globe–were interests "directly derived from the war powers of Articles I and II." (Citation omitted). In that court's view, because "Article III contains nothing analogous to the specific powers of war so carefully enumerated in Articles I and II," (Citation omitted), separation of powers principles prohibited a federal court from "delv[ing] further into Hamdi's status and capture," (Citation omitted). Accordingly, the District Court's more vigorous inquiry "went far beyond the acceptable scope of review." (Citation omitted).

On the more global question of whether legal authorization exists for the detention of citizen enemy combatants at all, the Fourth Circuit rejected Hamdi's arguments that 18 U.S.C. § 4001(a) and Article 5 of the Geneva Convention rendered any such detentions unlawful. The court expressed doubt as to Hamdi's argument that §4001(a), which provides that "[n]o citizen shall be imprisoned or otherwise detained by the United States except pursuant to an Act of Congress," required express congressional authorization of detentions of this sort. But it held that, in any event, such authorization was found in the post-September 11 Authorization for Use of Military Force. (Citation omitted). Because "capturing and detaining enemy combatants is an inherent part of warfare," the court held, "the 'necessary and appropriate force' referenced in the congressional resolution necessarily includes the capture and detention of any and all hostile forces arrayed against our troops." (Citation omitted)…

The Fourth Circuit denied rehearing en banc, 337 F.3d 335 (2003), and we granted certiorari. (Citation omitted). We now vacate the judgment below and remand.

II.

The threshold question before us is whether the Executive has the authority to detain citizens who qualify as "enemy combatants." There is some debate as to the proper scope of this term, and the

Government has never provided any court with the full criteria that it uses in classifying individuals as such. It has made clear, however, that, for purposes of this case, the "enemy combatant" that it is seeking to detain is an individual who, it alleges, was "'part of or supporting forces hostile to the United States or coalition partners' "in Afghanistan and who "'engaged in an armed conflict against the United States' "there. (Citation omitted). We therefore answer only the narrow question before us: whether the detention of citizens falling within that definition is authorized.

The Government maintains that no explicit congressional authorization is required, because the Executive possesses plenary authority to detain pursuant to Article II of the Constitution. We do not reach the question whether Article II provides such authority, however, because we agree with the Government's alternative position, that Congress has in fact authorized Hamdi's detention, through the AUMF.

Our analysis on that point, set forth below, substantially overlaps with our analysis of Hamdi's principal argument for the illegality of his detention. He posits that his detention is forbidden by 18 U.S.C. §4001(a). Section 4001(a) states that "[n]o citizen shall be imprisoned or otherwise detained by the United States except pursuant to an Act of Congress." Congress passed §4001(a) in 1971 as part of a bill to repeal the Emergency Detention Act of 1950, 50 U.S.C. §811 *et seq.*, which provided procedures for executive detention, during times of emergency, of individuals deemed likely to engage in espionage or sabotage. Congress was particularly concerned about the possibility that the Act could be used to reprise the Japanese internment camps of World War II. H. R. Rep. No. 92-116 (1971); *id.*, at 4 ("The concentration camp implications of the legislation render it abhorrent"). The Government again presses two alternative positions. First, it argues that §4001(a), in light of its legislative history and its location in Title 18, applies only to "the control of civilian prisons and related detentions," not to military detentions. (Citation omitted). Second, it maintains that §4001(a) is satisfied, because Hamdi is being detained "pursuant to an Act of Congress" – the AUMF. (Citation omitted). Again, because we conclude that the Government's second assertion is correct, we do not address the first. In other words, for the reasons that follow, we conclude that the AUMF is explicit congressional authorization for the detention of individuals in the narrow category we describe (assuming, without deciding, that such authorization is required), and that the AUMF satisfied §4001(a)'s requirement that a detention be "pursuant to an Act of Congress" (assuming, without deciding, that §4001(a) applies to military detentions).

The AUMF authorizes the President to use "all necessary and appropriate force" against "nations, organizations, or persons" associated with the September 11, 2001, terrorist attacks. (Citation omitted). There can be no doubt that individuals who fought against the United States in Afghanistan as part of the Taliban, an organization known to have supported the al Qaeda terrorist network responsible for those attacks, are individuals Congress sought to target in passing the AUMF. We conclude that detention of individuals falling into the limited category we are considering, for the duration of the particular conflict in which they were captured, is so fundamental and accepted an incident to war as to be an exercise of the "necessary and appropriate force" Congress has authorized the President to use.

The capture and detention of lawful combatants and the capture, detention, and trial of unlawful combatants, by "universal agreement and practice," are "important incident[s] of war." *Ex parte Quirin,* 317 U.S., at 28. The purpose of detention is to prevent captured individuals from returning to the field of battle and taking up arms once again. Naqvi, Doubtful Prisoner-of-War Status, 84 Int'l Rev. Red Cross 571, 572 (2002) ("[C]aptivity in war is 'neither revenge, nor punishment, but solely protective custody, the only purpose of which is to prevent the prisoners of war from further participation in the war'" (quoting decision of Nuremberg Military Tribunal, reprinted in 41 Am. J. Int'l L. 172, 229 (1947)); W. Winthrop, Military Law and Precedents 788 (rev. 2d ed. 1920) ("The time has long passed when 'no quarter' was the rule on the battlefield... It is now recognized that 'Captivity is neither a punishment nor an act of vengeance,' but 'merely a temporary detention which is devoid of all penal character.' ... 'A prisoner of war is no convict; his imprisonment is a simple war measure.' " (Citations omitted); cf. *In re Territo*, 156 F.2d 142, 145 (CA9 1946) ("The object of capture is to prevent the captured individual from serving the enemy. He is disarmed and from then on must be removed as completely as practicable from the front, treated humanely, and in time exchanged, repatriated, or otherwise released" (Footnotes omitted)).

There is no bar to this Nation's holding one of its own citizens as an enemy combatant. In *Quirin*, one of the detainees, Haupt, alleged that he was a naturalized United States citizen. 317 U.S., at 20. We held that "[c]itizens who associate themselves with the military arm of the enemy government, and with its aid, guidance and direction enter this country bent on hostile acts, are enemy belligerents within the meaning of... the law of war." (Citation omitted). While Haupt was tried for violations of the law of war, nothing in *Quirin* suggests that his citizenship would have precluded his mere detention for the duration of the relevant hostilities. (Citation omitted), Instructions for the Government of Armies of the United States in the Field, Gen. Order No. 100 (1863), reprinted in 2 Lieber, Miscellaneous Writings, p. 273 (contemplating, in code binding the Union Army during the Civil War, that "captured rebels" would be treated "as prisoners of war"). Nor can we see any reason for drawing such a line here. A citizen, no less than an alien, can be "part of or supporting forces hostile to the United States or coalition partners" and "engaged in an armed conflict against the United States," (Citation omitted); such a citizen, if released, would pose the same threat of returning to the front during the ongoing conflict.

In light of these principles, it is of no moment that the AUMF does not use specific language of detention. Because detention to prevent a combatant's return to the battlefield is a fundamental incident of waging war, in permitting the use of "necessary and appropriate force," Congress has clearly and unmistakably authorized detention in the narrow circumstances considered here.

Hamdi objects, nevertheless, that Congress has not authorized the *indefinite* detention to which he is now subject. The Government responds that "the detention of enemy combatants during World War

II was just as 'indefinite' while that war was being fought." (Citation omitted). We take Hamdi's objection to be not to the lack of certainty regarding the date on which the conflict will end, but to the substantial prospect of perpetual detention. We recognize that the national security underpinnings of the "war on terror," although crucially important, are broad and malleable. As the Government concedes, "given its unconventional nature, the current conflict is unlikely to end with a formal cease-fire agreement." (Citation omitted). The prospect Hamdi raises is therefore not far-fetched. If the Government does not consider this unconventional war won for two generations, and if it maintains during that time that Hamdi might, if released, rejoin forces fighting against the United States, then the position it has taken throughout the litigation of this case suggests that Hamdi's detention could last for the rest of his life.

It is a clearly established principle of the law of war that detention may last no longer than active hostilities. See Article 118 of the Geneva Convention (III) Relative to the Treatment of Prisoners of War, Aug. 12, 1949, [1955] 6 U.S. T. 3316, 3406, T. I. A. S. No. 3364 ("Prisoners of war shall be released and repatriated without delay after the cessation of active hostilities"). See also Article 20 of the Hague Convention (II) on Laws and Customs of War on Land, July 29, 1899, 32 Stat. 1817 (as soon as possible after "conclusion of peace"); Hague Convention (IV), *supra*, Oct. 18, 1907, 36 Stat. 2301 ("conclusion of peace" (Art. 20)); Geneva Convention, *supra*, July 27, 1929, 47 Stat. 2055 (repatriation should be accomplished with the least possible delay after conclusion of peace (Art. 75)); Praust, Judicial Power to Determine the Status and Rights of Persons Detained without Trial, 44 Harv. Int'l L. J. 503, 510-511 (2003) (prisoners of war "can be detained during an armed conflict, but the detaining country must release and repatriate them 'without delay after the cessation of active hostilities,' unless they are being lawfully prosecuted or have been lawfully convicted of crimes and are serving sentences" (citing Arts. 118, 85, 99, 119, 129, Geneva Convention (III), 6 T. I .A. S., at 3384, 3392, 3406, 3418)).

Hamdi contends that the AUMF does not authorize indefinite or perpetual detention. Certainly, we agree that indefinite detention for the purpose of interrogation is not authorized. Further, we understand Congress' grant of authority for the use of "necessary and appropriate force" to include the authority to detain for the duration of the relevant conflict, and our understanding is based on longstanding law-of-war principles. If the practical circumstances of a given conflict are entirely unlike those of the conflicts that informed the development of the law of war, that understanding may unravel. But that is not the situation we face as of this date. Active combat operations against Taliban fighters apparently are ongoing in Afghanistan. See, *e.g.,* Constable, U.S. Launches New Operation in Afghanistan, Washington Post, Mar. 14, 2004, p. A22 (reporting that 13,500 United States troops remain in Afghanistan, including several thousand new arrivals); J. Abizaid, Dept. of Defense, Gen. Abizaid Central Command Operations Update Briefing, Apr. 30, 2004, http://www.defenselink.mil/transcripts/2004/tr20040430-1402.html (as visited June 8, 2004, and available in the Clerk of Court's case file) (media briefing describing ongoing operations in Afghanistan involving 20,000 United States troops). The United States may detain, for the duration of these hostilities, individuals legitimately determined to be Taliban combatants who "engaged in an armed conflict against the United States." If the record establishes that United States troops are still involved in active combat in Afghanistan, those detentions are part of the exercise of "necessary and appropriate force," and therefore are authorized by the AUMF...

III.

Even in cases in which the detention of enemy combatants is legally authorized, there remains the question of what process is constitutionally due to a citizen who disputes his enemy-combatant status. Hamdi argues that he is owed a meaningful and timely hearing and that "extra-judicial detention [that] begins and ends with the submission of an affidavit based on third-hand hearsay" does not comport with the Fifth and Fourteenth Amendments. (Citation omitted). The Government counters that any more process than was provided below would be both unworkable and "constitutionally intolerable." (Citation omitted). Our resolution of this dispute requires a careful examination both of the writ of habeas corpus, which Hamdi now seeks to employ as a mechanism of judicial review, and of the Due Process Clause, which informs the procedural contours of that mechanism in this instance.

A.

Though they reach radically different conclusions on the process that ought to attend the present proceeding, the parties begin on common ground. All agree that, absent suspension, the writ of habeas corpus remains available to every individual detained within the United States. U.S. Const., Art. I, §9, cl. 2 ("The Privilege of the Writ of Habeas Corpus shall not be suspended, unless when in Cases of Rebellion or Invasion the public Safety may require it"). Only in the rarest of circumstances has Congress seen fit to suspend the writ. See, *e.g.*, Act of Mar. 3, 1863, ch. 81, §1, 12 Stat. 755; Act of April 20, 1871, ch. 22, §4, 17 Stat. 14. At all other times, it has remained a critical check on the Executive, ensuring that it does not detain individuals except in accordance with law. See *INS* v. *St. Cyr,* 533 U.S. 289, 301 (2001). All agree suspension of the writ has not occurred here. Thus, it is undisputed that Hamdi was properly before an Article III court to challenge his detention under 28 U.S.C. § 2241. (Citation omitted)...

B.

First, the Government urges the adoption of the Fourth Circuit's holding below-that because it is "undisputed" that Hamdi's seizure took place in a combat zone, the habeas determination can be made purely as a matter of law, with no further hearing or factfinding necessary. This argument is easily rejected. As the dissenters from the denial of rehearing en banc noted, the circumstances surrounding Hamdi's seizure cannot in any way be characterized as "undisputed," as "those circumstances are neither conceded in fact, nor susceptible to concession in law, because Hamdi has not been permitted to speak for himself or even through counsel as to those circumstances."... Further, the "facts" that constitute the alleged concession are insufficient to support Hamdi's detention. Under the definition of enemy combatant that we accept today as falling within the scope of Congress' authorization, Hamdi would need to be "part of or supporting forces hostile to the United States or coalition partners" and "engaged in an armed conflict against the United States" to justify his detention in the United States for the duration of the relevant conflict. (Citation omitted). The habeas petition states only that "[w]hen seized by the United States Government, Mr. Hamdi resided in Afghanistan." (Citation omitted). An assertion that one *resided* in a country in which combat operations are taking place is not a concession that one was "*captured* in a zone of active combat operations in a foreign theater of war," 316 F.3d, at 459 (emphasis added), and certainly is not a concession that one was "part of or supporting forces hostile to the United States or coalition partners" and "engaged in an armed conflict against the United States." Accordingly, we reject any argument that Hamdi has made concessions that eliminate any right to further process.

C.

The Government's second argument requires closer consideration. This is the argument that further factual exploration is unwarranted and inappropriate in light of the extraordinary constitutional interests at stake. Under the Government's most extreme rendition of this argument, "[r]espect for separation of powers and the limited institutional capabilities of courts in matters of military decision-making in connection with an ongoing conflict" ought to eliminate entirely any individual process, restricting the courts to investigating only whether legal authorization exists for the broader detention scheme. (Citation omitted). At most, the Government argues, courts should review its determination that a citizen is an enemy combatant under a very deferential "some evidence" standard. (Citation omitted)... Under this review, a court would assume the accuracy of the Government's articulated basis for Hamdi's detention, as set forth in the Mobbs Declaration, and assess only whether that articulated basis was a legitimate one....

1.

It is beyond question that substantial interests lie on both sides of the scale in this case. Hamdi's "private interest...affected by the official action," (Citation omitted), is the most elemental of liberty interests-the interest in being free from physical detention by one's own government. *Foucha* v. *Louisiana,* 504 U.S. 71, 80 (1992) ("Freedom from bodily restraint has always been at the core of the liberty protected by the Due Process Clause from arbitrary governmental action"); see also *Parham* v. *J. R.,* 442 U.S. 584, 600 (1979) (noting the "substantial liberty interest in not being confined unnecessarily"). "In our society liberty is the norm," and detention without trial "is the carefully limited exception." *Salerno, supra*, at 755. "We have always been careful not to 'minimize the importance and fundamental nature' of the individual's right to liberty," *Foucha, supra*, at 80 (quoting *Salerno, supra*, at 750), and we will not do so today.

Nor is the weight on this side of the *Mathews* scale offset by the circumstances of war or the accusation of treasonous behavior, for "[i]t is clear that commitment for *any* purpose constitutes a significant deprivation of liberty that requires due process protection," *Jones* v. *United States,* 463 U.S. 354, 361 (1983)... We reaffirm today the fundamental nature of a citizen's right to be free from involuntary confinement by his own government without due process of law, and we weigh the opposing governmental interests against the curtailment of liberty that such confinement entails.

2.

On the other side of the scale are the weighty and sensitive governmental interests in ensuring that those who have in fact fought with the enemy during a war do not return to battle against the United States. As discussed above, *supra*, at 10, the law of war and the realities of combat may render such detentions both necessary and appropriate, and our due process analysis need not blink at those realities. Without doubt, our Constitution recognizes that core strategic matters of warmaking belong in the hands of those who are best positioned and most politically accountable for making them...

3.

Striking the proper constitutional balance here is of great importance to the Nation during this period of ongoing combat. But it is equally vital that our calculus not give short shrift to the values that this country holds dear or to the privilege that is American citizenship. It is during our most challenging and uncertain moments that our Nation's commitment to due process is most severely tested; and it is in those times that we must preserve our commitment at home to the principles for which we fight abroad...

With due recognition of these competing concerns, we believe that neither the process proposed by the Government nor the process apparently envisioned by the District Court below strikes the proper constitutional balance when a United States citizen is detained in the United States as an enemy combatant. That is, "the risk of erroneous deprivation" of a detainee's liberty interest is unacceptably high under the Government's proposed rule, while some of the "additional or substitute procedural safeguards" suggested by the District Court are unwarranted in light of their limited "probable value" and the burdens they may impose on the military in such cases. *Mathews*, 424 U.S., at 335.

We therefore hold that a citizen-detainee seeking to challenge his classification as an enemy combatant must receive notice of the factual basis for his classification, and a fair opportunity to rebut the Government's factual assertions before a neutral decisionmaker... These essential constitutional promises may not be eroded.

At the same time, the exigencies of the circumstances may demand that, aside from these core elements, enemy combatant proceedings may be tailored to alleviate their uncommon potential to burden the Executive at a time of ongoing military conflict. Hearsay, for example, may need to be accepted as the most reliable available evidence from the Government in such a proceeding. Likewise, the Constitution would not be offended by a presumption in favor of the Government's evidence, so long as that presumption remained a rebuttable one and fair opportunity for rebuttal were provided. Thus, once the Government puts forth credible evidence that the habeas petitioner meets the enemy-combatant criteria, the onus could shift to the petitioner to rebut that evidence with more persuasive evidence that he falls outside the criteria. A burden-shifting scheme of this sort would meet the goal of ensuring that the errant tourist, embedded journalist, or local aid worker has a chance to prove military error while giving due regard to the Executive once it has put forth meaningful support for its conclusion that the detainee is in fact an enemy combatant…

We think it unlikely that this basic process will have the dire impact on the central functions of warmaking that the Government forecasts. The parties agree that initial captures on the battlefield need not receive the process we have discussed here; that process is due only when the determination is made to *continue* to hold those who have been seized. The Government has made clear in its briefing that documentation regarding battlefield detainees already is kept in the ordinary course of military affairs. (Citation omitted). Any factfinding imposition created by requiring a knowledgeable affiant to summarize these records to an independent tribunal is a minimal one. Likewise, arguments that military officers ought not have to wage war under the threat of litigation lose much of their steam when factual disputes at enemy-combatant hearings are limited to the alleged combatant's acts. This focus meddles little, if at all, in the strategy or conduct of war, inquiring only into the appropriateness of continuing to detain an individual claimed to have taken up arms against the United States. While we accord the greatest respect and consideration to the judgments of military authorities in matters relating to the actual prosecution of a war, and recognize that the scope of that discretion necessarily is wide, it does not infringe on the core role of the military for the courts to exercise their own time-honored and constitutionally mandated roles of reviewing and resolving claims like those presented here. Cf. *Korematsu* v. *United States*, (Citation omitted) ....

In sum, while the full protections that accompany challenges to detentions in other settings may prove unworkable and inappropriate in the enemy-combatant setting, the threats to military operations posed by a basic system of independent review are not so weighty as to trump a citizen's core rights to challenge meaningfully the Government's case and to be heard by an impartial adjudicator.

D.

In so holding, we necessarily reject the Government's assertion that separation of powers principles mandate a heavily circumscribed role for the courts in such circumstances. Indeed, the position that the courts must forgo any examination of the individual case and focus exclusively on the legality of the broader detention scheme cannot be mandated by any reasonable view of separation of powers, as this approach serves only to *condense* power into a single branch of government. We have long since made clear that a state of war is not a blank check for the President when it comes to the rights of the Nation's citizens. *Youngstown Sheet & Tube*, 343 U.S., at 587. Whatever power the United States Constitution envisions for the Executive in its exchanges with other nations or with enemy organizations in times of conflict, it most assuredly envisions a role for all three branches when individual liberties are at stake... Likewise, we have made clear that, unless Congress acts to suspend it, the Great Writ of habeas corpus allows the Judicial Branch to play a necessary role in maintaining this delicate balance of governance, serving as an important judicial check on the Executive's discretion in the realm of detentions. (Citation omitted). Thus, while we do not question that our due process assessment must pay keen attention to the particular burdens faced by the Executive in the context of military action, it would turn our system of checks and balances on its head to suggest that a citizen could not make his way to court with a challenge to the factual basis for his detention by his government, simply because the Executive opposes making available such a challenge. Absent suspension of the writ by Congress, a citizen detained as an enemy combatant is entitled to this process.

Because we conclude that due process demands some system for a citizen detainee to refute his classification, the proposed "some evidence" standard is inadequate. Any process in which the Executive's factual assertions go wholly unchallenged or are simply presumed correct without any opportunity for the alleged combatant to demonstrate otherwise falls constitutionally short. As the Government itself has recognized, we have utilized the "some evidence" standard in the past as a standard of review, not as a standard of proof. (Citation omitted). That is, it primarily has been employed by courts in examining an administrative record developed after an adversarial proceeding-one with process at least of the sort that we today hold is constitutionally mandated in the citizen enemy-combatant setting. See, *e.g.*, *St. Cyr, supra; Hill*, 472 U.S., at 455-457. This standard therefore is ill suited to the situation in which a habeas petitioner has received no prior proceedings before any tribunal and had no prior opportunity to rebut the Executive's factual assertions before a neutral decisionmaker...

Plainly, the "process" Hamdi has received is not that to which he is entitled under the Due Process Clause.

There remains the possibility that the standards we have articulated could be met by an appropriately authorized and properly constituted military tribunal. Indeed, it is notable that military regulations already provide for such process in related instances, dictating that tribunals be made available to determine the status of enemy detainees who assert prisoner-of-war status under the Geneva Convention... In the absence of such process, however, a court that receives a petition for a writ of habeas corpus from an alleged enemy combatant must itself ensure that the minimum requirements of due process are achieved. Both courts below recognized as much, focusing their energies on the question of whether Hamdi was due an opportunity to rebut the

Government's case against him. The Government, too, proceeded on this assumption, presenting its affidavit and then seeking that it be evaluated under a deferential standard of review based on burdens that it alleged would accompany any greater process. As we have discussed, a habeas court in a case such as this may accept affidavit evidence like that contained in the Mobbs Declaration, so long as it also permits the alleged combatant to present his own factual case to rebut the Government's return. We anticipate that a District Court would proceed with the caution that we have indicated is necessary in this setting, engaging in a factfinding process that is both prudent and incremental. We have no reason to doubt that courts faced with these sensitive matters will pay proper heed both to the matters of national security that might arise in an individual case and to the constitutional limitations safeguarding essential liberties that remain vibrant even in times of security concerns.

IV.

Hamdi asks us to hold that the Fourth Circuit also erred by denying him immediate access to counsel upon his detention and by disposing of the case without permitting him to meet with an attorney. (Citation omitted). Since our grant of certiorari in this case, Hamdi has been appointed counsel, with whom he has met for consultation purposes on several occasions, and with whom he is now being granted unmonitored meetings. He unquestionably has the right to access to counsel in connection with the proceedings on remand. No further consideration of this issue is necessary at this stage of the case.

The judgment of the United States Court of Appeals for the Fourth Circuit is vacated, and the case is remanded for further proceedings.

It is so ordered.

Abdullah al-Muhajir (Jose Padilla)

With the arrest of al-Muhajir, an American, the issue of race and terrorism reached a high point. He was born Jose Padilla in Brooklyn, New York to Puerto Rican parents. He apparently converted to Islam in 1992 after marrying a Muslim woman. On May 8, 2002, he was arrested when he arrived in Chicago from Pakistan. On June 10, he was arrested and charged with conspiracy to detonate a "dirty bomb." He was immediately declared an "enemy combatant" and placed in military custody. Under the rules governing this type of classification, he could be held indefinitely, without the benefit of counsel. This detention raised serious legal questions of whether military tribunals can try Americans. Another American of Saudi background, Yasser Esam Hamdi was captured on the battle field in Afghanistan and was being held in the same manner. Both of these men were being held indefinitely by the United States military as "enemy combatants." Yet, it was unlikely that the government would try Hamdi and Padilla in military tribunals. Federal regulations prohibited the trying of American citizens in these tribunals.[13]

The important question, however was why is Mr. Padilla being held indefinitely, while John Walker Lindh, a white defendant charged with conspiracy to kill Americans and providing support to the Taliban and Al Qaeda, had been tried in a Virginia federal court? Why had the Bush administration suspended the Constitutional rights of two Americans of color who had not been formally charged with an offense, but preserved those same rights for a white defendant? The white defendant had his day in court and was spared the death penalty and life imprisonment, while the other men of color were held indefinitely.

---

13   Adam Liptak, Accord Suggests U.S. Prefers to Avoid Courts, The New York Times, 7/16/02.

RUMSFELD v. PADILLA
SUPREME COURT OF THE UNITED STATES
542 U.S. 426 (2004)

Chief Justice Rehnquist delivered the opinion of the Court.

Respondent Jose Padilla is a United States citizen detained by the Department of Defense pursuant to the President's determination that he is an "enemy combatant" who conspired with al Qaeda to carry out terrorist attacks in the United States. We confront two questions: First, did Padilla properly file his habeas petition in the Southern District of New York; and second, did the President possess authority to detain Padilla militarily. We answer the threshold question in the negative and thus do not reach the second question presented.

Because we do not decide the merits, we only briefly recount the relevant facts. On May 8, 2002, Padilla flew from Pakistan to Chicago's O'Hare International Airport. As he stepped off the plane, Padilla was apprehended by federal agents executing a material witness warrant issued by the United States District Court for the Southern District of New York (Southern District) in connection with its grand jury investigation into the September 11th terrorist attacks. Padilla was then transported to New York, where he was held in federal criminal custody. On May 22, acting through appointed counsel, Padilla moved to vacate the material witness warrant.

In support of this action, the President invoked his authority as "Commander in Chief of the U.S. armed forces" and the Authorization for Use of Military Force Joint Resolution, Pub. L. 107-40, 115 Stat. 224 (AUMF), (Footnote omitted) enacted by Congress on September 18, 2001. June 9 Order 5a. The President also made several factual findings explaining his decision to designate Padilla an enemy combatant. ()Footnote omitted. Based on these findings, the President concluded that it is "consistent with U.S. law and the laws of war for the Secretary of Defense to detain Mr. Padilla as an enemy combatant." (Citation omitted.)

That same day, Padilla was taken into custody by Department of Defense officials and transported to the Consolidated Naval Brig in Charleston, South Carolina.(Footnote omitted). He has been held there ever since.

On June 11, Padilla's counsel, claiming to act as his next friend, filed in the Southern District a habeas corpus petition under 28 U.S.C. §2241. The petition, as amended, alleged that Padilla's military detention violates the Fourth, Fifth, and Sixth Amendments and the Suspension Clause, Art. I, §9, cl. 2, of the United States Constitution. The amended petition named as respondents President Bush, Secretary Rumsfeld, and Melanie A. Marr, Commander of the Consolidated Naval Brig.

The Government moved to dismiss, arguing that Commander Marr, as Padilla's immediate custodian, is the only proper respondent to his habeas petition, and that the District Court lacks jurisdiction over Commander Marr because she is located outside the Southern District...

The District Court issued its decision in December 2002. *Padilla ex rel. Newman* v. *Bush*, 233 F. Supp. 2d 564. The court held that the Secretary's "personal involvement" in Padilla's military custody renders him a proper respondent to Padilla's habeas petition, and that it can assert jurisdiction over the Secretary under New York's long-arm statute, notwithstanding his absence from the Southern District. (Citation omitted.) On the merits, however, the court accepted the Government's contention that the President has authority to detain as enemy combatants citizens captured on American soil during a time of war. (Citation omitted).

The Court of Appeals for the Second Circuit reversed. 352 F.3d 695 (2003). The court agreed with the District Court that Secretary Rumsfeld is a proper respondent, reasoning that in cases where the habeas petitioner is detained for "other than federal criminal violations, the Supreme Court has recognized exceptions to the general practice of naming the immediate physical custodian as respondent." (Citation omitted). The Court of Appeals concluded that on these "unique" facts Secretary Rumsfeld is Padilla's custodian because he exercises "the legal reality of control" over Padilla and because he was personally involved in Padilla's military detention. (Citation omitted). The Court of Appeals also affirmed the District Court's holding that it has jurisdiction over the Secretary under New York's long-arm statute. (Citation omitted).

Reaching the merits, the Court of Appeals held that the President lacks authority to detain Padilla militarily. (Citation omitted). The court concluded that neither the President's Commander-in-Chief power nor the AUMF authorizes military detentions of American citizens captured on American soil. (Citation omitted.) To the contrary, the Court of Appeals found in both our case law and in the Non-Detention Act, (Citation omitted) a strong presumption against domestic military detention of citizens absent explicit congressional authorization. (Citation omitted). Accordingly, the court granted the writ of habeas corpus and directed the Secretary to release Padilla from military custody within 30 days. (Citation omitted.)

We granted the Government's petition for certiorari to review the Court of Appeals' rulings with respect to the jurisdictional and the merits issues, both of which raise important questions of federal law. (Citation omitted).

The question whether the Southern District has jurisdiction over Padilla's habeas petition breaks down into two related subquestions. First, who is the proper respondent to that petition? And second, does the Southern District have jurisdiction over him or her? We address these questions in turn.

I.

The federal habeas statute straight forwardly provides that the proper respondent to a habeas petition is "the person who has custody over [the petitioner]." 28 U.S.C. §2242; see also §2243 ("The writ, or order to show cause shall be directed to the person having custody of the person detained"). The consistent use of the definite article in reference to the custodian indicates that there is generally only one proper respondent to a given prisoner's habeas petition. This custodian, moreover, is "the person" with the ability to produce the prisoner's body before the habeas court. (Citation omitted). We summed up the plain language of the habeas statute over 100 years ago in this way: "[T]hese provisions contemplate a proceeding against some person who has the *immediate custody* of the party detained, with the power to produce the body of such party before the court or judge, that he may be liberated if no sufficient reason is shown to the contrary." *Wales* v. *Whitney,* 114 U.S. 564, 574 (1885)...

In accord with the statutory language and *Wales'* immediate custodian rule, longstanding practice confirms that in habeas challenges to present physical confinement-"core challenges"- the default rule is that the proper respondent is the warden of the facility where the prisoner is being held, not the Attorney General or some other remote supervisory official. (Citation omitted).

If the *Wales* immediate custodian rule applies in this case, Commander Marr- the equivalent of the warden at the military brig-is the proper respondent, not Secretary Rumsfeld.... Neither Padilla, nor the courts below, nor Justice Stevens' dissent deny the general applicability of the immediate custodian rule to habeas petitions challenging physical custody. (Citation omitted). They argue instead that the rule is flexible and should not apply on the "unique facts" of this case. (Citation omitted). We disagree.

First, Padilla notes that the substantive holding of *Wales*-that a person released on his own recognizance is not "in custody" for habeas purposes-was disapproved in *Hensley* v. *Municipal Court, San Jose & nbhyph; Milpitas Judicial Dist., Santa Clara Cty.,* 411 U.S. 345, 350, n. 8 (1973), as part of this Court's expanding definition of "custody" under the habeas statute.(Footnote omitted). Padilla seems to contend, and the dissent agrees, (Citation omitted), that because we no longer require physical detention as a prerequisite to habeas relief, the immediate custodian rule, too, must no longer bind us, even in challenges to physical custody....

II.

We turn now to the second subquestion. District courts are limited to granting habeas relief "within their respective jurisdictions." 28 U.S.C. §2241(a). We have interpreted this language to require "nothing more than that the court issuing the writ have jurisdiction over the custodian." *Braden*, 410 U.S., at 495. Thus, jurisdiction over Padilla's habeas petition lies in the Southern District only if it has jurisdiction over Commander Marr. We conclude it does not...

The plain language of the habeas statute thus confirms the general rule that for core habeas petitions challenging present physical confinement, jurisdiction lies in only one district: the district of confinement. Despite this ample statutory and historical pedigree, Padilla contends, and the Court of Appeals held, that the district of confinement rule no longer applies to core habeas challenges. Rather, Padilla, as well as today's dissenters, (Citation omitted), urge that our decisions in *Braden* and *Strait* stand for the proposition that jurisdiction will lie in any district in which the respondent is amenable to service of process. We disagree...

This rule, derived from the terms of the habeas statute, serves the important purpose of preventing forum shopping by habeas petitioners. Without it, a prisoner could name a high-level supervisory official as respondent and then sue that person wherever he is amenable to long-arm jurisdiction. The result would be rampant forum shopping, district courts with overlapping jurisdiction, and the very inconvenience, expense, and embarrassment Congress sought to avoid when it added the jurisdictional limitation 137 years ago...

III.

The District of South Carolina, not the Southern District of New York, was the district court in which Padilla should have brought his habeas petition. We therefore reverse the judgment of the Court of Appeals and remand the case for entry of an order of dismissal without prejudice.

It is so ordered.

JUSTICE GINSBURG, dissenting from the denial of certiorari.

This case, here for the second time, raises a question "of profound importance to the Nation," (Citation omitted). Does the President have authority to imprison indefinitely a United States citizen arrested on United States soil distant from a zone of combat, based on an Executive declaration that the citizen was, at the time of his arrest, an "enemy combatant"? It is a question the Court heard, and should have decided, two years ago. (Citation omitted). Nothing the Government has yet done purports to retract the assertion of Executive power Padilla protests.

Although the Government has recently lodged charges against Padilla in a civilian court, nothing prevents the Executive from returning to the road it earlier constructed and defended. A party's voluntary cessation does not make a case less capable of repetition or less evasive of review. (Citation omitted)… Satisfied that this case is not moot, I would grant the petition for certiorari.

► Notes & Questions

In 2004 in the case of *Rasul v. Bush* the Supreme Court heard arguments in favor two Australians and twelve Kuwaitis who had been picked up in Afghanistan and held indefinitely at Guantanomo Bay. They were part of 600 individuals rounded up in Afghanistan. The Bush administration argued that they could be held indefinitely without charges but the Court ruled otherwise with an opinion written by Justice Stevens and joined in by Justices O'Connor, Souter, Ginsburg and Breyer. The Court ruled that the District Court had jurisdiction over the case. As reason it stated that the detainees were not "nationals of countries at war with the United States", and that habeas corpus petitions could be used by those held at Guantanomo Bay.

John Walker Lindh

When John Walker Lindh was captured by American authorities in Afghanistan on December 1, 2001, he had long hair and confessed that "He chose to embrace fanatics, and his allegiance to those terrorists never faltered."[14] Yet when he appeared before a federal judge on July 15, 2002, he was clean shaven, appearing like your average upper middle-class twenty-one year old white man. Lindh grew up in Fairfax, California to privilege and converted to Islam at the age of 16 after reading *The Autobiography of Malcolm.* Like Malcolm, he changed his name to an Islamic one: Suleyman Al-Lindh.[15] His parents paid for him to study Islam in Yemen and Pakistan. His parents had obtained some of the highest priced and most politically sophisticated and connected lawyers in the

---

14   David Johnston, "A Plea Suited to Both Sides," The New York Times, July 16, 2002.

15   Chris Gaither, "Back Home, Lindh Seen as no Terrorist," The Boston Globe, 7/16/02.

▶ Notes & Questions

United States. His lead attorney, James J. Brosnahan, was one of the best in the United States, according to Professor David D. Cole of Georgetown University Law School.[16] As a result, their son, who had once trained and fought with the Taliban, received a sentence of 20 years and a fine of up to $500,000.00 in exchange for his guilty plea to the crimes of providing service to Taliban. The United States government agreed to the sentence. The more serious charges of terrorism and conspiracy to kill Americans, including allegations of Lindh's involvement in the killing of Johnny Michael Spann, a Central Intelligence Agency officer on November 25, 2001, was dropped. Also, when Lindh was arrested he was carrying an automatic weapon, and two hand grenades, which was an indication that he was an active participant in a militant military organization.

Why did the United States government strike this deal with Lindh, when it was clear that Judge T.S. Ellis III of the Federal District Court in Alexandria, Virginia, was going to allow into evidence incriminating statements made by Lindh after his arrest? In these statements, Lindh indicated his wish to engage in Jihad (holy war), and that he had trained in a camp organized and financed by Osama bin Laden. He also indicated that he and others had been recruited to engage in terrorist activities in the United States.[17]

In addition, as a result of his agreement with the government, Lindh will be incarcerated in a prison near his parents' homes.[18]

---

16 Lyle Denniston, "Plea underscores role of legal aid," The Boston Globe, 7/16/02.

17 Neil A. Lewis, "Deal was worked out over weekend by Lindh lawyers," The New York Times, 7/16/02.

18 Denniston.

► **Notes & Questions**

This plea was approved by the highest levels of government, by George Bush himself. But, what of Bush's statements that the United States government would root out terrorists wherever they can be found? Here was an American who did more than harbor terrorists, but actually participated in a military scheme against American interests; yet, he was tried as a civilian and received a light sentence. Hamdi and Padilla, on the other hand, did not have a right to an attorney at all, neither were they allowed to see family members.

▶ Notes & Questions

Zacarias Moussaoui

Moussaoui, age 34, and a French national of Moroccan descent, was the first individual to be charged in the September 11th hijacking. He was arrested in August on immigration charges and was indicted for murder, conspiracy, conspiracy to destroy aircrafts, and the use of weapons of mass destruction. Four of the six charges carry the penalty of death. As a result, the French and German governments refused to cooperate with the United States in the prosecutions because they, along with the entire European Union, opposed the death penalty. What will make Mr. Moussaoui's defense even more difficult is his desire to represent himself or have a Muslim appointed to represent him. In his court papers he expressed his skepticism towards Jews and the United States.[19]

Mr. Moussaoui did eventually consult with Attorney Charles Freeman from Houston, an African-American and Muslim.

Class Problem: Hypothetical Scenario

A jury decided against death penalty after his conviction and he is currently serving a life sentence without a possibility of parole.

---

19   Philip Sheron, In Motions, Defendant Declares He is Hostile to Jews and U.S., *The New York Times*, June 18, 2002.

▶ Notes & Questions

It is the year 2004. The United States has just bombed Khartoum, Sudan, East Africa on the grounds that it is a haven for Islamic terrorists. Two weeks after the bombing a major news agency revealed that at least 700 civilians were killed by the bombing, including at least 100 children. The news of the atrocities quickly spread throughout the United States, causing major popular eruptions throughout the country. Numerous cities, including New York, Chicago and Los Angeles are in flames and civil disobedience appears to be the rule, instead of law and order.

In order to quell the violence, that was spreading rapidly across the country, the President of the United States signed a curfew order for inner city communities in the three cities most affected by the violence (New York, Chicago and Los Angeles). The order prohibited individuals from being on the public streets from 7pm until 6am each day. In addition, since the violence was very rampant in the Harlem section of New York City, the order required all residents to report to an assembly center where they were to remain until further notice. Anyone failing to abide by the order would be arrested and held without bail until the emergency was declared over. Entire communities refused to report to the assembly centers and were arrested and held without bail.

Furthermore, African students from countries that are predominantly Moslem have been ordered to leave the United States within 24 hours.

Moslem-Americans have been ordered to report to their local police departments, register and receive an identification card.

An African-American student, Mohamed Hasan, has been arrested in New York City on the grounds that he has been aiding and abetting a foreign organization, i.e. the Sudan People's Liberation Army (SPLA). Mr. Hasan has argued that as a Christian

▶ Notes & Questions

student he has been moved to action after learning of the suffering of the Sudanese people. For example, he stated that close to 2,000,000 Sudanese people have died as a result of the war against the Moslem north and resultant famine. He states that he has only organized campus and community fund-raisers for SPLA because it represents the Christians in the southern part of the Sudan who are fighting against the Moslem north. He believes that it is his Christian duty to support the Christians in the southern part of the Sudan. The United States Government has placed Sudan on a list of countries that it believes is sponsoring international terrorism. Mr. Hasan has therefore, been arrested after being detained for one week, without access to legal counsel.

You have been hired as a legal advisor to the group and have been asked to research their legal rights. In a memorandum of at least ten pages, outline and discuss the government's legal position and that of the defendants. What are the key legal issues that grow out of this case and controversy? Discuss the legal precedents and the moral and political issues that grow out of these events.